DATE DUE

Legitimism and the
Reconstruction of
French Society
1852–1883

Legitimism and the
Reconstruction of
French Society
1852–1883

STEVEN D. KALE

Louisiana State University Press

BATON ROUGE AND LONDON

Designer: Barbara Werden
Typeface: Linotron 202 Bembo
Typesetter: G & S Typesetters, Inc.
Printer and binder: Thomson-Shore, Inc.

Library of Congress Cataloging-in-Publication Data

Kale, Steven D., 1957–.
    Legitimism and the reconstruction of French society, 1852–1883 / Steven D. Kale.
        p. cm.
    Includes bibliographical references and index.
    ISBN 0-8071-1727-7 (cloth)
        1. France—Politics and government—19th century.   2. France—Social conditions—
    19th century.   3. Royalists—France—History—19th century.   4. France—Kings and
    rulers—Succession.
    I. Title.
    DC340.K26   1992   92-9297
    944.06—dc20   CIP

Several parts of this book appeared previously in somewhat different form in "The Monarchy According to the King: The Ideological Content of the *Drapeau Blanc*, 1871–1873," *French History*, II (1988), 399–426, used here by permission of Oxford University Press; and in "The Technique of *Encadrement*: The St. Vincent de Paul Society and the Problem of Social Reform in Nineteenth-Century France," *Proceedings of the Western Society of French History*, XV (1988), 341–53, and "Who Was Responsible for the Centralized State? The Legitimists and Tocqueville's *Ancien Régime*," *Proceedings of the Western Society of French History*, XVI (1989), 266–75, both used here by permission of the editor.

The paper in this book meets the guidelines for permanence and durability of the Committee on Production Guidelines for Book Longevity of the Council on Library Resources. ∞

*To my mother,
and to the memory of my father*

Contents

Maps

Tables

Preface

THE LONG LIFE, dramatic fall, and uncertain revival of monarchical government in France inevitably made those who continued to support the Bourbons in the modern era objects of controversy. In the nineteenth century the monarchy remained the focus of passionate loyalty and bitter opposition, and the Legitimist monarchists were characterized as obscurantists or men of good faith, anachronisms or patriots, men of principle or political imbeciles. Consequently, the study of Legitimism in France has often been encumbered by the living language and sentiments of long-standing political and social debates. At the same time, the historical failure of the Legitimists has made it too easy to dismiss Legitimism as a relatively insignificant political and intellectual tradition.

Scholarly preoccupation is a good indicator of this state of affairs. Fifteen years ago, there was very little important scholarly literature on Legitimism. René Rémond's now-classic study of the French "Rights" and André Jean Tudesq's magisterial work *Les Grands Notables en France, 1840–1849,* published in 1954 and 1964 respectively, were not studies of Legitimism per se but treated the Legitimists as part of the larger questions surrounding the nature of French conservatism and the composition of the French elite.[1] Both studies, however, showed Legitimism to be one of the great currents of French politics and integrated the Legiti-

1. René Rémond, *Les Droites en France* (4th ed.; Paris, 1982); André Jean Tudesq, *Les Grands Notables en France, 1840–1849: Etude historique d'une psychologie sociale* (2 vols.; Paris, 1964).

mists into the social, economic, and ideological universe of the French ruling classes. Between the early 1970s and the present, a number of significant studies on the nineteenth-century royalist tradition by French and Anglo-American historians have begun to paint a more complete portrait of a movement that now seems to have been as pervasive as it has since been neglected. David Higgs's work on ultraroyalism in Toulouse, Robert Locke's study of the Legitimist deputies in the National Assembly of 1871, and Michel Denis' monograph on the royalists of the Mayenne have provided both a general sketch of the Legitimists from the Restoration to the early Third Republic and a more detailed glimpse of royalist communities as they appeared in local contexts. More recent studies by Philippe Levillain on Albert de Mun, Hugues de Changy on Legitimism under the July Monarchy, and Higgs on the French nobility in the nineteenth century have added even greater dimension by illuminating the social values, ideological commitment, and political comportment of the Legitimists, as well as their relationship to the French class structure and nineteenth-century Catholicism. The appearance of Stéphane Rials' installment *Le Légitimisme* for the Que sais-je series in 1983, arriving well after earlier contributions on subjects like agricultural medicine, Russian grammar, and kayaks and canoes, seems finally to have given the topic an official imprimatur.

These works, though important, all tend to downplay the importance of ideology in favor of social and political factors. That approach has yielded indispensable data, but it has also left important factual and conceptual gaps in our understanding of nineteenth-century royalism. What, precisely, did the Legitimists want to accomplish, and what was the relationship between those goals and the place the Legitimists occupied in French society? How did they understand the impact of the French Revolution on the prospects for a monarchical restoration and on their own desire to play a wider and better-defined role in French public life? To address these questions, I have focused on the period between the coup d'etat of 1851 and the death of the Comte de Chambord, the Bourbon pretender, in 1883. Although the Legitimist movement had its nominal beginning in 1830 (its true historical origins reach back to the Revolution and, perhaps, beyond), it was only in the years following the Revolution of 1848 that its participants, and the French, had to face squarely the implications of industrial capitalism and cultural secularization at all levels of social and political life. Between 1851 and 1880, France was at the crossroads of modernity, and both the Legitimists and the rest of the French were obliged to come to terms with the persistence of a past they were striving to overcome and the anticipation of a future about which neither felt secure. What did it mean to support the restoration of the monarchy in the era of railroads, rural exodus, and the emergence of modern electoral politics? How did intelligent men of tradition and faith come to terms with change?

The progress of research on Legitimism has also done little to reconcile or dispose of the two great analytical narratives through which historians have tried to seize the larger significance of nineteenth-century royalism. Marxist and neo-Jacobin scholars have, in general, characterized Legitimism as the last gasp of an aristocratic and clerical reaction that can be traced back at least as far as the so-called aristocratic reaction of the late eighteenth century. From this perspective, Legitimism represented the "obsolete social forces" that Marx described as "nominally still in possession of all the attributes of power and continuing to vegetate long after the basis of their existence has rotted away."[2] Others, more or less influenced by Rémond's thesis, regard Legitimism as one changing yet essentially continuous dimension of a modern French conservatism whose values have found expression in every generation since 1789. More recent variations on these themes tend to come down on the side of persistence rather than decay but perpetuate the duality of a Legitimism made significant by the perenniality of its voice and a Legitimism rendered irrelevant by its attachment to declining social classes. Pierre Nora detects the persistence of what he calls the "monarchical nation," empowered by "eight centuries of temporal continuity" and locked in a struggle to "kill off" the revolutionary nation that has lasted until very recent events have permitted the "metamorphosis of a modern right wing prepared to accept the legacy of the Revolution."[3] By contrast, Arno Mayer, in what he characterizes as a "Marxist history from the top down," has suggested that movements such as Legitimism survived because European history in the nineteenth century reflected the persistence rather than the rotting-away of the essential economic, social, political,

---

2. Karl Marx, "Anti-Church Movement—Demonstration in Hyde Park," in *Marx and Engels on Religion,* ed. Reinhold Niebuhr (New York, 1964), 127.

3. Pierre Nora, "The Nation," in *A Critical Dictionary of the French Revolution,* ed. François Furet and Mona Ozouf, trans. Arthur Goldhammer (Cambridge, Mass., 1989), 749–50.

and cultural structures of the Old Regime.[4] Legitimists, however, were not ancien régime aristocrats, and Legitimism did not seek to restore the Old Regime. Indeed, they were obsessed with overcoming the contradictions of a monarchical tradition toward which they harbored a deep ambivalence. Moreover, they failed to institutionalize what they saw as a historic compromise between tradition and modernity not because their constituencies "rotted away" but because, in failing to make the monarchy the vehicle for a new social contract, many Catholics and peasants stopped voting for them. Shorn of the support of traditional constituencies, Legitimism began to resemble the counterrevolutionary intellectual tradition through which Rémond traces the persistence of the Legitimist Right.

Legitimism has left its mark on the values and priorities of certain elements of French conservatism. The Second Empire and the early years of the Third Republic witnessed an unprecedented ideological ferment as both the Right and the Left engaged in a collective examination of the implications of industrialization, urbanization, and democratization. Having participated in the collective reflection on the direction France was taking, the Legitimists themselves experienced a period of formidable ideological development, which, indeed, helped shape the content of a rightist critique of France's revolutionary and republican traditions, with a profound influence on those who continued to contest the legitimacy of the Republic during its turbulent existence. But was this critique necessarily Legitimist, and after traditionalist monarchism collapsed as an autonomous and viable political force in the 1880s under the pressure of democratic institutions, were those who kept the counterrevolutionary tradition alive able to rely on any of the certainties that had given Legitimism its presence earlier in the nineteenth century? As William D. Irvine has demonstrated, many of those who led the royalist movement after the death of Chambord were Bonapartists and royalism survived only at the price of some novel political alliances and ideological mutations.[5] If Legitimism survived as Rémond suggests, it did so in its Catholic integralist and social Catholic manifestations. Yet, as I

---

4. See Arno Mayer, *The Persistence of the Old Regime: Europe to the Great War* (New York, 1981).

5. See William D. Irvine, *The Boulanger Affair Reconsidered: Royalism, Boulangism, and the Origins of the Radical Right in France* (New York, 1989).

argue in this book, both tendencies had only tenuous links to political monarchism.

I am rather more inclined than Rémond to concede that Legitimism was a Right that did not continue. Despite the generic similarities between Legitimism and the social conservatism of Action Française or the traditionalism of Monsignor Lefebvre, it is difficult to draw a straight line between the well-entrenched movement Chambord had at his disposal and the phenomena of marginal twentieth-century intellectual and religious sects. I am rather more comfortable in seeking the long-term importance of Legitimism in its nineteenth-century persistence and in its ultimate failure and fragmentation. The *restauration manquée* of the 1870s and the subsequent *ralliement* of Catholics to the Republic eventually freed many Catholics to pursue social and religious goals unencumbered by the political ineptitude of the royalist party. For those French citizens who embraced their nation's liberal and republican traditions, the failure of the Legitimists to make common cause with the Orleanists saved French democracy from the kind of long abeyance it suffered in other European countries, like imperial Germany, where the alliance of iron and rye was consummated under the auspices of authoritarian institutions. In the context of Tory democracy in Britain, neoabsolutism and *Augleich* in Austria-Hungary, and Bismarckian nationalism in Germany, the triumph of democratic republicanism in France in this era of institutional adjustment and political realignment was no small failure for the notables of the monarchist Right.

The persistence of Legitimism in a country as economically diverse and politically unstable as France left an immense impression on the political adversaries of royalism, resulting in what is perhaps the Legitimists' most significant contribution to modern French history. The rhythm of revolution and reaction that characterized the nineteenth century gave republicans ample reason to take note of a segment of opinion for which the Republic was anathema. Republican discourse and policy were forged in a protracted dialectical struggle with a Catholic and royalist movement for which the Legitimists' systematic and intransigent antirepublicanism continued to have profound resonance. It was no accident that the Republic that emerged after 1880 institutionalized a secular political culture and a vision of civic engagement that sought systematically to exclude the political clericalism, Catholic solidarism, and traditionalist paternalism implicit in the Legitimist idea of monarchy. In that sense, the early Third Republic is incomprehensible without an understanding of the persistent enemy that represented to its founders their worst historical nightmares.

Researching Legitimism is not the best way to win friends, but I managed to make a few along the way. I am indebted to the graduate school and the history department at the University of Wisconsin–Madison for the years of financial and institutional assistance they provided. Special thanks must go to the Henry Vilas Foundation, the Wisconsin Alumni Research Foundation, and the Society for French Historical Studies for the funds they awarded me at critical points in the development of my work. The staffs at the Archives Nationales and the Bibliothèque Nationale deserve recognition for the courteous and valuable assistance they offer to American researchers.

I owe a special debt of gratitude to Professor Edward T. Gargan, whose patience, cooperation, intelligence, and constructive criticism served to dissolve certain mental habits and sharpen my thinking. I would also like to thank Professors Domenico Sella, Suzanne Desan, George Mosse, Murray Edleman, and Robert Locke for providing useful suggestions that have influenced the direction of my work. Throughout graduate school, I was fortunate to have a large number of bright, sympathetic, and friendly colleagues whose conversation and insights helped me past a few intellectual bottlenecks. Professors Tyler Stovall, Lisa Fine, Rosemarie Scuillon, David Wright, and Bud Burkhart helped make the atmosphere at Wisconsin truly noncompetitive and congenial. I am especially grateful in this regard to Professors Kathy Aliamo and Michael Berkowitz. I also want to thank members of the faculty and staff of the history department at Youngstown State University for their editorial assistance. Finally, Derrick Mancini, a research scientist with a valuable perspective on the past and a mania for computers, deserves partial credit—although no blame—for the quantitative aspects of my work.

This book is dedicated to my mother and to the memory of my father, neither of whom finished college. The value they placed on education, their moral and financial support, and their willingness to make sacrifices in exchange for the opportunity to enjoy the accomplishments of their children, as only great parents can, have made this book possible.

Legitimism and the
Reconstruction of
French Society
1852–1883

Introduction

ON MARCH 11, 1888, the funeral of the Comte de Falloux was held at the Collège de Juilly, where the former minister of public instruction had studied in his youth. In a eulogy by the Vicomte de Meaux, a prominent landowner from the Rhône department and a close political associate of Falloux, guests heard that Falloux had symbolized the "perpetuity of the Legitimist party in France," because, like the movement itself, he had taken an active part "in the development and progress" of his era. Firmly committed to the traditional monarchy, Falloux had nevertheless demonstrated that the Legitimists "were not exclusively backward old men, half-savage highlanders separated from the rest of the world, like the Jacobites immortalized by Walter Scott."[1]

If Meaux was correct—and for the most part he was—why was Legitimism so heavily burdened with the reputation of an anachronism? If indeed the Legitimists were not "Jacobites," then what were they? We are accustomed to thinking of modern French history in terms of a succession of five Republics whose numerical progression maps out the developing maturity of French democracy. Although the republicans clearly suffered reverses in 1800, 1815, 1851, and 1940, these have been seen as unnatural or criminal interruptions in the otherwise normal process by which France came to terms with the modern world. We know, of course, that a royalist option existed in the nineteenth century and that

1. Vicomte Marie Camille Alfred de Meaux, *Eloge de M. de Falloux prononcé au Collège de Juilly, le 11 mars 1888* (Paris, 1888), 13.

the Legitimists waited eagerly in the wings to end the cycle of revolutions that had separated the French from their "rightful" heritage. Yet we tend to think of them as quaint antiques or as dangerous historical misfits whose desire to turn back the clock was as ridiculous as it was unthinkable. We tend to forget, however, that until 1880, Legitimism constituted one of the few political options available to France and that the elite, convinced that the Republic always led to dangerous social upheaval, thought of their choices in terms of three possible monarchies: Legitimist, Orleanist, or Bonapartist. In fact, the nineteenth century was in no sense a republican century. Between 1789 and 1880, when the Third Republic seemed secure, the republicans had ruled for fewer than five years; throughout that period the possibility of a Legitimist restoration remained at the center of French political and intellectual life.

The strength of the Legitimists, which depended more on the weight of history than the real balance of social forces, permitted them to believe that they were vindicated by a glorious past. Their resulting confidence nourished a defiant assertion of "irrefutable" principles invulnerable to criticism and historical fact, and claiming special insight into the modern condition precisely because of a fidelity to the lessons of the past. Even in the 1970s, Pierre Debray, a member of Action Française, could assert that his royalism was not a consequence of "secret nostalgias" but rather was "due to an irrational or perhaps unreasonable confidence in man's future, in his creative power, in his inventive faculties." He continued, "By temperament, I am first of all a man of progress, and that is why I have become a man of tradition."[2]

Royalists have been defending themselves against accusations of historical retrogression for a long time. Declarations similar to Debray's by nineteenth-century Legitimists evoked only laughter and ridicule from liberals and republicans. Those claiming to be men of the times argued that the monarchy's historical tasks were accomplished and that it had to make way for modern forms of representative government or popular self-rule. Legitimists, and their clerical cousins, were viewed as superannuated reactionaries who were capable of offering France only a "grotesque spectacle of ideas from another age," and they could expect nothing better than to be despised by a nation anxious to liberate itself from

2. Pierre Debray, *Comment peut-on être royaliste aujourd'hui* (Paris, 1970), 2.

the past.[3] The Legitimists, many argued, had no organic ties to the modern world and could only justify their defiance, indeed their existence, by dragging France back to the Middle Ages. With a combination of ideological self-assurance and political savvy, the republicans ceaselessly announced that a Legitimist restoration would bring with it a revival of the hated dues and privileges of the Old Regime. In 1872, the republicans of the Tarn portrayed the Legitimist candidate, M. de Sonis, as a supporter of the *taille* and *cuissage;* in the Landes, voters were told that the monarchy would expropriate former noble property, reinstate aristocratic tax exemptions, and return the manorial hunting rights.[4] During the Second Empire, the administration used similar tactics against royalist candidates. In the local elections of 1869, the prefecture of Maine-et-Loire distributed posters announcing that the election of Falloux would bring back the Inquisition and the right of primogeniture, and in Caen during 1861 the Legitimist candidate, M. de Brécey, was accused by a government agent named Besnard of wanting to reestablish the notorious *droit de seigneur.* "Will you be happy," he asked, "if you had to give your young daughter to him?" At a local inn, Besnard was overheard telling patrons that Brécey, whom he called "un p—— et un grand p——," would "take your wife and have his way with her." Perhaps in recognition of the absurdity of these claims, perhaps because of Brécey's influence, Besnard was fined a hundred francs and forced to pay the candidate fifty francs in damages.[5]

Such canards were put to good use against the Legitimists during the electoral contests of the 1870s and 1880s. Although by then the Old Regime was a fading specter rather than a living memory, republican propaganda tapped a deep vein of antifeudalism in the political culture of the rural masses.[6] The Legitimists recognized the potency of the attacks and

3. See France, Assemblée nationale, *Annales parlementaires: Annales de l'Assemblée Nationale* (48 vols.; Versailles, 1871–76), March 25, 1873, XVI, 262, hereinafter cited as *Annales;* Charles Bigot, *Les Classes dirigeantes* (Paris, 1875), 42, 59.

4. Jean Faury, *Cléricalisme et Anticléricalisme dans le Tarn, 1848–1900* (Toulouse, 1980), 92–93; *Annales,* 1871, I, 287.

5. Lettre du procureur général de Caen, July 18, 1861, in BB (18) 1632, Archives Nationales, Paris, hereinafter cited as AN.

6. See André Siegfried, *Tableau politique de la France de l'Ouest sous la Troisième République* (Paris, 1913), 451; Albert Soboul, "Persistence of 'Feudalism' in Rural Nineteenth-Century France," in *Rural Society in France: Selections from the Annales Economies, Sociétés,*

felt helpless and humiliated when their efforts to counter them failed to persuade what they viewed as impressionable country folk. During the by-election of July, 1871, Léopold de Gaillard, then an editorialist for *Le Correspondant,* complained that he knew "of more than one candidate who . . . would be incapable of establishing, on acceptable grounds, that peasants do not exist only to beat water in a pond all night and that those who refuse to go to mass do not deserve to be burned alive." Nor were liberal notables immune from the impact of such rhetoric. A center-Left member of the National Assembly of 1871, Emile de Marcère, observed that even the more liberal Legitimists, who were "attached to political freedoms," evoked suspicion among a "large segment of the Right itself, which feared being compromised by the company of men who everyone said were partisans of a return to the past."[7]

The political value of presenting royalist opponents in this light was tested and demonstrated. Yet the positivist convictions that lent an air of philosophical respectability to republican exaggerations masked the more fundamental anxiety republicans felt over Legitimism's survival within the recurrent and troubling cycle of revolution and reaction that had afflicted France in the previous century, to the frustration of many hopes for democratic change. Indeed, the failure of the Revolution to destroy an unwanted past placed the Legitimists at the center of the historical dilemma of the liberal nineteenth century. How would it be possible to create a modern, unified, and secular society in harmony with revolutionary ideals without historically surmounting the persistent material and cultural realities whose demise the republicans' discourse had already anticipated? That is a question the French Left has always had difficulty answering, not least because of the pervasive assumption that the Right is always historically retrograde. After the conservative 1980s, it is well to be on guard against any analytical approach to political and social history which has no convincing way to account for the pattern of reaction and restoration that has enabled the Right to survive well beyond the erosion of the material structures that are supposed to have supported it. As long as the questions of what Legitimism was, what it

---

Civilisations, ed. Robert Forster and Orest Ranum, trans. Elborg Forster and Patricia M. Ranum (Baltimore, 1977), 50–71; Eugen Weber, *Peasants into Frenchmen: The Modernization of Rural France, 1870–1914* (Stanford, Calif., 1976), 16, 250–51.

7. Léopold de Gaillard, *Les Etapes de l'opinion, 1871–72* (Paris, 1873), 31; Emile de Marcère, *L'Assemblée Nationale de 1871* (2 vols.; Paris, 1904), II, 27.

wanted, and where it belongs in French history are posed in the traditional manner, the answers will always be the same and the issue will remain uninteresting.

Conceptual sclerosis is a legacy for which historians have to take credit. Writing at the turn of the century, Gabriel Hanotaux taxed the Legitimists with having an "often willful misunderstanding of the conditions of modern life" as well as "a vague regret for everything that has been and an invincible determination to close their eyes to the present and the future." In the 1930s, Daniel Halévy referred to the Legitimist deputies who came to Bordeaux in February, 1871, as "totally unknown vestiges of a bygone past who, in deference to the wishes of an exiled and aging Bourbon Prince, had remained on the periphery of national affairs."[8] It is indeed difficult to forget the compelling portrait of these deputies painted by J. J. Weiss, who after witnessing their arrival told of how worldly Parisian aristocrats had to find new clothes for their rustic comrades from the Breton interior. Their "unexpected Legitimist faces . . . looked as if they had been cut out of some pre-1830 tapestry."[9] Etched on the historical record, these impressions continue to influence historical judgment. Samuel Osgood has summed up the royalist program as "God and King, . . . a platform which needs no elaboration and brooks no compromise," and Theodore Zeldin has imagined Legitimism to be nothing more than a "web of personal and social relationships rather than a party with a program."[10]

The Legitimists in their own day greeted such notions with a mixture of incredulity, fear, and anger. As Gaillard pointed out, the Old Regime that the Legitimists purportedly hoped to restore was "so old . . . that no one really knew what it was. If it became necessary to reconstitute it, no one would be able to find the debris."[11] Indeed, if the Legitimists had been blind enough to support unalloyed reaction, they could simply have reprinted the old edits from a time that best represented their ideal past

8. Gabriel Hanotaux, *Histoire de la France contemporaine* (6 vols.; Paris, 1900), I, 35; Daniel Halévy, *The End of the Notables*, trans. Alain Silvera (Middletown, Conn., 1974), 8.

9. Quoted by Guy Chapman in *The French Third Republic: The First Phase* (London, 1962), 7.

10. Samuel Osgood, *French Royalism Since 1870* (The Hague, 1970), 10; Theodore Zeldin, *France, 1848–1945: Politics and Anger* (Oxford, 1979), 38.

11. Gaillard, *Les Etapes*, 34. See also Comte Alfred de Falloux, *L'Agriculture et la Politique* (Paris, 1866), 3; Claude Marie Raudot, *De la décadence de la France* (4th ed.; Paris, 1851), ii–iii.

and called this collection of documents a program. But like their republican opponents, the Legitimists predicated their thinking on the conviction that the Revolution had destroyed the old order and had inaugurated a new era in human history. Many royalists were quick to point out that the first act of the Restoration had been to recognize the demolition of ancient mores and institutions, since Louis XVIII had been anxious to accommodate new conditions by repudiating feudal rights and noble privileges.[12] Le Beschu de Champsavin, who believed that the reestablishment of the Old Regime in the mid–nineteenth century would entail a cumbersome and absurd legislative archaeology—as well as an enormous redistribution of property and wealth—wrote that few living nobles had ever known a regime of privilege, those grieving for the past being in their eighties.[13]

Old ideological skirmishes neither tell us very much about Legitimist intentions nor illuminate the context within which the Legitimist project was elaborated. France's willingness to refight the conflicts of the Revolution undoubtedly shaped the content of political debate, but the social categories and political stakes evoked were anachronistic at best. The survival, goals, and failures of Legitimism can best be understood if placed within the setting of nineteenth-century social and political realities, in order that the way prevailing preoccupations and rules of political conduct conditioned them may become clear.

As many have noted, nineteenth-century France was neither entirely modern nor completely archaic. French industrial growth, if steady, was hesitant and uneven. In 1851, 74 percent of the population lived in rural areas, with 53 percent of the labor force engaged in agriculture, as against 25 percent in the industrial sector. By 1881, the primary sector had declined by only five percentage points and the industrial sector had grown by only two.[14] Widely dispersed and highly concentrated, heavy industry was merely superimposed on an economy that remained largely traditional. The consequence was a myriad of regional contrasts. As Arno Mayer has pointed out, the capital-goods sector formed an "archipelago surrounded by a vast ocean of agricultural and traditional manufacture,"

12. Vicomte de La Boulaye, *Les six solutions* (Paris, 1851), 85–86.
13. Le Beschu de Champsavin, *La Peur des revenants: Des privilèges, des droits féodaux et des dîmes* (Rennes, 1851), 4–20.
14. Jean Claude Toutain, *La Population de la France de 1700 à 1959* (Paris, 1963), Tables 15, 33; Census of the French Population in 1866, C 2866, AN.

creating a kind of "mixed economy" in which market penetration was slow and uneven and where certain regions far outdistanced others.[15]

Instead of lessening social and ideological tensions, slow economic growth seems to have brought about the forced coexistence of rival political cultures. Structural and ideological heterogeneity accounted for the acute and repetitive nature of French political conflict. Elites, often responding to vastly different circumstances and responsible to opposed constituencies, continually confronted one another in intractable ideological battles in which the issues hardly changed. The pace of economic and social change served to stabilize the social structure, and the notables, secure in their predominance, could engage in bitter rivalries without risking their status. The advent of universal suffrage in 1848, according to André Jean Tudesq, "did not immediately put an end to the regime of the notables," inasmuch as political change did not necessarily follow from modifications in the pattern of social relations.[16] Although the development of industry in the 1860s caused some discrepancies between socioeconomic and political power, traditional rural elites, often willing to modernize their estates, lost little of their local influence. Economic evolution only served to illuminate the obstruction at the top of the social hierarchy, intensifying the ideological struggles between liberals and traditionalists who, with hope or apprehension, had begun to anticipate the new shape of French society and culture.

All French political parties, therefore, had to operate within a context of socioeconomic development that failed to exhaust any of the limited number of social, political, and economic options. In an era when it was difficult to know whether change or resistance to change had the greater impact in determining the direction of French life, protracted debates on the meaning and consequences of modernization recurred steadily whereas the outcome of each major political confrontation remained indeterminate. The Revolution, whose legitimacy was immediately contested, had brought neither stability nor consensus on the relationship

15. Arno Mayer, *The Persistence of the Old Regime: Europe to the Great War* (New York, 1981), 20. See also Clive Trebilcock, *The Industrialization of the Continental Powers, 1780–1914* (London, 1981); Alain Plessis, *De la fête impériale au mur des fédérés, 1852–1871* (Paris, 1979), 130–31; Maurice Agulhon, Gabriel Désert, and Robert Specklin, *Apogée et Crise de la civilisation paysanne, 1789–1914*, ed. Etienne Juillard (Paris, 1976), 13, Vol. III of Georges Duby and Armand Wallon, eds., *Histoire de la France rurale*, 4 vols.

16. André Jean Tudesq, *Les Grands Notables en France, 1840–1849: Etude historique d'une psychologie sociale* (2 vols.; Paris, 1964), I, 478, II, 666–67, 1233–34.

between state and society but had merely created different sets of rules by which elites could regulate internal rivalries and define their relationship to the nation as a whole. Revolutionary discourse anticipated forms of political comportment and social integration that were at variance with certain social and economic realities. A tentative politics, extending from the revolutionary era until the 1880s and reaching its apogee between 1848 and 1851 and again between 1871 and 1880, corresponded to the social and structural stagnation of the times. Conditions allowed a politically heterogeneous elite to agree tacitly to avoid mutual destruction by creating regimes that in their day seemed flexible enough to accommodate compromise and rigid enough to stave off further democratization.

Even though bitterly divided ideologically, most notables preferred coexistence to the risks of revolutionary change. But precisely because the rules of the game favored unseemly compromise and political moderation, groups on the extreme Right and extreme Left became alienated and were compelled to overturn the existing order and break the deadlock. French politics in many respects looked like those of Spain, where revolution became the normal means of rotating the executive: French liberals, who favored an English model marked by constitutional stability and a smooth alternation between sensible parties of the Right and the Left, remained frustrated in a system where the tyranny of moderation obliged them to accept regimes that were both exclusive and repressive. In the long run, the axis of French politics remained somewhere between the center Right and the center Left. Still, each political party remained loyal to one of the options created by the French Revolution. In such circumstances, no ideologically committed regime could claim to speak for a durable consensus. The tentative society that developed accounted for the strange contradiction between social stability and political instability which characterized France in the nineteenth century.

During the long impasse, political instability, despite being universally condemned, served the interests of the parties, each of which had experienced the satisfaction of power and the bitterness of exclusion. Between 1815 and 1880, France produced a series of regimes that failed to rally national support and were thus provisional in the eyes of those outside official spheres of power who questioned the legitimacy of governments that rested on only an imperfect consensus about the nature of political organization and about policy goals. During the Restoration, the July Monarchy, and the Second Empire, the moderate opposition—

including liberal Legitimists—preferred to avoid the uncertainty of a new revolution and forced the regime to liberalize just enough to accommodate minimum reforms like "free" instruction, decentralization, and greater civil liberties. By contrast, radical republicans, socialists, and intransigent Legitimists did not compromise so easily and preferred to engage in either clandestine activity or, more often, to remain in internal exile hoping that the next revolutionary crisis would bring them to power.

The politics of the tentative society were most evident during the Second Republic (1848–1852) and the first ten years of the Third Republic because political crisis had reshuffled the deck and allowed all contenders to participate in parliament and influence the administration without renouncing their social goals or their desire for constitutional revision. Legitimists understood the opportunity as well as anyone. In 1851, Falloux noted that the republican form of government "is not the regime that divides us least, it is the regime that allows us to remain divided."[17] Claude Marie Raudot, elected to the Chamber as a Legitimist in 1849 and 1871, explained his support for the Second Republic by pointing out that the regime was an "anonymous and irresponsible government" that owed "nobody anything" while being supported by everyone. The Republic, he felt, could "break through the abuses" that other regimes, held down by vested interests, could not touch.[18] In 1871, when "all of France's old regimes . . . emerged miraculously from the native soil," the deputies instinctively returned to the political form of 1848 and enshrined ultimate power in a National Assembly. The monarchist majority was willing to call this regime a republic, but the label was meant to signify the absence of a solution to the constitutional question and thus had a purely academic connotation, in which a republic is merely a state through which power is exercised. The party truce arranged by President Louis Adolphe Thiers, the Pact of Bordeaux, was initially accepted because, as one deputy explained, it afforded a terrain on which the parties

17. Comte Alfred de Falloux, *Discours de M. de Falloux à l'Assemblée Nationale* (Paris, 1851), 14. Similarly, Charles Muller argued that under the Second Republic the election of Louis Napoleon in 1848 did not necessarily "prepare the way for the Empire" but could also have "left the field open to public opinion" (*L'Empire et les Légitimistes* [Paris, 1864], 18). For Vicomte de La Boulaye, the presidential election of 1848 "decided nothing about a future that was always ready to change in new storms" (*Les six solutions,* 70–71).
18. Claude Marie Raudot, *De la grandeur possible de la France, faisant suite à la décadence de la France* (Paris, 1851), 13–14.

"did not cease to struggle among themselves for preeminence."[19] Even the Legitimists, who mistrusted Thiers but were unable to restore the monarchy, demanded the retention of what they called the *provisoire* and opposed every attempt by the radicals to challenge the constituent powers of the Assembly.[20] Henri de La Broise wrote in 1871 that the Republic "only subsists provisionally through the tacit accord of the monarchist parties, who can meet on this neutral ground without abdicating their respective hopes and who force it to exist in spite of itself . . . by paralyzing the attempts of its lost children who would waste no time in dragging it into the abyss if they got hold of it."[21]

As long as French politics was hobbled by tentativeness, the Legitimists, who never had the power to rule alone, could exploit opportunities to have an effect on the contours of French government and society. Such circumstances negate most of the myths that have colored later impressions of nineteenth-century royalism. First, the Legitimists were not fixated on the restoration of God and king to the exclusion of all else. They promoted a larger agenda that defined the monarchy in terms of social, cultural, and institutional changes extending well beyond the bounds of institutional and constitutional questions. Second, if many Legitimists exiled themselves to the interior after 1830, their absence was short-lived and their reemergence into public life in the 1840s and again in the 1860s and 1870s involved them in a wide range of ongoing struggles through which their idea of a monarchical restoration took on elaborate practical implications. Only in this period was the meaning of the "legitimate" monarchy in the nineteenth century fully articulated. (That is why I have chosen to limit my discussion to the years between 1852 and 1883.) Once the republicans put an end to the tentative society in the 1880s by denying royalist notables access to power, the state of affairs arising out of the rivalries of the nineteenth-century elite was replaced by an emerging ideological and administrative monopoly under which the axis of French politics shifted to the left, creating what Odile Rudelle has

---

19. Marcère, *L'Assemblée Nationale*, II, 152, 168, 283. See also Halévy, *The End of the Notables*, 7; Odile Rudelle, *La République absolue: Aux origines de l'instabilité constitutionnelle de la France républicaine, 1870–1889* (Paris, 1982), 7; Claude Nicolet, *L'Idée républicaine en France: Essai d'histoire critique* (Paris, 1982), 162; P. d'Yvon, *Monarchie-République: Quelques Vérités sur la situation politique de 1871* (Bordeaux, 1874), 16–18; and *Annales*, 1871, I, 6.

20. See *Annales*, 1873, XVI, 270, 380.

21. Henri de La Broise, *République ou Monarchie* (Laval, 1871), 49.

called "la République absolue."[22] Although the Third Republic suffered
repeated aftershocks that the discontented yet impotent monarchist opposition helped intensify, it managed to survive longer than any previous
regime, without sharing real power with its sworn enemies. The 1880s
also saw the social and economic pendulum swing definitively toward
the advancement of industrial capitalism and urbanization; the old rural
order and the Catholic church could no longer resist the structural and
cultural changes wrought by modernization. Although France did not
experience an end to the rule of the notables such as Halévy has supposed, it did abandon the tentative society in which traditional elites retained predominance. Political power was transferred from one elite to
another without catastrophe or revolution for the first time in French
history.

If nineteenth-century French politics evinced regulated instability and
tacit indetermination, and if none of the questions raised by the French
Revolution were fully settled, the period did not witness a battle between
the forces of change and those of reaction. In fact, the French were forced
to choose not between the Old Regime and the Revolution but rather
between various political families that proposed alternative forms of political and social organization in response to the realities of nineteenth-
century life. All political parties were reformist, because modernization
provided no fixed point of reference. Meanwhile, *Old Regime* was a hol-
low term of abuse, and a language and practice that seized the precise
implications of the Revolution had to be invented. In this context, it was
no harder to imagine the persistence of Legitimism than to account for
the ultimate success of the republicans.

One question remains. In what sense were the Legitimists reformists
rather than reactionaries? Their intellectual heritage, inspired by Joseph
de Maistre and the Vicomte de Bonald, certainly marked them as counterrevolutionaries who denounced industrialization, democracy, and secularization and who valued gradual change in conformity with custom
and tradition. Yet such a description plays semantic tricks, because neither the words nor the society they refer to is stable or transparent.
Albert de Mun once compared French history to a river that in a storm
overran its banks, ruptured dikes, and flooded plains after flowing

---

22. See Rudelle, *La République absolue.*

steadily from the same source for centuries. The disaster, he added, occurred only because the river ceased to follow its natural course. After the storm subsided and calm returned, workers could begin to repair the dikes. At the same time, "the river returns to its bed and retakes its majestic course."[23] Yet Mun failed to remark what he undoubtedly knew: that after a flood the landscape is radically altered. New dikes and good weather are sufficient to return the river to its bed, but even long years of recultivation can never re-create the antediluvian landscape. As Mun commented elsewhere, "The Old Regime is dead along with its merits and abuses, and if it is true that after a century of revolutions, we need a social reorganization, it is no less true that this is only possible . . . through an intimate accord between tradition and the actual conditions of society."[24]

The paradox of the traditionalist discourse is that in France it became necessary to reconstruct a tradition through language that took its point of reference from a past that itself had to be reconstituted and from "actual conditions of society" whose objective ties to the past were only remote. Under those necessities, actual tradition was lost and the pretense of continuity and conservation unraveled and became a call for radical change. Legitimist efforts to speak about a restoration are a case in point. La Broise claimed, "The world is too old to be remade," but at the same time he called for a "general return" to traditional social and political principles. Undoubtedly, the practical modalities of a "general return" implied that the world had in some sense to be remade.[25]

The recurring use of words like *regenerate, reorganize, reconstitute,* and *reconstruct* in the vocabulary of the Legitimists is a good indicator of the reformist intent inherent in the monarchical restoration they sought. The implications were clear to Jules Simon when he characterized the Legitimists as "radicals . . . on the other end of the [political] horizon." Thiers expressed the thoughts of many liberals in 1872 when he declared that the restoration of the monarchy "will be a new revolution."[26] Far from being conservatives, the Legitimists envisioned a radical reformation of

23. "Discours d'Albert de Mun à l'Assemblée des Catholiques de 1888," in René de La Tour du Pin-Chambly's *Le Centenaire de 1789: Etude d'économie sociale* (Paris, 1888), 13.

24. Albert de Mun, *Dieu et Roi: Discours prononcé à Vannes, le 8 mars 1881* (Paris, 1881), 30.

25. Henri de La Broise, *Le Vrai et le Faux Libéralisme* (Paris, 1866), 303–306.

26. Jules Simon, *La Politique radicale* (Paris, 1868); *Annales,* November 13, 1872, XII, 17.

French politics, culture, and social life going well beyond, or rather, sub-suming, the idea of a monarchical restoration.

The tension between conservatism and radicalism resulted from Le-gitimism's source in the questioning of tradition. Ideally, the Legitimists wanted a monarchy that rested on, and functioned according to, the un-learned convictions, religious principles, and conservative instincts of a well-ordered society. Such a moral order, as they conceived it, would have eliminated the need for an ideology designed to invent antidotes to the disruption of the social order. The restoration, they hoped, would, like the *chouannerie* of 1792, be an expression of the "instinct of conser-vation," in which "social resistance" was determined not by theory but by a natural revulsion against the "crumbling social order" and by the unexamined desire to defend home and hearth, religion and the king.[27] The royalists' attempt to devise a praxis that would allow society to re-gain its moral order was an admission that the French were no longer governed by the immediacy of received tradition and religious faith. The Revolution had forced tradition to justify itself in the free market of elec-toral politics, and Legitimism, no less than any other modern ideology, was the product of a historical transformation that shifted the focus of social discourse from an emphasis on customary social experience to an articulation of speculative descriptions of alternative societies. Since the Old Regime was no longer a point of reference and the monarchy the Legitimists desired did not exist, it was necessary to invent tradition and to project a new order capable of encompassing the totality of relation-ships and social bonds that could exist between individuals, society, and the state. In that sense, the Legitimists had to become sociologists who did fieldwork on their estates and in their factories and who presented their findings in legislative committees. Ideology became the last anchor for the Legitimists precisely because their ties to the larger social order were being eroded by modernity.

Their use of history confirms this point. Cut adrift from usable his-torical models, the Legitimists chose the so-called reform movement of the late eighteenth century as their point of reference. In the period ex-tending from the meeting of the Assembly of Notables in 1787 to the Tennis Court Oath, of June, 1789, and the installation of a "usurpatory" National Assembly, the Legitimists recalled what they believed had been

27. Muller, *L'Empire et les Légitimistes,* 87.

a beneficial legal effort to eradicate the abuses of royal absolutism and lay the foundations for national regeneration within the framework of customary practices and monarchical legitimacy. It was the restorative effort they sought to resume that permitted them to speak of the restoration as an opportunity to reform the existing order. By adopting both the reform movement and the myth of France's "ancient constitution," they endeavored to overcome the ambiguity of their claim to speak for tradition. They had formulated a model that at once satisfied their desire for continuity and supported their urge to reorganize French society and institutions.

Inspired by events that they saw as marking a new beginning, they chose to give clarity and purpose to their projects by employing the metaphor of the architect rather than the archaeologist. The Revolution, they argued, had destroyed the social edifice, leaving only ruins upon which it was impossible to rebuild. What was needed was "solid cement" and a "new plan of general reconstruction," because the Old Regime could not serve as a blueprint.[28] Le Beschu de Champsavin asserted, "Privileges, the *dîme,* feudal rights are dead, like so many other human institutions that have appeared on earth, lasted as long as they were useful, and been annihilated when they were exhausted or became harmful." He continued, "There is no ingratitude here. It is like the house you knock down even though it has over centuries sheltered every generation of a family." But a new revolution was not an option. Champsavin believed that "the utility of change in human institutions can never justify the violence and cruelty of innovators," and he represented Legitimist goals as being like those of the rebuilders after the fire that destroyed Rennes in 1720. Despite the "frightful calamity, no one dreamed of opposing the design that laid out spacious streets and gave a new architecture to the houses. We rejoice now in the wisdom of our predecessors. Sixty years ago, a storm carried off our aging institutions. During the reconstruction of the new edifice upon the old site, we are searching for an organization in accord with our sentiments, mores, and civilization."[29]

This study examines the Legitimists' attempt to design and create a

28. Henri de Gavardie, *Etudes sur les vraies doctrines sociales et politiques* (Pau, 1862), 22–23; Alexandre Denis de Saint-Albin, *Les Libres-penseurs et la Ligue de l'Enseignement* (Paris, 1868), 87; Léopold de Gaillard, "L'Obstacle," *Le Correspondant,* LXXVI (1868), 7.
29. Le Beschu de Champsavin, *La Peur des revenants,* 30–31.

new architecture for French society in the mid–nineteenth century. Like Roger Chartier, I do not insist that "mental structures" are dependent "on their material determinations," because the relationship between thought and action in politics and social life seems to validate his claim that "the representations of the social world themselves are the constituents of social reality."[30] Yet the Legitimists' ideology was indeed an attempt to codify a certain social experience. The more the immediacy of that social experience faded, the more important their interpretation of it became as an instrument of social and cultural reconstruction. Legitimist ideology, therefore, expressed and responded to certain contextual constraints and depended, to some degree, on the framers' sense that their own social experience confirmed its validity. Part One will examine the Legitimists' place within the French elite and their relationship to the wider social order, along with their reflections on how social realities had created practical opportunities to redefine social authority and redesign social relationships. Part Two will provide an intellectual history of Legitimist social reconstruction and an analysis of the legislative programs that envisioned the practical implementation of the Legitimists' plans. In that regard, the three interrelated goals of administrative decentralization, the elaboration of a theory and practice of Christian social action, and the development of ways to protect rural France from a growing urban society are the most important.

It was the conclusions the Legitimists drew from their experiences as *propriétaires*, industrialists, general counselors, legislators, and Catholic social activists that shaped their understanding of the significance of the monarchy. Royalist politics in the 1860s and especially the 1870s revealed the Legitimists' growing preoccupation with the centrality of social and cultural matters. Part Three, which will examine the Legitimists' conception of politics, will reveal how their understanding of restoration as a social and cultural transformation—elaborated during the long years in which a restoration was impossible—contributed to both Chambord's rejection of the white flag in 1873 and the fragmentation of the Legitimist party into those who favored electoral politics, those who placed greater emphasis on social action, and those who hoped to preserve the principles of legitimacy against all practical contingencies. It will become clear

---

30. Roger Chartier, "Intellectual History or Sociocultural History? The French Trajectories," in *Modern European Intellectual History: Reappraisals and New Perspectives,* ed. Dominick LaCapra and Steven L. Kaplan (Ithaca, N.Y., 1982), 30.

that the monarchy mattered less than the ideals it represented and the architecture it was supposed to guarantee.

It is indeed strange to see that people who placed the restoration of the Bourbons at the center of their aspirations conceived of a social order for which the monarchical form of government was irrelevant. Nonetheless, as René Rémond observed long ago, Legitimism gained its "profound significance" in French history by proposing a "conception of society" rather than a "form of government" once the passing of the Bourbon Restoration destroyed the political hopes of one of France's principal political traditions.[31]

31. René Rémond, *Les Droites en France* (4th ed.; Paris, 1982), 58.

PART ONE

The Foundations of French Legitimism

CHAPTER I

Legitimists as Notables

ALTHOUGH THE Legitimists were united by a common de-
sire to place the Comte de Chambord upon the throne of his ancestors,
they did not constitute a homogeneous social class. The Legitimist
ranks included *hobereaux* from Brittany, *négociants* from the south, great
industrialists from the north and east, and a variety of bourgeois professionals, all of whom were part of a national movement held together
by the conviction that the monarchy was the key to France's salvation. Social diversity proved that the Legitimist appeal could cross class
boundaries. It also forced the royalist leadership to accommodate a broad
range of interests and forge a vision of French society that rejected the
corporate privileges of the Old Regime in favor of prevailing nineteenth-
century standards of class, wealth, and merit. This was especially apparent in the Legitimists' concept of the role and composition of the ruling
class. In what sense did the Legitimists belong to a wider society of notables, and what did they think about the social composition and purpose
of the elite, among which they inevitably numbered?

A PARTY OF NOTABLES

The survival of Legitimism was due to the Legitimists' standing as a party of notables. On all the evidence, the image of brood-
ing aristocrats cut off from the mainstream of French society must be
replaced by one of a group of ideologically distinct notables socially
and materially integrated into the nineteenth-century elite. The Vicomte

Table I   Professions of 510 Legitimist Notables

Professional Group	Number	%
Propriétaires/agriculteurs	271	53.1
Businessmen/industrialists	42	8.2
Minor functionaries	21	4.1
Higher functionaries	2	0.3
Magistrates	31	6.0
Lawyers/attorneys	67	13.1
Members of other liberal professions	44	8.6
Military officers	32	6.3
Total	510	99.7

SOURCES: Conseillers généraux de 1870, in F (I) b 230, 1–20, AN; G. Cougny and A. Robert, *Dictionnaire des parlementaires français* (5 vols.; Paris, 1889); Angot, *Dictionnaire historique de la Mayenne, 1900–1914* (4 vols.; Laval, 1975–77); Maurice Briollet, *Les Zouaves pontificaux du Maine, d'Anjou et de la Touraine* (Paris, 1968–69); Gustave Vapereau, *Dictionnaire universel des contemporains contentant toutes les personnes notables de la France et des pays étrangers* (6th ed.; Paris, 1893); Michel Belanger, *Les Conseillers généraux de Charente sous le Second Empire* (Angoulême, 1969); Robert R. Locke, *French Legitimists and the Politics of Moral Order in the Early Third Republic* (Princeton, 1974); André Jean Tudesq, *Les Grandes Notables en France, 1840–1849: Etude historique d'une psychologie sociale* (2 vols.; Paris, 1964).

de Meaux rejected in his memoirs the notion that the Legitimists belonged "to a single class" or a "caste." Many, he wrote, "possessed obscure names," lived in modest conditions, and engaged in "manual trades."[1] In an important respect, Meaux was wrong. Legitimists could be found in all classes and all regions, but the active cadres of the party possessed a more exalted social profile, dominated by the *grands propriétaires.*

Table I records that the Legitimists, despite a preponderance of *propriétaires,* occupied a number of different professions but that these were largely the ones traditionally filled by the French notables.[2] Legitimism gained the support of a coalition of wealthy landed proprietors

1. Vicomte Marie Camille Alfred de Meaux, *Souvenirs politiques, 1870–1877* (Paris, 1905), 10.
2. This sample was compiled from short biographical sketches of 543 Legitimist deputies, general counselors, minor civil servants, journalists, *hommes des lettres,* and papal

who often had diverse business interests and links to the business community, a small number of industrialists, and a section of the provincial professional bourgeoisie. In a predominantly rural society that was undergoing a slow process of industrialization and that included numerous

---

zouaves active in public life between 1848 and 1880. The average age of these Legitimists was fifty-three in 1870; most (77 percent) were born between 1800 and 1829.

The figures in Table I are in substantial agreement with those established by Robert R. Locke, who studied 186 Legitimist deputies in the National Assembly of 1871 (*French Legitimists and the Politics of Moral Order in the Early Third Republic* [Princeton, 1974], 127), and Louis Girard, who offered a professional breakdown for 415 Legitimist general counselors serving in 1870 (*Les Conseillers généraux en 1870: Etude statistique d'un personnel politique* [Paris, 1967], 197–98). Many of the subjects of those two studies are included in the present survey, since they were the most prominent Legitimists, but the addition of 92 others does not significantly alter the picture.

All three samples are similar in composition and suffer equally from the exclusion of Legitimists in the department of the Seine, an inclusion of which presumably would have increased the number of businessmen and liberal professionals. In Paris, however, the Legitimists were neither numerous nor politically influential. In February, 1871, only 2 Legitimists out of a delegation of 43 representatives were elected to the National Assembly from the Seine, and in my sample only 16, or 2.9 percent, resided there throughout the year. Those Legitimists who did live part time in the Parisian faubourgs almost always maintained châteaus in the provinces, and if they sought public office, they did so in their departmental districts.

Locke's sample includes a lower percentage of *propriétaires* and a higher percentage of businessmen, because he chose to classify the deputies according to which category "best reveals their relationship to the economy," explaining that *propriétaires* with important financial or corporate interests were classed as industrialists on the grounds that "association with big business is more significant than other occupations." I have chosen to group the Legitimists with multiple occupations according to the first occupation listed in the sources. For example, Joseph de Foresta, Chambord's political agent in the Bouches-du-Rhône, was involved in the railroad and armaments industries in Provence, but the administration considered him above all a *grand propriétaire terrien*. Girard's sample includes rather obscure general counselors who were apt to be landowners influential only in their cantons, whereas Locke's deputies were often prominent national leaders residing in towns where electoral lists were drawn up. In my sample, 85, or 32 percent, of those designated as *propriétaires* in Table I possessed more than one source of income; of these, 14 were industrialists, 34 were members of the professions (mainly lawyers), and 14 were officials in the administration or the judiciary. Out of a total of 513 Legitimists, 188, or 36.3 percent, had more than one occupation, in the military (50 percent), business (13 percent), agriculture (23.7 percent), or the professions (39.8 percent).

All three surveys demonstrate the exclusion of the Legitimists from the upper reaches of the state bureaucracy. Although 512 Legitimists were elected to political office a total of 1,056 times between 1830 and 1876, they received only 191 administrative appointments, 168 of which were as *maires* under the July Monarchy and the Second Empire. There were only 4 subprefects and 1 ambassador.

small- and medium-size towns, there was nothing anomalous about this particular group of notables.

The typical Legitimist was identified not only as a *propriétaire* but as a member of the Old Regime nobility. Although there is a reason to argue that the nineteenth-century French nobility was distinguished from other social groups by its choice of professions, its tastes, its matrimonial alliances, and its preference for Legitimism in politics, the Legitimists and the nobles were not one and the same group.[3] André Jean Tudesq and Robert Locke have demonstrated the high percentage of bourgeois in the ranks of Legitimists. Moreover, as Tudesq has demonstrated, the nobles and bourgeois at the top of France's social hierarchy became "amalgamated" into a "society of notables."[4]

Undeniably, more nobles were attracted to Legitimism, either by family tradition or by choice, than to any competing ideology. The aristocracy constituted a majority of the party's leadership. The Orleanists had their share of representatives from the *ancienne noblesse,* including the Duc de Broglie, Comte d'Haussonville, and Duc de Noailles, but no group apart from the Legitimists could claim the membership of so many descendants of the old noble families, like the Goutant-Birons, La Monnerayes, or La Rouchfoucauld-Bisaccias. Louis Girard has shown that 69.5 percent of the Legitimists who were general counselors in 1870 were nobles, whereas nobles made up only 28 percent of the Orleanists, 14 percent of the liberals, and a paltry 3.7 percent of the republicans and social democrats.[5] In March, 1871, Hippolyte de La Grimaudière self-consciously warned the editor of the *Journal de Rennes* that the electoral list of the *comité royaliste* of Ille-et-Vilaine read a bit too much like the

3. See David Higgs, "Politics and Landownership Among the French Nobility After the Revolution," *European Studies Review,* I (1971), 116; David Higgs, *Nobles in Nineteenth-Century France: The Practice of Inegalitarianism* (Baltimore, 1987); Thomas Beck, "Occupation, Taxes, and a Distinct Nobility Under Louis-Philippe," *European Studies Review,* XIII (1983), 403–22; and Ralph Gibson, "The French Nobility in the Nineteenth Century—Particularly in the Dordogne," in *Elites in France: Origins, Reproduction, and Power,* ed. Jolyen Howorth and Philip Cerney (New York, 1981), 6–45.
4. See especially Locke, *French Legitimists,* 54–139; Tudesq, *Les Grands Notables en France,* I; Gérard Gaudin, "Le Royalisme dans les Bouches-du-Rhône, 1876–1927" (Thèse, 3rd cycle, Université de Aix-en-Provence, 1978); Michel Denis, *Les Royalistes de la Mayenne et le Monde moderne, XIXe–XXe siècles* (Paris, 1977); and Y. M. Hilaire, *Une Chrétienté au XIXe siècle? La Vie religieuse des populations du diocèse d'Arras, 1840–1914* (2 vols.; Lille, 1977).
5. Girard *et al., Les Conseillers généraux en 1870,* 139.

Almanach du Gotha and suggested the addition of some "names taken from the bourgeoisie."[6]

But the social diversity of the Legitimists is equally important. Locke has found that 55 percent of the Legitimist deputies elected in 1871 were nobles and that 45 percent "had no claim to noble status."[7] My own research shows that out of 543 Legitimists active in public life between 1848 and 1876, 198, or 36.5 percent, were nobles and 238, or 43.9 percent, were members of the bourgeoisie. Whatever the precise ratio, it is clear that nobles made up no more than half the Legitimists, and it is the coexistence of two social groups in a single ideologically defined movement that seems most significant. Bourgeois Legitimists like Emmanuel Lucien-Brun in Lyon, Charles Kolb-Bernard in Lille, Ferdinand Béchard and Louis-Numa Baragnon in Nîmes, Maurice Aubry and Jacques Hervé-Bazin in the Vosges, and Henri Carron in Rennes were influential party leaders. Legitimist propaganda in the 1870s was quick to point out that the monarchy had always been served by distinguished *roturiers* from Denis Frayssinous to Antoine Berryer, and Orleanists interested in a political alliance with the Legitimists reminded liberal monarchists of the "essentially popular character" of many prominent Legitimists like Charles Chesnelong, Octave Depeyre, and Edmond Ernoul.[8] In Marseille, the chamber of commerce was controlled for a long time by a local Legitimist merchant-and-banking oligarchy that included men with close ties to the clergy and to powerful charitable organizations.[9] Through southern commerce and banking, northern industry, journalism, charitable activity, letters, politics, and law, many provincial bourgeois associated with influential nobles and made their way to prominence in the royalist movement. As Table II shows, however, they often differed from their aristocratic counterparts in profession and economic status.

6. Hippolyte de La Grimaudière to Barthélemy Pocquet, March, 1871, in *Légitimistes parlementaires: Correspondance politique de Barthélemy Pocquet, rédacteur du "Journal de Rennes," 1848–1878*, ed. Barthélemy A. Pocquet du Haut-Jussé (Paris, 1976), 145.

7. Locke, *French Legitimists*, 70–72.

8. See Prosper Vedrenne, *Vive le roi!* (Toulouse, 1871), 34; Ferdinand Bernard, *Le Parlementairianisme, la Dictateur et la Monarchie légitime* (Poitiers, 1882), 24. Vedrenne wrote that the "greatest party of men" who "fight for the royal cause" were "men of popular origin." Bernard, an Orleanist, called the effort to restore "Henri V" a "national movement" arising "from the profound feelings of the people."

9. See Bernard Jacquier, *Le Légitimisme dauphinois, 1830–1870* (Grenoble, 1976), 30–31; and Tudesq, *Les Grands Notables en France*, I, 158–59, 173, 195–96.

Table II   Income and Professions of Noble and Bourgeois Legitimists

Yearly Income in Francs	Bourgeois	Nobles
500–5,000	17	3
5,001–10,000	41	3
10,001–30,000	40	47
30,001–50,000	12	19
50,001–80,000	4	14
80,001–100,000	2	4
Above 100,000	5	19

Profession	% of Bourgeois	% of Nobles
Agriculture	37.2	70.2
Business	8.3	4.2
Administrative	3.0	3.0
Liberal	36.8	12.8
Military	4.0	9.5

SOURCE: Conseillers généraux de 1870, in F (I) b 230, 1–20, AN.

Few Legitimists were industrialists, but there were not many industrialists in France anyway. That did not mean, though, that the Legitimists, noble or common, isolated themselves from the world of business and industry or from the general economic expansion of the nineteenth century.[10] Even before the Revolution, the nobility had actively participated in mercantile exchange, capital investment, and stock trading. Its ranks possessed by far the largest surpluses of wood, wine, and wheat in the kingdom.[11] In the nineteenth century, Legitimist nobles continued this traditional economic involvement by joining in the expansion of the industrial sector.[12] With members like Charles de Wendel, Benoist d'Azy,

10. See Mme. Sontade-Rouger, "Les Notables en France sous la Restauration," *Revue d'histoire économique et sociale,* XXXVIII (1960), 98–110; Girard et al., *Les Conseillers généraux en 1870,* 80–82; Tudesq, *Les Grands Notables en France,* I, 261–313; Locke, *French Legitimists,* 98–139; and Plessis, *De la fête impériale,* 166–67.
11. Guy Richard, "La Noblesse d'affaires en France de 1750 à 1850," *Revue internationale d'histoire de la Banque,* XIII (1976), 2–7. See also Guy Chaussinand-Nogaret, *The French Nobility in the Eighteenth Century: From Feudalism to Enlightenment* (London, 1985), Chapter 5; and Denis, *Les Royalistes de la Mayenne,* 11.
12. See Tudesq, *Les Grands Notables en France,* I, 194–95, 423–24, 630–31.

Table III   Income of 319 Legitimists

Yearly Income in Francs	Number	%
100–5,000	24	7.5
5,001–10,000	58	18.1
10,001–20,000	87	27.2
20,001–50,000	93	29.1
50,001–100,000	34	10.6
Above 100,000	23	7.2
Total	319	99.7

SOURCE: Conseillers généraux de 1870, in F (I) b 230, 1–20, AN.

and Roger de Larcy, the Legitimist aristocracy included some of the richest industrialists of their day.[13] In the early stages of industrialization, aristocratic wealth was one of the few sources of capital available.[14]

But great wealth was no more reliable a correlate of Legitimism than noble origins. Legitimist notables engaged in a wide variety of economic and professional activities across the country, and consequently large differentials of wealth existed among them. Far from being exclusively rich landowners and businessmen, the group was hospitable to the coexistence of extremes, as Table III makes plain.

Lawyers, notaries, doctors, and state officials tended to be less wealthy; *propriétaires* and industrialists had relatively large fortunes. Although *pro-*

13. The Wendels ran one of the largest metallurgical enterprises in France, comparable in size to Le Creusot. By the end of the Second Empire, Wendel's mines employed 9,200 workers and were producing 134,000 tons of cast iron and 112,000 tons of pig iron, while the Schneiders were producing 130,000 tons and 100,000 tons respectively. Only of recent noble lineage, Charles de Wendel married the Comtesse de Commingues-Guitant, who came from the ancient Legitimist nobility. See Guy Palmade, *French Capitalism in the Nineteenth Century,* trans. Graeme M. Holmes (London, 1972), 155–56.

14. See Locke, *French Legitimists,* 105–15; Tudesq, *Les Grands Notables en France,* I, 92–94, 417–35, 630–31; André Jean Tudesq, "Les Survivances de l'ancien régime: La Noblesse dans la société française de la 1er moitié du XIXe siècle," in *Ordres et Classes: Colloque d'histoire sociale, St. Cloud, 1967,* ed. D. Roche and C. E. Labrousse (Saint-Cloud, 1974), 210–13; Mayer, *The Persistence of the Old Regime,* 104–105; Adeline Daumard, "La Fortune mobilière en France selon les milieux sociaux, XIXe et XXe siècles," *Revue d'histoire économique et sociale,* XLIV (1966), 388–89; Ralph Gibson, "The French Nobility in the Nineteenth Century—Particularly in the Dordogne," in *Elites in France,* ed. Howorth and Cerney, 28–31; and Fernand Braudel and Ernest Labrousse, eds., *Histoire économique et sociale de la France* (4 vols.; Paris, 1970–82), Vol. III, Part 2, p. 937.

priétaires appear in each income category, their presence increases as fortunes become larger. Of the richest individuals, with annual incomes of
50,000 francs or more, *propriétaires* made up 72.8 percent of the total.
Clearly, though, industrialists had the most wealth. Only three industrialists had incomes below 50,000 francs a year; eight appear in the highest
rank, representing 45 percent of all the industrialists in the group. They
possessed an average annual income of 228,125 francs, whereas lawyers
earned an average of 10,140 francs and *propriétaires* fell in the middle,
with an average of 50,088 francs. In reality, the fortunes of most *propriétaires* and industrialists were probably closer, since the largest industrial
incomes raised the average for the industrialists while the average income
of *propriétaires*—whose annual earnings ranged from 1,200 to 800,000
francs a year—masks the fact that the wealthiest Legitimists drew their
income primarily from their estates. Thus, among nineteenth-century
Legitimists, large landowners and industrialists together occupied the
summit of the party's social hierarchy by the criterion of economic power.

The same, however, could be said about the summit of the French
ruling class as a whole, indicating a certain integration of Legitimists
with the wider world of notables. As Girard has observed, among the
general counselors of 1870 the "great capitalist" and the "great propertied noble" were "at the same level" and "great landed fortunes" were
"often tied to great capitalist enterprises."[15] Apart from the larger number of titled noblemen in their ranks, the Legitimists were in most respects socially indistinguishable from the notables as a group. This was
true not only for the upper reaches of the Legitimist party but for Legitimists in general. By 1870, the French ruling class had undergone a long
process of "amalgamation," expansion, and diversification which not
only permitted the emergence of a stable, confident, and wealthy elite
but also presaged the integration of more modest elements into positions
of influence. That process did not weaken the fundamental barrier between the notables and the people, because it was well regulated by a
restrictive economic, educational, and political channeling of social mobility. With the social and economic fusion of the rich nobility and the
haute bourgeoisie, and the expansion of the elite to include a diverse collection of bureaucrats, officers, traditional professionals, modest business-

15. Girard *et al., Les Conseillers généraux en 1870,* 81–82. See also Tudesq, *Les Grands
Notables en France,* I, 428–32, 194.

men, and influential technicians, the composition of the *classes dirigeantes* came to reflect the growing complexity of a capitalist society with a large service sector. It now seems clear that Legitimism was not untouched by the process.

The fusion of the upper classes occurred not only on the boards of major industrial concerns, as Tudesq has noted, but also in countless localities where a common interest in economic progress and a shared social conservatism allowed elites to collaborate on matters, such as road construction, that were not overtly political.[16] Michel Denis has argued that in the Mayenne, with the decline of traditional manufacture and commercial activity during the Revolution and the Empire and the eclipse of many former *seigneurs,* the local propertied classes became more homogeneous. The royalist of the early nineteenth century was more likely to be a gentleman bourgeois than a freewheeling absentee landlord. By 1815, the differences between the nobles and the bourgeoisie became virtually imperceptible, at least in terms of net wealth, and the typical royalist, whatever his prerevolutionary antecedents, lived "more or less on [his] rents."[17] Even if political differences became more inflexible after the Revolution of 1830, "the chatelains became farmers, the richest liberal merchants acquired a château. . . . Whites and Blues saw their interests come together even though they still mistrusted each other."[18] According to Gustave de Bernardi, a Legitimist from the Vaucluse, the "Third Estate had forced the Second Estate to renounce its traditions and to adopt the mores and the *métier* of the shopkeeper."[19] As the distinction between noble and bourgeois, so prominent in the political conflicts of the Restoration, came to matter less and less in public affairs, many liberals followed François Guizot into a rigid conservatism, and parliamentary Legitimists and Catholics like Alfred de Falloux, Antoine Berryer, and Charles de Montalembert appeared in the Chamber of Deputies to act in concert as the Party of Order against the threats of electoral reform, social unrest, and democracy.

The reaction against the social experiments of the Second Republic,

16. Tudesq, *Les Grand Notables en France,* I, 422–31. Tudesq sees no separation between "the great proprietors who commercialize their agricultural production and the manufacturers whose clientele is more national than local," and he emphasizes landed wealth as a common source of investment capital in industry.

17. Denis, *Les Royalistes de la Mayenne,* 27–35.

18. *Ibid.,* 247.

19. Gustave de Bernardi, *La Révolution* (Paris, 1873), 116–17.

the rise of republican anticlericalism, and the religious fervor of the 1850s and 1860s revealed splits in the middle class which favored Legitimist recruitment. Many provincial bourgeois joined a large segment of the clergy in viewing a restoration as the best means to save society and the church from revolutionaries, secular nationalists, and freethinkers; the integration of these "clerico-Legitimists" into the old royalist party expanded its middle-class base. The clericals were younger, less wealthy, and less inclined toward compromise than the moderate Legitimists and liberal Catholics who dominated the party before 1848. While *propriétaires* made up 41.7 percent of the moderates, they constituted only 24 percent of the clerico-Legitimists, whose ranks included a far higher number of professionals (48.1 percent, compared with 25.5 percent) and a greater number earning between a thousand and twenty thousand francs per year (66.4 percent, against 8.3 percent). Of the moderates, 33.3 percent had incomes in excess of a hundred thousand francs, but only 2.2 percent of the clerico-Legitimists fell into that category. Nobles were also in a clear minority (12.2 percent) among the clerico-Legitimists; they dominated the older, more moderate group (58.3 percent).

The advent of universal suffrage, the expansion of the political class after 1848, and the steady growth of business activity and educational opportunities under the Second Empire continued to draw new elements into the elite. The economic boom of the 1850s and 1860s created an ever-increasing number of small- and medium-size enterprises that served to increase the clout of the middle class.[20] Secondary-school enrollments grew considerably, with the total number of students rising from 70,500 to 154,700 between 1842 and 1876.[21] Such increases provided many from the "lower ranks of the middle class" with the opportunity to slip through the formidable barrier between the notables and the masses.[22]

20. Adeline Daumard, "L'Evolution des structures sociales en France à l'époque de l'industrialisation," *Revue historique*, DII (1972), 326–41; Braudel and Labrousse, eds., *Histoire économique et sociale de la France*, Vol. III, Part 2, pp. 870, 905.
21. Fritz Ringer, *Education and Society in Modern Europe* (Bloomington, Ind., 1979), 134–36, 316; Robert D. Anderson, *Education in France, 1848–1870* (Oxford, 1975), 102–103.
22. Patrick J. Harrigan, *Mobility, Elites, and Education in French Society Under the Second Empire* (Waterloo, Ont., 1980), 7, 150–57; Robert D. Anderson, "New Light on French Secondary Education in the Nineteenth Century," *Social History*, VII (1982), 148–51, 162–63; Anderson, *Education in France*, 12–13; Robert D. Anderson, "Secondary Education in Mid Nineteenth-Century France: Some Social Aspects," *Past and Present*, LIII (1971), 132–35, 144–45; Patrick J. Harrigan, "Elites, Education, and Social Mobility in France During the Second Empire," *Proceedings of the Western Society for French History*, IV

Politics, and especially Bonapartist politics, also helped diversify socially the *classes dirigeantes,* by expanding the central bureaucracy and by establishing a system of official candidates that aimed at detaching the rural masses from their party allegiances. The strategy often failed in regions, like Brittany, where notables hostile to the regime were politically entrenched, but it encouraged the shifting of local loyalties, disturbed established ties of patronage, and forced the Legitimists as well as other notables accustomed to an obedient constituency to enter political contests and compete for votes they had previously taken for granted.[23] Bonapartist authoritarianism had the consequence of democratizing French politics and diversifying the available hierarchies of political leadership, for it permitted cooperative *roturiers* to break into the system and it weakened the power of the old monarchist political cadres.[24]

These forces did not cause dramatic changes in France's social structure, but they tended to create strong similarities in the composition of the various political parties. Girard's study of the general counselors of

---

(1976), 334–41. Legitimists feared that secondary education would give many *bacheliers* a taste for the professions, which they considered "much too encumbered" already. They also hoped, however, that secondary education would provide industry, agriculture, and technical fields with more able workers and managers. Thus, for the Legitimists the concern over *déclassement* had more to do with the nature of French secondary education and the fear that the public schools would produce a generation of liberals than with the question of mobility per se. See, for example, Gavardie, *Etudes sur les vraies doctrines sociales,* 96–97.

23. See especially Theodore Zeldin, *The Political System of Napoleon III* (London, 1958), 16–19; Zeldin, *France, 1848–1945,* 164–81; and Judith Silver, "French Peasant Demands for Popular Leadership in the Vendômois (Loir-et-Cher)," *Journal of Social History,* XIV (1980), 277–94. C. B. Dupont-White, who was one of the principal theoreticians of Napoleonic centralization, saw the state as a primary instrument of social progress, with the duty to rise above the political melee and serve the interests of society against the "castes," the church, the corporations, the aristocrats, and the provinces (*La Centralisation* [Paris, 1860]). The regime of Napoleon III generally feared independent local power and often tried to neutralize local influences by appointing officials from outside the area where they were to serve. They could thus create an alternative network of patronage. For examples of that, see Bernard Menager, *La Vie politique dans le département du Nord de 1851 à 1877* (3 vols.; Dunkerque, 1983), I, 186; and Henri Goallou, "Les Déboires de la candidature officielle," *Annales de Bretagne,* LXXVII (1970), 305. For the Comte de Falloux' reaction to Bonapartist methods, see his "L'Agriculture et la Politique," in *Etudes et souvenirs* (2 vols.; Paris, 1885), II, 275–76.

24. Maurice Duverger, *La Démocratie sans le peuple* (Paris, 1967), 195; Rémond, *Les Droites en France,* 108–109; Michel Belanger, *Les Conseillers généraux de Charente sous le Second Empire* (Angoulême, 1969), 18, 22–28. In 1865, Xavier de Fontaines observed that in each successive municipal election, "the job of counselor falls . . . to an inferior class" (La Broise, *Le Vrai et le Faux Libéralisme,* 81n).

Table IV   Income of Counselors and Legitimists

Yearly Income in Francs	% of Counselors	% of Legitimists
0–5,000	9.4	7.5
5,001–10,000	19.8	18.2
10,001–15,000	17.9	13.8
15,001–20,000	8.0	13.4
20,001–30,000	16.9	15.9
30,001–50,000	12.6	13.1
50,001–100,000	9.4	10.6
Above 100,000	6.1	7.2

SOURCE: Conseillers généraux de 1870, in F (I) b 230, 1–20, AN; Louis Girard *et al.*, *Les Conseillers généraux en 1870: Etude statistique d'un personnel politique* (Paris, 1967), 197–98.

1870 shows that *propriétaires* had proportionally almost as much of a presence (31.7 percent) among the Orleanists as among the Legitimists (45.5 percent) and that businessmen had a modest representation in both camps.[25] Many among the Orleanist deputies of 1871, Locke found, "were no more important as financiers, industrialists, or small businessmen than their Legitimist colleagues."[26] *Propriétaires* remained predominant within the elite through the nineteenth century, but the role of the professionals grew steadily, accounting for about 20 percent of the deputies in the Chamber in 1840 and 49 percent of those in the National Assembly in 1871.[27] Table IV illustrates the striking similarities in the income levels of Legitimist general counselors and general counselors as a group in 1870.[28] Thus, by 1875, Charles Bigot, a supporter of Léon

25. Girard *et al.*, *Les Conseillers généraux en 1870*, 47–53. Of the electors paying more than a thousand francs in *cens* in 1840, only 16 percent were businessmen or industrialists, but their influence was greater than their numbers suggest. For the social origins of the Orleanists, see Sherman Kent, *Electoral Procedure Under Louis Philippe* (New Haven, 1937), and Locke, *French Legitimists*, 128–32.

26. Locke, *French Legitimists*, 128.

27. See Mattei Dogan, "Les Filières de la carrière politique en France," *Revue français de sociologie*, VIII (1967), 472.

28. Girard *et al.*, *Les Conseillers généraux en 1870*, 47, 197–98; André Jean Tudesq, *Les Conseillers généraux en France au temps de Guizot* (Paris, 1967), 115–17, 232–36; Georges Dupeux, *Aspects de l'histoire sociale et politique du Loir-et-Cher, 1848–1914* (Paris, 1962), 138–43; Braudel and Labrousse, eds., *Histoire économique et sociale de la France*, Vol. III, Part 2, pp. 914–15, 936–37; Philippe Levillain, *Albert de Mun: Catholicisme français et catholicisme romain, du syllabus au ralliement* (Rome, 1983), 196, 207; Daumard, "La Fortune mobilière," 392.

Gambetta, could conclude that the *classes dirigeantes* were "three classes": a nobility without legal rights and a dubious economic advantage, a rich bourgeoisie of "great landed *propriétaires* and great holders of financial stock," and a *moyenne bourgeoisie* of "lawyers, notaries, doctors, functionaries, *rentiers,* and merchants on the make." [29]

The French elite was small by definition, but it had a degree of internal social heterogeneity that owed to contrasts in wealth, rank, and life-style based on stable yet open professional hierarchies. Never threatening the political and social predominance of the established elites, newcomers to positions of status quickly joined in the elites' commitment to maintain the rigid distinction between themselves and the masses. Since stability was seen as a supreme good, distinctions of social rank ceased to determine political and ideological allegiances. Legitimists, Orleanists, and Bonapartists were in general agreement that nobility was above all an honorific distinction, and although nobles often intermarried, titles, family histories, and matrimonial affairs increasingly became private preoccupations. The Comte de Puységur saw his own title as a *culte de famille,* and the Alsatian journalist Charles Muller affirmed that the importance of titles did not reach beyond "salons" and "questions of marriage." [30] The elites attended the same schools and mixed publicly—in church-related activities, salons, electoral committees, political assemblies, corporate boardrooms, and agricultural and literary societies.[31] Jean Dubois found that in the late 1860s and early 1870s, unlike thirty years earlier, the political vocabulary usually referred to the *noblesse* and the bourgeoisie together as the *classes élevées* and even the republican press often called the monarchists *gentilhommes bourgeois* to "underline the integration of the nobility into the largest class of wealthy persons." [32] Well-reasoned ideological principles were worth fighting for, but smart people knew that considerations of rank were too unimportant to com-

29. Bigot, *Les Classes dirigeantes,* 20–21. See also Adeline Daumard, "Les Fondements de la société bourgeoise en France au XIXe siècle," in *Ordres et Classes: Colloque d'histoire sociale, St.-Cloud, 1967,* ed. D. Roche and C. E. Labrousse (Saint-Cloud, 1974), 220.

30. Auguste de Chastenet de Puységur, *La Fusion* (Toulouse, 1851), 41; Muller, *L'Empire et les Légitimistes,* 18–19.

31. See Adeline Daumard, "Les Elèves de L'Ecole Polytechnique de 1815 à 1848," *Revue d'histoire moderne et contemporaine,* V (1958), 226–31; Gaudin, "Le Royalisme dans les Bouches-du-Rhône," 26; and Rémond, *Les Droites en France,* 136.

32. Jean Dubois, *Le Vocabulaire politique et sociale en France de 1869 à 1872* (Paris, 1962), 14, 65. Similarly, Comte Adrien de Mailly, Marquis de Nesle, wrote that "the upper classes include . . . the French aristocracy in its generality" (*La Révolution est-elle finie?* [Paris, 1853], 81).

plicate the already difficult task of fashioning the institutions through which the notables would rule.

The Legitimists understood that they were part of a society of notables united by their accord on the permanent nature of social inequalities and disturbed by continual constitutional instability and social unrest. The rivalries among the notables were more ideological than social, and the pressure of coalition politics merely heightened the Legitimists' desire to stress what united them to other elites and to forgo prattle about privileges and titles. For them, the monarchy represented an ideological *main tendue,* since they believed they could sell the idea of a restoration as the best means of stabilizing French politics and society and of preventing a repetition of the bloody factional conflicts that the Revolution had brought. They felt that the "revolutionary spirit" could gain partisans even among the "most cultivated" and that "rationalist ideas" could seduce "honest men" regardless of class distinction. They believed that values, and not rank, were responsible for the dangerously intractable division within the elite.[33] "Wealth, rank, and state of mind mean nothing," wrote Monsignor Louis de Ségur about the disposition of the conscience. "One can be a revolutionary at any degree on the social scale: it is a matter of principles and of conduct" to stay "outside the camp of the Revolution."[34]

French notables, Legitimist and not, had come to recognize the right of each party to claim membership in the political class, to exercise social power, and to govern the nation. To a Legitimist, the republicans were dangerous not because they were bourgeois but because they were "social atheists." At the same time, a kind of schizophrenia arose within the elite which produced a constant fission of coalitions, along with repeated appeals for unity. The principal question raised by the social integration of the notables was how to coexist politically in light of ideological divisions, in order to preserve a collective hegemony in the face of revolutionary social democracy. Except for socialism, the major French ideologies of the nineteenth century—with their common emphasis on stability, institutional consolidation, and the arrest of the Revolution at a certain point of its articulation—formed around a common recognition that the social and ideological diversity of the elites made it necessary to nurture their unity of purpose by creating institutions that would allow

33. *Revue indépendante,* February 15, 1865, p. 450; Guillaume Véran, *La Question du XIXe siècle* (Paris, 1866), 369.
34. Louis Gaston Adrien de Ségur, *La Révolution* (4th ed.; Paris, 1872), 113.

them to overcome their historic failure to resolve disputes among themselves. Far from being on the fringe of French political discourse, Legitimism shared equally in the collective obsession with disunity. The Legitimists' notion of the composition and purpose of the *classes dirigeantes* was forged in the general search for a political consensus compatible with the social makeup of their party and of the society of notables overall.

IN SEARCH OF A CLASSLESS ELITE

In a debate before the Corps Législatif in 1858 on regulating the authenticity of titles, M. Miral, a Bonapartist deputy, suggested that nobility signified no "material reality" and that the hierarchy of functions created by the development of the French state mitigated the necessity of re-creating a nobility, since that in effect already existed by virtue of the notables' control over the levers of power. For most notables, a viable ruling class was already in place and titles merely provided signs of distinction to honor prevailing social conditions.[35] The Legitimists could generally concur with that idea: they accepted the collapse of the society of orders and recognized that the existing nobility could not rule alone. For them, it was not a question of changing the ruling class but of redefining the ends to which it devoted itself.

The Legitimists made a point of declaring their acceptance of the most basic "conquests of 1789." Highly critical of the Revolution, Amédée de Margerie, a professor on the faculty of letters at Nancy, nevertheless agreed that the upheaval had swept away the most "oppressive" aspects of the Old Regime. But he thought that the defects of the system were already "in the process of disappearing" in 1789 and that the monarchy had had every intention of redressing them. "Royalty," he wrote in 1873, "has not given itself the task of resuscitating the dead." To believe that the monarchy wished to reestablish noble privileges was an insult to those who supported it. "It will treat men according to their talents and their character, not according to their titles of nobility, and the bourgeois who fears that it prefers the titled gentleman to the gentleman is no less credulous than the peasant who fears that it will send him out at night to silence the frogs in the moats of the châteaus."[36]

In a polemic fashion, Margerie was repeating what had been stated in

---

35. Rapport du M. Miral au Corps Législatif, 1858, quoted by Nicolas Batjin in *Histoire complète de la noblesse de 1789 à 1861* (Paris, 1862), 320.

36. Amédée de Margerie, *La Solution* (Paris, 1880), 50.

the letters and manifestos of the Comte de Chambord since the 1840s. In 1848, the pretender reassured the Duc de Noailles, a leading Orleanist, that the national regeneration envisioned by the monarchy would require the cooperation of all "distinguished men." He continued, "I understand how time and events have shaped the conditions of contemporary society; I recognize the multitude of new interests that have been created in France and the social rank that is legitimately acquired by intelligence and capacity. Exempt from prejudice . . . I will try to bring together all the talent and all the intellectual forces of Frenchmen to cooperate in the prosperity and glory of France." In 1850, he wrote, "How after this can people still suspect me of being the king of a privileged caste or . . . the king of the Old Regime, the old nobility, and the old court?"[37] For positive effect, Chambord pledged himself in 1851 to the "maxims" that parliamentarians had discussed at the tribunal: "equality before the law, freedom of conscience, free access for all who merit to all positions, honors, and social advantages"; these, he said, were the "great principles of an enlightened and Christian society." In his famous manifesto of 1871 he declared once again his respect for the "lessons of history" and for equality before the law, and he reminded the notables that the old monarchy had always practiced that principle by taking "its ministers from all ranks of society." He asserted, "In modern society, the situation must be the same for all, there can be no personal privilege, and sovereigns must be able to choose freely from among all classes."[38]

Such pronouncements were frequent in 1848–1851 and in the 1870s and were, of course, preeminently political, calculated at once to combat propaganda about the reactionary intention of the Right and to assure the liberals that their interests would be respected. The Legitimists wanted to convince the notables of their sincere desire for a social and political, if not an ideological, fusion that would enable the monarchist parties to bar the way to Bonapartists and republicans and restore Chambord through a parliamentary majority. Politics aside, Chambord's declara-

37. Comte de Chambord, *La Monarchie française: Lettres et Documents politiques* (Paris, 1908), 32–35; Jean Dubosc de Pesquidoux, *Le Comte de Chambord d'après lui-même: Etude politique et historique* (Paris, 1887), 106–109. Meaux explained that the "fruits of time, progress, and Christian civilization" had resulted in the "union of classes" and the effacement of all divisions and insurmountable social barriers. He saw this achievement as "the brightest honor of 1789" (*Annales,* March 5, 1872, VIII, 185).

38. Ferdinand Jacques Hervé-Bazin, *La Monarchie selon le programme du roi* (Paris, 1882), 72.

tions paradoxically restated the concept of an aristocratic monarchy developed by such eighteenth-century thinkers as François Fénelon, Marie Chevreuse, and the Duc de Beauvilliers, the last of these a bitter opponent of the absolutism of his ancestors. The Legitimists, who looked to the aristocratic critiques of the Old Regime and to the *cahiers* of the Second Estate as sources of inspiration, found in Chambord a monarch tailored to their aspirations. They often returned to the themes outlined in Chambord's letters to affirm what they saw as the proper conditions of political and social leadership.

In a pamphlet entitled *La Peur des revenants* (1851), directed at republicans who argued that the monarchy would be run by nobles and priests, Le Beschu de Champsavin tried to show empirically that demographic changes and the growth of the French state rendered impossible any plan to confine state and ecclesiastical positions to the nobility. French kings, he explained, had always chosen their administrators "under the rigorous standards adequate to those functions." Since 1789, he wrote, the "population of France has grown by more than a quarter; commerce and industry have developed marvelously." In addition, the military, the courts, and the administration required a much larger personnel. In such circumstances, the nobility, diminished in size and unreplenished by the ennoblements of the Empire and the Restoration, could not possibly fill every vacancy. The crown would never sacrifice its interest in effective government to the few "ghosts" who still thought a return to privilege possible, especially since "the majority . . . knows quite well that a return to privilege is impossible." He compared those who said that the king and the nobility wanted to reestablish privileges to a builder who thought that a single worker could transport a thousand kilograms of granite on his shoulders. Besides, he argued, even if public opinion permitted it, a nobility large enough and strong enough to serve the state would have to be as numerous as "in the time when feudalism dominated France" and that would require the king "to ennoble among the propertied and educated bourgeoisie a number of families nearly equal to those . . . who . . . formed the electoral corps" under the July Monarchy.[39] In 1851, the Comte de Montel, at one time a minister of Charles X, told Charles Muller that the "aristocratic regime" was dead because the nobility constituted neither the "necessary gears of the government machine" nor the

39. Le Beschu de Champsavin, *La Peur des revenants,* 6–11.

"most enlightened and influential part of the nation." In England, where conditions were different, the nobility had a raison d'être, but in France no class had a monopoly on intelligence or state service. The monarchy, he said, which in the past had not asked Colbert "if he had ancestors," would do well "to seek its ministers among the most eminent men, without being preoccupied with their origins."[40] Muller himself believed that civil and political equality would have triumphed in France without the Revolution, because "the aspirations of the French monarchy have always been democratic"; aristocratic power was a "transitory fact" in French history accepted by the monarchy only as a remnant of a decaying feudalism. Lacking a "determined place" in the state and the authority of a "constitutive element," the aristocracy was never a fundamental institution and its effacement had a negligible impact on the "genius of our national organization."[41] According to Louis d'Armailhac, France's natural democratic inclinations and the leveling effects of economic progress should have prevented Napoleon and Louis XVIII from introducing a hereditary peerage, but "the *parvenu* loved to mimic the Old Regime" and Louis XVIII, exiled in England, granted France an "English charter without bothering to question whether it suited our mores, our traditions, our accomplishments, or our aspirations for the future."[42]

Public opinion and new circumstances required new measurements of social authority and a new language with which to speak about social status. Discarding the term *nobility,* the Legitimists preferred to speak of the *classes supérieures,* the elite, or the *classes dirigeantes,* by which they meant those who were the best in everything, qualified by their wealth, virtue, and intelligence to direct the affairs of society. By changing the terminology, the Legitimists announced their acceptance of new criteria. Comte Albert de Mun defined the *classes dirigeantes* as "those on whom the advantages of education, knowledge, and wealth . . . confer, vis-à-vis those who lack these gifts, an authority, an influence, in a word, the means of moral and material action, the precise use of which constitutes social leadership."[43] While Mun saw wealth, talent, and intelligence as an

---

40. Quoted by Charles Muller in *La Légitimité* (Paris, 1857), 243.

41. *Ibid.,* 247–48.

42. Louis d'Armailhac, *La Légitimité et le Progrès, par un économiste* (Bordeaux, 1871), 87–91.

43. Albert de Mun, *Ma vocation sociale: Souvenirs de la fondation de l'Oeuvre des Cercles Catholiques d'Ouvriers, 1871–1875* (Paris, 1908), 83.

obligating gift, Berryer saw them as serving to distinguish the notables from the masses.[44] The social effect, however, was the same. What seems most important was the greater Legitimist focus on the themes of education and virtue and the reduced focus on wealth and experience after midcentury. Margerie stressed a "liberal education" and an "intellectual culture" as well as wealth among the criteria for elite status, and A. de Béchade asserted that "the great modern nobility is the nobility of education."[45]

As for titles, Falloux thought that whatever implicit advantage they had given toward securing a place in state service no longer existed, and he pointed out that young nobles often found their titles to be "inconveniences and obstacles." Legitimists preferred "bourgeois" standards for determining social authority, he maintained, because they shared with other notables the assumption that success in social competition exhibited the superior virtue of those who earned a place at the top of the social hierarchy. Legitimists who believed public office to be closed to them, he suggested, should rejoice in the bourgeois standards because "personal values" counted more than birth and on that criterion there was no group more worthy on the whole to exercise authority than they.[46] Prince Auguste de Croy-Chanel argued that civil equality benefited the nobility because it made possible the association of titles and merit and thus ended the harmful perception of the nobility as parasitical.[47] Moreover, bourgeois standards of success conformed to contemporary social realities: by opening the elite to all who could demonstrate merit and good character within narrowly prescribed material boundaries, old rivalries had been quelled and new links had become feasible. At midcentury, Falloux was observing that "emulation" had replaced "base jealousies" in the competition for social rank, and Muller testified that many nobles had been converted to the new thinking upon realizing that "sixty years of egalitarianism" had not reduced their "importance in the world," an importance that under modern conditions "no longer ex-

44. Antoine Berryer, quoted in *Histoire économique et sociale de la France,* ed. Braudel and Labrousse, Vol. III, Part 2, p. 942.
45. Amédée de Margerie, *La Restauration de la France* (Paris, 1872), 61; A. de Béchade, *Le Noeud gordien: Légitimité au radicalisme* (Bordeaux, 1873), 3.
46. Comte Alfred de Falloux, "Les Républicains et les Monarchistes depuis la Révolution de février," *Revue des deux mondes,* XXI (1851), 398.
47. Prince Auguste de Croy-Chanel, *La Noblesse et les Titres nobiliaires dans les sociétés chrétiennes* (Paris, 1857), 14–15.

cite[d] so much jealousy and hatred" against those who seemed "to hold a hereditary monopoly."[48]

Modern criteria were more likely to be successful in establishing social demarcations than the criteria of the past, it was thought, because authority would be conferred on the basis of proven capacity. The Legitimists often argued that the social model of the Old Regime and the material qualifications of the Empire and of the *monarchies censitaires* were no longer tenable because the middle class had absorbed both the nobility and certain popular elements.[49] Property qualifications had served only to offend the egalitarian sensibilities of the masses, they conceded, and wealth by itself was not an index of the moral qualities necessary for leadership. The Legitimists' emphasis on morality largely depreciated older distinctions of rank and fostered a discourse that nullified the ideological importance of external signs of social status. Most Legitimists believed that the Revolution had dismantled the old social hierarchy less by abolishing privileges than by instilling in the people a new spirit of equality that threatened to sever social bonds and overturn the notion of authority itself. Thus, in rejecting a legally defined nobility, they emphasized that a democratic society needed a "new aristocracy" of virtue and of acquired respect to hold the anarchic passions of the masses in check. Appealing to the standards of antiquity, Ferdinand Béchard declared that the "false aristocracy is irrevocably condemned" because "the jealous mores of our century only recognize proven virtue: Nobilitas cognita virtus." The "new aristocracy" had to reconquer the esteem, the power, and the influence necessary to integrate morally a society shattered by egalitarianism and universal suffrage.[50] In that task, titles were deemed meaningless; when opinion and comportment determined everything, democratic aristocracies could rule only by moral example.[51] Bernardi

48. Falloux, "Les Républicains et les Monarchistes," *Revue des deux mondes,* XXI (1851), 398; Muller, *La Légitimité,* 232.

49. In 1889, on the eve of the centenary of the French Revolution, Mun argued that social classes were divided along professional lines because social authority no longer corresponded to social rank: "The bourgeoisie has received certain satisfactions from the Revolution, the nobility has lost its rank in the state, but in the end, dissolved into the bourgeoisie, it participates in the condition of the latter" (Discours prononcé par Albert de Mun, in *Le Centenaire de 1788* [Paris, 1889], 10).

50. Ferdinand Béchard, *De l'administration intérieure de la France* (2 vols.; Paris, 1851), I, 89–91.

51. Margerie, *La Restauration,* 113.

believed that in modern society the aristocracy could not be a "superior caste" but had to include "all who distinguished themselves by the most excellent qualities," qualities that imparted "legitimate preeminence, consideration, and advantage." Such advantages do not exist naturally, he held, but are conferred on those who, through "their honesty, their justice, their continence, and their work," courageously set an example of virtue worthy of respect and deference in a Christian society. "For the needy," he wrote, "the rich man is the aristocracy; . . . for the impious, for the squanderer, for the drunkard, the aristocracy comprises the religious, the thrifty, the sober."[52]

On this view, the ideal social authorities were to be found not in traditional aristocratic institutions like salons and the Jockey Club but in Christian schools, charitable societies, and the provincial châteaus. The benevolent *propriétaire* who guided his peasants, conducted local affairs with attention to the moral needs of the people, and remained indifferent to personal advancement and uncorrupted by the lure of the city was more likely to understand his social obligations than the high bureaucrat or the idle rich who frequented *la société mondaine*. Margerie preferred the students of the Catholic *collège* at which he taught to the gilded youth of the capital who spent their time reading novels rather than books of law, who sat in the cafés smoking and playing cards instead of occupying their time with the innocent pleasures of study or commerce. The Comte de Mailly, the Marquis de Nesle, thought that the sons of the new aristocracy should be educated in the countryside in traditional Christian values, and he condemned the swarm of city slickers, dandies, and weaklings who waited anxiously for the next opening in the offices of the Conseil d'Etat.[53] For the Legitimists, the aristocracy was not synonymous with privilege but was associated with patronage and a recognition

52. Gustave de Bernardi, *La Vérité divine et l'Idée humaine; ou, Christianisme et Révolution* (Paris, 1870), 317–18. Muller, who stated that the nobility no longer had a "proper value," portrayed the Legitimists as a party more inclined to honor "grand traditions" than to revere the spirit of a "caste." He wrote, "It respects the heraldry that is respectable, but it puts, in its esteem, the lowest farm worker of the Vendée above a Biron who commanded the revolutionary army sent against the royalist and Catholic army" (*La Légitimité*, 249–50).
53. Margerie, *La Restauration*, 63–64; Mailly-Nesle, *La Révolution est-elle finie?* 71–75. Antoine Blanc de St. Bonnet saw the members of the conferences of the Saint Vincent de Paul Society as the "precious vegetation of a new aristocracy" (*La Légitimité* [Tournai, 1873], 389–92).

of the Christian duty of social and moral stewardship. According to Croy-Chanel, the concept of nobility in modern society was the opposite of the feudal "right of domination of one man over another"; modern nobles had to embrace an ideal of service toward society in harmony with the "dogma of evangelical fraternity." Antoine Blanc de St. Bonnet even recommended that virtuous members of the bourgeoisie who had served the common good be ennobled in order to encourage a process of emulation that would wean the middle class from revolutionary principles.[54]

The Legitimists, by defining moral qualities as they did, replaced an exclusivity of social rank with an exclusivity of ideological purity. The aristocracy they desired could be of diverse origins but could demonstrate merit only by rejecting the spirit of 1789. The Legitimists were more concerned with the philosophical revolt of the bourgeoisie than with threats to the social preeminence of the nobility. The crisis of leadership and authority in France, they believed, was not due to a conflict of classes but rather resulted from the way certain notables infected the masses with the virus of insubordination and tried to translate the destructive principles of the Revolution into law. The continued attachment of a portion of the elite to secular liberalism had undermined conservative principles and encouraged an unending cycle of subversion and revolution.[55] "If the social order is unsettled," wrote Louis de Kergolay, "it is at the summits of society, and not in the indoctrinated populations below, that one must seek the sources of evil." Guillaume Véran, a Legitimist journalist, repeated the charge and the metaphor: "The ruling classes have lacked faith, hope, and charity. Perverted values first appeared at the summit . . . and like torrents, they have ravaged the plain."[56] The message to the notables was clear. Only a strict moral unity would allow the ruling classes to work in concert to diffuse proper models of comportment among the masses and erect institutions embodying a historic renunciation of the revolutionary spirit. The legitime monarchy alone could achieve the desired ends, because it incarnated the true ideal of authority. The acceptance by all notables of the principles of legitimacy would symbolize the historic reconciliation of elites and would

54. Croy-Chanel, *La Noblesse,* 14–15; Blanc de St. Bonnet, *La Légitimité,* 625–29, 510–15, 394–97.

55. Bernardi, *La Révolution,* 79–80.

56. Louis de Kergolay, "Aux abonnés," *Revue provinciale,* II (August, 1849), 480; Guillaume Véran, *La Légitimité devant le catholicisme* (Angers, 1880), 39.

constitute a barrier to future revolutions. La Broise appealed especially to "industrialists, manufacturers, capitalists, and merchants" to get over their fear of a return to the Old Regime and to recognize that they had inherited the mantle of social responsibility by virtue of their dominance over the working classes. "Today," he proclaimed, "you are the new aristocracy. . . . Recognize that you are the ones with privileges. Better yet, let us forget designations that have been manipulated to perpetuate the deplorable antagonisms of the ruling classes and that strengthen the enemies of society. Unite in a common love of *la patrie,* and let there be between you no other rivalry than in serving it better" by repudiating the "insane and culpable revolt" that, in overthrowing the monarchy, "delivered us to ceaseless agitation and created the divisions from which we still suffer today."[57]

Clerico-Legitimists only accentuated the emphasis on morality, venturing that Catholicism could be the foundation for the new moral unity that would restore the monarchy. To them faith presented itself as a terrain of interaction and reconciliation for France's political parties. They expected conversion to create a new Christian elite that would be willing to reject the "false dogma of 1789" and look to the Syllabus of Errors, of 1864, and the decrees of the Vatican Council of 1870 as foundations for a Christian monarchy. In emphasizing faith over social rank, the clerico-Legitimists joined other Legitimists in a search for a social vocabulary that excluded traditional social categories and gave life to the idea of a reconstruction of French society by "men of goodwill" and of a political and moral rechristianization of the notables and the masses.[58]

57. La Broise, *Le Vrai et le Faux Libéralisme,* 288.

58. See Emile Keller, *L'Encyclique du 8 décembre 1864 et les Principes de 1789; ou, L'Eglise, L'Etat et la Liberté* (Paris, 1866), 311; Bernardi, *La Vérité divine,* xi; Armailhac, *La Légitimité et le Progrès,* 11; Margerie, *La Restauration,* 164–65, 170–71, 212–17; and Jean Brunet, in *Annales,* March 8, 1872, VIII, 246–48. For Margerie and other clerical Legitimists, the rechristianization of the notables was the more urgent objective. Margerie argued that, however honest and intelligent liberal elites like Prévost-Paradol were, they continued to hold that "religion tends always to decrease" in society "by the singular effect of reason and philosophy." Even though some conservatives spoke of moral regeneration, their fatalistic view of the consequences of the spread of "enlightenment" expressed their lack of faith and their fundamental belief that France would never return to Christianity. To the cause of order, therefore, they could contribute not their heart and soul but only their money and sympathy. Margerie continued, "The decisive contribution, that of example and action, they can never lend, because in their eyes there is nothing true in the ensemble of mysterious dogmas by which religion sustains and gives life to the idea of God in men's

The displacement of Legitimist notions of social demarcation toward morality and faith bore not only on the notables. What the Legitimists feared most was not that they might lose their place in the social hierarchy but that democratization and secularization might undermine their links to, or outright control of, the elements of French society that could provide the social foundations for the restoration. The Catholic clergy and the religious peasants, workers, and bourgeois constituted the Legitimists' most important connection with the rest of society and helped ensure that their movement amounted to more than a pastime for a handful of stubborn aristocrats and hidebound country squires.

souls, nothing serious and obligatory in the ensemble of disciplinary precepts under the guard of which it puts the observance of social duties. Thus, between their attitude as men and their attitude as mayor or proprietor there is an inevitable contrast; hence the contribution that they refuse neutralizes the one they offer, and their abstention does more harm to religious ideas then their subvention does to serve them" (*La Restauration,* 214–16).

CHAPTER II

 The Social Geography of
Legitimism

IN JUNE and July, 1862, officials in Riom and Lyon, and the
press in Moulin, reported a flurry of activity among the Legitimists
on the occasion of Chambord's sojourn in Switzerland. The *procureur
général* of Puy-de-Dôme told superiors of press announcements regarding "3,500 to 4,000 persons" on their way to the frontier to visit the
pretender; from Lyon, police noted that 1,200 Legitimists and church
officials, including the bishop of Angoulême, passed through Geneva en
route to the Hôtel des Berges in Lucerne, where 4,000 visitors "demonstrated their sentiments in a noisy and provocative manner," like a "kind
of riotous mob." The Midi, Brittany, and the Vendée, they observed,
were "naturally best represented" among the travelers, especially since
the entourage included Charles de Charette, a descendant of the Vendean
hero, at the head of a contingent of papal zouaves. They remarked, "The
Legitimist party wanted to prove that it still exists and that it extends its
hand to the clerical party."[1]

The reports attest not only to the vitality of Legitimism under the
Second Empire but also to the principal reasons for its persistence
through the nineteenth century. Well entrenched in its regional strongholds and allied by sympathy to political Catholics and many elements
within the church, the Legitimists remained a political force to be reck-
oned with, at least until the collapse of the Moral Order and the resig-

1. Rapport du procureur général de Riom, July, 1862, in BB (18) 1654, AN; Rapport
du procureur général de Lyon, June 29, 1862, in BB (18) 1654, AN.

nation of President Marie de MacMahon in 1879. Why did Legitimism flourish in some regions while being considered irrelevant in others? Was there a particular social context that contributed to its success? What role did the church play in sustaining Legitimist notables, and why, if only regionally successful, could the Legitimists go on believing that they represented an alternative capable of gaining national support?

ROYALIST FRANCE

The resilience of the Legitimists was demonstrated most clearly by their repeated electoral successes in certain regions. The political geography of Legitimism, like that of the Left, remained relatively stable from the 1830s until the collapse of the movement in the 1880s, when Legitimism merged with the conservative opposition under the Third Republic (Map I). Elections in a number of core departments, including the Nord, Pas-de-Calais, Morbihan, Mayenne, Ille-et-Vilaine, Loire-Inférieure, Maine-et-Loire, Tarn, Haute-Garonne, Gers, Hérault, Gard, and Averyon, repeatedly gave evidence of Legitimist strength. In Normandy, Dauphiné, the Massif Central, Aquitaine, and along the western slopes of the Rhône valley through Allier, Nièvre, and the Yonne, Legitimism was a constant and visible, if not a predominant, feature of local politics. Only in the south did the pattern change. Before 1848, Provence was among the principal *terres fidèles* (Maps II–V), but during the Second Republic a dramatic erosion of popular royalism occurred, especially in the Var and the Bouches-du-Rhône, as the peasants turned to the democratic and republican Left.[2] Although Legitimism re-

2. Royalist demonstrations against the July Monarchy occurred in the West and the Midi in the summer of 1830, recalling the events of the White Terror of 1814. In a report drawn up in 1830 assessing the potential for an insurrection to the benefit of the overthrown dynasty, Bertier de Sauvigny identified the rural areas of nine western departments (Morbihan, Mayenne, Ille-et-Vilaine, Loire-Inférieure, Maine-et-Loire, Côtes-du-Nord, Vendée, Deux-Sèvres, and the western Sarthe) and fourteen southern departments, including Var, Vaucluse, Basses-Alpes, and Bouches-du-Rhône, as well as various towns in Provence like Aix, Marseille, Arles, Tarascon, and Avignon, as the "most disposed to arm themselves for the good cause." In the general elections of 1816 and 1827 and in the municipal elections of 1837, Provence gave the royalists either a majority or a strong plurality (Map III). Yet, by 1849, the Legitimists, while confirming their influence in the west, Flanders, and Lower Languedoc, had lost their position in Provence, where a preference for the Left was revealed again in the resistance to the coup d'etat of 1851. For the geography of the insurrection of 1830, see G. Bertier de Sauvigny, *La Conspiration des légitimistes et la duchesse du Berry contre*

mained a force to contend with in Marseille, Aix, Tarascon, and Arles, its support nearly vanished in the rural areas.[3] Subsequent elections during the Second Empire confirmed the persistence of Legitimism in its other traditional strongholds but also the evaporation of royalist support in the extreme southeast (Maps VI–IX).[4]

What characteristics did Brittany, Anjou, the northeast, and Languedoc share that distinguished them from the regions where the Legitimists

---

Louis-Philippe, 1830–1832: Rapport de Ferdinand de Bertier au roi sur les chances et les moyens d'une restauration, 25 séptembre 1830 (Paris, 1965), 13; and Hugues de Changy, *Le Soulévement de la duchesse de Berry, 1830–1832: Les Royalistes dans la Tourmente* (Paris, 1986). On the Legitimists' electoral strength under the July Monarchy, see Tudesq, *Les Grands Notables en France*, I, 132–33; and Rémond, *Les Droites en France*, 62. On the republicanization of Provence, see especially Maurice Agulhon, *The Republic in the Village: The People of the Var from the French Revolution to the Second Republic*, trans. Janet Lloyd (Cambridge, Mass., 1982).

3. See Philippe Vigier, *La Seconde République dans la région alpine: Etude politique et social* (2 vols.; Paris, 1963); Gaudin, "Le Royalisme dans les Bouches-du-Rhône."

4. Map VI suggests certain refinements in the profile of western Legitimism. Lacking deep popular roots in Finistère and Côtes-du-Nord, which, much like Normandy, tended to vote conservative, Legitimism had its principal base in Upper Brittany, Maine, and Anjou, where it played an important role in the social and political life of both the towns and the countryside. Although most towns in the west remained Blue, the Legitimists were strong in Vannes, Nantes, Laval, Château-Gontier, Angers, Pontivy, Auruy, and Rennes. Like Toulouse in the south, Rennes was the winter domicile of many Legitimist aristocrats and a center of royalist-dominated commerce and intellectual life. The distribution of Legitimist general counselors in 1870 (Map VII) offers an even more precise profile, because the local elections of 1868 and 1870 were held under relaxed administrative pressure. Present in every department except Alpes-Maritime, Vaucluse, Basses-Alpes, Drôme, Charente, Bas-Rhin, and Haut-Rhin, Legitimist general counselors tended to cluster in certain arrondissements within their traditional enclaves as well as in regions where they were less numerous. In the northeast, they were much more numerous in the Flemish-speaking areas of Flanders and Artois, around St. Pol, Arras, and the industrial triangle of Lille, Roubaix, and Tourcoing. South of Cambrai, their influence was negligible. In Normandy, Legitimists were elected only in the far western end of the province, within a line running from Vire to Mont-Saint-Michel to the canton of Balleroy in the Marche. In Brittany, their principal redoubts were around Morlaix, the *pays gallo* of southern Morbihan, the Croan, the area southeast of St. Brieuc, the arrondissement of Redon, and the area southeast of Nantes. In addition to their concentration in urban areas of Languedoc and Béarn (Pau, Toulouse, Albi, Nîmes, Carcassonne, Auch, and Montpellier), the Legitimists held scattered support along the west bank of the Rhône and in Burgundy, the western Jura, southern Haute-Saône, and the southeastern regions of the Massif Central. See Reports on the general counselors elected in 1870, in F (1) b 230, fols. 1–20, AN; Girard *et al., Les Conseillers généraux en 1870*, 141–42; Y. M. Hilaire, *Une Chrétienté au XIXe siècle?* II; and P. Huot-Pleuroux, *La Vie chrétienne dans le Doubs et la Haute-Saône de 1860 à 1960* (Besançon, 1960).

Map I   Persistence of Legitimism, 1830–1880

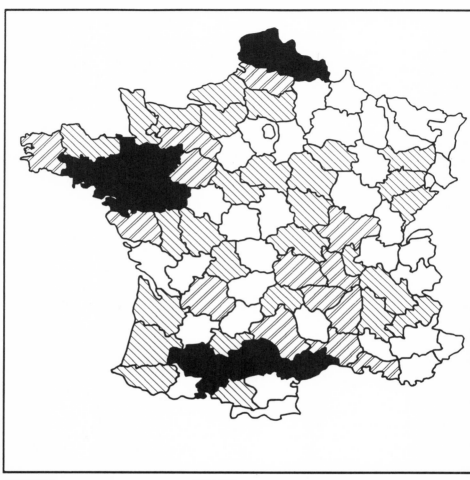

Strong representation
throughout period

Minority tendency, but
persistent representation

Strong minority
representation

Weak or sporadic
representation

Map II   Royalist Deputies Resigning from Office or Refusing
Serment in 1830

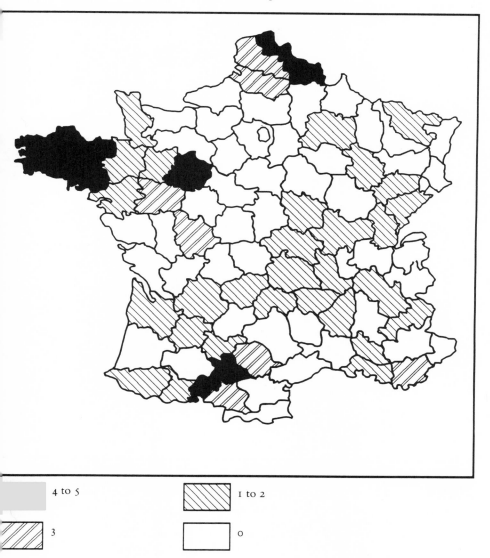

4 to 5

1 to 2

3

0

Adapted from *La Soulèvement de la duchesse de Berry, 1830–1832: Les Royalistes dans le Tourmente,* by Hugues de Changy (Paris, 1986), 31. By courtesy of Albatros et Diffusion-Université-Culture.

Map III   Legitimist General Counselors in 1837

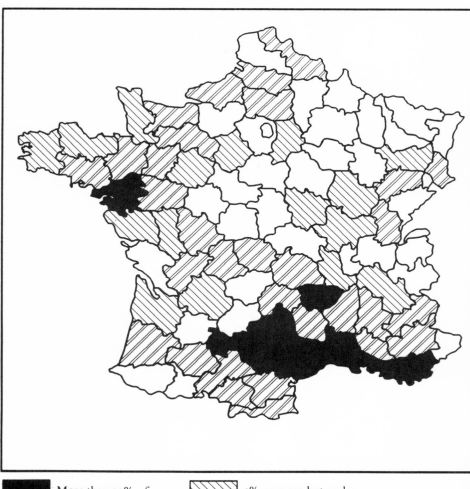

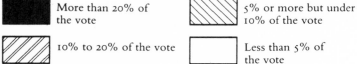

More than 20% of
the vote

5% or more but under
10% of the vote

10% to 20% of the vote

Less than 5% of
the vote

Adapted from *Les Grand Notables en France, 1840–1849: Etude historique d'une psychologie sociale*, by André Jean Tudesq
(2 vols.; Paris, 1964), I. By courtesy of Presses Universitaires de France.

Map IV   Legitimist General Counselors in 1840

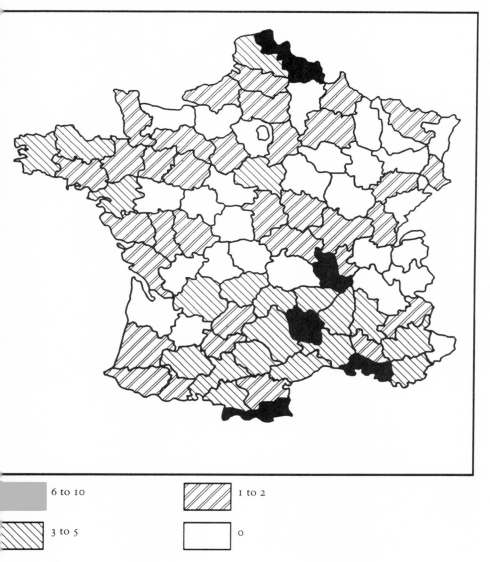

6 to 10

3 to 5

1 to 2

0

Adapted from *Les Conseillers généraux en France au temps de Guizot,* by André Jean Tudesq (Paris, 1967), 231. By
courtesy of Presses de la Fondation Nationale des Sciences Politiques.

Map V   Petitions of the Amis du Droit National in 1850

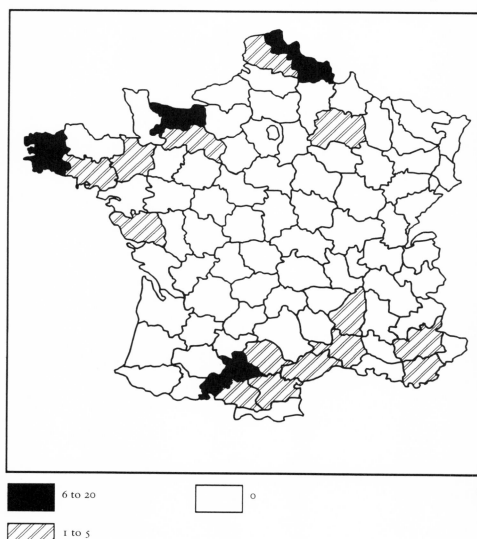

■ 6 to 20   □ 0

▨ 1 to 5

Based on data from Archives de l'Assemblée Nationale, C 2288, AN.

Map VI   Legitimist and Clerical General Counselors in 1870

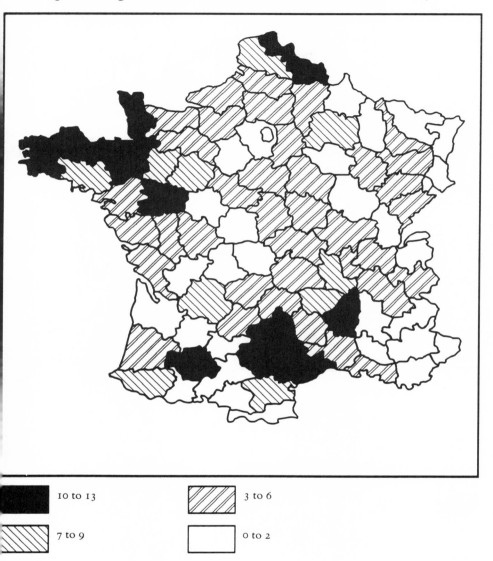

	10 to 13		3 to 6
	7 to 9		0 to 2

Adapted from *Les Conseillers généraux en 1870: Etude statistique d'un personnel politique,* by Louis Girard *et al.* (Paris, 1967), 142. By courtesy of Presses Universitaires de France.

Map VII   Legitimist Deputies in 1871

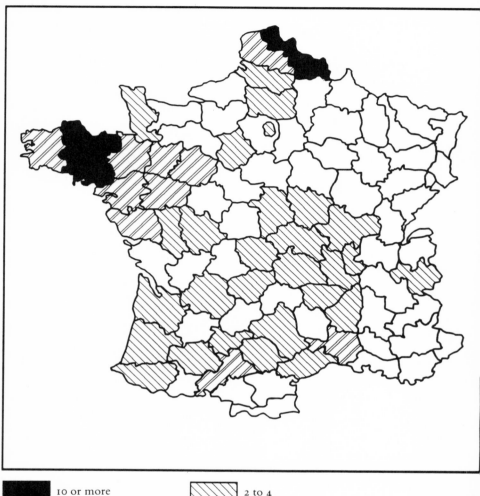

10 or more   2 to 4

5 to 9   0 to 1

Based on data from France, Assemblée Nationale, *Annales parlementaires: Annales de l'Assemblée Nationale* (48 vols.; Versailles, 1871–76), I, 23–37.

Map VIII   Petitions in 1873 for Reestablishment of
Monarchy

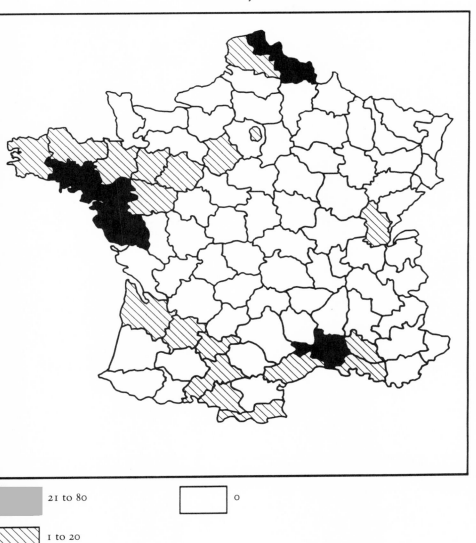

21 to 80

0

1 to 20

ased on data from Archives de l'Assemblée Nationale, C 4259, 4260, 4271, AN.

Map IX Legitimist Deputies in 1876

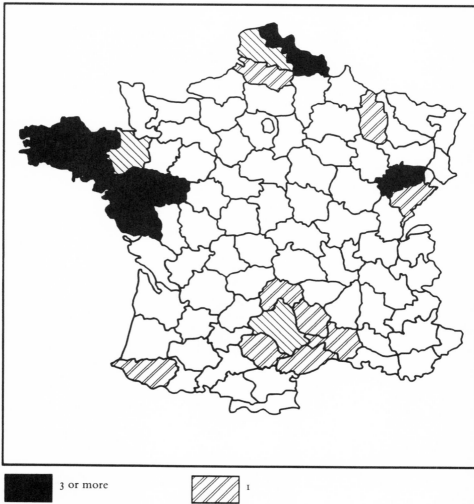

3 or more

2

1

0

Adapted from *French Legitimists and the Politics of Moral Order in the Early Third Republic,* by Robert R. Locke (Princeton, 1974), 258. By permission of Princeton University Press.

Map X   Poorest Departments by Tax Revenue per Hectare
in 1857

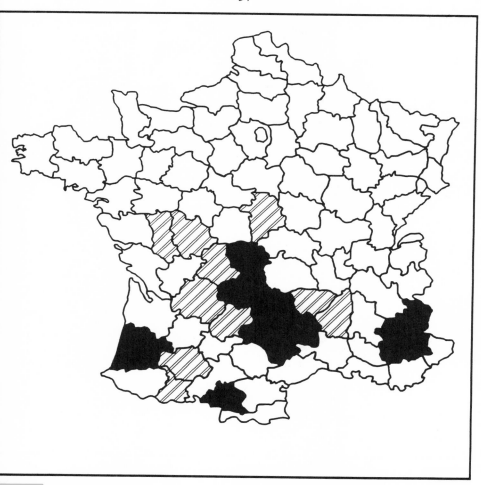

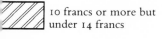 Less than 10 francs

10 francs or more but
under 14 francs

dapted from *Peasants into Frenchmen: The Modernization of Rural France, 1870–1914,* by Eugen Weber (Stanford, Calif.,
•77), 181. By courtesy of Stanford University Press. The national average for tax revenue was 31 francs.

Map XI Gross Agricultural Revenue in 1864

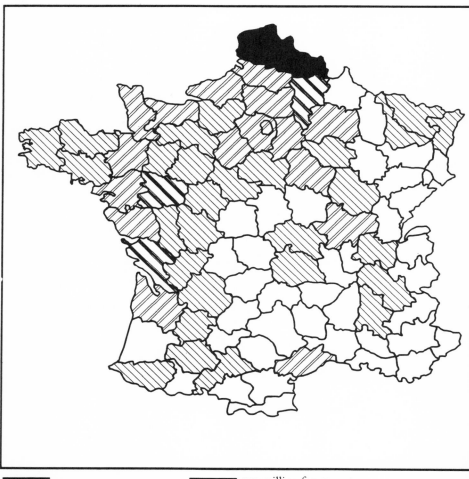

 250 million francs
or more

 200 million francs
or more but under
250 million francs

 150 million francs
or more but under
200 million francs

 100 million francs
or more but under
150 million francs

 Less than 100 million
francs

Adapted from *Atlas historique de la France contemporaine, 1800–1965*, ed. René Rémond and P. M. Boyer (Paris, 1966),
67. By permission of Armand Colin.

Map XII   Population Engaged in Large-Scale Industry
in 1851

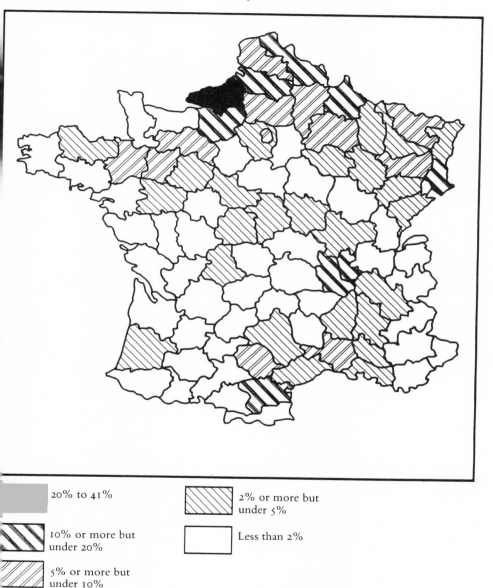

20% to 41%

2% or more but
under 5%

10% or more but
under 20%

Less than 2%

5% or more but
under 10%

dapted from *Atlas historique de la France contemporaine*, ed. Rémond and Boyer, 46. By permission of Armand Colin.

Map XIII General Counselors from Nobility in 1870

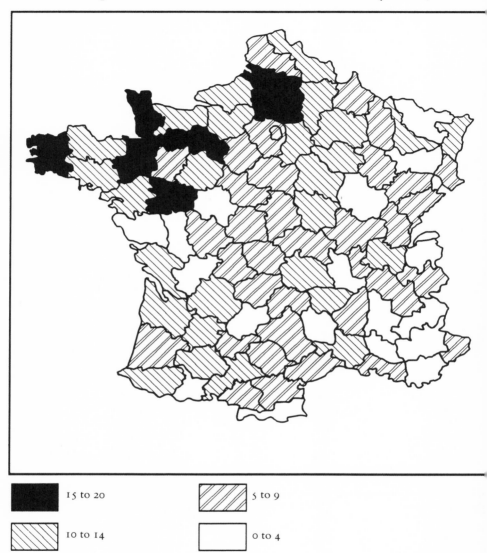

| | 15 to 20 | | 5 to 9 |
| | 10 to 14 | | 0 to 4 |

Adapted from *Les Conseillers généraux en 1870*, by Girard *et al.*, 128. By courtesy of Presses Universitaires de France.

Map XIV   Nobles in National Assembly of 1871

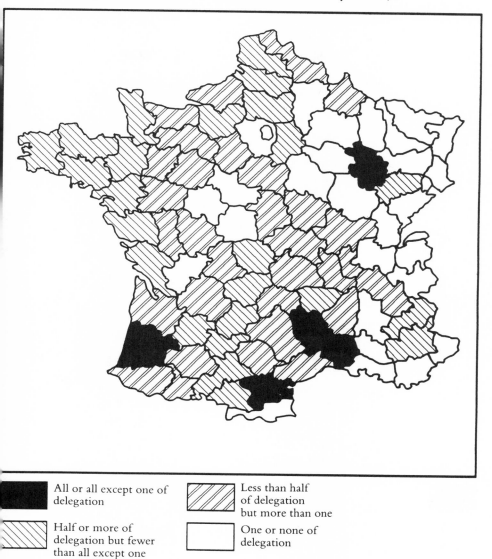

All or all except one of
delegation

Half or more of
delegation but fewer
than all except one

Less than half
of delegation
but more than one

One or none of
delegation

ased on data from "Noblesse et Représentation parlementaire: Les Députés nobles de 1871 à 1968," by Jean Bécarud, *evue française de science politique*, XXIII (1973), 972–99.

Map XV   *Côtes* of over 100 Hectares in 1884

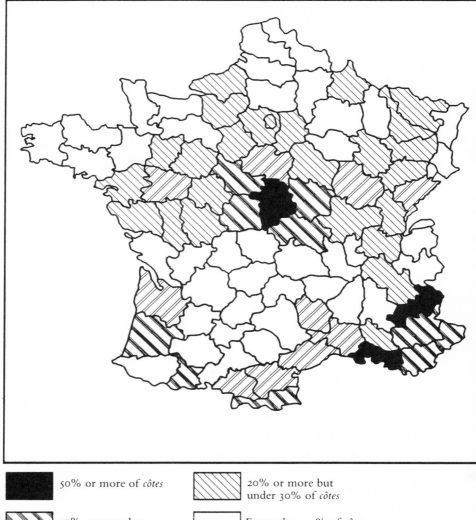

■ 50% or more of *côtes*

▨ 40% or more but under 50% of *côtes*

▨ 30% or more but under 40% of *côtes*

▨ 20% or more but under 30% of *côtes*

□ Fewer than 20% of *côtes*

Adapted from *Atlas historique de la France contemporaine,* ed. Rémond and Boyer, 48. By permission of Armand Colin.

were only a coterie of isolated notables? Contrary to the traditional view of Legitimism as accompanying socioeconomic underdevelopment, Chambord's partisans did not represent the archaic or backward rural departments exclusively. The Legitimists were in fact more successful in areas of average or above average economic development, and even in the most economically advanced regions (Maps X–XII). If backwardness was associated with Legitimism in the Southern Massif, that was certainly not the case in the Nord and the Pas-de-Calais. In some of the poorest rural areas, like the Limousin, peasants resisted domination by Legitimist *grands propriétaires;* according to Alain Corbin, "certain very isolated zones constituted the bastions of 'advanced' ideology."[5] In 1867, the *procureur général* of Limoges reported that "actually, here there exists only an infinitely limited number of people who still maintain some attachment to the principles of Legitimacy."[6] In the Var, Maurice Agulhon has found that democracy advanced far more quickly than modernity and has concluded that the radicalization of the department did "not appear to owe anything to progressivist economic development."[7] Brittany was not economically stagnant in the nineteenth century, and after 1830 the region underwent something of an agricultural boom, with taxable income rising nearly 61 percent between 1851 and 1879, compared with 23.8 percent in the Paris region during the same period.[8] Paul Bois has found that in the Sarthe it was the more prosperous western half of the department that remained *pratiquant* and voted for the Right; in the east, "the greatest unbelief and the greatest poverty coincided" with the estrangement of the poor from traditional social authorities.[9]

If Legitimism was not equivalent to underdevelopment, neither was it strictly dependent on the presence of a large noble population. None of the departments with the largest delegations of noble general counselors in 1840 (Ain, Cher, Indre-et-Loire, Marne, Basse-Pyrénées, Seine-et-Marne, Yonne, Seine) were Legitimist bastions, and F. J. Gibson has shown that the largest percentage of nobles among the electors of 1820

5. Alain Corbin, *Archaisme et Modernité en Limousin au XIXe siècle* (2 vols.; Paris, 1975), II, 991, I, 31–32.
6. Rapport du procureur général de Limoges, February 11, 1867, in BB (18) 1746, AN.
7. Agulhon, *The Republic in the Village,* 295.
8. Agulhon, Désert, and Specklin, *Apogée et Crise de la civilisation paysanne,* 248–49; Roger Price, *The Modernization of Rural France* (London, 1983), 392.
9. Paul Bois, *Paysans de l'Ouest: Des structures économiques et sociales aux options politiques depuis l'époque révolutionnaire dans la Sarthe* (Paris, 1971), 68–69.

resided outside the principal White regions.[10] In 1870, noble general counselors were indeed concentrated in Brittany, Lower Languedoc, and along the Rhône, but also in the Moselle, the Rhinish departments, and especially in Normandy and the Paris Basin (Map XIII). In the National Assembly of 1871, nobles and Legitimists did not coincide geographically (Maps XIV, VII).

Neither entirely rural nor exclusively aristocratic, the apparently complex character of Legitimism casts doubt on André Siegfried's well-known thesis linking the survival of Legitimism to the persistence of "great feudal property" in the west. Siegfried had tried to show that in the Vendée and Brittany the existence of large estates owned by nobles usually went with royalist electoral success and thorough religious conformity because rich aristocratic landowners were able to dominate the peasantry and check the independence of the clergy. Contrariwise, he had suggested that a pattern of small property holding created a "democratic atmosphere" that allowed the peasants and the clergy to escape the "irresistible pressure" of the *grands propriétaires*.[11] Bois, who has submitted Siegfried's conclusions to a systematic critique, has demonstrated that in the Sarthe large property holding was "nowhere a necessary condition" for a royalist political orientation, and he has given examples of areas, like the canton of Léon, where the absence of large noble property corresponded to a pattern of conservative and royalist electoral success. Re-

10. Of a total of 2,399 general counselors in 1840, 180 were Legitimists and 414 were nobles, among whom the "Legitimists were a minority." Among the Legitimists, nobles were surprisingly rare; the party was represented by lawyers and journalists, like Ferdinand Béchard, Duffours, and Vincent Audren de Kerdrel. The noble counselors of 1840 constituted part of an "Orleanist nobility, favorable to the July Regime and often attached to members of the new dynasty" (Tudesq, *Les Conseillers généraux en France au temps de Guizot,* 223–24).

Gibson drew a map of the geographical distribution of the nobility based on a list of noble electors compiled by a genealogist named Hozier in 1820, then added up the number of names for each department and expressed the total as a number per ten thousand of each department's population in 1821. He found that nobles were concentrated around Paris, in Normandy and the western interior (but not the Armorican peninsula), in the center (Cher, Indre, Allier), in the Gard and Hérault, and in an arch running southeast from Maine-et-Loire to Haute-Vienne and then southwest to Lot-et-Garonne. See Tudesq, *Les Conseillers généraux en France au temps de Guizot,* 162–67, 223–24; and F. J. Gibson, "The French Nobility in the Nineteenth Century—Particularly in the Dordogne," in *Elites in France,* ed. Howorth and Cerney, 17–18.

11. Siegfried, *Tableau politique,* 367, and *passim*.

jecting the determinism implicit in Siegfried's analysis, Bois has traced the long-term political behavior of the Sarthe to the bitter struggles between town and country that occurred during the Revolution.[12]

Despite a narrow geographical focus, Siegfried had tried to formulate a general explanation for French political behavior. His analysis has some merit, especially regarding the west, but the overall correlation between *grande propriété* and Legitimism does not close the book on Legitimism's social foundations. Noble estates in Brittany, if numerous, were small in comparison with those in Berry, Landes, Provence, and Ile-de-France. If the size of landholdings had been the key factor, Legitimism would have been much more potent in departments like Cher, Indre, Aude, Landes, and Hautes-Alpes, instead of being confined to small aristocratic minorities and their clients (Map XV).

For both Siegfried and Bois, however, land tenure is only part of the story. They have also been concerned with the cultural foundations of lower-class deference to traditional social authorities. Bois has concentrated on Siegfried's tendency to overstate the importance of land tenure in order to highlight the centrality of "psychological elements" that contributed to the acceptance or rejection of hierarchical social deference. But in underscoring the role of *grande propriété,* Siegfried does not completely ignore personal relations, collective memory, and ideology as reinforcements of economic power. The problem is that he depicts a social and cultural universe in which the only possible outcome could be submission, religious conformity, and political traditionalism.[13] What Bois contests is the suggestion that large estate ownership determined these "psychological" realities and the assumption that the people who were enlightened, independent, and free from subjugating economic structures would naturally reject the straitjacket of conservatism imposed by the notables. The peasants, he maintains, had an autonomous political culture that complemented that of the notables with whom they coexisted in a morally integrated community.[14]

Yet Siegfried was not the first to assume that the peasants of the west

12. Bois, *Paysans de l'Ouest,* 14–19, 48–49.
13. Siegfried, *Tableau politique,* 361–408.
14. Bois has noted that Siegfried attributed to the peasants only a "mysterious" temperament or a "tendency," which seemed to suggest the lack of clear and independent popular attitudes (*Paysans de l'Ouest,* 28–29).

were encased in a "feudal armature." His conclusions gave coherence and scientific stature to a tradition deeply ingrained in nineteenth-century French liberalism and republicanism. For the Blues, whose ideas Siegfried's family shared, the depths of the Breton and Vendean countryside were figuratively and literally shrouded in fog and mystery because they resisted the impulse of progressive human liberation that animated the liberals' political faith. Siegfried describes the arrondissements of Vannes and Plöermel as "Shakespearean lands of rose heathers, . . . granite crosses, isolated and mysterious farms hidden behind their hedges, . . . whose sparkling and delicate atmosphere recalls an inland sea on the coast of Japan."[15] Since the west appeared distant, exotic, out of joint, and separate from the mainstream of French life, progressive Frenchmen decided that nobles and priests had to be responsible for the cruel malformation they detected. Of course, they considered the "feudal elements" historically irredeemable; what they found intolerable was that, under the weight of the château and the presbytery, the peasant farmer "was not free" and "popular rancor [was] so deeply buried that it [was] practically unthinkable."[16] Siegfried, despite admirable efforts, has no more penetrating a view than the *procureur général* of Poitiers who attributed the success of a Legitimist in the local election of 1867 not to hostility toward the government but to the peasants' fear of losing the "generosities of M. Laurenceau," or the subprefect of Castelsarrazin, in the Tarn, who described the local population as "ignorant and influenced by the priests and the Carlists" when they elected a Legitimist in 1842.[17]

What bothered these officials was the persistence of the Legitimists' "social power."[18] Supported by a complicated system of patronage based on wealth, knowledge, family connections, and political ties, their power to dominate the lower classes was neither the fault of the people themselves nor the exclusive privilege of the Legitimist notables. Much of

15. Siegfried, *Tableau politique,* 112–13. For a discussion of similar imagery in the works of Victor Hugo, see Jeffrey Mehlman, *Revolution and Repetition* (Berkeley and Los Angeles, 1979).

16. Siegfried, *Tableau politique,* 114–15.

17. Rapport du procureur général de Poitier, January 2, 1867, in BB (18) 1757, AN; Tudesq, *Les Grands Notables en France,* I, 152.

18. For definitions of social power, see Jean Lhomme, *Le Grande Bourgeoisie au pouvoir, 1830–1880* (Paris, 1960); Bertrand Hervieu, "Le Pouvoir au village," *Etudes rurales,* LXII–LXIII (1976), 15–30; and Tudesq, *Les Grands Notables en France,* I, 475.

rural France in the nineteenth century was afflicted by limited mobility and opportunity, isolation, economic hardship, stultifying routine, illiteracy, and family and community constraints, so that a sense of changelessness and resignation formed a convenient context for dependency and coercion.[19] The notables' ownership of the means of production, their education, and their monopoly on certain technical skills endowed them with a preeminent role in local economies. As the principal providers of employment, they held command over the livelihood of a population with whom they were periodically in direct contact.

In addition, the notables provided services from which the lower classes derived tangible benefits. That too worked to consolidate the existing social structure. Large landowners not only collected rents, they were called upon to arbitrate disputes and mediate between the people and the local authorities. They could use their influence to get a community favors resulting in roads, schools, medical assistance, or military exemptions for peasant boys.[20] In times of economic crisis and shortage, they often purchased grain from distant markets and sold it below market prices.[21] By increasing the productivity of their estates, they offered the peasants an example of efficiency. That, along with the technical advice they could make available, allowed smaller producers to improve their

19. See the portrait of peasant society painted by Weber in *Peasants into Frenchmen*, and by Barnet Singer in *Village Notables in Nineteenth-Century France: Priests, Mayors, and Schoolmasters* (Albany, N.Y., 1982), 3–6.

20. See, for example, Pocquet du Haut-Jussé, *Légitimistes parlementaires*, 211.

21. Tudesq, *Les Grands Notables en France*, II, 956. During the economic crisis of 1846–1847, many Legitimists in the Mayenne distributed money and bread to the peasants to alleviate hardship. At Chantrigne, the Marquis de Hauteville gave the curé 250 decaliters of wheat, 600 fagots, and clothes to distribute among the poor. Other Legitimist *propriétaires* allowed the unemployed to set up camps on their estates. The authorities of the regime saw all this as an attempt by the Legitimists to gain recruits. See Denis, *Les Royalistes de la Mayenne*, 247.

In Vienne, the generosity of the Comte de La Rochethulon came with strings attached. He told the agricultural inquiry of 1866 that it was advantageous "to buy a house and some surrounding land for the good worker. By annuities calculated and agreed between us, he has to repay me over the long term all my expenses with legal interest. I incur no risk, the property remains mine until its complete amortization, and I pledge myself the punctual remittances of my buyer over the long term. If his commitments are not fulfilled, I am free to give him back his annual payments and keep, besides the entire property, the benefit of the interest paid" (Deposition orale de M. de La Rochethulon, in France, Ministère de l'Agriculture, *Enquête agricole: Enquêtes départementales* [38 vols.; Paris, 1867–72], Serie 2, Part 10, p. 53, hereinafter cited as *Enquête agricole*).

yields. Moreover, wealthy landowners, prosperous businessmen, and the clergy undertook acts of private generosity and eventually built impressive local and national charitable instruments that often provided the only emergency relief, welfare, and medical services the poor could obtain.[22] The Legitimists were especially active in charitable organizations and customarily attended local agricultural fairs, contributed to the preservation of historic monuments, and allowed their estates to be used for wedding celebrations. They often provided the food for feast days and officiated when the occasion arose—for instance, at a bishop's pastoral visit or the opening of a new Catholic school.[23] By participating in the rites of passage and the festive life of the village, a notable could integrate himself into a ritual structure that enacted the community's special identity.

The Legitimists saw their local patronage as a means of maintaining ties with other social groups and of creating a pattern of social relations that could thwart attempts by rival elites or the central administration to establish their own followings.[24] Out of awareness of the effectiveness, or indispensability, of the kind of patronage they practiced, they elevated their local activities into a system of social thought. At the center of this doctrine stood the *propriétaire* himself, whose paternal example they counted on to create the proper climate of unity and social deference regardless of other social factors. For the Legitimists, it was not *grand propriété* but the *propriétaire* himself that produced the salutary influence. In 1862, Falloux attributed the conservatism of the Vendée to the "rec-

22. In an article on the need to integrate the methods and principles of private charity into public assistance, Anatole de Melun noted that in rural communes, peasants who suffered sickness or accident consulted *la dame* more often than the doctor. See Anatole de Melun, "Application de la mutualité à l'assistance dans les campagnes," *Annales de la charité,* VI (October, 1873), 8.

23. On October 9, 1864, the Comte de Charette held a great feast at his château of Cornfret, near Concorret. Three hundred guests, including many peasants from the surrounding countryside and the *maire* of Concorret, were invited to feast on mutton supplied by their generous host. According to the police, Charette turned the occasion into a "demonstration in favor of the temporal power of the pope." Outside the dining hall, the white flag of the Bourbons hung over the door, and Charette carried another such flag as he walked among the crowd. See Rapport du procureur général de Rennes, October 11, 1864, in BB (18) 1702, AN.

24. See Austin Gough, "The Conflict in Politics," in *Conflicts in French Society: Anticlericalism, Education, and Morals in the Nineteenth Century,* ed. Theodore Zeldin (London, 1970), 94–168; and Cour Impériale de Poitiers, August 11, 1858, in BB (30) 421, AN.

ognition of ancient and uninterrupted bonds between the landowner and his tenant" and characterized Brittany, Anjou, and Provence as the "provinces where a gentleman most habitually resides on his lands, where he craves least for changes of the heart, where he shows the most impatience to return to die in the modest foyer of the paternal manor after leaving the army, the magistrature, or the administration."[25] The connection between residence and social power was not an illusion. Agulhon has found that in the Var the presence of numerous aristocratic and bourgeois landowners served to maintain the ascendancy of conservative forces, whereas in towns where absenteeism "had left the proletarians without any effective 'patronage' . . . liberal elements were masters of the field."[26] Bois feels that the presence of *propriétaires* upheld a consensus on the legitimacy of the social hierarchy and the *mentalités* that supported it, creating a "sort of tacit accord" that both sustained the influence of the notables and morally integrated them into the life of a community.[27]

In this lay the key to the Legitimists' social comportment and the foundation of their political strategy. Chambord in letters to his partisans consistently preached against absenteeism and supported Catholic social action and agricultural progress, reminding his readers that "revolutionary seductions especially ravage populations abandoned by their natural protectors." He went on to explain, "Short visits can never replace real affection in relations, disinterestedness in service, and follow-ups on earlier advice." The pretender saw monarchy as the supreme paternity and reasoned that a fatherly and conscientious landowner living among the people and guiding them toward an understanding of their moral and social duties would constitute a political pedagogy superior to anything royalist propaganda could confect.[28] Chambord enjoined the Legitimists to abstain from participation in public affairs, precisely because he believed that the other work they could accomplish at the local level was the best way to regain the loyalty and respect of the people after the

25. Comte Alfred de Falloux, "Dix ans d'agriculture," *Le Correspondant*, LXXIV (1862), 658–59.
26. Agulhon, *The Republic in the Village*, 261–62. See also Denis, *Les Royalistes de la Mayenne*, 247.
27. Bois, *Paysans de l'Ouest*, 23, 84. See also P. M. Jones, "Political Commitment and Rural Society in the Southern Massif-Central," *European Studies Review*, X (1980), 338–39.
28. Dubosc de Pesquidoux, *Le Comte de Chambord*, 246–47.

political disaster of 1830. Public office under a "revolutionary" regime like the July Monarchy or the Second Empire would, he feared, merely turn the *propriétaires* into rootless functionaries detached from the masses and would neither "improve the lot of the agricultural classes" nor "render to landed property the portion of influence that belongs to it."[29]

The restriction on political participation was the obverse side of Chambord's denunciation of absenteeism. The failure, during the Second Republic, of liberal Legitimists led by Berryer and Falloux to demonstrate that the monarchy could be restored through parliamentary measures taken by an alliance of Legitimists and Orleanists convinced Chambord and his exiled courtiers that electoral action and full participation in public affairs threatened the unity of the royalist movement and placed parliamentary liberals in a position to negotiate the conditions of monarchical fusion. After the coup of 1851 and the apparent *ralliement* of a number of prominent Legitimists to the regime of Louis Napoleon in 1852, Chambord reorganized the Legitimist party by removing the liberal majority from the party's executive committee and replacing them with more authoritarian members of his personal entourage like the Duc de Lévis and the Duc Des Cars. He also established direct communication with a series of departmental *comités royalistes* presided over by hand-picked—and mostly aristocratic—supporters, to which he could communicate his wishes through a passive six-member liaison committee called the Bureau du Roi. It was between April and October, 1852, once the new structure was in place, that Chambord sent his series of letters and manifestos ordering the Legitimists to abstain from voting, from accepting administrative appointments, and from running for elected office.

The man who aspired to be Henri V fully intended the Legitimists one day to assume political control of France through moral conquest, and he believed that political abstentionism, joined to a program of charitable social action, would allow them to accede to power with the support of a morally regenerated population. Grateful for the devotion of a worthy and benevolent elite, the people were to reject the egotistical rule of the liberal bourgeoisie and greet the restoration of the monarchy as a deliverance from oppression and self-indulgence. Upon assuming office,

29. Comte de Chambord to Comte de Turenne, June 27, 1841, in Dubosc de Pesquidoux's *Le Comte de Chambord,* 425.

the new ruling cadres would have the moral training for leadership that only charity and *la vie agricole* could provide.[30] For Chambord, who obstinately maintained this policy in its broad outlines until the fall of Napoleon III in 1870, those who abstained from government participation gave the masses an example of obedience to authority and were most likely to have internalized the kind of loyalty that merited the pretender's consideration, confidence, and respect.

Outstanding moderate Legitimist politicians like Berryer accepted abstentionism during the 1850s, when the opposition had little chance of mounting an independent and effective strategy, but they worried that the party would become isolated and irrelevant. When conservative support for Napoleon III wavered in the wake of the emperor's Italian policy in 1859–1860, moderates who were anxious to join the emerging Liberal Union and who hoped to encourage the liberalization of the regime all but begged Chambord to reverse the abstention order and allow the Legitimists to place themselves at the head of the Catholic and liberal forces that aimed at modifying the empire's domestic and foreign policy. Although the pretender gave the Legitimists permission in 1862 to vote for independent Catholic candidates who were aligned with Legitimist principles, he continued to bar them from active participation. In 1863, Berryer and other liberal royalists broke rank and sought election to the Corps Législatif, but most Legitimists, including Falloux, remained loyal to the policy of abstention and sought to give substance to Chambord's vision of a restoration through moral conquest by performing acts of social patronage and by persistently condemning the idleness and egotism of the rich. Edouard de La Bassétière spoke of the *propriétaire's* special mission to remain "at the center of his domains" and to preserve "this solidarity of interests, this community of mores, between the different classes of society."[31] Falloux tried to reconcile his personal misgivings about abstentionism and his loyalty to the prince by urging "*pro-*

30. See Chambord's letter of March, 1866, on the *enquête agricole,* in Chambord's *La Monarchie française,* 93.

31. Déposition écrite de M. de La Bassétière, *Enquête agricole,* Série 2, Vol. I, Part 3, Documents annexes, 152–53. Falloux wrote that the landowner's first duty was the "attentive management" of his properties because as a *propriétaire* he naturally possessed an obligation to attend to the well-being of those attached to him. "If the capitalist loses his capital, it is a great private misfortune, but the command of souls is not involved. If, by contrast, [a landowner] cannot understand or fulfill his mission, it is more than a private misfortune, it is public bankruptcy" ("Dix ans d'agriculture," 650).

priétaires voluntarily or involuntarily exiled from the political hierarchy" to treat the management of their estates as a "political function," and he placed the conscientious landowner "at the first rank among the servants and even the restorers of a shaken society."[32] Others who might have agreed with Chambord's objectives held that service on the municipal and departmental councils was the best way for Legitimists to remain in contact with the vital affairs of the nation while developing the moral strength of the people and gaining practical experience and esteem. Armand de Melun recommended the *mairie* over the Corps Législatif as a "very natural and very acceptable means of reasserting the influence of conservative and moral ideas" and told Madame de Caramen in 1868 of his astonishment at what he could accomplish as mayor of Bouvelingham: "Here, a *propriétaire* can truly find a career full of activity and interest. Whoever wishes to devote himself to improving the morality of the commune would not regret either his time or the talent he expended."[33] Margerie felt that if "the patron in his workshop and the *propriétaire* on his country estate" lived among the people according to the "precepts of fraternal charity," electioneering would not be necessary: "On election day, some will come on their own to ask for advice in which they already have faith." Others would vote for "sane ideas" without even having to seek guidance.[34]

Legitimist views about patronage, charity, and residency made a virtue of necessity. Kept from high political office, the Legitimists used all the means at their disposal to preserve their local influence and gain allies or clients in their effort to avoid political isolation. Yet the Legitimists understood that such methods worked best in regions where distinct historical experiences and high levels of religious observance predisposed the populations to recognize the legitimacy of old-fashioned paternalism. These historical and cultural conditions seemed to create common identities on which vertical patterns of social deference could be built and sustained.

The political geography of Legitimism corresponded much more

32. Comte Alfred de Falloux, *Dix ans d'agriculture* (Paris, 1863), 6, 44–46. Falloux frequently expressed the idea that the *émigration à l'intérieure* was a fabrication, since even if a Legitimist abstained from political participation, he "understood that a fruitful and great career could still be open to him in the accomplishment of his social duties" (*Mémoires d'une royaliste* [2 vols.; Paris, 1888], I, 149).

33. Armand de Melun to Mme. de Caramen, July 2, 1868, in A. d'Andigné's *Un Apôtre de la charité: Armand de Melun* (Paris, 1962), 344.

34. Margerie, *La Restauration,* 314–15.

closely to the regional distribution of the Counterrevolution than to rural poverty or aristocratic predominance (Map XVI). The Legitimists sustained memories of the Counterrevolution partly because it had rallied a cross section of the people in militant defense of faith and tradition. A great many Legitimist families harbored bitter personal memories of the Revolution, recalling each year, in prayer, the death of a relative or a parent at the hands of the Jacobins. The recollection, often shared by entire communities, was kept alive from one generation to the next through oral tradition, family history, and the education young Catholics received at home and in private religious schools. The ranks of the Legitimist party were filled with descendants of veteran counterrevolutionary heros like François Charette, the Comte de La Rochejacquelein, Mortemart, Georges Cadoudal, and Vicomte Joseph Walsh. Henriette Déan de Ligne, the wife of Charles Marie Tresvaux Du Fraval, recounted how her great-grandmother and three aunts were either shot or condemned to death for harboring a refractory priest. Although not guillotined by the Terror, Henri Foucault Des Bigottières' father, a former member of the Assemblée de la Noblessee of Angers, had all his goods sequestered when he emigrated in 1790. The Mayol family's property was left intact, but the suppression of the monasteries and convents left bitter family resentment against the Revolution and sent many relatives into "pious retirement."[35] Civil war, confiscation, and emigration affected entire regions and deepened existing animosities. These did not dissipate during the nineteenth century.[36]

The Counterrevolution was, in many respects, a reaction against the imposition of Parisian centralization and urban values, which peripheral regions had resented even before 1789. Not surprisingly, Legitimism also flourished in territories within the former *pays d'états* where a degree of political and cultural autonomy had survived under the Old Regime (Map XVII). The persistence of Legitimism in regions where a patois continued to be spoken by a majority of the population indicates that particularist traditions supported Catholic royalism (Map XVIII). Legitimists counted on the social and cultural cohesiveness bred by strong regional identities and believed that extensive administrative decentralization would encourage stability and traditionalism by putting power in

---

35. Jéhan de Mayol Du Lupé, *La Maison de Mayol: Mémoires familiaux* (Rome, 1913).
36. See Bois, *Paysans de l'Ouest,* 83–89; Brian Fitzpatrick, *Catholic Royalism in the Department of the Gard, 1814–1852* (Cambridge, Mass., 1983), 14–21; Tudesq, *Les Grands Notables en France,* I, 293; and Denis, *Les Royalistes de la Mayenne,* 125–26.

Map XVI   Executions During French Revolution

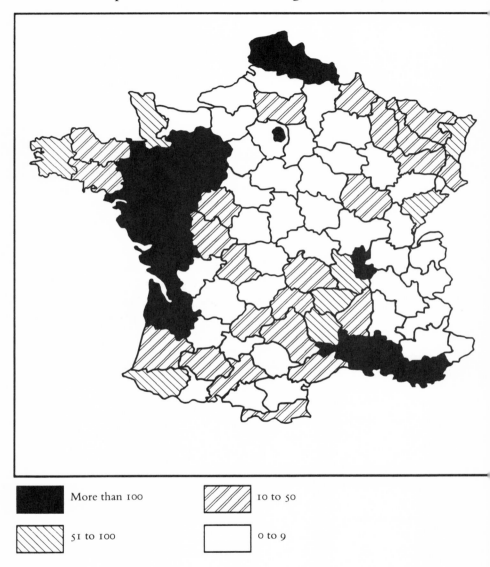

More than 100

51 to 100

10 to 50

0 to 9

Modified with permission of the publishers from *The Incidence of the Terror During the French Revolution: A Statistical Interpretation,* by Donald Greer, Cambridge, Mass.: Harvard University Press, Copyright © 1935 by the President and Fellows of Harvard College. Rpr. Gloucester, Mass., 1966.

Map XVII   The *Pays d'Etat* of the Old Regime

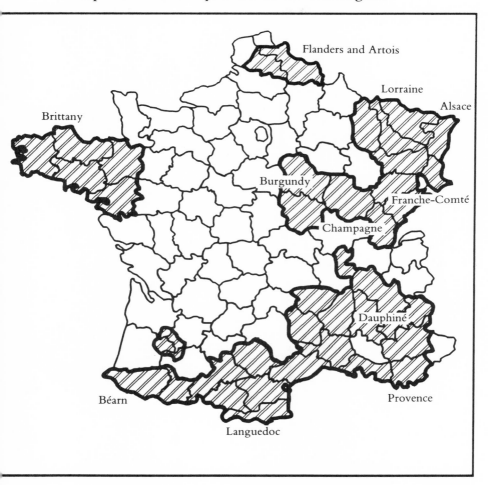

Flanders and Artois

Lorraine

Alsace

Brittany

Burgundy

Franche-Comté

Champagne

Dauphiné

Béarn

Provence

Languedoc

Map XVIII Patois-Speaking Communes in 1863

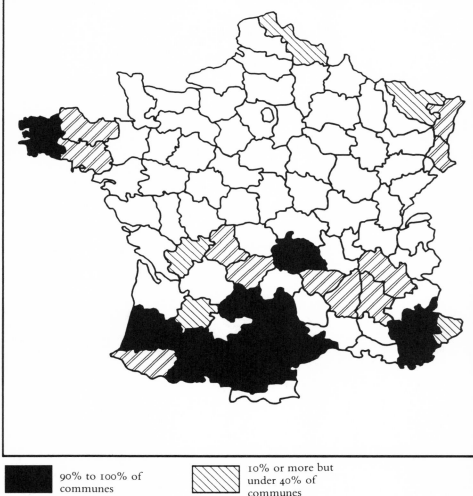

 90% to 100% of
communes

10% or more but
under 40% of
communes

40% or more but
under 90% of
communes

Fewer than 10% of
communes

Based on data from *Peasants into Frenchmen,* by Weber, 498–501; Ministère de l'Instruction Publique, F (17) 3160, AN

Map XIX   Religious Practice in Rural Areas in 1950

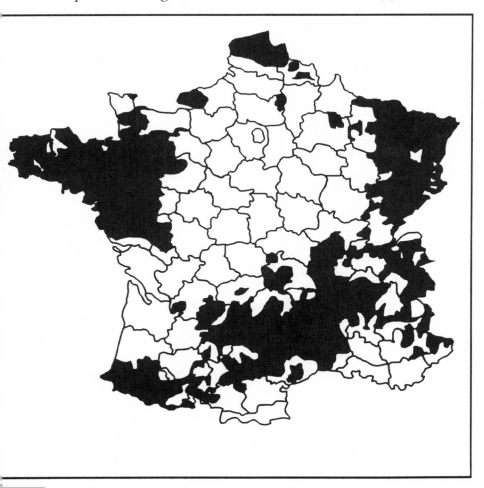

Strong Catholic areas

Weak Catholic and "missionary" areas

dapted from *Essor ou Déclin du clergé français,* by F. Boulard (Paris, 1950), 169. By permission of Editions du Cerf.

the hands of local elites (see Chapters 3 and 4). Decentralist sentiment meshed with regional resentments that the Legitimists could encourage and exploit. Bernard Menager has found that the urban Flemish notables of the Nord embraced Legitimism as a way to express their attachment to former municipal liberties.[37] Notwithstanding the region's commercial and industrial vitality, in 1844 the prefect of the Nord wrote, "French Flanders . . . remains profoundly imbued with old prejudices. . . . Lille is a conquered land and has not completely forgotten it. In the language of the people, France means the rest of the kingdom in opposition to Flanders."[38]

In solidarity with such sentiments in the west, Vincent d'Audren de Kerdrel and Arthur de La Borderie, both graduates of the Ecole des Chartes, helped found the Association Bretonne in 1843 to encourage the study of Breton literature and history. A. de Blois, M. de Courson, and Hérsart de La Villemarque, who directed the archaeological section of the association, devoted much of their efforts to a revival of the Breton language. Arcisse de Caumont and Louis de Kergolay directed the Institute des Provinces, for the preservation of provincial art and literature, and Gabriel de Belcastel was a principal member of the Academie des Jeux Floraux, at Toulouse, dedicated to the promotion of Occitain literature and poetry. Henri Fournier founded the *Revue de Berry* in 1864 to renew interest in the history and culture of the old province, and many of the Legitimists' regional "gazettes" carried the names of the former provinces on their mastheads.

The Legitimists praised the survival of regional particularism and equated it with the persistence of local mores in defiance of the atomizing and homogenizing impulse of the central government. Kergolay and Arthur de Gobineau judged France too vast, its dialects too various, and its local *esprit* too strong for all Frenchmen to be the same; they denied that the nation could "accommodate itself to a single set of regulations." Eugène Forcade, a businessman from Marseille, asserted that France's "second city" was too proud of its economic success and its "cultural originality" to submit to the dictates of the distant Parisian administration.[39]

37. Menager, *La Vie politique*, I, 418–23.

38. Report quoted by Tudesq in *Les Grands Notables en France*, I, 275.

39. Arthur de Gobineau and Louis de Kergolay, "Introduction," *Revue provinciale*, I (September, 1848), 1; M. Forcade, "La Centralisation et les Intérêts marseillais," *Revue provinciale*, I (October, 1848), 126.

Ferdinand Béchard and Claude Marie Raudot noted that the Revolution had failed to crush the "indomitable" resilience of regionalist sentiments among people who still referred to themselves as Bretons, Gascons, and Languedocians despite the irrevocable destruction of the old provinces. As a young native of Avignon in the 1870s, Frédéric Mistral turned to Legitimism because of his desire for a "resurgent Provence" and his hatred for the "centralized Jacobin republic."[40]

For the Legitimists, fidelity to the Bourbons was itself an expression of regionalism. Living amid the enduring signs of ancestral glory, customs, and loyalties gave people a natural love and respect for the past, they believed. Falloux thought that the Craon region of his birth was an "ardent and pure foyer of monarchical traditions" because its geography, character, and history exuded royalist sentiment and validated a sort of populist idiom that escaped rational political choices: "The land itself speaks an intelligible and cherished language, . . . and the native province [is] loyally and distinctly loved along with the entire nation." Falloux' neighbor Veillon de La Garraullaye was so "passionately attached to his native soil" that he joined the rising of the west in 1815 and again in 1832 "through a devotion that was so natural to him that he would not have understood that anyone could abstain from it or take any credit for joining it."[41] La Borderie asserted that it was his attachment to his native region that made him a monarchist and his attachment to the monarchy which made him French.[42] During the celebration of the Fête Dieu in June, 1855, peasants in Moellan carried white flags through the commune bearing the fleur-de-lis and the inscription God and King in French and Breton.[43]

History, regionalism, and monarchism were seen as inseparable from a special allegiance to the Catholic church. The most striking aspect of royalist political geography was that it reflected Legitimism's greatest strength in areas that were not only conservative and particularist but

40. Béchard, *De l'administration,* II, 268; Claude Marie Raudot, in *Annales,* April 27, 1871, I, annexe 183, p. 949; Charles Mesliand, "Le Félibrige, la République et l'Idée de décentralisation, 1870–72," in *La Décentralisation: 6ème Colloque d'histoire, Aix-en-Provence, 1961* (Gap, 1964), 119–64.

41. C. B. Pitman, trans. and ed., *Memoirs of the Count de Falloux, from the French* (2 vols.; London, 1888), I, 10–11, 15–16.

42. See Jack Reece, *Bretons Against France: Ethnic Minority Nationalism in Twentieth-Century Brittany* (Chapel Hill, N.C., 1977), Chapter I.

43. Cour Impériale de Rennes, June 21, 1855, in BB (30) 410, AN.

profoundly Catholic as well (Map XIX). The pattern was extremely stable throughout the nineteenth century. With the exception of parts of upper Normandy and the Midi, which experienced a regression in religious practice, the religious map of France was as unchanging as that of France's political orientation.[44] Together, historical experience, regional identity, and Catholicism formed what F. Boulard and Jacques Gadille have called a "compost" that nourished an interrelated attachment to certain religious, cultural, and political traditions. Catholicism was especially important in this regard, not only because of the power of the church but because religious comportment was a manifestation of collective social activity, which implied a community, with faith shaping the larger social environment in such a way as to preserve and expand a personal internalization of the evangelical message.[45]

The Legitimists recognized the link between history, locality, social conditions, and religious practice, but that did not by itself tell them how to create conditions favorable to a restoration of the monarchy. Rooted in a specific past and bound to regional particularities in a diverse country, the conditions that would aid them could not be reproduced everywhere. Or could they? Nineteenth-century Legitimists were convinced that changes in the way France was governed would let a moral and paternalistic elite—in conjunction with a church that was free to evangelize the masses—reconstruct the nation in the image of royalist France. If historical experience and regional memories were not transferable, religion and the social environment it helped structure were. Thus, the key to Legitimist social reconstruction seemed to lie in transplanting to the

44. See especially Gabriel Le Bras, *Etudes de sociologie religieuse* (2 vols.; Paris, 1956), I, 370–71; Rémond, *Les Droites en France,* 420–21; and F. Boulard, *An Introduction to Religious Sociology: Pioneer Work in France* (London, 1960), 15. The intensity of religious practice varied greatly from region to region. François Lebrun writes that for the years 1830 to 1850, Easter attendance was as low as 6 percent at Versailles and 13 percent at Orleans, and as high as 85 percent in the diocese of Nantes and 69 percent in the rural areas of the Tarn. See François Lebrun, ed., *Histoire des catholiques en France du XVe siècle à nos jours* (Toulouse, 1980), 322–27. Lebrun stresses both the diversity of practice and the stability of percentages throughout the nineteenth century. Recent scholarship has shown that the rate of religious observance was quite high in some urban areas and among the working class in the nineteenth century. See especially Gérard Cholvy and Y. M. Hilaire, *Histoire religieuse de la France contemporaine* (3 vols.; Paris, 1986), I.

45. F. Boulard and Jacques Gadille, "Sociologie et Histoire religieuse de la France aux XIXe et XXe siècles: Introduction générale," in *Matériaux pour l'histoire religieuse du peuple français, XIX–XX siècles,* ed. F. Boulard and Jacques Gadille (Paris, 1982), 11–12.

rest of the nation the pattern of social relations existent in areas of high religious observance. That placed sociology at the center of the royalist program.

VERTICAL COMMUNITIES

Legitimism flourished in cities, towns, and rural villages where strong and respected traditional institutions helped create, and were sustained by, a pattern of social relations that tended to integrate the communities vertically rather than stratify them horizontally. The Legitimists believed that reinforcing and establishing local and national institutions that patterned social relations and social encounters so as to "moralize" the masses could overcome diversity, individualism, and class conflict. Catholic monarchism, they presumed, would regain national support if a pattern of hierarchical influences that shielded the lower classes from the agents of subversion and brought them into frequent and efficacious contact with the agents of moral reinforcement could be adapted to diverse socioeconomic settings. Ferdinand Béchard envisioned that form of social reconstruction when he wrote that human passions were best deflected from evil when the "society" surrounding the individual encouraged "moral sentiments" that "forewarned" man against his baser instincts. Devotion "to family, sociability, religion," he explained, were all "natural inclinations that combat in us the appetites of the senses and the disorder of the spirit." Those forces "will acquire greater strength by our interaction with our fellow man and by the effect of habits that will bind us to all things worthy of esteem and respect."[46]

The Legitimists' presumptions about vertical social relations do not appear out of line with the views of social analysts studying nineteenth-century France who have employed contrasting models of vertical or horizontal social integration to account for the regional diversity of French political and religious behavior. Gabriel Le Bras has observed that the "linear relations" in "closed" local societies, largely shielded from external contacts, favored religious conformity, but he has conceded that when associations—families, corporations, municipal institutions—created an *esprit* serving to unite a community through deference to tra-

46. Ferdinand Béchard, *De l'état du paupérisme en France et des moyens d'y remédier* (Paris, 1852), 59.

ditional authority, there was the same hospitality to religion. Where a "hierarchical sentiment" animated the social structure, "vertical liaisons" were strong enough to "associate socially unequal people on the plane of equality."[47] By contrast, Agulhon found that in the Var a pattern of association that united artisans, workers, and peasants and challenged the hegemony of the conservative landowners created a situation conducive to the diffusion of republican ideology and secured the political predominance of the bourgeoisie. The radicalization of the Var, he writes, resulted from "social . . . influences that passed from one social class to another" through the "intermediary milieus" of artisans and petit bourgeois intellectuals who had established "intermediary networks of influence [and] patronage" in the form of new associations. Their more democratic horizontal structure contrasted with the vertical social alignment of Siegfried's west and suggests that the success of the Right depended above all on its ability to prevent the transition from traditional to democratic patronage.[48]

Thus associations played an important role in creating patterns of social interaction on the margins of class encounters. Indeed, Legitimists and republicans, Catholics and freethinkers viewed politics largely in terms of such patterns. Albert de Mun dreamed of an alliance between the *classes dirigeantes* and the *classes inférieures* forged by the social Catholic action of his Oeuvre des Cercles Catholiques des Ouvriers while Jules Macé, president of the republican Ligue de l'Enseignement called for more "intercourse . . . between the people and the bourgeoisie."[49] As Katherine Auspitz has observed, associational conflicts were fought "for control of the rudimentary apparatus of social services," communications, and patronage, to determine which group of elites would be able to shape France's agencies of socialization.[50]

The politics of patronage and influence let intermediately placed groups, especially the clergy and the middle class, hold the balance of

47. See Le Bras, *Etudes,* I, 317–22.

48. Agulhon, *The Republic in the Village,* 148, 297, 302–303. See also Corbin, *Archaisme et Modernité,* I, 533–34, II, 798–99, 998.

49. Mun, *Ma vocation sociale,* 83; Mun, *Discours prononcé par le comte Albert de Mun à l'inauguration du Cercle de Montmartre-Clignancourt, le 16 juin 1872* (Paris, 1872), 3; Jules Macé, quoted by Katherine Auspitz in *The Radical Bourgeoisie: The Ligue de l'Enseignement and the Origins of the Third Republic, 1866–1885* (Cambridge, Mass., 1982), 25.

50. Auspitz, *The Radical Bourgeoisie,* 25.

power. Clergymen, often recruited from the lower middle class, not only
on occasion acted as electoral agents for the royalist landowners and industrialists but used their pastoral function and their position in Catholic
charitable organizations to maintain lower-class sympathy for conservative elites. Especially in the towns, where the direct and personal ties of
dependency characteristic of the countryside were often lacking, the
church provided, in the words of Ronald Aminzade, the "social nexus
which linked workers to the patronage, though not the person, of the
urban aristocracy." He sees the "mediation of the clergy and the church-
based cultural institutions" as having played a key role in maintaining
Legitimist influence in Toulouse. Religion, he has concluded, was the
foundation of popular royalism in Haute-Garonne: "The Church was a
powerful institution possessing strong moral authority which maintained
a popular tradition productive of vertically integrated solidarities between aristocrats and workers." Only with the emergence of associations
based in the working class and unconnected with the older Catholic and
royalist networks of clientage did the republican and socialist movements
in Toulouse gain strength and influence.[51]

It is not surprising, therefore, that the Legitimist aristocracy tried to
create its own bourgeois intermediaries by relying heavily on the clergy
and by recruiting members for such organizations as the Saint Vincent
de Paul Society from among the middle class. With over thirty-two
thousand members in 1859, the Saint Vincent de Paul Society attracted
not only aristocrats but shopkeepers, artisans, and employees of the
church, along with businessmen and civil servants.[52] Clement Myionnet,
a founding member of the society in Angers, looked for *confrères* among
the "good young people coming out of the seminaries of Combrée" as
well as "among the commercial professions, the bourgeoisie, and the
nobility."[53] Legitimist-sponsored charitable organizations tried to envelop precisely those social elements that, in other circumstances, could
break the vertical chain of solidarities and undermine the patronage of

51. Ronald Aminzade, *Class, Politics, and Early Industrial Capitalism: A Study of Mid-
Nineteenth-Century Toulouse, France* (Albany, N.Y., 1981), 52–63.
52. Austin Gough, "The Conflict in Politics," in *Conflicts in French Society,* ed. Zeldin, 110.
53. Charles Maignen, *Clement Myionnet, premier membre de la Congrégation des Frères de
St. Vincent de Paul d'Angers: Sa vie, ses oeuvres, d'après sa autobiographie annotée et complétée*
(Paris, 1925), 51–52.

conservative elites. Where the chain held, Legitimists reaped important social and political dividends. The *procureur* of Aix, a royalist stronghold, called the "*oeuvres de bénéfaisance* and other organizations" run by the "religious or lay congregations" a "veritable army on which [the clerical party] exercises its action and its control" and warned his superiors of the danger of not taking measures to curtail them.[54] Similar political considerations led the government of Napoleon III to try to detach the clergy from the Legitimists and to break up the centralized bureaucracy of the Saint Vincent de Paul Society in 1861. Rather than eliminate the society, the regime abolished its central secretariat and, in search of its own clients and intermediaries, placed men loyal to the Empire at the head of the local conferences.[55]

The same concern about the role of bourgeois intermediaries meant that *laique* clubs and Masonic lodges, usually dominated by middle-class republicans, were bound to become a focus of Legitimist hostility.[56] Edouard Pie, the ultramontane bishop of Poitiers, traced the true social peril not to the "uncouth greed of the lower classes" but to "irreligion among that so-called conservative category that in each town is represented by the mayor, the schoolteacher, the notary, the doctor, and various landowners whose defiance toward the clergy is unbeatable."[57] Since Legitimism and anticlericalism fed on each other, they flourished

54. Rapport du procureur général d'Aix, February 19, 1861, in BB (18) 1598, AN. The report calls special attention to the Mission de France, directed by Père Tissier, whom the official protrayed as the "soul" of a network of charitable organizations supported by members "from big business in Marseille and from the class of *propriétaires*" close to the Legitimist party. According to the report, these members were always "ready to extend a hand to the worker . . . in order to win men over to its undertakings." Tissier's societies were "numerous" and could "make a perfectly appreciable impact during elections." The local director of customs told the *procureur* that members of the Mission's mutual-aid society who worked for the customs office were passing official certificates of illness back and forth so that they could collect an indemnity equal to their salary from the association each time they reported ill. By such means, the official continued, Tissier and his patrons hoped "under a government based on universal suffrage, to find in numbers a power that they previously looked for in the government itself."

55. See Albert Foucault, *La Société de St. Vincent de Paul: Histoire de cent ans* (Paris, 1933), and Abbé J. Schall, *Un Disciple de Saint Vincent de Paul au XIXe siècle: Adolphe Baudon, 1819–1888* (Paris, 1897).

56. See Faury, *Cléricalisme et Anticléricalisme,* 371–73; and C. Marcilhacy, *Le Diocèse d'Orléans au milieu du XIXe siècle: Les Hommes et leurs mentalités* (Paris, 1964), 202–209.

57. Louis Baunard, *Histoire du Cardinal Pie, évêque de Poitiers* (2 vols.; Paris, 1901), I, 334.

in the same regions; clerical Legitimists and anticlerical republicans—
Clemenceau, Briand, and Waldeck-Rousseau were all from the west—
who rose to national prominence understood the central role played by
such associations in local power struggles. In launching the Oeuvre in
1871, Albert de Mun, another westerner, likened the Catholic *cercles* to
Masonic lodges: "They create revolutionary clubs, we create Catholic
cercles."[58]

If the middle class had been solidly republican or liberal, the Legitimists could not have hoped to maintain a bourgeois following. But the
middle class was divided ideologically, especially after 1848, and many
joined the religious and political reaction that gripped the notables in the
wake of the June Days. The emergence of a politically vocal Catholic
bourgeoisie during Napoleon III's intervention in Italy in 1859 helped
sustain and invigorate the fortunes of Legitimism at a time when few
comfortable people were searching for political alternatives. United by
religious sentiments and by concerns about political instability and cultural secularization, Legitimists and clericals formed a powerful, although tenuous, alliance during the 1860s and 1870s. Michel Denis has
found that the religious question and events in Rome reduced the cohesion among a once solidly liberal middle class in the Mayenne and caused
a number of former republicans to follow the lead of the clergy. The
more religion became an issue in Mayenne, the more former liberals
joined religious associations and moved closer to the Legitimists politically. The realignment added both to the ranks of the royalist party and
to the importance of the issues political Catholics deemed especially urgent. The Legitimists were thus led to place increased emphasis on the
school question and on the role of the church in society in order to reflect
the concerns of their new constituency.[59] Aggressive denunciations of
freethinkers and socialists, accompanied by the rise of a new religious
piety, allowed the Legitimists to "recover an audience among the Catho-

58. Mun, *Ma vocation sociale,* 74.
59. See Denis, *Les Royalistes de la Mayenne,* 399–407; and Stéphane Rials, *Le Légitimisme*
(Paris, 1983), 27. In 1861, shortly after the clerical reaction against the Empire's foreign
policy, an official in Aix spoke of the alliance of the Legitimist party and the clerical party
as "a consequence of the general state of mind today as well as a bit of the history of our
times." The alliance, he commented, had always existed because of the sentiments shared
by the Legitimists, the clergy, and conservative Catholics, "but it was not ostensible the
way it is today" (Report of February 19, 1861, in BB [18] 1598, AN).

lic masses by assuming the principal role in the defense of the pope."[60]
By 1870, liberal Catholics like the Comte de Montalembert and Alfred
de Falloux had lost ground in the party to ultramontanes, like Louis
Veuillot, who saw the restoration of the monarchy not as an end in itself
but as a means to protect the church. Meanwhile extreme Legitimist
"inseparatists" like Guillaume Véran were declaring, "One cannot be
Catholic without being royalist."[61]

Legitimists fought to expand authoritarian patronage and maintain
vertical social integration because that is what seemed to work in regions
where they remained politically successful. Where they failed to make
that effort or where the possibilities for it never existed, as in Dauphiné
or Orléanais, their party was isolated and ineffective.[62] In the 1880s, the
prefect of the Vendée still traced royalist strength to the way influence
"goes out from the presbytery, is exerted by it on the château, and by
the château on the sharecroppers."[63] Mun saw the absence of this hierarchical pattern as the reason certain areas of the Vosges were inaccessible
to Legitimist influence: "The big landowners are nothing more than big
businessmen, five-sixths of whom are sectarians, radicals, or simply
pleasure-seekers. The bourgeoisie, flattered by the [Republic], are envi-
ous and full of hatred over being reduced to toeing the line. The people
of the countryside, deprived of traditions, are in lockstep with the actions
of the administration, upon which they are entirely dependent."[64] In Poitiers, the population was described as "instinctively attracted to royalist

60. Denis, Les Royalistes de la Mayenne, 400–401. The ideological diversity of the French
bourgeoisie was also related to the growing number of middle-class youth entering Catholic secondary schools after the passage of the Falloux Law in 1850. See Ringer, Education
and Society in Modern Europe, 316; and Robert Gildea, Education in Provincial France,
1800–1914: A Study of Three Departments (Oxford, 1983), 188–98.
    61. Véran, La Question du XIXe siècle, 516–18. On the issue of separatism and inseparat-
ism, see Rials, Le Légitimisme, 39–43; Etudes Maurrassiennes, VIIe Colloque Maurras (Aix,
1983); and E. Catta, La Doctrine politique et social du Cardinal Pie, 1815–1880 (Paris, 1959).
    62. See Jacquier, Le Légitimisme dauphinois; Marcilhacy, Le Diocèse d'Orléans au milieu du
XIXe siècle; and Le Bras, Etude, ix–xiii.
    63. Prefect of the Vendée, quoted by Jacques Gadille in La Pensée et l'Action politique des
évêques françaises au début de la IIIe République, 1870–1883 (2 vols.; Paris, 1967), I, 185.
    64. Albert de Mun to the Comte de Chambord, quoted by Levillain in Albert de Mun,
716n. According to the procureur of Pau, the election in 1856 of the Marquis de Cornulier
to the general council occurred because of his network of supporters, which included workers on his "very important properties," the Legitimist organization, the clergy, and even
the maire, the adjunct, and the garde champêtre. The government's candidate did not receive
a single vote. See Lettre du procureur général de Pau, April 23, 1856, in BB (18) 1543, AN.

ideas"; in Haute Garonne, the prefect in 1849 reported that "in other regions there are few Legitimists except among wealthy aristocratic families, whereas here there are Legitimists among the people."[65] At Grenoble, by contrast, the Legitimists were "not very numerous, their opinions a pale reflection of a respectable but forgotten past"; engaged in "vain abstention . . . , they do not attract the masses." In Montluçon, the Legitimists were reported not to have the "initiative to encourage the manifestation of popular sentiment" and to be distinguished only by their "profound obscurity."[66]

The Legitimists believed that they could make all of France like the western *bocage,* the Midi *blanc,* and the pious plains of Flanders, because it was evident from those regions' diverse regional and social features that traditionalism could persist irrespective of the size of landholdings, the existence of factory production, and the extent of the aristocratic presence. If Legitimism was rural in the west, urban in parts of the Midi, and compatible with industrialization in the Nord, economic conditions did not by themselves determine a region's political culture. The Legitimists, by understanding their own survival in social and cultural terms, came to a confidence that large cities could be made to function like devout rural communities and factories like paternalistic estates. What was needed was for conservative elites and the church to be free to construct economic and social institutions that could replace the social structures of moral suasion lost by recalcitrant communities. There was no other way for Legitimists to regard their fate. To concede that their influence, and that of the church, would always be restricted by certain economic structures, historical traditions, and regional particularisms would have been to admit the impossibility of forging a national consensus in favor of a restoration of the monarchy.

In 1852, Falloux told the Duc Des Cars that the Legitimists could not simply withdraw into internal exile because Louis Napoleon had succeeded in consolidating his regime. Royalists, he wrote, had failed to restore the monarchy on top of the rubble of the Second Republic because they had failed to prepare French society to accept their leadership in advance. Legitimists, he held, should avoid the same mistakes by

65. Cour Impériale de Poitiers, June 15, 1859, in BB (30) 422; Prefect of Haute-Garonne, quoted by Aminzade in *Class, Politics, and Early Industrial Capitalism,* 54–55.
66. Rapport du procureur général de Isère, 1867, in Jacquier's *Le Légitimisme dauphinois,* 70; Cour Impériale de Riom, June 21, 1866, in BB (30) 423, AN.

working "to reconstitute a France capable of receiving a monarch."[67] Much of the work the Legitimists undertook in this regard did not begin under the Second Empire, but it was only after 1852 that the combination of political repression and a growing sociological bent compelled them to concentrate on the problems presented by restoring the monarchy in what they perceived as a damaged civil society.

67. Falloux, *Mémoires d'une royaliste*, II, 213.

PART TWO

 The Ideological
Reconstruction of
Royalist France

CHAPTER III

⚜ Decentralization

THE GOAL of decentralization reflected the Legitimists' desire to break with the historical options of monarchical absolutism and revolutionary centralization by creating an administrative system that better suited a return to an orderly hierarchical society. From the beginning of the Bourbon Restoration, decentralization had been part of the royalist project. Administrative reform figured prominently in the Legitimists' first program, published in the *Gazette de France* in 1832. Yet, even though all Legitimists supported decentralization, it became the special object of study for only a handful of royalists whose shared faith in local self-government and whose administrative and legal experience gave them a greater degree of interest and expertise in such matters. Strongly influenced by Alexis de Tocqueville and Pierre Paul Royer-Collard, they were heard at the critical moments in 1848 and 1871 when the opportunity emerged to refashion the administrative order.

Claude Marie Raudot was perhaps the most outspoken and persistent advocate of decentralization in the nineteenth century. When he told the National Assembly that it seemed to him as if some people had been calling for decentralization all their lives, he drew laughter from his colleagues, who knew that Raudot had to be speaking about himself. Born in 1801 at Saulieu, Côte d'Or, Raudot was the son of the *maire* of Avallon. His father was to be a member of the *chambre introuvable* of 1815. After 1852, Raudot, who began his career as a *substitut* to the *procureur du roi* at Auxerre, was intermittently in a position to observe firsthand the workings of the French state. At the time of the July Revolution, he, as a loyal Legitimist, resigned in protest his post of magistrate at Versailles.

But his preoccupation with public affairs and his inclination toward the parliamentary Legitimism of Antoine Berryer prevented him from remaining inactive. Between 1842 and 1871 he sat on the general council of the Yonne and the municipal council of Avallon, was the *maire* of Avallon, and represented his department in the legislatures of 1848, 1849, and 1871. His numerous publications included articles for the prestigious *Journal des économistes* and *Le Correspondant,* as well as a study of Napoleon I. His most influential work, *De la décadence de la France* (1850), was a comprehensive critique of French administrative practice and a call for the drastic reduction of the central government's role in economic and political life. He carried his obsession with decentralization into practice when he headed a *comité de décentralisation* in 1849, participated in the extraparliamentary Commission on Decentralization set up in 1870 under the Ollivier ministry, and was the author of a comprehensive decentralist proposal submitted to the *commission de décentralisation* of the National Assembly of 1871.

Raudot was joined in his enthusiasm for administrative reform by Ferdinand Béchard, Roger de Larcy, Louis de Kergolay, and Arthur de Gobineau. Gobineau collaborated with Kergolay in editing the strongly decentralist *Revue provinciale* between 1848 and 1851 before becoming preoccupied with racial theory under the Second Empire. Béchard (1799–1870), Kergolay (1804–1880), and Larcy (1805–1882), who all served as deputies either in 1849 or 1871, had important state positions that brought them into closer contact with the administration than many Legitimists enjoyed. Kergolay, who entered the Ecole Polytechnique under the Restoration, became an officer at the Ecole d'Application in 1826. Although he left politics after participating in the failed Legitimist insurrection of 1832, living as a country squire and keeping in touch with Tocqueville until that writer's death in 1859, he returned from internal exile in 1871 to take a seat as a deputy from the Oise. Béchard, a prominent member of the bar at Nîmes, became a lawyer at the Cour de Cassation in 1840 and later at the Conseil d'Etat, the very pinnacle of the administrative structure. His publications included *L'Administration de la France* (1851), a lengthy plea for extensive municipal autonomy, and a number of pieces on municipal law in France, Switzerland, and the United States, as well as historical studies of communal law during antiquity and the Middle Ages. The son of a subprefect, Larcy was a member of a prominent noble family and served as president of the general council of the Gard under Louis Philippe and as the minister of public works under Louis Adolphe Thiers and the Duc de Broglie in the 1870s. Collectively, these Legitimist decentralizers had a prominence in public affairs that contrasted with the abstentionism of others of their party and the merely local experience of those who accepted minor elected positions.

The concrete encounter with administrative authoritarianism under Napoleon III placed decentralization at the center of Legitimist hopes for the establishment of a new order, because it promised to alleviate their political isolation and solve the problems arising out of the relationship between the exercise of political authority and the structure of society. The Legitimists saw decentralization as a means of reviving the power of conservative elites by giving them a dominant role in local life and by preventing the central administration from further damaging established local power relations. Government by a cadre of "natural" elites, they believed, would renew the governing capacity of the notables and would offer the people practical lessons in obedience and civic duty.

Decentralization was not, however, merely a political expedient for a class that had suffered from political isolation and the erosion of an advantageous social structure. In a larger sense it was a response to the historic problem of institutional and social instability, and in this respect it was an attempt to institutionalize an alternative form of social integration. Decentralization corresponded in the minds of Legitimists to an image of a society with a diffused pattern of vertically stratified power relations, the compartmentalization of territorial, economic, and cultural spaces, and the depoliticization of government. The Legitimists' preference for that kind of social structure grew out of their critique of the centralized state, their own experience, and their sense of history. How did they pose the question of decentralization in historical terms? To what degree was decentralization compatible with monarchical government and how was it to address the special problem of instability with which all French elites were concerned?

DECENTRALIZATION AND
THE MONARCHY:
THE PROBLEM OF CONTINUITY

In 1888 Albert Du Boys told an audience gathered to commemorate the 1788 Assembly of Vizille—which among other things had sought to revitalize provincial estates—that the French must cease to be

revolutionaries even though they would always be *frondeurs*.[1] Du Boys'
distinction pointed to the importance the Legitimists placed on breaking
the historical link between the Bourbon monarchy and bureaucratic absolutism. Although they searched France's past for examples of stable
and durable institutions, they also embraced every occasion to imitate
their ancestors in trying to transform the French state. What the Comte
de Chambord called, in his manifesto of 1871, the "great reform movement of the last century" often served as a starting point for monarchist
decentralist proposals. The reform movement's legacy implicitly raised
the question of whether the monarchy was necessary for, or even compatible with, a decentralized administration; the answer the Legitimists
gave rested ultimately on how they assessed the historical role of France's
monarchical institutions in forming the modern state.

Decentralist theories naturally required a retrospective glance not only
at the revolutionary state, either Jacobin or Bonapartist, but at the monarchy of Richelieu and Louis XIV. Royalists were often very selective
about which monarchy they admired and usually pointed to the reign of
Henri IV and the blossoming of the Estates of Languedoc and Burgundy
as the springtime of local liberties. Others took note of how the monarchy developed in the seventeenth century but sought a way to be both
counterrevolutionary and antiabsolutist by invoking the sanction of historical continuity afforded by the tradition of provincial liberties, and by
arguing that carrying such a tradition forward required a monarchical
restoration.

The misconduct of history posed problems for any royalist justification of decentralization, since as the Legitimists, along with Tocqueville,
readily acknowledged, the Old Regime had begun the process of centralization that the Revolution and Napoleon had refined and completed.
The problems were all the more urgent since the opponents of Legitimism argued that royalist hopes for decentralization were historically un-
founded and the Bourbons would never abandon their inclination toward
absolutism. Republicans, unwilling to grant the Legitimists any historical credibility, viewed decentralization as a reactionary scheme to restore
the power of locally entrenched aristocrats, while liberals who favored
decentralization felt that the Revolution had only reinforced a centraliz-
ing tendency whose origins lay with the Bourbons.

The Legitimists saw the issue differently. Raudot recognized the mon-

1. Albert DuBoys, *Le Centenaire de l'assemblée de Vizille et son véritable esprit* (Lyon,
1888), 26.

archy's faults but held that, political unity during the Middle Ages having been too tenuous, it was not the Old Regime but the Revolution that had led France to the "opposite excess."[2] Guillaume Véran argued more dogmatically that despotism had never been a natural feature of the monarchy. According to him, the true monarchy had always respected provincial franchises, and centralization had been forced upon the Bourbons by feudal Protestant barons during the Wars of Religion and by the Protestant powers of Europe during the wars of the sixteenth and seventeenth centuries. After the reign of Henri IV, royal power "took up arms against rebellion, and the glorious despotism of Richelieu and Louis XIV deflected France from its natural traditions." For Véran, the same Protestant assault on tradition that had forced the monarchy to transform itself into the centralized and despotic ancien régime culminated in the revolutionary excesses of popular sovereignty in 1793.[3]

Others, like Béchard, Kergolay, and Larcy, looked to the reform movement of the 1780s, when the notables strove to return France to its ancient constitution and the king recognized municipal and provincial franchises and the need to reduce the power of the *intendants*. Béchard and Kergolay sought to demonstrate how Louis XVI greeted with "extreme favor" projects initiated in 1779 and 1787 that aimed at the reconstruction of intermediary powers through local assemblies in the *pays d'état* and in the *pays d'élection*. The culmination of this movement was to have been the Estates General of 1789, following in the same spirit as the "insurrectional assembly of Vizille," whose chief goal was the "reestablishment of the Provincial Estates of Dauphiné." The *cahiers,* many Legitimists believed, unanimously seconded the demand to revive the provincial estates. Kergolay was certain that up until the very moment when the delegates to the Estates General arrived in Paris, the desire for the preservation of local liberties and provincial self-administration remained strong. Therefore he believed that by decreeing on the night of August 4 the suppression of the provincial estates, the National Assembly betrayed the mandate it had received from the people.[4]

Despite some variation, each of these interpretations suggests that the monarchy, regardless of its absolutism, had preserved within its tradi-

2. Claude Marie Raudot, "La Décentralisation: Première Partie," *Le Correspondant,* XLV (1858), 459.
3. Véran, *La Question du XIXe siècle,* 386–87.
4. Béchard, *De l'administration,* II, 21–22; Louis de Kergolay, "Des états provinciaux de l'ancienne monarchie," *Revue provinciale,* I (November, 1848), 203–205; Roger de Larcy, "La Décentralisation de 1789 à 1870," *Le Correspondant,* LXXXII (1870), 7.

tions and institutional principles the potential for the reemergence of an administration based on local liberties and viable provincial assemblies. The "great reform movement" was thought indicative of decentralization's latency in the monarchy. Since the Legitimists believed that Louis XVI had embraced the goals of the Assembly of Notables, the failure of 1789 seemed all the more tragic and, in their minds, tied excessive centralization all the more firmly to the work of the Revolution. Larcy wrote that the institutions of the Old Regime "possessed that principle of autonomy so vigorously demanded today"; in 1789, all that was needed was for that principle to be "rejuvenated and regularized."[5] But with the Revolution those dormant institutions were fully discountenanced and systematically abolished. If the monarchy was responsible for a certain measure of centralization, Larcy believed, it had at least guarded and sheltered what it had encouraged in better times. The Revolution, by contrast, stood as the point of no return, since by instituting centralization, revolutionaries gained a vested interest in an instrument of power that severed the link between French society and its monarchical institutions. Gustave de Bernardi argued that the "administrative organization" created by "imperial genius" had become a tool by which liberals established the hegemony and permanence of revolutionary reforms. "This organization," he suggested, "persisted untempered across each change of regime" because it served to perpetuate the social and cultural disorder upon which "the regime of eighty-nine" thrived.[6] Larcy viewed the destruction of local liberties, estates, and guilds as an attempt to clear away social and political obstacles to the hegemony of the state but pointed out that, having destroyed the social order, the revolutionaries were forced back upon an "administration without roots, entirely elective, initially dominated and soon carried along with the revolutionary wind."[7] Raudot asserted that only before the Revolution was French society reasonably well endowed with independent social bodies—the clergy, the municipalities, a nobility and bourgeoisie with private wealth, and a church that directed education and public assistance—that could resist any proclivity the monarchy had toward arbitrary action.[8]

5. Larcy, "La Décentralisation de 1789 à 1870," *Le Correspondant*, LXXXII (1870), 7.
6. Bernardi, *La Révolution*, 81–82.
7. Larcy, "La Décentralisation de 1789 à 1870," *Le Correspondant*, LXXXII (1870), 7.
8. Claude Marie Raudot, *La France avant la Révolution: Son état politique et social en 1787 à l'ouverture de l'assemblée des notables et son histoire depuis cette époque jusqu'aux Etats Généraux* (Paris, n.d.), 8–18.

It is clear why Tocqueville's thesis presented embarrassments for Legitimist notables. Despite the "fund of benevolence" with which the Legitimists greeted *The Old Regime and the French Revolution* when it appeared in 1856, Legitimist newspapers seldom offered more than a selective reading of it, focusing only on Tocqueville's condemnation of the Revolution's zeal for centralization and its destruction of the historic opportunity of 1789.[9] They did not deny—what Tocqueville had shown—that the king and his council, local agents, *intendants,* and *subdélégués* directly administered the *pays d'élection* and took active steps to reduce the prerogatives of the provincial estates, which were eventually suppressed, but they pointed out that neither Richelieu nor Louis XIV nor any king had destroyed by a "stroke of the pen" a province or a traditional body, no matter how dormant or ineffective it might have become. Moreover, unlike Tocqueville, who observed that monarchical centralization had undermined aristocratic government prior to 1789 by weakening or destroying provincial institutions, the Legitimists argued that the reform movement revealed both the vitality of these institutions and the ability of the notables to reclaim their function as effective political elites. As Charles Maurras later wrote, "These bodies would have persisted. But it was these very bodies, their principle much more than their reality, that the Revolution attacked in their entirety."[10] If the monarchy had been careless of local liberties, the Republic and the Empire were their sworn enemies.

Tocqueville's perception of a continuity between the Old Regime and the Revolution also challenged the Legitimists' reading of the historic significance of 1789. Unlike the Legitimists, Tocqueville viewed the so-called reform movement of 1787–1789 not as a stillborn revival of France's ancient constitution but as a dress-rehearsal for the destruction of monarchical power and noble privilege, in which the nobility participated by defending deformed and discredited institutions.[11] Still,

---

9. Alexis de Tocqueville to Louis de Kergolay, August 28, 1856, in Alexis de Tocqueville, *Correspondances d'Alexis de Tocqueville et de Louis de Kergolay,* ed. André Jardin (Paris, 1977), Part 2, p. 310, Vol. XIII of Tocqueville, *Oeuvres,* 27 vols.

10. Charles Maurras, *L'Enquête sur la monarchie* (Paris, 1900), quoted by Henri Morel in "Charles Maurras et l'Idée de la décentralisation," *Etudes Maurrassiennes,* I (1972), 122–23. See also Arthur de Gobineau, "Etudes sur les municipalités," *Revue provinciale,* I (October, 1848), 111.

11. Alexis de Tocqueville, *The Old Regime and the French Revolution,* trans. Stuart Gilbert (Garden City, N.Y., 1955), 141–42; John Lukacs, ed., *The European Revolution and the Correspondence with Gobineau* (Gloucester, Mass., 1968), 42–44, 55–58, 72–73.

nineteenth-century supporters of a monarchical restoration were no less consistent than republicans in considering the Revolution a radical break with the past, because a Jacobin perspective allowed them to argue that the true restoration of local liberties was organically tied to French's monarchical past. Since the Legitimists defined decentralization as a reparative process designed to heal the "large and deep wound" the Revolution had opened "between the past and the future of France," they found Tocqueville's thesis insupportable. For them, the restoration of a monarchy that to their mind had historically been the vessel of ancient liberties would redress the impetuous errors of the Revolution and "reconnect the chain of time" by increasing the power of local government.[12]

Cast in these terms, however, the Legitimists' proposition oscillated between holding that decentralization was a necessary prerequisite to a restoration and holding that a restoration was needed to create conditions favorable to the reformation of the administrative system. To put it another way, was local autonomy and decentralization consubstantial with the monarchy or did institutional structures configure a preexisting political culture? The question was especially troublesome in the mid–nineteenth century, since it was far easier for the Legitimists to influence the details of legislation than to gain an ultimate political victory. Both Raudot and Béchard, the two principal architects of Legitimist decentralization, judged a coordination of legislative action and royalist politics impracticable, since any outcome of royalist maneuvers was far from predictable. In fact, both men were more disturbed by the relationship between centralization and what they saw as the precipitous decline of French society than with the machinations of the Bureau du Roi, and both set about designing administrative reforms in a way that did not overtly presuppose a particular form of government. The political realities within which the Legitimists had to work served to reinforce the tendency of some of them to assume that institutions create their own moral foundations once they have been put into place. In an illuminating

12. Gobineau, "Etudes," 111; Arthur de Gobineau, "De la création de comités provincaux," *Revue provinciale,* II (January, 1849), 333; "Bulletin départementale," *Revue provinciale,* II (May, 1849), 227. Raudot's proposals for administrative reform (see Chapter IV), endorsed by Kergolay, were admired by him because they were modeled on the Belgium system, which was the "result of a sort of compromise between the centralist, governmental ideas of our modern times and the barely effaced memories of these ancient franchises that shine nowhere more brilliantly than in these very lands" ("Des institutions communales de la Belgique: Premier Article," *Revue provinciale,* II [July, 1849], 322).

exchange of letters on the subject of English self-government in 1857, Kergolay told Tocqueville that it would be possible for the French to emulate the British system when elites gained a "practical competency for the day-to-day details of local government." Since the practice of wise self-administration was seen as a natural consequence of self-administration, the mere effective use of local institutions by qualified notables was itself a positive argument for decentralization, according to Kergolay. Like most Legitimist decentralizers, he assumed that the "elite of society" were already predisposed to exercise power through local institutions and that they merely lacked the opportunity to do so effectively because the Second Empire had deprived them of any real political function. It followed that a revival of local institutions depended on "its practical realization in the great debates of the political rostrum"; once in place, local institutions would engender the potential for self-perpetuation when the "light" that "completely instructs the elite of society . . . descends on the masses."[13]

By embracing the myth of the reform movement, the Legitimists were not calling for a return to the institutions of the past. As Kergolay admitted, the task was not to "reproduce what was" but to write legislation and create new institutions consistent with the "physiognomy" and "essence" of "our era."[14] What Legitimist decentralizers wanted was not an excuse to resurrect the Old Regime but a face-saving way to cover their break with a bothersome past and a way to allow the old *frondeur* to coexist with the loyal royalist. As long as Chambord fully endorsed decentralist reform based on the spirit of the "great reform movement," it was possible to count on the docility of the future monarch and to tinker

13. Louis de Kergolay to Alexis de Tocqueville, August 11, 1857, March 15, 1858, both in Tocqueville, *Correspondances*, Part 2, pp. 329, 335. Decentralization and Legitimism were not equivalent. Only for the Legitimist writers examined here was the success of decentralization linked to the viability and stability of a monarchist regime. As the ideas of Béchard and Raudot demonstrate, it was possible to imagine a decentralized regime without a monarchical form: from a purely practical point of view, the Legitimist critique of centralization touched only the function and not the nature of the executive. Indeed, many decentralizers were not monarchists—Pierre Joseph Proudhon and Odilon Barrot are two examples—and in later republican regionalist movements such as the Fédération Régionaliste Française of Jean Charles-Brun, the absence of monarchism did nothing to modify the practical arguments in favor of decentralization. See Jean Charles-Brun, *Le Régionalisme* (Paris, 1911).

14. Arthur de Gobineau and Louis de Kergolay, "De la politique rétrospective," *Revue provinciale*, II (June, 1849), 242–52.

with an administrative structure created by a revolution that had obliterated the old monarchy. Such tinkering would, the Legitimists imagined, allow them to instate the monarchy their ancestors had always wanted.

THE LEGITIMIST CRITIQUE OF
THE REVOLUTIONARY STATE

Although the Legitimists were careful to assert the historical rationale behind their pursuit of decentralization, they followed Kergolay in not taking the past to offer a complete model for the reform that French administration needed. Under the impact of day-to-day experience, the inspiration of the reform movement favored an innovative assault on prevailing administrative practices. The revisionist nature of Legitimist traditionalism is evident in the Legitimist critique of centralization and in the solutions it generated, which were rooted in the concerns of the day and envisioned nothing less than the remaking of French public life.

The Legitimists' conviction that the bureaucratic state was partly responsible for the debasement of French culture and society made the need for radical administrative reform all the more urgent in their eyes. Many of them saw centralization as a national malady that had left France a deformed misanthrope with an enormous head atop a weak and sickly body. The anatomical metaphor graphically put centralization at the heart of France's progressive moral decay. Raudot made a point of calling centralization "one of the greatest causes of the decadence of France"; in amplification, he blamed everything from an increasing crime rate to artistic and literary decline on its debilitating effects.[15] For Henri de La Broise, centralization was responsible not only for despotism and individualism but for a loss of national energy, the corruption of public morals, an obsession with luxury and indulgence, and the growth of anticlericalism.[16]

The succession of revolutions in the nineteenth century and France's defeat in a war against a federated Germany reinforced the sense of decadence. For the Legitimists, the Napoleonic refinements upon the revo-

15. Raudot, *De la décadence de la France,* 28–32.
16. La Broise, *République ou Monarchie,* 95–97.

lutionary state, which had been intended to make future revolutions impossible, had instead seriously weakened France's resistance to upheaval by debasing the country's elite, turning it into a corps of procedure-obsessed bureaucrats and frustrated job seekers. Centralization disrupted villages and families as the best men had to abandon home to find government employment. This inevitably created a class of uprooted misfits and malcontents among those whose ambitions went unfulfilled. Encouraged to seize control of the state by virtue of the geographical concentration of the state's power, vagabond notables turned into revolutionaries in order to rectify the wrong done them by a regime that did not recognize their talent. For Raudot, the mendicancy of the rich and the concentration of power in Paris were enough to explain the coup d'etat of 1851. Amédée de Gouvello went even farther by attributing the fall of every regime after 1789 to the centralist system the political parties were all exploiting for their own purposes.[17] On his view, a system that was designed to end revolution had actually become its principal cause.

Since Paris was synonymous with state power, urbanization, and revolution, it naturally became the focus of Legitimist discontent. The Legitimists, often with justification, voiced a distinct hostility toward the great metropolis. The smaller communes in which they customarily resided suffered a chronic shortage of the resources to keep up local buildings, repair monuments, and initiate public works, and the departmental *chefs-lieux* like Toulouse and Nantes, once true cultural and political centers, increasingly became no more than regional economic and administrative centers with little political clout. The state distributed national resources unequally, favoring large cities and wealthier departments, especially the Seine. Paris and other urban centers received more than half the total funds for public assistance. Raudot calculated that in 1847, out of a budget of 297,000 francs for the *bureaux de bienfaisance,* poor departments, like the Cantal and Lozère, received a pittance while the more prosperous Eure got 13,300 francs. In 1849, Paris acquired 1,960,000 francs out of a *fonds commun* of 13.5 million, while the Gers obtained only 35,000.[18] In the Charente, Edgard de Champvallier, a Legitimist general

17. *Annales,* June 28, 1871, III, 668–69; Amédée de Gouvello, *Vues sur la réorganisation de la France* (Vannes, 1871), 3.
18. Raudot, *De la décadence de la France,* 38–39. The *fonds commun* was revenue distributed to the departments by the central government from taxes. It was to be used according to local discretion.

counselor, fought a long battle with the central government during the 1860s for permission to levy municipal taxes and tolls that would enable the departments to construct and maintain secondary roads. Most funds collected for this purpose were remitted to the state and distributed for projects like national road construction, which did not directly benefit the Charente. Local construction faltered, Champvallier observed, and poor communes received next to nothing for secondary roads, while departments along imperial routes were lavished with funds collected from tolls in all departments.[19] The Legitimists, therefore, argued that the only thing that would ensure a fair distribution of resources was a halt to, and a reversal of, the accumulation of economic and political power in the capital. For that, a comprehensive effort to alter the structural trends favoring Parisian expansion would be needed. As Raudot put it, "Each new social need, each improvement, becomes the occasion for creating new services and new functionaries and for putting still more millions of francs at the disposal of the central power."[20]

It was recognized that to cut off the flow of people, money, and power to Paris would entail a thorough revision of economic practices that had their origins under the Old Regime. The structure of the transport system that was developed in the eighteenth and nineteenth centuries and the unification of the national market tended to exacerbate the imbalance between town and country, concentrating wealth and commerce in Paris and a handful of other large cities while smaller, more regionally oriented market towns stagnated or declined. All tax revenues were placed in the state treasury, the state tobacco monopoly fed copious funds to the government, and the increase in the number of state-run manufacturers swelled the bureaucracy, increased taxes, and created formidable competition for private industry. Banking became more and more centralized in Paris and credit institutions such as the Crédit Foncier, designed ini-

19. Edgard de Champvallier, *De quelques questions de vicinalité: De l'assimilation des chemins de grande communication de la Charente aux routes départementales* (Niort, 1868).

20. Claude Marie Raudot, "La Décentralisation en 1870," *Le Correspondant,* LXXXII (1870), 193–94. The number of employees of the central state grew from 477,000 in 1851 to 628,000 in 1866, and to just under 700,000 by the end of the Second Empire. The totals do not include the members of the clergy who collected a salary. Apart from the career army personnel (approximately 360,000), the civil service had more than doubled between 1851 and 1870, from 122,000 to 265,000 employees. Much of the increase was in the police force and resulted from the growth of the larger cities—a development not confined to the Second Empire. See Plessis, *De la fête impériale,* 59.

tially to help farmers, used their capital to finance urban public-works projects. In Raudot's opinion, the cumulative effect of the state policies was to make Paris a voracious threat to the economy: "Commerce tends to become centralized in Paris, just as finance and politics; big business is concentrated there; the Bourse, that temple of money, receives so many fanatic worshipers that the service charges of sixty brokers, the priests of the place, are worth more than sixty million."[21] He argued that such a concentration of money and workers inevitably denuded the countryside and choked off the effort to improve agriculture, forcing people to turn to urban elites and government officials rather than rural *propriétaires* for guidance and leadership. Meanwhile the population of Paris had swelled by nearly a million in the first half of the nineteenth century—largely poor, rootless migrants who filled the ranks of the revolutionary multitudes.[22]

The Legitimists found Parisian arrogance cultural and literary as well as economic, since the city had made itself the arbiter of fame and a conduit for provincial talent. They complained that all the nation's greatest museums, libraries, universities, and artistic and literary academies were located in the capital and expressed admiration for Germany, where local centers such as Weimar and Munich remained important focal points of cultural achievement. Vicomte de Meaux told the National Assembly that in the United States the cultural leadership of New York City detracted nothing from the esteem of Washington, D.C., the center of government.[23] Véran called for a "literary and artistic decentralization" to restore the dignity of the provinces and the quality of letters. A provincial "renaissance" might be achieved, he said, by the establishment of "free academies" in which "liberty, authority, and religion would be defended by writers chosen by the electors of the communes, cantons, and provinces instead of being chosen because of their invisible ties to . . .

21. Raudot, "La Décentralisation en 1870," *Le Correspondant,* LXXXII (1870), 193–94.
22. For Raudot, Parisian centralization in the final analysis presaged the triumph of socialism, because it created the conditions for socialist institutions by overstepping the traditional boundaries of the state's role. The French state, instead of limiting itself to defense, diplomacy, and the maintenance of public order, willingly embarked upon educating youth, directing the economy, and ultimately transforming the character and destiny of the nation. Paraphrasing François Babeuf, Raudot remarked that the French state meant "to play the role of providence." The result of "this wonderful system" was to make the state the "harbinger of communism" ("La Décentralisation en 1870," 194).
23. *Annales,* September 7, 1871, V, 446–47.

the influence of a coterie and a party systematically hostile to truth, order, and progress."[24]

Various plans that the Legitimists proposed for territorial reorganization sought to eliminate the political, geographical, and economic causes of regional disequilibrium. Béchard maintained that the division of France into departments was economically harmful because it destroyed regional harmony and encouraged an unequal distribution of material and human resources. Unable to function as self-supporting economic systems, the departments were at the mercy of the central government, whose practice of administrative and legislative uniformity tended, in his judgment, to worsen existing inequalitites.

Béchard's territorial solutions were motivated by what he saw as empirical economic realities, and not by a sentimental attachment to the lost provinces of the Old Regime. The economy, he observed, was not nationally uniform and open, but compartmentalized. Trade and production usually occurred on the scale of regional markets, and prices for the transport of goods varied from region to region.[25] When interregional trade occurred, it was usually at the expense of less productive areas or those far removed from heavily traveled routes. Béchard felt that administrative divisions established for political rather than economic purposes led to regional economic conflicts and bitterness between the departments and that these would end if all regions were on an equal economic footing. He proposed the creation of provincial divisions that traced out coherent, complementary economic zones that, given the support of national legislation fairly regulating interregional trade, would flourish on their own. The historic provinces, with their different sizes, populations, and resources, were at odds with economic equity. What were needed were new provinces, each of which would be an *ensemble complet,* with the internal strength to resist outside dependence and domination.[26]

In 1850, Béchard suggested a plan for consolidating the departments into twenty-one economically compatible *circonscriptions divisionaires*

24. Véran, *La Question du XIXe siècle,* 127–28.

25. See Price, *The Modernization of Rural France,* especially Chapter 8. The society to which Béchard fitted his project was the one of fractured spaces and precapitalist economic conditions described by Eugen Weber: "Most of the circulation was limited in scope. Goods and products were exchanged whenever possible between neighboring complementary regions, say, cattle and chestnuts traded for wine and grain; and the greater part of the tonnage moved only over small distances" (*Peasants into Frenchmen,* 198).

26. Ferdinand Béchard, *Autonomie et Césarisme: Introduction au droit municipal modern* (Paris, 1869), 178.

(Map XX) that were to subdivide France's five great geographical river basins.[27] Each of the *circonscriptions* was to contain roughly 1.5 to 2 million inhabitants, and they were to be roughly equal in size, each a *contrée entière*. For example, the three departments of the Vosges, Haut-Rhin, and Bas-Rhin, close to the German frontier, were to constitute a territorial and economic whole shaped by its unique commercial relationship with foreign countries. The new divisions, Béchard said, would also correct economic disparities inside France. The relatively wealthy departments of Allier and Nièvre would be united to the poorer departments of the Rhône Valley. The depressed departments of the Landes and Corrèze would share in the prosperity of the Gironde and the Dordogne. In the attachment of the Orne to Normandy, an area "badly cultivated would find in its reunion with Calvados, one of the richest and best cultivated departments of France, advantages that would profit both." By including the Eure, Seine-Inférieure, the Somme, and the Oise in one division, Béchard hoped to create a new economic triangle consisting of Rouen, Amiens, and Beauvais, with regional markets, local resources, and less dependence on public and private consumers in Paris. Economic centers like Lyon were to gain a new, larger economic hinterland that could sustain its vitality and independence from Paris, and the southern viticultural region of Lower Languedoc was to have the territorial coherence and political freedom to turn Montpellier and Nîmes (Béchard's home) into significant commercial focal points for the southern wine and grain trades. Unique regional personalities were to be maintained and encouraged in such divisions as Brittany and the Upper Rhône (Jura, Haute-Saône, Côte d'Or, Saône-et-Loire), with the Upper Rhône preserving its special relationship to the Swiss and subalpine regions.

To maintain equilibrium, uniformity in economic policy was to be replaced with zones of shifting commodity-price scales that would ensure an adequate and fair return to producers whose markets reached across regional boundaries.[28] In that way, Béchard hoped to end the local economic and demographic evacuations encouraged by centralization and free trade. He felt that the proposed *circonscriptions,* with the political autonomy necessary to decide their own economic destinies, would promote general economic progress over regional imbalance.

Jean Brunet's plan focused less on economic disequilibrium and more

27. Béchard, *De l'administration,* II, 312–35. The five basins are of the Rhône, the Seine, the Loire, the Rhine, and the Garonne.
28. Béchard, *Autonomie et Césarisme,* 70.

Map XX   Béchard's Consolidation

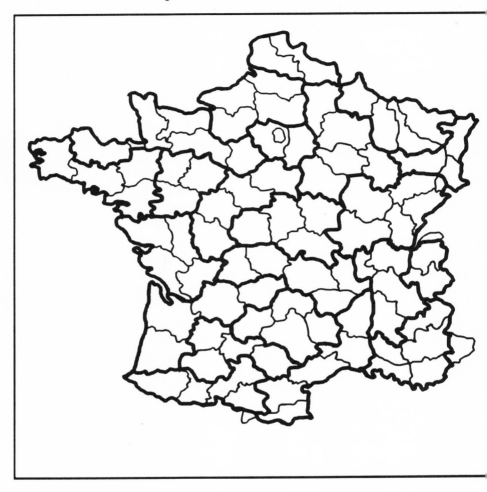

Based on proposals in *De l'administration intérieure de la France,* by Ferdinand Béchard (2 vols.; Paris, 1851), 312–15.

on the demographic inequality between departments.[29] As long as administrative divisions were unequal in population, Brunet argued, it would be "impossible to establish the least bit of similarity of rights and power" between them. He held that the "territorial undertaking of 1789" was only an "incomplete outline" that needed to be corrected as time reshaped the distribution of the French population. In this sense, his project was designed in the same spirit as that of 1789: far from concerning itself with tradition, it sought to revise and rationalize existing territorial divisions. For Brunet, the departments amounted to a hastily constructed and "mutilated France" that was incapable of resisting the violent political earthquakes originating in Paris. The old provinces had been strong and had endured because they were "complete organs" with roughly equal populations, Brunet observed. Accordingly, only "vigorous organic centers" acting as the "necessary intermediaries between individuals and the central authority" could ensure stability in the future, he reasoned. His proposal was to replace the communes, cantons, and departments with a hierarchy of territorial units of equal population and size at each level. The new communes would have an average population of 6,250. Smaller ones would be annexed, and larger ones broken up. The communes would be combined into four hundred cantons of 80,000 inhabitants each, which would be grouped into forty "tribes" of 900,000 each, named after their *chefs-lieux:* Rennes, Brest, Arras, for instance. Each tribe—obviously a biblical reference—would be part of one of twelve regions of between 2.5 and 3.5 million inhabitants (Map XXI), and the tribes themselves would become "real centers of power and strength, managing themselves with their own general councils and resources of all sorts."[30]

The Legitimists' preference for radical revisions in France's territorial, economic, and political organization was accompanied, especially after the Paris Commune of 1871, by a desire to move the capital from Paris to a more geographically central, politically safe, and culturally representative city. Before 1871, this aspiration had been given only sporadic ex-

29. Jean Brunet, an army officer born in Limoges and residing in Paris, a graduate of the Ecole Polytechnique and a republican deputy in 1848, underwent a conversion to Catholicism and royalism in 1871 and sat in the National Assembly with the extreme Right.

30. No one in the National Assembly of 1871 seemed to support Brunet, although his project worked its way through committee. The details of his proposal vary; I have used those presented in *Annales*, February 2, 1872, VII, annexe 871, pp. 141–42.

Map XXI   Brunet's Groupings

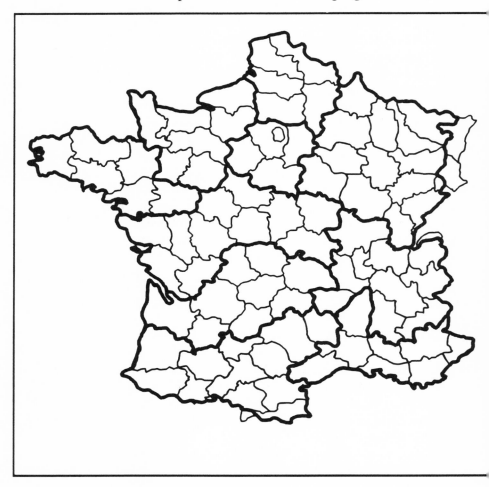

Based on data from France, Assemblée Nationale, *Annales parlementaires*, XIII, 66.

pression, but the need to move the government to Bordeaux, and then Versailles, during the *année terrible* sparked an outpouring of appeals from the Legitimist Right to relocate the capital permanently. The moment was ripe for a debate on the topic, since the monarchists knew that a return to Paris after the armistice of January, 1871, would threaten their control of the National Assembly. For Legitimists, the Commune merely confirmed what earlier revolutions had taught. As Emmanuel Lucien-Brun put it, the center of government had to distance itself from the "influence of the streets" so that a riot in Paris did not place a revolutionary burden on the entire nation.[31]

The campaign to reduce Paris to just another city is further evidence that the counterrevolutionary goals of the Legitimists favored solutions without precedents. Despite Paris' long history as the political center of France, the nineteenth-century royalists had concluded that stability was impossible as long as a nation's principal institutions were located in a large urban area. Paris would always remain the "depot where the centuries have accumulated the treasures of the work and genius of a people," but life there was incompatible with the normal process of government because of "its ebb and flow, its convulsions, and its periodic fever and constant agitation." For Vicomte de Meaux, it was precisely because Paris was the "liveliest part of the country" that it could never express or represent the real nature and desires of the nation as a whole.[32] Whereas Paris was the "seat of organized revolt," the provinces were usually calm and therefore had to be protected from the impertinent impulses of the capital.[33] Since the true France was in the provinces, its government had to be located there, in a place that expressed both the unity of the nation and the character of its people. The Legitimists searched for a town in the geographical and temperamental center of France, like Blois, Orléans, or Bourges. La Broise argued that it was unimportant that these towns were rather small since, "after decentralization, the governmental mechanism being extremely simplified and most business being retained in the departments or in the provinces, the

---

31. *Annales,* September 8, 1871, V, 466.

32. *Annales,* September 7, 1871, V, 446. See also the introductory letter to subscribers from A. Fournier in *Revue de Berry,* I (1864), 3.

33. *Annales,* September 7, 1871, V, 335. See also *Annales,* September 7, 1871, V, 446; Gaillard, *Les Etapes,* 320; and Arthur de Gobineau and Louis de Kergolay, "Introduction," *Revue provinciale,* I (September, 1848), 6–7.

personnel and the material of the ministries will be diminished considerably." With a decentralized administration, the new capital would be not a giant city but merely a sleepy administrative center on a par with the provincial capitals. Paris would be contained and would cease to "take from the provinces all the eminence they hold and denude the country for its own profit."[34] La Broise's fantasy was, therefore, consistent with those of Béchard and Brunet, since each believed that decentralization would create an alternative socioeconomic order in which the differences between town and country would be reduced, demographic and social change moderated, and France spared the horror of seeing Paris as prefiguring its future.

Nevertheless, the Legitimists found very little support for these ideas. In 1871, the National Assembly followed Thiers to Versailles, from which the repression of the Commune could be directed by an entity endowed by the centralized administration with enormous powers of coordination. In 1879, though, once the republicans gained a firmer grip on the Republic, the government returned to Paris. In the meantime the Legitimists sought to create an administrative structure for the capital that would eliminate or tame its revolutionary potential. If France could not be decentralized, at least the forces that made Paris a danger could be blunted by federalizing the city or breaking it up into smaller communes.

Brunet proposed a strategy. He suggested that the department of the Seine should be abolished and the population of Paris portioned out into "several administrative centers" so that a "certain number of distinct departments" could be fused with "purely . . . rural elements." In that way, he explained, Paris would be absorbed into the Ile-de-France: a "compact block consisting only of city dwellers" would be replaced by the "precious system of social . . . unity that prevails in the other French departments."[35] Raudot, who like Meaux believed that politics were incompatible with the performance of administrative tasks, proposed on the other hand that Paris could be kept under control by dividing it into distinct harmonious communities where there were no conflicts of interest and

---

34. La Broise, *République ou Monarchie,* 103–106. "If the ministers, senators, and deputies of the latest empire had had to reside in Bourges or even in Tours, instead of at Paris," wrote Gouvello, "their positions would have been less coveted by superfluous men and by rakes. The affairs of the country would have been no worse off for all that" (*Vues sur la réorganisation de la France,* 33).

35. *Annales,* November 7, 1873, XXXVII, 37.

where elites could manage local affairs for the good of the inhabitants. Instead of continuing as one large, unified city, Paris could be divided into twenty arrondissements, each with its own budget and "patrimony." The collective receipts of the city would be distributed to the arrondissements according to their population and the size of their initial contribution after sums necessary for paying the city's common debt had been deducted. Services of common interest, like sewage, the police, and street maintenance, would be periodically regulated by a commission composed of leaders chosen from each district.[36] Paris would cease to be a single municipality, conquered and prostrate before the bureaucracy, and would begin to take on some of the characteristics of a peaceful rural commune. Once order reigned in Paris, conservative France could breathe more easily.[37]

What unites these schemes is an element of radicalism and experimentation, albeit for conservative ends, that is at odds with the traditionalism with which Legitimism has been identified. This aspect of the Legitimists' envisioned decentralization was not overlooked by men who were themselves quite conservative. Anselme Batbie and Richard Waddington, who headed the National Assembly's Commission of Decentralization, called Raudot's ideas concerning the city government of Paris an unworkable "innovation" that would undo "by a stroke of the pen" what was "constituted by the work of sixty years."[38] Although liberals were just as likely to favor decentralization as Legitimists, they believed that the existing system required only adjustments, not a complete overhaul. But the Legitimists wanted not a fine-tuning of the state but the emancipation of the agents of social conservation, for which they considered the surgical removal of the revolutionary state from the body of French society necessary. During a period of serious discussion of decentralization in 1851, Raudot had said that France had enough tinkers and masons, carpenters and laborers; what it needed were architects to plan a general reconstruction of the social edifice.[39] In 1873, when it became clear that the type of reconstruction he was calling for was out of reach,

36. *Annales,* March 31, 1871, II, annexe 99, pp. 200–205.
37. Raudot looked to the example of the London parishes, which were ruled by aldermen in the absence of any strong centralized administration. See *Annales,* 1871, II, 337.
38. Rapport fait au nom de la commission chargée d'examiner le projet de loi rélatif aux élections municipales en France, par M. Batbie, in *Annales,* March 31, 1871, II, annexe 99, p. 205.
39. Raudot, *De la décadence de la France,* 36–37.

he lectured the National Assembly for making only meaningless refinements and thereby missing another chance to establish a solid "general base." Centralization, he declared, had to be confronted "in all its details," in how it "entangled all men and [took] away their independence."[40] Meaux made the far-reaching objectives of Legitimist decentralization even more obvious when he announced that "everything can . . . be a matter of decentralization" and that he was interested in a decentralist plan that would account for "all the intermediary circles between the citizen and the state, . . . traversing all these administrative circles and causing liberty to penetrate life without jeopardizing political unity."[41]

The decentralist initiatives of the early 1870s came after many years of debate during the Second Republic and again during the 1860s, at the time of the liberalization of the Second Empire. Legitimists joined Orleanists and moderate republicans in an effort to loosen the grip of the Bonapartist administration and to carve out a larger governing role for local elites. The attempts to design and implement a new administrative order revealed the profound ideological gap separating the Legitimists from their conservative allies on the nature and role of the state.

40. *Annales,* July 2, 1873, XIX, 3; *Annales,* June 28, 1871, III, 668.
41. Rapport fait au nom de la Commission de Décentralisation, par M. le vicomte de Meaux, in *Annales,* April 13, 1871, I, annexe 131, p. 478.

CHAPTER IV

Reconstructing Local Power

TOCQUEVILLE GREW more pessimistic about the possibility of institutional change in France toward the end of his life. Convinced that Old Regime despotism had long before sapped the public spirit of the aristocracy, he was not at all inclined to think that the relentless centralization of the nineteenth century had prepared the Legitimists, or any other group of notables, to make good use of institutional reform. The British experience with local government indicated to him that it was a "passion to be one's own master," not procedural details, that sustained institutional practice; the French, he decided, had a thirst not for political liberty but only for personal freedom. Having very little faith in institutions, he thought it foolish to search for the "precious piece of paper that would contain the recipe" allowing the French to govern themselves.[1]

The Legitimists had much more confidence in pieces of paper. When Napoleon III began to search for a larger base of support by liberalizing his regime in the 1860s, the Legitimists joined a coalition of liberal notables to push for greater local autonomy. When it became clear by the end of the Empire that the liberal decentralist blueprint would leave the foundations of the existing administration intact, Raudot and other Legitimists became convinced that the notables had complacently agreed to govern badly and separated themselves from the apparent liberal consen-

1. Alexis de Tocqueville to Louis de Kergolay, February 27, 1858, in Tocqueville, *Correspondances,* Part 2, p. 333; Alexis de Tocqueville to Claude François de Corcelle, September 17, 1858, in *Alexis de Tocqueville: Selected Letters on Politics and Society,* trans. James Toupin and Roger Boesche, ed. Roger Boesche (Berkeley and Los Angeles, 1985), 294.

sus on the administrative legacy of the Revolution. The more resilient
old administrative habits proved to be, the more emphatically Legitimists began to link decentralization with radical modifications of existing
institutions.

THE DISMAL TRIUMPH OF LIBERAL DECENTRALIZATION

Neither the Ultras of the Restoration nor the Legitimists ever
thoroughly rejected the four major administrative divisions bequeathed
by the Revolution. The municipal councils, and especially the departmental councils, became the central organizational components of each
of their decentralist plans. For all the talk by Legitimists of provincial
estates, they never demanded that the estates be restored and tended to
see them only as affording models for local self-government. It was impracticable and politically unwise for those accused of jeopardizing the
political and territorial integrity of the nation to call for the return of
provincial assemblies that historically were tied to lands originally separate from the French crown and that had preserved features of their early
independence until their demise. Moreover, the Legitimists understood
that the old estates were linked to a complex system of administrative
divisions and privileges, and ultimately to the society of orders. It had
been the resurrection of the power of traditional elites under Napoleon
and the Restoration—in a way, however, that did not lead to the rebirth
of older institutions—that made it unnecessary to insist on the revival of
the provincial estates. The departmental general councils, as they evolved
into the principal base of power for royalists, became the Legitimists' best
means of resistance against the central bureaucracy and the revolutionary
capital.[2]

The laws of June 21–22, 1833, which stipulated that both the *conseillers
d'arrondissement* and the general counselors would be elected by voters
paying the *cens,* confirmed and deepened the notables' hold over local
bodies. Even though Orleanist, and later Bonapartist, prefects used
whatever expedients they could to reduce the chance that Legitimists

2. See Denis, *Les Royalistes de la Mayenne,* 117–18. Denis quotes an Ultra deputy from
the Mayenne, Le Clerc de Beaulieu, who in 1823 maintained that "the division by departments, mentioned in the Charter, already has the merit of an institution grown old by time
and rooted in the spirit of the people" (p. 117).

would obtain places in the local councils, the presence of Legitimists there grew steadily after 1833, especially after 1848. In 1840, out of 2,399 counselors, there were 257 Legitimists or Legitimist *ralliés* and a total of 691 opponents of the regime. By 1870, when the number of general counselors had reached 2,688, Legitimist and clerical candidates claimed 415 seats, or 14.8 percent of the total, and numbered more than half the 957 counselors who were either cool or hostile toward the Empire. Under the Second Empire, the Legitimists maintained a presence in the general councils unmatched by any other organized party.[3] As early as 1848, the Legitimist press in Nantes referred to the men who composed the general councils as the "responsible elite of the nation."[4]

Under the Second Republic, several decentralist initiatives were debated in the legislature, and as in 1871, standing committees were set up to redesign the administrative order. Legitimists like Larcy and Raudot, as well as liberals like Odilon Barrot and Michel Chevalier, played a prominent role in the discussions. Although the coup of 1851 suspended the deliberations, they confirmed the common political interests of the monarchist notables and helped forge a coalition of Orleanists and moderate Legitimists that survived the authoritarian Empire of the 1850s to reemerge as part of the liberal opposition in the 1860s.

The call for decentralization, along with the demand for civil liberties, became the centerpiece of the Liberal Union's program, in which the *grands notables* attempted to chip away at aspects of the imperial system that denied them political liberty and an access to real power within the administration. In 1865, a group of local officials in the east that was associated with the Orleanist Alexandre de Metz-Noblat, drew up a cautious program for decentralization—the Nancy Program—which was signed by nineteen local notables representing a cross section of the local liberal elite. Only three of them held positions in the regular administration, either as subprefects or *maires*. The final draft was published along with fifty-eight letters of support from influential and nationally known members of the opposition, including republicans (Sadi Carnot, Jules Favre, Jules Ferry, Jules Simon, Eugène Pelletan, Louis Antoine Garnier-Pàge), Orleanists (Victor de Broglie, François Guizot, Odilon Barrot, Ernest Duvergier de Hauranne), and Legitimists (Ferdinand Béchard,

---

3. Girard *et al.*, *Les Conseillers généraux en 1870*, 7; Tudesq, *Les Conseillers généraux en France au temps de Guizot*, 221–27; Tudesq, *Les Grands Notables en France*, II, 1123.
4. "Bulletin départementale," *Revue provinciale*, I (October, 1848), 79.

Antoine Berryer, Alfred de Falloux, Léopold de Gaillard, Roger de Larcy, Armand de Melun, and Claude Marie Raudot).

The Nancy Program gained attention because it gave the opposition a way to take a stand in anticipation of the upcoming debate on administrative reform. In 1858, during a speech at Limoges, the emperor had stirred the hopes of decentralists by suggesting that it was harmful for the activity of the government to become a substitute for the "acts of social life" since it weakened "all personal initiative, under the tutelage of an exaggerated centralization."[5] In 1863, with the first steps toward liberalization and the revival of a broad-based liberal opposition, Eugène Rouher, the president of the Conseil d'Etat, denounced excessive regulation and announced his intention to transfer to the prefects a portion of the powers previously held by the ministries. Lest people mistake the so-called deconcentration of power for real decentralization, the opposition sought to make clear that they wanted a greater autonomy for elected local councils, not stronger prefects. Critics charged that the Empire's decree would only increase the grip of the administration over the departments and would do nothing to alter the authoritarian nature of centralization.[6] The Nancy Program elaborated a liberal definition of decentralization as distinct from deconcentration and gained symbolic significance as an act of true civic initiative rather than an acceptance of gifts from on high. Moreover, the adherents to the program were especially well known in the arenas of elite power out of the reach of the central government—the academies, the local councils, the press. Thus the decentralists were able to attract the attention of all the important newspapers and reviews and to "arouse a current of opinion too general and forceful for the government to ignore."[7]

The Nancy Program defined a decentralist minimum involving the election of *maires* and presidents of the general councils and leaving aside the mode of suffrage. It demanded that the local assemblies be allowed to publish their deliberations, that cantonal councils be given real power

5. Quoted by B. Basdevant-Gaudemet in *La Commission de Décentralisation de 1870: Contribution à l'étude de la décentralisation en France au XIXe siècle* (Paris, 1973), 24.

6. For Ferdinand Béchard, the reforms of March 25, 1861, "called decentralization," represented merely "resistance to local influences and an increase in the personal power of the prefects" (*Du projet de décentralisation administrative annoncé par l'empereur* [Paris, 1864], 139).

7. Odette Voilliard, "Autour du programme de Nancy, 1865," in *Régions et Régionalisme en France du XVIIIe siècle à nos jours: Actes publiés par Christian Gras and Georges Livert* (Paris, 1977), 292–93; *Nancy: Un Projet de décentralisation* (Nancy, 1865), 5.

to supervise communal affairs, and that executive departmental councils be created to advise the prefects and to take over some of their administrative functions. Although these goals were mild enough to be nonpartisan, insofar as they represented a consensus among traditional elites, the regime immediately suspected that the *grands notables* were trying to recapture the social predominance Napoleon III had denied them. Newspapers loyal to the regime denounced the Nancy Program as a monarchist effort to reestablish the influence of the aristocrats, who wanted to turn France over to a clique of local oligarchs ensconced in the general councils. *Le Siècle* treated the program as a plot by nobles to return control over political life "to the sacristy, the château, and the factory," while the republican *L'Opinion nationale* accused the Legitimist party of hatching a project developed by the Catholic party, which found its principal spokesmen among prominent Orleanists.[8]

The polemics were simplistic, but they pointed to the fact that the Nancy Program expressed a common desire on the part of the regime's most powerful political opponents for revenge against the Napoleonic police state and for the restoration of the hegemony of the former local oligarchies. Yet the propagandists of the regime were wrong to suggest that Legitimists, Catholics, and Orleanists were in lockstep on the issues. The Nancy Program neither demanded fundamental modifications in the structure of the administration nor challenged the basic liberal assumption that political individualism and the rule of law were enough to repair the damage centralization had inflicted on the French political community. A fair number of liberals and republicans saw the laws of July 18, 1866, and July 24, 1867, which enlarged the administrative role of the municipal and general councils, as an important step toward their goal of "parliamentizing" local government. The centrists who continued to speak in favor of decentralization would hardly go beyond the framework laid down by the Nancy Program in 1865.

To the Legitimists, however, it was the administrative structure itself, which gave the central government the final say on local matters and which did not distinguish between the nation's governing bureaucracy and the organs of local government, that had to be demolished, since it was revolutionary centralization and not just Bonapartist authoritarianism that destabilized French society and threatened the social order. To

8. Jacques Droz, "Le Problème de la décentralisation sous le Second Empire," in *Festgabe für Max Braubach* (Münster, 1964), 787–88.

get at the root of the problem, they argued, localities had to be free to decide on their own needs and power had to emanate from organic and autonomous local communities where the absence of bureaucratic intrusion encouraged the moral cohesion of a naturally hierarchical social order. Local power, according to this view, should not initiate goals that had to be sent on to be sanctioned by the state but should be the final voice of civil society. As Stéphane Rials has pointed out, the Legitimist concept of decentralization assumed from the start that society was familial and hierarchical;[9] thus Béchard could affirm that the commune, as the "link that ties the family to the state," was the first component in a larger "political family" that knew itself better than the functionaries who were assigned to arbitrate the fate of the entire nation did. As far as Béchard was concerned, local autonomy was a matter not of introducing "some improvements into the administrative mechanism" but of "regenerating society from the base" by allowing the natural relations created by the *esprit de famille,* the *esprit de corps,* and the *esprit de cité* "to penetrate viscerally into the nation." Only in that way could decentralization make each commune a "fortress against central despotism."[10] If the purest forms of human solidarity were possible only at the level of the family and the commune, then the nation-state should not place obstacles in the path of the expression of the family's and the commune's natural political instincts. Béchard was persuaded that the sort of elected intermediary bodies the liberal decentralizers wanted would do just that.

What the Legitimists contemplated was a form of decentralization that would enforce political conservatism and moral conformity by freeing a class society to form and maintain its own basic social restraints. They wished to encourage the internalization of the prevailing cultural norms in the thousands of places in which individuals lived before they made contact with the wider world. Daniel Halévy reminds us that the Legitimists never spoke of liberty in the abstract but were intent on "scattered and specific liberties—the type which . . . would be influenced by local and traditional forces."[11] Béchard wanted the commune to be the "pri-

9. Rials, *Le Légitimisme,* 56–57.
10. Béchard, *De l'administration,* I, 46, II, 120–21.
11. Halévy, *The End of the Notables,* 38. See also Albert du Boys, *Des principes de la Révolution française considérés comme principes générateurs du socialisme et du communisme* (Lyon, 1851), 5–6. Du Boys characterized the liberties demanded and obtained by the medieval communes and provinces as "determined and precise." By contrast, he represented "liberty" as a "vague abstraction that never seems to be able to take on a genuine firmness; it is a phantom that flees more and more as one tries to approach it and seize it."

mary school where inhabitants of a free country ought to develop the apprenticeship of social life, where each citizen . . . accomplishes his domestic, professional, religious, and municipal duties." He went on to explain, "It is necessary to reattach men to the places that present their habits and their memories to them"[12]

In 1865, the Legitimists were too weak and too politically isolated to pursue their own ends when the liberal opposition was mobilizing to force the Empire to recognize the "necessary liberties" of free speech and assembly. Once the Ollivier ministry, by organizing an extraparliamentary commission, gave increased credibility to the regime's willingness to sponsor decentralization, the incompatibility of liberal and Legitimist interests began to emerge more clearly.[13]

Liberals, from Madame de Staël to Lucien Anatole Prévost-Paradal, François Guizot, and Louis Adolphe Thiers, who shared Tocqueville's skepticism about the capacity of a radical institutional reconstruction to cure France's ills, felt justified in seeking to preserve the existing admin-

12. Béchard, *De l'administration,* I, 46–47; Béchard, *Du projet de décentralisation administrative,* 32. The Legitimists rejected the notion that suffrage could express the autonomous moral judgment of the individual. They argued that the sort of education the republicans hoped would emancipate the peasantry was more likely to deform the collective expression of political preferences through the intrusion of uncustomary, mostly urban influences. To the Legitimists, it seemed the absence of such outside interference that preserved freedom and morality. Local communities, with their unique conditions, were as important for the cultivation of *la morale* as was formal education. Communities, families, and churches were also schools, and though formal education had its place, neither laicity nor independent moral judgment was compatible with the genuine expression of a community's political values. Consequently, Béchard opposed the "arbitrary" division of cities such as Lyon, Nancy, Lille, Grenoble, and Tours (but not Paris) into separate electoral districts for the purpose of political representation arguing that such divisions would negate their "communal individuality" (*Du projet de décentralisation administrative,* 42–44; see also Béchard, *De l'état du paupérisme*).

Using the same rationale in 1871, Lucien-Brun argued that since each district of Lyon—the *rive droite,* the old city, and Croix-Rousse—formed distinct areas marked by different habits, traditions, and populations, the city should be divided into three different communes. Of course, the Legitimists feared the existence of single municipal councils in large cities in the wake of the Paris Commune. Yet what seems most noteworthy is the assumption that each district would be politically safe because it was historically distinct. See *Annales,* 1871, II, 409–12.

13. In order to counter the initiative taken at Nancy, the more radical Legitimists held their own reunion in Lyon in 1869 on the initiative of Charles Garnier, editor and owner of the Legitimist journal *La Décentralisation.* This Congrès de la Presse Provinciale Indépendante, not unlike the gathering held in Paris in 1847 by the royalist journalists close to Genoude and Lourdoueix, of the *Gazette de France,* stressed the need for autonomous local councils freed from bureaucratic control. See Basdevant-Gaudemet, *La Commission de Décentralisation,* 29.

istrative order. The Orleanist aristocracy was ambivalent about the work of the first Constituent Assembly and of Napoleon but in the main focused its critique not on the state apparatus but on the way the procedures centralization created encouraged the despotism of the Napoleonic regimes and were inimical to the political habits that prosper with individual initiative and a spirit of public service. Such concerns had been addressed by the Nancy Program and were reflected in the procedural adjustments approved by the Orleanist-dominated Commission on Decentralization set up by the government in 1870, which added a call for the nomination of *maires* and the election of local officials by universal suffrage.[14] At the same time, Raudot, a member of the commission, was appealing for the abolition of the prefectorial system, the restoration of the old provinces, and the erection of a federalized administration whose effective power would reside in the general councils. The liberals seemed content to gain effective control over some local administrative matters in order to obstruct or facilitate general policy on certain controversial issues such as education and public assistance; they wanted to leave intact the principal agencies of administrative uniformity—the Conseil d'Etat, the ministry of the interior, the councils of the prefecture, the *fonds commun,* and the state tax and financial organization—which they saw as inseparable from the revolutionary idea of national unity. Legitimist asseverations that only the provincial governments could provide a counterweight to Paris by enabling the provinces to mount "political resistance" were seen by the majority as a threat to national unity and met with either silent indifference or frank hostility.[15]

Support for the schemes of Raudot was nonexistent, therefore, among the established elites. During the deliberations of the Commission of 1870, he played the role of constant dissenter, frequently monopolizing the debate while other members politely waited to continue. Emile de Marcère recalled that during similar discussions in the National Assembly after 1871 the deputies listened to the sixty-year-old Raudot "with the deference men in good company accord to a passion for ideas, how-

14. Basdevant-Gaudemet, *La Commission de Décentralisation,* annexe 4, p. 142. The six Legitimists who sat on the commission were Benoist d'Azy, Charles Garnier, Amédée Lefèvre-Pontalis, Albert Maussarbe, Comte de Mortemart, and Claude Marie Raudot. The recommendations of the commission are summarized by Basdevant-Gaudemet in *La Commission de Décentralisation.*

15. For earlier examples of hostility toward the Legitimists' decentralist ideas, see Béchard, *De l'état du paupérisme,* 165; and Gobineau, "Etudes sur les municipalités," *Revue provinciale,* I (1848), 122.

ever chimerical, and to the ardor of sincere convictions."[16] In June, 1871, the Commission of Decentralization, organized by the National Assembly to continue the work of the Ollivier commission that had been cut short by the fall of the Empire, reported that "the idea of forming provinces containing several departments . . . does not respond to a single present need," especially since "public opinion" saw in such proposals "a return to the past, a threat to national unity, or a new administrative cogwheel and a new series of functionaries added to so many others."[17]

The liberals' hostility to extensive decentralization is instructive because it shows how Tocqueville's doubts about radical administrative reform conformed to the general apprehension of liberal elites. In contrast to what the Legitimists believed, the liberals were convinced that it was only the endurance of the centralized state that had saved French institutions and society from the successive waves of political upheaval after 1789. In *The Old Regime and the French Revolution,* Tocqueville asserted that the centralized administration had survived despite the "debacles of political systems" because fear and habit resisted modifications in the "course of day-to-day affairs."[18] Elsewhere, he adverted to the administration's ability to "keep running even when the central motor was shut off."[19] Marcère, a member of the center Left in the National Assembly, touched on the larger implications of this when he wrote, "It has been the internal organization of the country, conceived by the Caesarean brain of Napoleon, that has, in reality, served as the constitution of France." Centralization, for all the scope it allowed authoritarian abuse, was the concrete embodiment of the organized power of the notables and sustained the uniformity of culture and national purpose that was the most deliberate, explicit, and durable legacy of the French Revolution. As Marcère also observed, attempts at administrative decentralization encountered serious opposition from men like Thiers who

> by temperament and by habits contracted under the July Monarchy
> are opposed to any reformist spirit. In their resistance, they always
> find support in the republican party, which has remained Jacobin,

16. Marcère, *L'Assemblée Nationale,* II, 280.
17. Rapport fait au nom de la commission de décentralisation chargée d'examiner de lois rélatives à l'organisation et aux attributions des conseils généraux, in *Annales,* June 14, 1871, II, annexe 320, p. 398.
18. Tocqueville, *The Old Regime and the French Revolution,* 202.
19. Tocqueville, quoted in *The European Revolution and the Correspondence with Gobineau,* ed. Lukacs, 152–53.

and among a great number of partisans of a constitutional monarchy like that of the reign of Louis Philippe. For more than a century, no government in France has ever established itself and endured with the unanimous assent of the entire nation. In truth, the
legitimacy and power of every government has rested on foundations other than those of the capricious and ephemeral opinion of
factions now vanquished, now triumphant. Each of them has had
its only serious basis of support in the administrative hierarchy, the
only organized constitutive force since the Revolution.[20]

In August, 1871, Thiers even scolded the Orleanists on the Commission
of Decentralization for supporting the concept of elected advisers to the
prefects. "At my age," he said, "I will not lend my name to the disloca-
tion of the French administrative system. . . . I have always been a resolute supporter of French administration. There is not another in Europe
as good as ours. In each of our revolutions everything would have collapsed into disorder without it."[21]

Such views expressed what Tocqueville had implied: that men who
were concerned with liberty as an ideal were nevertheless obliged to retain the essentials of the centralized system because the Revolution, and
the monarchy before it, had destroyed the social and moral basis of free
self-government. The Legitimists, who in effect considered themselves
the only remaining link with an administrative structure and a symbol of
central authority that preserved the latency of aristocratic government,
could never accept that judgment. The importance of this disagreement
should not be underestimated, for it amounted to a fundamental ideological split at the top of France's social structure. The Legitimists, no
less than the liberals, were preoccupied with the possibility of creating a
durable institutional and social order in France. To do that, however, the
Legitimists demanded that the notables dismantle what most of them had
come to see as the only foundation of political and social stability. The
Legitimists' critique of modern France was perhaps best expressed in
their assertion that the centralized state, which for them was the most
conspicuous creation of the Revolution, was the source of France's pro-

20. Marcère, *L'Assemblée Nationale*, II, 182, 280–81, 34–35.
21. Thiers before the Commission on Decentralization, August 2, 1871, in Herbert F.
Brabant's *The Beginnings of the Third Republic: A History of the National Assembly, February
to September, 1871* (New York, 1940), Appendix, 515–22.

gressive decline. As early as 1861, Raudot, writing in *Le Correspondant,* had concluded that "liberals of every nuance" were the "greatest obstacle to the success of decentralization" because they "regard centralization as the work, the triumph, the holy arch of the Revolution."[22]

The decentralist law that passed the National Assembly on August 10, 1871, instituted a watered-down version of what liberals had called for in the Nancy Program and the Commission of 1870.[23] In 1884, the republicans realized their own version of decentralization when the Chamber of Deputies provided for the election of *maires* by the communes. When extensive decentralization was finally implemented by President François Mitterand in 1981, Pierre Mauroy, then first minister, said it had become possible to decentralize because "the men in the châteaus are gone now."[24]

THE RAUDOT PLAN: PROVINCES AND PROPER AUTHORITIES

Raudot's single-minded pursuit of decentralization was not deterred by the polite smiles of his colleagues. In 1871, the daunting decentralist proposal he submitted to the National Assembly outlining a comprehensive reconstruction of the French administrative order gave mature expression to many years of hope and reflection.[25] In this proposal, Raudot, as in his previous work, developed a hierarchical system of local councils that functioned within the framework of twenty-five

22. Claude Marie Raudot, "La Décentralisation: Seconde Partie," *Le Correspondant,* LIII (1861), 242–43.

23. The law called for the creation of departmental commissions and larger powers for the general councils. Yet, another law, passed in 1871, stated that the "executive power in the department" would continue to be "in charge of the first command of the affairs of the department, as well as the execution of the decisions of the general council and the departmental commission" (Basdevant-Gaudemet, *La Commission de Décentralisation,* 94–95).

24. Frank J. Prial, "France Loosens Centralized Rule," New York *Times,* July 17, 1981, Sec. I, Part 1, p. 1. According to Pierre Mauroy, an outspoken advocate of decentralization, the socialist reforms sought to create a "new citizenry" through the "reactivation of our collective life." But Mauroy held that possible only "thanks to [our] Jacobin past, thanks to this centralist tradition that has seen the Republic and democracy descend from Paris toward the provinces, that has seen the emancipation of the workers and socialism spread from the working-class faubourgs toward the countryside" (*C'est ici le chemin* [Paris, 1982], 121, 96–97).

25. Proposition de loi sur la décentralisation, présentée par M. Raudot, in *Annales,* April 29, 1871, I, annexe 183, pp. 949–55.

semiautonomous provinces linked to a central government that had virtually no control over local administrative matters. The system centered on the communes and the departments, which were to elect officers with broad powers over their respective domains, and knitted them together through the supervisory and appointment responsibilities of councils and committees at the levels of the canton, the arrondissement, and the province. Officials were to come from the locality in which they were to serve, and locally elected or appointed officials were to supervise the work of lower bodies. Thus, *maires* and adjuncts of each commune were to be named by the municipal council from among its own members, cantonal councils were to be composed of local *maires* and general counselors, and general counselors were to dominate the executive commissions of the newly revived provinces. All local administrators, including those who managed schools, hospices, hospitals, charitable establishments, and local associations, and those whose purview included market days, fairs, communal property, public works, public assistance, flood relief, reforestation, roads, highways, railroads, bridges, river navigation, and tolls, would be appointed by one or more of the elected local councils that had complete or partial control over extraordinary taxation, tax collection, borrowing, salaries, and other budgetary matters. With control over the compilation of lists for criminal and civil juries and the nomination of justices of the peace falling to the arrondissement and the provincial governors, and with general counselors taking over the responsibilities of the prefectorial councils, the central government was on Raudot's plan effectively to lose its role in most local matters, and local organs were to replace prefects and subprefects.

With the abolition of the prefectorial system, Raudot planned for the general councils to control all matters not strictly related to national policy. Indeed, Legitimist decentralizers reserved their most strenuous objections for the prefectorial system. For Raudot, the presence of the prefect in the department as both the principal administrator and a political agent of the central government had destructive repercussions. It politicized administrative functions and imported ideological divisions and political conflict into localities that, if left to themselves, would arrive naturally at solutions to problems that, essentially technical in nature, were in any case to be solved by community consensus. Usually an outsider ignorant of local conditions and without affective attachment to the community, the prefect busied himself with all the details of local life, thus depriving the locality of its autonomous vigor and its freedom.

Moreover, Raudot asserted, the central bureaucracy, of which the prefect was only the most visible and deleterious manifestation, invited social and political instability by using state patronage to dissolve social ties and by educating the people to look away from their neighbors for guidance and favors. The dependence the bureaucracy fostered led to the general impression that the state was the primary engine of social arrangements and compelled natural community leaders either to seek government appointments or to resign themselves to social and political oblivion. In times of crisis, the concentration of state power instantly made the administration the focus of discontent and forced the government to take responsibility for the least administrative error or social injustice. Raudot felt that, among other things, decentralization would lift many grievances against the state and would orient people toward regulating their own affairs and solving their own problems instead of hoping for remedies through revolutions.

Sharing Béchard's view of the commune as the primary self-governing entity, Raudot thought that the department could act as an intermediary between it and the nation, thereby shielding the communal "family" from the depredations of bureaucratic government. With the commune's executive council meeting all year long and its administrators acting on the needs and enforcing the obligations of the community, the general councils could be made into a "diminutive form of our old estates."[26] In studying the ancient estates of his native Burgundy in 1861, during his retirement from politics, Raudot concluded that general counselors were analogous to the "general electors of Burgundy," with material and family interests giving them natural "consideration" in their *pays,* and a permanent sense of responsibility flowing from the knowledge that "their actions will last as long as the lifetime they spend among their compatriots."[27] From Raudot's historical perspective, the general councils had to command the central role in governing France. In his

26. "Bulletin départementale," *Revue provinciale,* I (December, 1848), 319; Raudot, "La Décentralisation: Première Partie," *Le Correspondant,* XLV (1858), 479. In the Commission on Decentralization of 1871, Raudot told his colleagues, "In the old *pays d'état,* the local administration nominated the architects, the engineers, and the contractors of the province; the results were admirable. These lands were infinitely better administered than the *pays d'élection.* It is the very same today in the countries that still practice true liberty, and the reward is the greatest stability, because the government is not held responsible for everything the prefects does badly" (Commission de la Décentralisation, procès-verbaux, April 28, 1871, in C2866, AN).

27. Raudot, "La Décentralisation: Seconde Partie," *Le Correspondant,* LIII (1861), 268.

proposal, matters concerning administrative justice that had once been submitted to the prefectorial councils or the Conseil d'Etat would be dealt with by the ordinary judicial system appointed by the general councils. The general councils would have perpetual rather than periodic control over the details of departmental administration, with their own budgets and finances separate from the finances of the state—eliminating the *fonds commun*. They would have the right to initiate their own public works projects, with a locally appointed staff of architects, engineers, surveyors, public health officials, public assistance personnel, school inspectors, teaching faculties, and economists.

Raudot wanted to restore the provinces in order to ensure that the link between the eighty-six semiautonomous general councils and a much-diminished central government would be indirect (Map XXII). Each province was to be headed by a governor—only one of two local officials named by the central government—who would take over the small number of prefectorial responsibilities not assigned to other bodies and who would have a purely political and surpervisory role devoid of any administrative initiative. As a further guard against the governor's independence, he was to be guided by a council the members of which the central government was to choose, three from each department, out of the present and former *maires* of the *chefs-lieux* and the general counselors. This body was to assume the tasks of the prefectorial councils not yet appropriated by the general councils. The governor was to be completely accountable to yet another council—the provincial council—nominated by the general counselors of the province to deliberate on all provincial affairs, allocate expenses between the departments, decide the routing of provincial roads and railroads, and nominate candidates for the provincial *cour d'appels*. All administrative, judicial, and financial matters were ultimately to be controlled by the eighty-six general councils or by officials elected or appointed at or below the level of the department.[28]

Raudot hoped that the restoration of the provinces, besides filling the void created by eliminating the prefects and besides establishing federal ties between the twenty-five provinces and the central government, would prevent any centralized "Asiatic government" from further effacing particularist identities. The Legitimists saw French national unity as a spontaneous manifestation of the free governing activity of smaller so-

28. Raudot, "La Décentralisation en 1870," *Le Correspondant,* LXXXII (1870), 200.

Map XXII Raudot's Proposal for Restoring Provinces

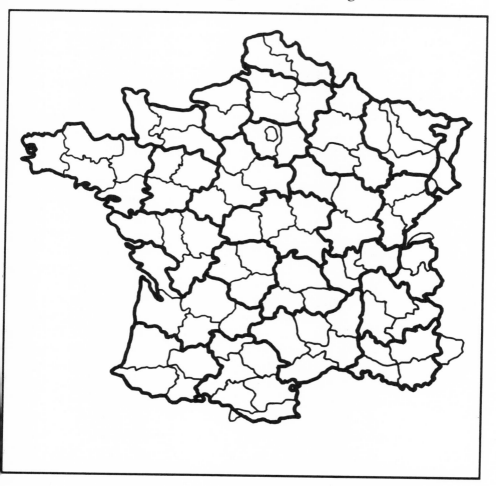

Based on proposals in *De la grandeur possible de la France, faisant suite à la décadence de la France,* by Claude Marie Raudot (Paris, 1851).

cial units; these had historically been allowed to evolve according to in-
digenous traditions despite the ill-advised extension of royal power under
the Old Regime. After the Revolution destroyed the foundations of local
autonomy, national unity became "mechanical, violent, routine, and
consequently deceitful," the Legitimists complained. By stifling the
"provincial spirit" and preventing the circulation of the "mutual intelligence" of the various departments, the concentration of power in Paris
caused, in their view, regional antagonisms that threatened the "complete fusion that alone constitutes the moral unity of a . . . free people."[29]
Raudot conceived of his project as a "transaction with the past" that
would provide a form of administration compatible with the greater
unity demanded by modern communications, transport, and regional interdependence but that would concurrently "reestablish glorious names"
and reanimate the honors of the past.[30]

But the intention of Raudot's proposal was primarily social. In assigning functions to the various local bodies, he sought not only to eliminate
the interference of the central government but to institutionalize the predominance of departmental notables through a vertically stratified political hierarchy. In place of an artificially imposed central administration
dictating to society, Raudot's plan envisioned a society in which the natural leaders of the people would administer the *administrés* and "enlighten
the central power." Decentralization was, besides, to stabilize the social
order by creating a place for "free intermediary authorities" who by their
activity would restore respect for social authority and reintegrate the
conservative notables into natural, cohesive, and well-ordered commu-

29. M. Forcade, "La Centralisation et les intérêts marseillais," *Revue provinciale,* I (October, 1848), 126–27.

30. *Annales,* April 29, 1871, I, annexe 183, p. 950; Raudot, *De la grandeur possible de la
France,* 55–57, 73. "Our departments now, through the passage of time, have become too
small. When they were instituted, the means of communication were not easy, highways
were badly maintained, there were no telegraph lines, there were none of the facilities of
transport and communication the administration disposes of today. In 1789, we created
eighty departments; now that there are railroads, telegraph lines and excellent highways,
should the old organization be preserved, when for so many things it is useless?

"But we must absolutely administer by more economic means. We no longer need
eighty prefects and a multitude of functionaries; today, thanks to our mastery over distances, they can be reduced to a smaller number. I have therefore proposed only progressive
measures and have nowhere placed federalism in my proposition of one governor per province containing several departments" (*Annales,* July 10, 1871, III, 884).

nities that would not need the coercion of the ministry of the interior to get them to behave.[31]

By endowing the elite with a new freedom and importance, decentralization was to "ennoble" those who "enjoy the leisure of an independent fortune," by allowing them to serve society.[32] Raudot had always deplored that when centralization turned social authorities into functionaries, it sapped their sense of confidence and civic responsibility. Uprooted, bullied, and psychologically debilitated—like "certain savages deformed by their parents"—the elite who became functionaries lost the habit of appealing to their own conscience to make choices and came to be ruled only by the ambition "to get a piece of the power and the budget."[33] As Raudot told the National Assembly, centralization "deprived the elite of French society of a domestic foyer"; they were forced to neglect, abandon, or even sell "all their rural properties, to spend their life in the thrall of ceaseless advancement, and to cause profound irritation among the people."[34] By contrast, decentralization would, according to Charles Muller, open a "career other than pleasure to those referred to as the blessed of the earth" and combat the "habits of laziness that waste them," by "giving them state employment to occupy their leisure with tasks whose honor will be the best remuneration."[35]

The Legitimists acknowledged that decentralization would not ensure the power of the notables as long as individualism and egalitarianism eroded social harmony. They therefore favored restrictions on local suffrage which might afford "moral guarantees," such as requiring a certain length of domicile or a form of corporatist representation designed to salvage "from electoral contests all the higher interests of society, [by holding] them in an inaccessible region, sheltered from the hazards of voting, outside what Bossuet called the cruel whim of the multitudes."[36]

---

31. Raudot, "La Décentralisation: Seconde Partie," *Le Correspondant*, LIII (1861), 267.
32. Muller, *La Légitimité* (Paris, 1857), 224–25.
33. Raudot, *De la décadence de la France*, 32–37.
34. *Annales*, 1871, I, annexe 183, pp. 943–44.
35. Muller, *La Légitimité*, 225–26.
36. Hilaire de Lacombe, "Le Suffrage universel et la Représentation des intérêts," *Le Correspondant*, CL (1876), 600. The Legitimists devised numerous ways of ensuring dominance by the conservative notables without, strictly speaking, eliminating universal suffrage. Gouvello recommended that half of each municipal council be composed of the highest taxpayers in the commune. See his *Vues sur la réorganisation de la France*, 82–

Yet they assumed that a revitalized local elite would eventually obviate the need for such measures, since by virtue of these men's status and service they would have no need to agitate local communities in seeking votes or to disrupt the social order by competing for positions. Motivated only by the desire to serve and sharing the larger interests of the community, the notables would be freed from political preoccupations when people saw that they were the best choice universal suffrage could make. Since the need to solicit votes would vanish, so would ambition and demagoguery; the voter would recognize the notables' capacity as notables, and their election would merely register a social fact.[37] The lack of competition would create unity at the top of the social hierarchy; men of worth would see public service as an end in itself rather than as a springboard to higher office. Ideological divisions would cease to impede government operations and imperil institutions, because the attainment of office and the exercise of power "would have nothing artificial about it."[38] Chambord could consequently proclaim that decentralization would make the attainment of rank in society depend on capacity and merit, at the same time that it would stimulate an "incessant competition of emulation, informed by devotion, intelligence, and activity, in careers always open to all" within a "natural, flexible hierarchy, in conformity . . . with the spirit of [civil] equality among us."[39]

Until the notables were secure in their predominance, they hoped to use their existing local power to "erect a dike against future revolutions" by devolving the central power into the hands of the general councils in the event of a seizure of government in the capital.[40] During the Com-

86. General Douhet proposed that all married electors with children have three votes so that wives and children were represented in the communes as well. See *Annales*, June 12, 1874, XXXII, 146–47. See also Armand Fresneau, in *Annales*, June 17, 1874, XXXII, 235–36; and Charles de Franclieu, in *Annales*, July 7, 1873, XIX, 59–61.

37. M. de Ventavon described his ideal candidate for the municipal council as a "magistrate who resides in the *chef-lieu* of the department and who possesses properties in a rural commune. He would reside there frequently. He would be a disinterested family counselor, the arbiter of all differences. It is he who would have the most influence in the *pays*. Well, I ask all serious minds if, in this eminent position, he would have to go solicit votes in order to figure twelfth on the list of candidates" (*Annales*, 1871, II, 314).

38. Comte de Chambord, Lettre sur la décentralisation, November 14, 1862, in *La Monarchie française*, 72.

39. *Ibid.*

40. Voilliard, "Autour du programme de Nancy," 229.

mune, Amédée de Gouvello pointed with favor to the contrast offered by Austria in 1849, when "good Jellachich came to deliver the capital from its oppressors."[41] Under the Second Republic, Béchard had endorsed a plan by a group of Legitimists to put France under the rule of an executive body constituted of locally elected officials and military commanders in the event of "whatever dire threat"; the Legitimist *L'Union de l'Ouest* supported decentralization as a means to create local institutions strong enough to carry out passive resistance against Paris.[42] In 1872, four Legitimist deputies sponsored a plan that in effect called for letting a military dictatorship reestablish law and order and "legitimate authority" in case of "exceptional circumstances." The emergency dictatorship was to be controlled by the regional commanders under the direction of the general counselors. The plan's goal was to secure the continuity of the notables' power and to bring to an end the chain of revolutionary "days" and coups d'etat that had punctuated French history after 1789.[43]

The Legitimists also believed decentralization would virtually eliminate whatever pockets of political radicalism had formed in the localities. The Legitimists tended in their crankier moments to see republicans as representing the frustrated debris of a disintegrating social order whose ideology was merely the subversive and corrosive reasoning of those who did not fit in. One Legitimist counted republicans only among gendarmes reduced in rank, schoolteachers hounded by the church and the *mairie* for offenses against public morality, *clercs d'hussier* retired to the countryside to save money, village dandies, self-deluded big shots, and small landowners captivated by the fancy that they deserved the *mairie*. Conservatives, by contrast, included the "good merchant who has by a lifetime of work and probity acquired some comfort that he wants to shield from disruptions in order to leave something to his children," the retired soldier whose life has been "one long school of duty," the Catholic priest, the landowner hardened by work, or even the lawyer who has

41. Gouvello, *Vues sur la réorganisation de la France*, 24.
42. Béchard, *De l'administration*, II, 292–96; L'Union de l'Ouest, in "Bulletin départementale," *Revue provinciale*, II (June, 1849), 300–301.
43. Rapport fait au nom de la commission chargée d'examiner les propositions de M. le vicomte de Treveneuc, M. Vetillart, M. de Aboville, M. Depeyre relative au rôle éventuel des conseils généraux dans des circonstances exceptionnelle, par Henri Fournier, in *Annales*, 1872, V, annexe 659, pp. 274–75.

maintained a reputable practice for fifty years—in short, all who have remained innocent of the aspiration to seek influence because of the misplaced pride that manifests itself in "rancorous speech."[44]

Hence, Raudot believed that extensive decentralization could succeed in a country that for long had been inhospitable toward local autonomy. The Legitimists were convinced that political conflict sprang from the mischief of those who wanted to disrupt society for their own ends, and therefore they rejected the notion that the social conditions prevailing in "well-ordered societies" could ever be the source of antagonisms. Once the centralized state was checked, the social order could be repaired, they had no doubt, and administrative efforts would be eased by consensus rather than hobbled by greedy manipulation. The elites, given the chance to exercise their right "to manage the affairs of their departments with devotion, activity, and economy," would cease to contest each other's power in a debate on fundamental principles, because the goals they pursued would reflect the moral unity of a society that was pleased to let them govern.[45]

FROM ARISTOCRATS TO ASSOCIATIONS

If Raudot's proposal seemed utopian in the context of French political realities, it was nevertheless perfectly consistent with the Legitimists' concept of social reconstruction. In the past, they believed, local liberties and social stability had been protected in France by an aristocracy governing in conjunction with the monarchy through a system of representative institutions. That belief led Charles Muller to suggest that the government of the Bourbon Restoration could have arrested the erosion of intermediary bodies and the power of traditional elites if in fashioning the terminology for "designating the administrators of our de-

---

44. Yvon, *Monarchie-République,* 25–27.

45. Raudot, "La Décentralisation: Seconde Partie," *Le Correspondant,* LIII (1861), 268; Louis de Kergolay, "Des institutions communales de la Belqique: Seconde Article," *Revue provinciale,* II (August, 1849), 436–37. According to Kergolay, decentralization worked in Belgium because a consensus existed between Catholics and liberals. Moreover, the Belgian people were "truly religious" and did "not bring into communal life any of these inspirations we call the revolutionary spirit. They have an ancient, deep, and sincere taste for their local liberties; they love them for themselves and not in view of the political intrigues to which they might devote their intelligence" ("Des institutions communales de la Belgique: Seconde Article," 436–37).

partments," it had invoked the "titles consecrated by centuries of habit
. . . and enjoying a prestige that has survived all our revolutions" instead
of resorting to administrative ranks based on "qualifications adopted by
a legislative caprice without resonance in our history." "It would have
been no more difficult," he wrote, "to accustom the population to the
commands of a *comte* than to those of a prefect," and "the effect produced
in mores and ideas would have been enormous."[46] But the Legitimists
realized that it would take more than deft nomenclature to reconstitute
the social order, effectively free elites from the fetters of bureaucratic
control, and erase the schism within the upper classes over how best to
govern the nation. Since the Revolution had undermined the notables'
confidence in liberty by irrevocably destroying the institutional guarantees of the past, the Legitimists believed that it was necessary to replace
the nobility, the provincial estates, and the enfranchised towns with surrogates in the form of corporative associations or local institutions that
could perform the same functions.

    In the distant past, Roger de Larcy argued, representative and stable
government in France was assured by an agreement between the monarchy and the aristocracy to protect and preserve local liberties. Under Car-
olingian feudalism, however, that consensus was abandoned, the nobility
desiring "only to govern its fiefs in the greatest possible independence
from royal power" and the crown, in seeking to extend its power, more
and more disregarding the ancient constitution of the nation. The failure
of the eighteenth-century reform movement and the triumph of the
Revolution, according to Larcy, deprived France of the chance to reestablish the ancient compromise. That happened because both the crown
and a portion of the elite turned to bureaucratic despotism as a defense
against anarchy.[47]

    If the French aristocracy had been more like its English counterpart,
France like England might have had the "strongest political institutions,
which alone resolve in a durable manner the problem of free and representative government," Larcy believed. Across the Channel, the old feudal aristocracy, modifying its role through the centuries, had understood
how to preserve real power along with an essential function in the constitutional order. "One knows that in England," Larcy explained, "the

46. Muller, *La Légitimité,* 231–32.
47. Roger de Larcy, *Des vicissitudes politiques de la France: Etudes historiques* (Paris, 1860),
ix; "Bibliographie," *Le Correspondant,* LIII (1861), 799.

high aristocracy constituted itself as a peerage, an individual but hereditary magistrature, conferring privileges only on those who exercised
functions; the rest of the nobility were indistinguishable from the rest of
the nation. This combination, assigning a fixed and restrained role to the
rights of the aristocracy, made these rights easier to support, and with
this exception the upper classes were obliged to merge with the lower,
sparing the susceptibilities of one and favoring the ascendancy of the
other." In France, however, he went on,

> nobles of every degree ended by forming a distinct body, electing
> its own representatives to the Estates General. The way its privi-
> leges separated it from other citizens with whom it was constantly
> in contact led to many occasions for mild confrontation. Arrogant
> of its rights in its relations with them and feeling that it had noth-
> ing to obtain by exercising influence over them, it did not perceive
> the need to attach them to itself by bonds of patronage. Besides,
> having no determined political function and badly united itself,
> without permanent organization, it could never hope to exercise
> real power [*une action reélle*] and assist in the government of the
> state. Despite its brilliant qualities, its courage, and its services, it
> was more like a jealous caste than a respected institution.[48]

Larcy judged that by not breaking definitively with the society of orders
in 1789, the monarchy and the aristocracy had lost the opportunity to
base the ascendancy of the elite on a national consensus and had allowed
their own survival to become the issue that launched a revolution striking
at the roots of the Old Regime and in the end toppling the entire "ancient
constitution." When the Revolution was over, Larcy contended, many
institutions that had been proscribed came back to life, but the old aristocratic order—which, reformed, he believed could have been the vital
element of any new organization—was irretrievably lost. The lesson was
clear: a successful restoration of the monarchy and the power of the notables depended on their common support for local institutions that
could unite the upper classes in permanent commitment to the service of
society and the protection of provincial liberties.

The decentralized monarchy, then, was Larcy's answer to the problem
of how to create liberty and order in an egalitarian society that had for-

48. Larcy, *Des vicissitudes,* x–xi.

ever lost the "aristocratic element" that had guaranteed stability in the past.[49] Although the Legitimists conceded that the idea of aristocratic government could never be reconciled "with the exigencies of modern times, such as they were manifested in 1789," they also believed that the bureaucratic despotism and egalitarianism that had accompanied the aristocracy's demise could be balanced through the creation of "intermediary collective forces" and the "free association" of the notables and the people within civil society.[50] Hilaire de Lacombe declared that, having destroyed "hereditary power condensed into a class or a race" by abolishing the corporations and the aristocracy, the Revolution "left no resources to societies but the forces of all grouped together by association."[51] Municipal councils, provincial administrations, charitable associations, professional corporations, productory cooperatives, and mutual-aid societies could take the place of powerful aristocrats by organizing, within their sphere of influence, the patronage of local notables, the community bonds, and the self-reliance required to impede bureaucratization and mass politicization. Civil society could in that way constitute itself apart from inordinate state control and ultimately protect itself from the ravages of despotism and the resulting threat of democracy. As Chambord cautioned in 1862, "The more democracy gains ground, the more it is urgent to regulate and organize it in order to preserve the social order from the perils to which it could be exposed."[52]

Still, although decentralization could provide the Legitimists and

49. "The absolute disappearance of the aristocratic element was, we believe, a misfortune for true liberty" (*Ibid.*, ix).

50. Larcy, "La Décentralisation de 1789 à 1870," *Le Correspondant*, LXXXII (1870), 10–11. These expressions were taken from the work of M. de Serre and M. Desmaret, whom Larcy cited to support his thesis. Béchard stated that "respect for individual liberties is undoubtedly the first duty of a government; nevertheless, it is to the association rather than the individual that one must look for the counterweight to centralization" (*Autonomie et Césarisme*, 148).

51. Lacombe, "Le Suffrage universel et la Représentation des inérêts," 623. Véran wrote that "the question of communal emancipation rests on the right of association" (*La Question du XIXe siècle*, 101), and Antoine Berryer, in a letter to Odilon Barrot commenting on Chambord's decentralist manifesto, spoke of the need to "reconstitute in this leveled society a class that can serve as a rallying point in a great crisis, that has traditions, and that can defend something. This class . . . can be produced only as a result of services rendered and of the influences that such services have in our cities and our countryside. But the only cadres in which these influences can be formed are free municipal institutions" (Quoted by Charles de Lacombe in *Vie de Berryer* [3 vols.; Paris, 1895], III, 479).

52. Chambord, *La Monarchie française*, 73.

other notables with the power and autonomy to organize social patronage, it was merely one precondition for social reconstruction, since freedom from bureaucratic interference by itself neither entailed the creation nor defined the nature of the "free associations" that might, without resorting to state repression, curb social disorder and reestablish the traditional values of deference and faith. If the Legitimists intended decentralization to settle how France would be governed, their encounter with the social question forced them to think about how to revive and maintain traditional values and hierarchical social relations in the era of industrialization.

CHAPTER V

Social Legitimism

FOR LEGITIMIST social Catholics, the unraveling of the social order had far more to do with industrialization and the emergence of the urban proletariat than with the centralized state. While Legitimist decentralizers like Raudot were part of a long tradition of struggle between the local and central authorities, those who confronted directly the implications of industrial capitalism had to navigate uncharted waters. Nevertheless, developing a response to the social transformation of the nineteenth century, and to the ideology that recommended it, was central to the Legitimists' effort to project royalism as a viable alternative to the liberal capitalist order, for the concept of monarchy they were defining was grounded in the hope that civil society could generate the conditions for a successful conservative polity. But just how did the problem of nineteenth-century economic and social change enter the Legitimist discourse on social reconstruction, and what were the priorities that guided Legitimist social activity? How were the solutions the Legitimists envisioned related to the larger goals of the royalist program?

THE SOCIAL CATHOLIC MILIEU

Legitimists often tried to distinguish themselves from other monarchist notables by declaring their Catholic faith and their devotion to the plight of the lower classes, rather than by emphasizing their fidelity to the Comte de Chambord. According to one of Chambord's biographers, the pretender himself was more absorbed by the "social

135

question" than by "the mode of government or the machinery of politics."[1] Alfred de Falloux, with evident pride, asserted in his memoirs that the Legitimist party had consistently furnished Catholic charitable undertakings with the "largest contingent" of supporters, and he affirmed that social leadership such as the party had provided was as important for notables as the political management of the state.[2] In the 1850s, when the papacy was on friendly terms with the regime of Napoleon III because of his conciliatory religious policies, Bishop Edouard Pie rejected Rome's criticism that he showed too much amity toward the Legitimists of Poitiers because the Legitimists were especially apt "to accomplish their religious duties" and "put themselves at the service of Catholic charities."[3]

The preponderance of Legitimists in the conservative social Catholic movement seems incontestable. Jean Baptiste Duroselle, admitting that he could not find a single Orleanist among the early conservative social Catholics, concluded that the Catholic piety of the Legitimist aristocracy made it more likely to be concerned about poverty than were the Voltaireans, the Protestants, or the Jews who dominated the industrial *patronat* of the July Monarchy. By the 1840s, he argued, the Legitimists were compelled to respond to the social question because of their tradition of aristocratic paternalism, their long-standing involvement in charitable activity, and their habit of contrasting the miseries of contemporary society against an idealized image of Old Regime corporatism and class harmony. The Legitimists were also strongly inclined to politicize the visible poverty of the lower classes under the July Monarchy in order to criticize the regime and strengthen the outrage against the egotism of the bourgeoisie.[4] René Rémond thinks it natural that *grands propriétaires,* former feudal lords "accustomed to the respect of their peasants" and "always ready . . . to come to their aid," should have been the first on the Right to raise the social question.[5]

1. Dubosc de Pesquidoux, *Le Comte de Chambord,* 179.

2. Pitman, trans. and ed., *Memoirs of the Count de Falloux,* I, 156.

3. Baunard, *Histoire du cardinal Pie,* I, 369. Pie's comments were addressed to the Abbé de Solesmes, who wrote from Rome in 1852 calling Louis Napoleon's coup d'etat "this rainbow of hope."

4. Jean Baptiste Duroselle, *Les Débuts du catholicisme social en France* (Paris, 1951), 198–200; Tudesq, *Les Grands Notables en France,* I, 576. See also Lebrun, ed., *Histoire des catholiques en France,* 350.

5. Rémond, *Les Droites en France,* 129.

Such explanations of the Legitimists' social involvement have the merit of recognizing the link between it and a certain aristocratic self-consciousness that animated Legitimist attempts to define the conditions of social leadership. But they also take the Legitimists' own mythology too seriously. The social conditions of the early nineteenth century presented themselves to French notables as a "social question" precisely because past experience did not vouchsafe a reliable response to anything that unprecedented. Most Legitimists were provincial chatelains who in the beginning had no direct contact with the emerging industrial world, and the majority of rural *propriétaires* remained silent on urban social issues until forced to confront them head on during the Revolution of 1848.[6] The handful of Legitimists who articulated the first distinctly Catholic and conservative approach to the social question were less concerned about aristocratic manners and Old Regime corporatism than about reconciling the realities of a liberal society with the social implications of their faith. Thus, in the 1840s Legitimist social Catholics had more to do than simply make the psychological transition from feudal seigneur to Catholic patron; they had to discover social content in a religious tradition that offered no direct answers to the problems of free labor, wage slavery, family dissolution, and factory organization. Albert de Mun, the principal Legitimist social Catholic of the late nineteenth century, had to discover his "social vocation" before he could define the relevance of paternalist and corporatist traditions.

Hence, Legitimist social Catholicism seems to have had more to do

---

6. Although agriculture was the dominant occupation of 53 percent of the 512 Legitimists in my sample, social Catholic activists were not so completely associated with rural life. Of 41 social Catholics, only 32.5 percent were *propriétaires* and only 20 percent had agriculture as their sole profession. Nearly half were members of the professions, reflecting the fact that charitable activities were concentrated in towns and cities. Moreover, 22.5 percent, compared with fewer than 10 percent from the larger sample, were bankers, industrialists, or merchants exclusively. Social Catholics, with only 36.6 percent of their number titled noblemen and 48.8 percent non-nobles, were quite often of bourgeois origins and because of their professions lived in closer proximity to urban conditions than did most Legitimists. Quite a few, like the Comte de Juigné, president of the Jockey Club, Benoist d'Azy, and Joseph de La Bouillerie, were aristocratic industrialists who sponsored Catholic associations and initiated social projects in their own industrial establishments. See Denis, *Les Royalistes de la Mayenne,* 444; and Pierre Pierrand, "Un Grand Bourgeois de Lille: Charles Kolb-Bernard, 1799–1888," *Revue du Nord,* XLVIII (1966). For biographical sources, see Table I and Bibliography.

with the developing sensibilities of French Catholics than with the political economy of Orleanism. This can be seen in the generational shift of
focus that took place between the 1840s, when Armand de Melun was
the most visible social Catholic, and the 1870s, when Albert de Mun
emerged as the leader of the social Catholic Right. Melun and Mun, born
in 1811 and 1841 respectively, exemplify two different stages in the
Catholic response to capitalism, one associated with the liberal Catholicism of the 1830s and the 1840s and the other tied to the reaction that
grew against liberalism in the 1860s. During the earlier stage, social Catholicism simply meant making a commitment to the lower classes part
of Christian comportment. Melun, Falloux, and Adolphe Baudon, the
general secretary of the Saint Vincent de Paul Society between 1848 and
1878, were each attracted to an ecclesiastical vocation in their youth, but
they all reported that when they had to choose a career, they were
gripped by the idea that Catholics had a special mission to serve the material and spiritual needs of the poor. Catholics, they believed, could
solve the social question by leading the proletariat back to the church,
and they could revitalize the faith by inspiring lay Catholics to devote
themselves to society. Melun saw what his life's mission was when Sister
Rosalie of the Sisters of Charity showed him the "hope" that charity
brought to the poor of Paris.[7]

The generation of Melun and Falloux, coming of age under the July
Monarchy, remained attached throughout their political lives to the liberal Catholicism of the Comte de Montalembert, Père Ravignan, and
Jean Baptiste Lacordaire. Their outlook was formed in the salon of Madame Swetchine, a Russian émigré converted to Catholicism, with
whom both Melun and Falloux maintained an extensive correspondence.
The salon was the center of apprenticeship for many young notables,
including Tocqueville, who through its influence undergirded their faith
with a commitment to live a "seriously Christian life."[8] Much of the
discussion in this period centered on the growing materialism of the age
and especially on the religious indifference of the upper classes, which
Legitimists believed was related to the July Revolution. Concern about
that was conjoined with a mounting apprehension that the intensifying
class conflict threatened to end in the overthrow of the bourgeoisie by

7. Andigné, *Un Apôtre de la charité*, 37.
8. Pitman, trans. and ed., *Memoirs of the Count de Falloux*, I, 154.

the proletariat, just as the moral decline of the late eighteenth century had led to the bourgeoisie's supplanting the aristocracy in 1789. The *cercles* and salons of the time served as seminaries for a new generation of lay Catholics who set as their mission the salvation of society—through charity—from the social antagonisms created by materialism and free enterprise.[9]

The early debates on the social question in the 1830s and 1840s gave Melun's generation a spirit of optimism and even experimentation, but the older generation never abandoned the faith in individual action untainted by state intervention which was prevalent among the wider society of notables. Saint-Simonian and Fourierist ideas were openly discussed in a climate that permitted the enunciation of socialist views to parallel the moral critique of capitalism deployed in Catholic circles. As the social and economic crisis of the 1840s deepened, Catholic and socialist idioms mixed in a shared enthusiasm for the part the church could play in bringing about universal fraternity. Observing a priest hold out his hand to the workers at a meeting of the Saint Francis Xavier Society in the cellar of Saint Suplice in 1846, Maurice Maignen thought he was witnessing a social "renovation": "There I shared in this impulse, and there I could see the realization of my socialist dreams, but through Christ and his church."[10]

Born in time to be impressed by the intellectual and social reaction that set in after the Revolution of 1848, Mun and his protégé René de La Tour Du Pin were much more skeptical than Melun's generation of the possibility of a rapprochement between Catholicism and secular ideology and far more willing to link social disorder to liberalism and the stewardship of the bourgeoisie. If Melun's conversion to social Catholicism came as he saw alms distributed to workers by the Sisters of Charity, Mun

9. Schall, *Un Disciple de Saint Vincent de Paul*, 30.
10. Charles Maignen, *Maurice Maignen, directeur du Cercle Montparnasse, et les origines du mouvement social catholique en France, 1822–1890* (2 vols.; Luçon, 1927), I, 26. Maurice Maignen, according to his brother Charles, later alluded to this incident by noting that he had been "early attracted by [the socialists'] humanitarian theories and strongly impressed by their lamentations on the misery of the workers. . . . By what wonderful prejudices was my heart inclined toward the generous side of these doctrines: the love of the oppressed and the devotion to their suffering. How could my weak and ignorant mind resist the poison of these impious and detestable theories?" Maignen also believed that he was drawn to the socialists by their use of a "certain Christian jargon" that hid from him the danger their doctrines posed to his salvation. See Charles Maignen, *Maurice Maignen*, I, 26n.

embraced his "social vocation" after reading Emile Keller on the incompatibility between the Syllabus of Errors and the principles of 1789.[11] Legitimists who became prominent in the conservative social Catholic movement after 1870 matured during a time of growing militancy in the church, when the struggles against anticlericalism in the 1860s, the loss of the papacy's temporal power, and the catastrophe of the Paris Commune seemed to presage a recrudescence of the dechristianizing impulse of 1793. Increasingly counterrevolutionary and ultramontane, Mun's generation came to see the salvation of society as inseparable from a defense of the social and political power of the church and lay Catholics to organize a "Christian social order" capable, by breaking with individualism, of providing permanent, and often authoritarian, solutions to the problems of class conflict and social disintegration.[12]

Despite such shifts, however, conservative social Catholics held a number of basic assumptions in common. Their different plans of action stemmed not from disagreements on fundamental goals but rather from conflicts over the practical and philosophical implications of a few fixed ideas.

THE SEARCH FOR A DOCTRINE

From the time of the Restoration, social Catholics were aware that their criticism of laissez-faire capitalism imposed on them the obligation to frame an alternative to the emerging system of production and its social relations. Alban de Villeneuve-Bargemont, who served as prefect of the Nord between 1828 and 1830 and who was the first to bring the question of misery among the working class before the Chamber of Deputies, in 1840, argued that France had to find an alternative to the "English system" of capital accumulation and labor exploitation more appropriate to French mores and religious values. He called for a new "Christian political economy" based on the "practical and general application of the principles of justice, morality, humanity, and charity" to be achieved through the encouragement of producers' cooperatives, the ex-

---

11. Mun, *Ma vocation sociale*, 21. Andigné, who makes no secret of his preference for the ideas of Mun, mirrors the attitude of Mun's generation in commenting that for Melun, "the principles ceaselessly affirmed by the sovereign pontiffs do not seem ever to have had a social import" (*Un Apôtre de la charité*, 412).

12. Andigné, *Un Apôtre de la charité*, 412.

tension of state-funded public assistance, and the passage of social legislation that could soften the rigors of the system.[13]

Villeneuve-Bargemont's practical recommendations were widely accepted by conservative elites later in the century, but the set of Christian economic principles he sought in order to respond to liberalism on theoretical grounds proved far more difficult to attain. In 1845, Armand de Melun launched the Société d'Economie Charitable to study the social question from a Christian perspective and to search for "all the proper means to diminish suffering, facilitate work, and efface stubborn misunderstandings."[14] Composed of Orleanist and Legitimist activists, including Prosper de Barante, Falloux, and Alexis Chevalier, the group became a debating society that organized conferences on social issues and got bogged down in discussions of free trade, public assistance, and *livrets* for workers, with little advance to the intellectual breadth or stature of Catholic social theory. To emphasize the theoretical concerns of the society, Melun in 1860 changed the title of its publication from *Annales de la charité* to *Revue d'économie charitable,* but the society found it far easier to plan small changes in public social policy than to theorize about what it was doing. It produced an impressive quantity of commentary on contemporary social issues, but it examined them one by one and merely added to the proliferation of schemes for the application of private and public charity while failing to provide the sort of theoretical foundation Melun had hoped for. Questions such as what constituted a fair wage, the nature of value, and the limits of property ownership were largely neglected.

Why was Melun so concerned with theoretical soundness when, by his own account, Catholics had made great strides in organizing charitable associations whose operations were successful? It is significant that he should have reached a positive prognosis for socialism among the working classes at a time when far more people went to mass and took alms from the church than read socialist newspapers. Like most notables

13. Duroselle, *Les Débuts du catholicisme social,* 60–62. See Alban de Villeneuve-Bargemont, *Economie politique chrétienne; ou, Recherche sur la nature et les causes du paupérisme, en France et en Europe, et sur les moyens de le soulager et de le prévenir* (3 vols.; Paris, 1834).

14. *Annales de la charité,* 1846, referred to by Andigné in *Un Apôtre de la charité,* Preface. This type of activity was continued with greater theoretical significance by Albert de Mun's Oeuvre des Cercles after 1870, under which La Tour Du Pin established and directed the Conseil de Jésus-Ouvrier, with ecclesiastical and lay directors. The Conseil published a journal entitled *Revue catholique des questions ouvrières.*

educated in the Catholic tradition, he believed that principled social action by elites would be able to impart normative social values effective in
shaping the behavior of the masses, and that led him to perceive the
socialists as successful: they had advanced a "theory that appears as a
revelation for the renewal of society."[15] Without a system of ideas, he
wrote in 1871, Catholics would continue "to speak in vague terms, in
sermons," and would be unable to seize the imagination of the masses.[16]
Though he praised the social work Catholics had excelled at from the
1840s on, he feared that "this admirable action . . . saves individuals"
but does not "suffice to save society." He later wrote, "While the enemy
attacks our beliefs, our ideas, our principles, we do not prepare our ammunition. Each day, it fights us with its economic doctrines, its social
theories; we remain immobile and silent. But our repose is not a contemplation that consolidates and enlivens the forces of struggle; it is rather a
somnolence which neglects to take its part."[17] In 1869, J. Bourgeois, an
editor of the *Gazette de France,* lamented the growing dominance of liberalism in social life and exhorted Catholics to create a true "Catholic
science" uniting religion and the "economic order" by clearly defining a
Catholic position on matters like value, profits, rent, interest, credit, and
the organization of labor. Ancient theological solutions, he argued, true
in essence, were from a time when economic and social conditions differed greatly from the nineteenth century and did not respond to its
needs. "We must," he concluded, "formulate them in a new way that
can be applied more exactly to the present, without weakening our principles." The moral principles of Christianity not only had to be true and
eternal, they had to be "justified by economic considerations."[18]

Many Legitimists and Catholics frankly resented the notion, however,
that Christians had to elaborate a new political economy to compete with
the liberals and the socialists. The source of the aversion to extending
Villeneuve-Bargemont's approach was not strictly intellectual. The Legitimists were strongly divided on social issues, and many were content
to suppose that social amelioration would result from applying tradi-

---

15. Armand de Melun to Comte Edouard Le Camus, July 25, 1871, in Duroselle's *Les
Débuts du catholicisme social,* 655.

16. Duroselle, *Les Débuts du catholicisme social,* 655.

17. Armand de Melun, "De l'économie charitable et chrétienne," *Revue d'économie charitable,* I (1869), 7–17.

18. J. Bourgeois, *Le Catholicisme et les Questions sociales* (Paris, 1867), 158–59.

tional values to social ills. Their doctrinal timidity also had roots in their material interests. As Bourgeois suggested, the doctrines of the church of the time were unclear, contradictory, or silent on many details of economic life, and the spiritual principles it supported—charity, social reconciliation, respect for authority—were open to interpretation when applied to social conditions. Some decided that the way a small group of Christian socialists around Félicité Robert de Lamennais and Philippe Buchez had joined the movement for economic and social democracy exposed the hazard of any departure from a rigid adherence to orthodoxy and strict papal authority. Many conservative social Catholics, no matter how charitable, were concerned, as *propriétaires* and industrialists, with profits and social status. They were more than happy to contribute time and money to social causes, but wanting to preserve their own freedom of action, they persuaded themselves that Catholic social teachings addressed the inner conscience and not the law of supply and demand. Many concluded that Catholicism did not challenge but rather supported the operations of a free economy, leaving the *patron* free to choose how much to do for his workers. As Henri Rollet has written, "The immense majority of Catholics in this period saw in the existing order the intangible work of the Revolution and did not believe possible a secular transformation of political and economic conditions."[19]

But the stongest resistance to attention to economic theory came from social Catholic leaders, like Mun and Maignen, who flatly rejected economic liberalism and the unrestricted rights of the entrepreneur but feared that a kind of idolatry of ideas would deflect Catholics from an understanding of the higher source of their social obligations. This attitude was expressed by Charles Chesnelong in 1873, when he asked the Assemblée Général des Comités Catholiques de France,

> Are we searching for a new truth? No, we have a sure, immutable doctrine, and there is no other on this or that side of the prime meridian as lofty as God from whom it emanates, as imperishable as the human soul for which it is the supreme law and for which it proclaims the immortal vocation. As disciples of this doctrine, we rest our honor in recognizing that there is nothing above it, because there is nothing above the work of God, guarded by the infallible head of his church. We do not aspire to a truth that would

19. Henri Rollet, quoted in Andigné's *Un Apôtre de la charité*, 112.

be our own personal achievement; we possess a truth that was taught to us and that we preserve as our dearest treasure.[20]

The thinking was that for true Catholics a theory of political economy already existed in Scripture and the doctrines of the church; it consisted of the application of Christian truths to the economic and social order. On this view, Melun was misguided to hold that unless Catholics worked out a theoretical "system," they had no "right . . . to preach to others." Was it not enough to preach the gospel and call on society to obey the "rights of God" rather than the Rights of Man? Why, many Catholics must have wondered, should Christianity need to be "justified by economic considerations"? Neither the normative operations of the liberal economy nor the theoretical conclusions of the most learned Christian economist should overrule a social practice grounded in faith; what Catholics should argue about was what they were already arguing about: how to institutionalize the application of Christian principles to create a Christian social order. As far as doctrine was concerned, Mun, for one, found all the theoretical knowledge he needed in the Syllabus of Errors.[21]

The inclination to see in church doctrine a sufficient response to the social question explains the aloofness of Mun and other Legitimists from conservative social theorists like La Tour Du Pin, Frédéric Le Play, Charles Périn, and Claudio Jannet. Many Legitimists greeted Le Play as a farsighted thinker who had given coherent form and intellectual respectability to conservative principles. Chambord himself was said to have greatly admired Le Play's work.[22] Mun appreciated Le Play's opposition to the principles of 1789, his "profundity of perception," and his

20. Discours de M. Chesnelong, May 19–24, 1873, in *Comité catholique de Paris: Assemblée général des comités catholiques de France, 1872–1873* (Paris, 1872–73), 22.

21. Mun, *Ma vocation sociale,* 70–71. As Benjamin F. Martin points out, Mun's motive for taking this position reflected political considerations as well. The Oeuvre des Cercles, he writes, "had very early placed the association under the tutelage of the church and had attracted the attention of Pius IX with their specific praise of the Syllabus in their first appeal. The Pontiff in turn had blessed the *cercles* in a note to de Mun in January 1872. This approbation forestalled the episcopal disfavor that had handicapped earlier social Catholic efforts and was vital to the success of the *cercles.* Joseph Guibert, cardinal-archbishop of Paris, and Felix Dupanloup, bishop of Orleans, . . . had both opposed de Mun's scheme when he had approached them about it in December 1871." Martin adds that "if the *cercles* were to retain the favor of the Holy See, their leader had to tread a narrow doctrinal line" (*Count Albert de Mun: Paladin of the Third Republic* [Chapel Hill, N.C., 1978], 18).

22. See Marvin L. Brown, *The Comte de Chambord: The Third Republic's Uncompromising King* (Durham, N.C., 1964), 15, 164.

"breadth of knowledge," but he felt that the theoretician's words did not sufficiently express "the passion of faith and the impulse of the struggle." He wrote, "The laws of the Decalogue are not sufficient for my soul, smitten with Catholic truth; the experimental method does not grip my intelligence, avid for doctrinal affirmations."[23] Le Play's empirical *économie sociale,* built with an assemblage of artificial word-concepts like *famille souche* and *authorités sociales,* demystified traditional social structures and asked social Catholics to be field investigators rather than militant social activists. For Gabriel de Chaules, Le Play's pretensions as a man of science and an impartial observer threatened Catholic priorities: "Sometimes the economist dominates the philosopher, the utilitarian too readily absorbs the moralist; I would be tempted to say that he has in some measure taken the cause for the effect, and that he attaches too much importance to political economy and not enough to the delicacy of the human conscience."[24] Maignen thought of La Tour Du Pin— who admired Le Play—as more a sociologist than a Christian thinker and spoke of Périn, a Belgian liberal Catholic economist, as a defender of economic liberalism cloaking his ideas in the language of Christian charity.[25]

There was a strong propensity for social Catholics to fear in social

23. Mun, *Ma vocation sociale,* 54.
24. Gabriel de Chaules, "Bibliographie," *Revue Indépendante,* IV (August 1, 1865), 104–105. Le Play, always mentioned and respected, nevertheless remained something of an intellectual exile in the 1870s, being at once too positivist for the Legitimists, too clerical for the republicans, and too reactionary for the liberals. Melun, speaking of Le Play's So-ciété d'Economie Sociale in his *Mémoires,* wrote, "In their sermons, they associate testamentary rights with the Decalogue—a quite troublesome idea that goes so far as to involve the Credo with an economic dogma in which people feel the presence of the Old Regime and the revival of the *droit d'ainesse*" (Andigné, *Un Apôtre de la charité,* 409).
25. Charles Maignen, *Maurice Maignen,* II, 820. Maignen criticized the social Catholic doctrines of the "German school" and the "Austrian school" of La Tour Du Pin, Monsignor Ketteler, Count von Blôme, and others for attempting to "proclaim a positive science." In 1884, he wrote to his brother Charles, "You tell me to buy Le Play, Charles Périn, and Claudio Jannet [a member of the Société d'Economie Sociale]. That's not where to search for the truth but where to take cognizance of modern errors. M. Le Play, of Saint-Simonian origins, arrived at the discovery of the Decalogue after thirty years of social observation. M. Charles Périn is the doctor of Belgium liberalism in political economy" (Maignen, *Maurice Maignen,* II, 820). Mun in a letter to his close associate, Félix de Roquefeuil, in 1877 referred to both the theories of "the Le Play school" and those of liberal Catholic economists like Périn as an "attempt at conservative deism designed to organize a society independently of the church" (Albert de Mun to Felix de Roquefeuil, July 9, 1877, in Charles Mollet's *Albert de Mun, 1872–1890: Exigences doctrinales et Préoccupations sociales chez un laic catholique* [Paris, 1970], Documents, p. 168).

theory the rise of an autonomous intellectual authority apart from Christian doctrine and spirituality. Social theorists, instead of submitting their speculations to the authority of doctrinal exegesis, tended to "move some principles borrowed from moral theology to the level of a sociopolitical theory constructed by natural reason."[26] Within the social Catholic movement, the opposition between the two attitudes to social theory often signalized a power struggle between lay social Catholics and clergymen over control of the character and structure of Catholic organizations. The activists were also divided ideologically between men of ideas like La Tour Du Pin, who believed that institutional reconstruction was crucial and that the social order could be shaped according to certain theoretical positions, and men of practical concern like Melun and Mun, who were interested in results and believed that the relationship between faith and action was experiential and provided for a certain degree of flexibility in the application of principles.

The Legitimists' rejection of social theory also stemmed from their contempt for the abstract and from their certainty that the elements of a durable social reconstruction lay in concrete examples from the past. The opinions they invoked in their opposition to modern French bourgeois society often had more to do with nostalgic romanticism and native anticapitalism than with any well-reasoned Christian doctrine. As Marx understood, proponents of "feudal socialism" were above all concerned with how the "bourgeois regime" created class antagonisms and a revolutionary working-class consciousness "destined to destroy, root and branch, the old order of society."[27] Antoine Blanc de St. Bonnet, an obscure Legitimist writer, made the same observation when he accused the "aristocracy formed by the Revolution" of creating a "people in its own image" who were becoming the "enraged hordes who will one day devastate Europe."[28] As landowners with commercial interests or small-town professionals, most Legitimists had one foot in traditional society and the other in the changing world of capitalist relations. They participated in and accepted the economic results of commercial and industrial capitalism but rejected its social, political, and cultural ramifications. Legitimists wanted a tempered capitalism that could generate profits and

26. Mollet, *Albert de Mun,* 134.
27. Karl Marx and Friedrich Engels, *The Communist Manifesto,* trans. Samuel Moore (Middlesex, Eng., 1967), 106–107.
28. Blanc de St. Bonnet, *Le Légitimité,* 25–26.

progress while preserving the moral order of society. As Falloux told an audience in Angers, competition in business had its advantages but also its disadvantages: "Labor is more independent, but it is more exposed; it encounters fewer obstacles, but it is surrounded by fewer means of support. One can get rich overnight, but one can also more easily, more blindly rush toward ruin."[29] Bourgeois accepted the reality of industrial concentration, but he warned that "desperate competition" created among entrepreneurs an ethic of neglect that contributed to working-class poverty and restlessness. Capitalism, he argued, was irrational and anarchic because it resulted in individual enrichment at the expense of social and economic stability: "Nothing is more agitated, more unstable than the world of business."[30]

Legitimists feared industrial capitalism not because it exploited the productivity of labor and enriched the bourgeoisie but because it created social environments that traditional social institutions could not easily contain. The proletariat was vulnerable to socialism, they argued, because it had become detached from the craft affiliations that had protected native skills, encouraged religious observance, ensured a minimum livelihood, and forced employers to collaborate with employees to regulate working conditions. Moreover, crowded urban slums, long working hours, and unemployment had destroyed family relations by upsetting the reciprocal bonds between parents and children and had led to a breakdown of social discipline not only in the home but also in the factory and the city. In such an environment, they decided, religious and social authorities could neither hold the respect nor shape the moral habits of the community. By disrupting the influences that promoted morality, capitalism seemed destined to deny generation after generation the faith and hope of spiritual consolation; the Legitimists feared that in the wake of the human and cultural desolation capitalism spawned, "insane doctrines" would find willing adherents. Consequently, social Legitimism was less concerned with theorizing about the nature of capitalism than with building a social and institutional infrastructure capable of combating its consequences. What the Legitimists articulated as Christian principles constituted not a doctrine that could stir the masses but a set of architectural guidelines answering to their conviction that the in-

29. Comte Alfred de Falloux, "Discours prononcé à la distribution des prix des Ecoles Chrétiens d'Angers," in *Discours et Mélanges politiques* (2nd ed.; 2 vols.; Paris, 1882), I, 377.
30. Bourgeois, *Le Catholicisme et les Questions sociales,* 51.

frastructures of the past could help establish the kind of society they preferred.

The Legitimists cannot be charged with viewing the misery of the working class as a recompense for individual moral failings. France's social ills, they concurred, were seated not in moral debauchery or laziness but in a milieu conducive to impoverishment, deracination, and dechristianization. If the Legitimists spoke of "moralizing" the proletariat, their object was not simply to induce sound behavior but to create a physical and social environment that could give decisive support to class harmony and traditional values. Their use of terms like *charitable economy* and *Christian social order* was meant to suggest a reconstruction of an economic and associational life effective in eliminating the systemic causes of the moral laxity—indecency, drunkenness, illegitimacy—that, as André Jean Tudesq has documented, many conservatives and liberals deemed at the heart of the social question.[31]

The Legitimists tended to see social problems as proceeding less from the depravity of the poor than from the carelessness and egotism of the rich, whose responsibility it was to improve society, not destabilize it through a blind pursuit of personal gain. For the Legitimists, the term *bourgeoisie* denoted not a specific social category but a political class that governed to the detriment of the common good: it had demonstrated its failure as a ruling class by allowing social relations to degenerate into class warfare. According to Georges de Cadoudal, the Revolution replaced the "tutelary privileges of the old landed proprietors" with the "most odious and corrupt feudalism, that of the bank and the factory." Under the rule of the bourgeoisie, "natural relations founded upon a mutual exchange of obligations and favors, on protection and respect, which in the old social hierarchy united all estates and ranks from the sovereign to the most humble brothelkeeper, disappeared to make way for the relations established by the Code of Procedure, relations of landlords to renters, of debtors to creditors." In a society where "the value of a man was measured by that of his strongbox," where law and language were reduced to a "commercial expression," and where the ruling class practiced fraud and speculation in full view of the public, "the sacred word *duty* . . . fell into disuse" and ceased to have an "all-powerful

31. *Ibid.*, 34–50; Tudesq, *Les Grands Notables en France*, I, 566–71.

influence on the spirits." How, in this context, could the masses learn the value of work, piety, and probity?[32]

The importance of this Legitimist antibourgeois rhetoric lay not so much in its evocation of an ideal past as in its depiction of a society where values and models of behavior descended from above. Legitimism discovered in the behavior and ideology of the bourgeoisie a full explanation of the rejection of authority, of inequality, and of property rights among the masses. It also detected there the reason for socialism's progress among a proletariat justified in thinking it had nothing to gain from the existing order. If a more solid social order was dependent on the compassion and good example of the rich, the solution to the social question was plain: it rested on upper-class paternalism, Christian charity, and the kind of general rechristianization that would permit the internalization of the values necessary for squelching insubordination. By assuming that elites were ultimately responsible for all social ills and gains, the Legitimists endorsed a kind of trickle-down theory of culture that served as the foundation of all their responses to the social question.

Since the Legitimists' own discourse and interests constrained them to formulate paternalistic solutions to the social question, there is little surprise in their lack of interest in promoting democratic and working-class organizations. The Legitimists inevitably viewed democratic action, popular leadership, and working-class participation in Christian-based social organizations as antithetical to their goal of vertical ties of dependence and influence. Moreover, it was impossible for them to imagine that associations based purely on popular initiative could ever be financially sound, let alone effective, untruculent, and suited to a society that operated along lines of organic affinities rather than conflicting class interests. Melun was willing to accede to the demands he anticipated for working-class participation in the management of cooperatives and mutual-aid societies only because he felt it necessary to humor the "prejudices" workers harbored against authority. Even so, he never relinquished his certainty that such associations needed the financial and

---

32. Georges de Cadoudal, *Esquisses morales, historiques et littéraires: Souvenirs de quinze années, 1845–1861* (Paris, 1862), 61–62. Melun saw capitalism as corrupting the morals of the rich because of the vulnerability of "the weak side" of "our society" to the "avidity for money" (Armand de Melun to the Duchesse de Caramen, October 1856, in Andigné's *Un Apôtre de la charité*, 138).

moral patronage of "honorary members" drawn from the elite.[33] In the elaborate models projected by conservative social Catholicism, the working-class *associés* whom the notables were to organize never acquired a human aspect but were either shrouded in silence or presented in stereotyped images vague enough not to jar the notables' sensibilities. The workers who inhabited Legitimist discourse lived in parables: the bad worker, absent from church on Sunday, absent from work on Monday, given over to alcoholism and a complete disregard for family life; or the Christian worker, obedient, respectful, churchgoing, and content to spend the Sabbath around the family hearth. As Jean Baptiste Duroselle has commented, social Catholicism, at least before 1870, "was outside the world of the worker," and the worker, "whatever the diversity of his inclinations, remained foreign to the church and for the most part hostile to it."[34]

In effect, social Legitimism was only partly an attempt to better the condition of the poor. Legitimists were also concerned with redefining the role and function of the notables in French society. Since they believed that the stewardship of the materialistic bourgeoisie had caused the social question to be raised in the first place, the Legitimists sought to force the notables to justify their social authority before God by serving the masses and guiding them toward moral enlightenment. The new ethic, they hoped, would mobilize the ruling class to save itself and France from the next revolution.[35] As Bourgeois explained, the danger faced by society "does not result from the theories of this or that sect; it lies above all in the religious and moral state not of the popular masses alone but of the entire society." To accuse the lower classes of materialism, lack of foresight, or violent intentions was, he declared, so much "hypocritical ranting." If the masses cease to be Christian, "if the multitudes are prey to the spirit of revolt, the example has come from above; if the nations tremble, if the people everywhere foment conspiracies, it is, as David once announced, that the kings of the earth have risen up and that the powerful are in league against the Lord and his Christ."[36]

33. See Rapport fait au nom de la commission chargée d'étudier la situation des classes ouvrières en France, in *Annales,* July 27, 1875, XLIV, annexe 3283.

34. Duroselle, *Le Débuts du catholicisme social,* 706. See Pierre Pierrand, *L'Eglise et les Ouvriers en France, 1840–1940* (Paris, 1984), 19–259.

35. Pierrand, *L'Eglise et les Ouvriers,* 283. See Levillain, *Albert de Mun,* 233.

36. Bourgeois, *Le Catholicisme et les Questions sociales,* 14–15.

This appeal to the ruling class to recognize its social duties gave Legitimist charitable endeavors much of their character and continuity. Melun wrote in his *Mémoires* that the reconciliation of modern society and the church depended on creating for "men of good will a new function, the aim of which would be to call the neglectful into the house of God, to lead them to the threshold, to place them once again, docile and faithful, between the hands of the ministers of religion." He added, "From now on this task must belong to lay Catholics."[37] The manifesto that launched Mun's Oeuvre des Cercles Catholiques des Ouvriers in 1871 reminded "men of the privileged classes" that they "had duties vis-à-vis the workers," and in 1878 Mun told his troops that the "devotion of the upper classes to the popular classes" was a "social paternity" that formed the "fundamental basis of our action."[38] Indeed, Mun asserted that superior social status was a manifestation of God's grace but that it was not to be enjoyed for personal benefit. Rather, he explained, such "received grace" implied a contractual obligation on the part of those who benefited from it to care for and protect "those who are below." His suggestion was that God, in his providential wisdom, had created social inequality in order that men of faith might will themselves to solve the contradiction between rich and poor in accordance with Scripture.[39]

The Legitimists' idea of paternalism was directly linked to the conservative social Catholic conception of charity as a model for sound social relationships. Charity not only could "attenuate [the] age-old antagonism between misery and opulence and fill the gap between those who swim in abundance and those who lack necessities," it could create a reciprocal bond between giver and receiver that the Legitimists felt had the power to redefine the nature of social encounters.[40] Christian giving accorded well with the Legitimists' concern about creating social conditions that engendered respect for authority, social deference, compassion by the elite, and class harmony. But charity encompassed more than almsgiving and philanthropy; it came to serve the Legitimists as an or-

37. Armand de Melun, in Duroselle's *Les Débuts du catholicisme social,* 213.

38. Mun, *Ma vocation sociale,* 73; Gabriel de Belcastel, Charles Chesnelong, and Albert de Mun, *Aurore du salut de la France dans les trois oeuvres des Cercles Catholiques d'Ouvriers, des Comités Catholiques et du Voeu National au Sacré Coeur* (Perpignan, 1878), 21.

39. Albert de Mun, "Discours de clôture de la IIIe assemblée générale de l'Oeuvre des Cercles," in Pierrand's *L'Eglise et les Ouvriers,* 283–85.

40. Barthélemy Pocquet, *Essai sur l'assistance publique, son histoire, ses principes, sa organisation actuelle* (Paris, 1877), vii.

ganizational principle that could be applied to the operations of a Catholic social organization, to the factory, and to society at large. For social Catholics, charity was above all a collective enterprise, and it had the same place in Legitimist thinking that fraternity had in the social conceptions of the republican Left. As *fraternité* projected an image of society in which class barriers were effaced through democracy, egalitarianism, and patriotism, charity signaled a concept of social bonds that were equally constitutive of civil and political society but that did not imply an equality of conditions or a social cement based purely on the human will. As the social principle behind Legitimist efforts to build a Christian social order, charity came to stand for the totality of reparative social activity undertaken to defuse class conflict and evangelize the masses. Having framed the solution in this way, social Catholics committed themselves to a broad social apostolate that had to address the moral and social consequences of economic forces that were transforming the material conditions and cultural values of an entire society.[41]

It is tempting to interpret social Legitimism as, at best, a pious and self-righteous strategy of social control and, at worst, a quixotic attempt to hold back social and economic change. Tudesq has argued that, by asking the social question in moral rather than social terms, the Legitimists were compelled to seek solutions to social indiscipline, debauchery, and vice rather than poverty and exploitation.[42] Brian Fitzpatrick has asserted that Legitimists in the Gard exercised a form of "social control" over the peasants that was more subtle than what other notables were prone to, because the Legitimists employed "traditional paternalism" rather than "brutal police repression."[43] Though it is true that the Legitimists deplored social violence as a symptom of, rather than a remedy for, social disintegration, it is an oversimplification to take their preference for "moral solutions" as an alternative attempt to manage social change and quell lower-class rebelliousness. The Legitimists also wanted a qualitatively different society from the one liberal capitalism promised, because they feared that the nineteenth century was well along in the unprecedented experiment of producing a working class with no links to the Christian past. The Legitimists were, therefore, compelled to become not social managers but architects of rechristianization. Catholicism in-

41. Bourgeois, *Le Catholicisme et les Questions sociales*, 144.
42. Tudesq, *Les Grands Notables en France*, I, 217–21.
43. Fitzpatrick, *Catholic Royalism*, 128.

evitably led social Catholics beyond liberalism and the status quo because the interaction of faith and the principles of nineteenth-century political economy left the principles of political economy transformed.[44]

What role would the monarchy play in the social reconstruction? Just as the Legitimists hoped that a restored monarchy would accede to their decentralist plans, they also wanted a regime that would authorize and validate the Christian regeneration of society. For all their criticism of the Empire and the Republic as godless states, their ultimate vision of a Christian social order did not necessarily imply a particular form of government. That the social Catholics and clericals momentarily opted for a Christian prince was only a consequence of tradition and an accident of history rather than the result of profound conviction. As will become apparent, the elaboration of a Christian response to the social question was far more compelling to many Catholics than was the blundering royalist political strategy.

44. DuBoys, *Des principes de la Révolution française*, 283.

CHAPTER VI

 The Method of *Encadrement*

PATERNALISM, CHARITY, and rechristianization constituted the ideological foundations of social Legitimism. The practical application of these principles underwent significant modification as Legitimist social Catholics came to deploy charitable and paternalist solutions to an ever-widening range of social and economic problems. Time-honored and personal acts of charity continued to be practiced and recommended, but the crises of the 1840s revealed that the social question involved much more than the existence of indigence, that charitable giving, even if organized on a grand scale, was insufficient to the needs it addressed, and that the social and cultural damage wrought by bourgeois liberalism and industrial capitalism would require the active and constant intervention of *propriétaires, patrons,* and the state in order to construct institutions to regulate the lives of the workers and the poor while materially assisting them. The diversification of Legitimist social activity and the growing statism and antiliberalism of leading social Catholics manifested itself in the creation of organizations, societies, and associations that were meant to guide workers, children, and other *assistés* from the cradle to the grave.

ORGANIZED CHARITY AND PATRONAGE FOR THE WORKING CLASS

In 1868, Georges de Cadoudal, a descendant of the Vendean hero, published the story of a certain Marquis de L—— whose generosity toward the poor youth of his commune brought reproach from his

154

friends, who derided his "charitable follies." Smiling as always, the good marquis responded that he was merely fulfilling the duty imposed by his birth. One day, as he was sitting at table, a young peasant, Paul, tremblingly asked to speak with him. The marquis rose and invited the stranger to join in the meal. After dinner, Paul revealed that he intended to leave the village, where he was employed as a tailor, to seek his fortune in Paris. The boy's mother had sent him to the marquis because, knowing his reputation, she foresaw that he would give her son aid and counsel. The marquis attributed Paul's illusions to his age and the times, and encouraged him to return to his family. He offered the youth a small gift of charity to help him in his quest for happiness. "In Paris," he said, "city of both good and evil, for every 2 who get rich, 998 disappear. How they survive God only knows." But the youth was confident of his strength to overcome the obstacles; he asked only that the marquis have the same confidence. "Paris it is," the marquis acceded, and as the peasant left he was discreetly handed a "heavy purse."

But the tale is not finished. Twenty years later, the tailor had realized his dreams; meanwhile the marquis, always prodigal, was reduced to a disquieting impoverishment, which he bore without complaint. One sunrise, the old man received a letter from Paul, whom he had entirely forgotten: "Paul offers to the marquis a government bond that rightly belongs to the recipient in remembrance of a sacred debt contracted by a little peasant he helped with a paternal solicitude that will not be forgotten until that youth's last breath."[1]

In its simplicity and its sentiment, this quaint parable captures the desired essence of charity: personal, mutually beneficial, morally salutary, a sacred bond between two souls. Yet it tells more about the moral universe of the obscure Breton nobles of which Cadoudal wrote than about the organized, collective charitable networks in which so many of his peers collaborated. In 1868, while Cadoudal was waxing sentimental about Paul and the marquis, an editor of the Legitimist *Gazette de France* declared that individual acts of charity "could never suffice for all the needs of a numerous society." Indeed, to keep Paul on the right track, the purse offered by the marquis would never be enough. Who would ensure him an elementary Christian education, care for him in sickness,

1. Georges de Cadoudal, *Faits et Récits contemporains: Nouveau Recueil anecdotique* (Paris, 1860), 87–88.

and prevent unforeseen difficulties from robbing him of his savings? For that, charity had to be more than a personal and individual act; it had to be a collective and massive effort on the part of the church, lay Catholics, and perhaps even the state.[2]

In 1868, exhortations about the insufficiency of private charity were not new, but they carried ever greater urgency because the Legitimists believed too few Catholic notabìes had made an effort to support the extensive array of charitable organizations founded from the 1830s on. The earliest, largest, and most durable of those was the Saint Vincent de Paul Society, established in 1833 by the liberal Catholic Frédéric Ozanam and a small group of young *universitaires* and law students.[3] Going beyond earlier charitable groups like the Saint Joseph Society, which was linked to the government of the Restoration and concentrated on encouraging acts of personal charity among the elite, the new society sought to organize a reconciliation of classes by creating "conferences" in which members might fortify their faith and the faith of the poor through the practice of charity in common. From the beginning, the Saint Vincent de Paul Society espoused a degree of centralization unseen among earlier organizations.[4] The original members, mostly students and young liberal Catholics, sought to separate clearly the church and Catholic activities from politics, and especially from Legitimism, and indeed they were seen as upstarts by the Legitimist notables who dominated existing charitable groups. But as the society gained adherents and vigorously recruited among dedicated young Catholics, it inevitably attracted a large number of the Legitimist aristocracy and bourgeoisie, who constituted the "segment of the world of the notables most attached to Catholicism."[5]

Expansion slowly changed the character of the Saint Vincent de Paul Society. "The movement of young students," writes François Lebrun, "became an association of Catholic notables, often Legitimists."[6] Although it remained nominally apolitical, the Legitimist presence among its leadership led to a growing association between social Catholicism and royalism in the minds of many officials during the 1840s, and the

2. J. Bourgeois, *Le Catholicisme et les Questions sociales,* 183–84.
3. For the history of the Saint Vincent de Paul Society, see Schall, *Un Disciple de Saint Vincent de Paul,* and Foucault, *La Société de St. Vincent de Paul.*
4. Lebrun, *Histoire des catholiques en France,* 344.
5. Tudesq, *Les Grands Notables en France,* I, 439–40.
6. Lebrun, *Histoire des catholiques en France,* 344.

organization remained suspect under the successive regimes. Between 1839 and 1844, the society's general council in Paris came to include such royalists as Vincent de Paul de Bailly, J. Gossin, de Baudicourt, Alban de Villeneuve-Bargemont, Henri de Raincey, Armand de Melun, and Adolphe Baudon alongside liberals like Frédéric Ozanam; by 1848, Baudon, son of a *receveur général* and a regent of the Bank of France, became its general secretary. The same royalist evolution occurred in major urban conferences in Lyon, Montpellier, and Marseille, all centers of considerable Catholic and Legitimist influence. In Montpellier, the young students in the organization were superseded in 1843 by the ruling landed Legitimist oligarchs of the region, men like Charles de Sainte-Maure, the Vicomte de Vögué, and Victor de Bonald.[7] In Marseille, where efforts to establish a conference floundered until 1844, the first success was achieved by Legitimist merchants and landowners—Henri Bergasse, the Marquis de Sabran, Barthélemy de Camprieu, Félix de Chomel, François Marie de Roux, and Gavoty de Philemon—who constituted a representative sample of the "high society of Marseille."[8]

The society experienced impressive growth between the 1840s and 1861, when the Second Empire dissolved the general council in an attempt to weaken the group and contain what was seen as a threat to the state's political control of the working class. In 1854, the *Bulletin* of the Dijon conference had admitted that the expansion had been "no where foreseen" and attributed it, of course, to the "invisible hand of providence." The *Bulletin* continued, "What is noteworthy is that this progress is being accomplished under the most diverse conditions, in the countryside as well as in the cities, in the heart of completely agricultural regions as well as in commercial centers and in places of manufacture, often under circumstances that one would find accidental."[9] In 1839, there were already 32 conferences—12 in Paris—and 1,068 *confrères;* by 1843 there were 127 conferences and 3,479 active members.[10] In 1844, the urban conferences counted no fewer than 5,000 members. As of the start of 1852, the society included 490 conferences in France and 878 in foreign

7. Tudesq, *Les Grands Notables en France,* I, 199–201; Lebrun, *Histoire des catholiques en France,* 344.
8. *La Société de St. Vincent de Paul à Marseille: Histoire d'un siècle, 1844–1944* (Marseille, 1944), 8–9.
9. *Société de St. Vincent de Paul: Conseil central de Dijon* (Dijon, 1854), 4–5.
10. Tudesq, *Les Grands Notables en France,* I, 439–40.

countries, and by the time of the Persigny circular in 1861 disbanding the general council, the society had 1,549 French conferences and 3,406 abroad, with a total membership, according to Jean Baptiste Duroselle, of approximately 32,500.[11]

Provincial centers flourished as well. In 1853, the central council of the diocese of Dijon reported 37 conferences, 1,023 active members, 339 honorary members, 76 aspiring members, and total receipts of over 56,700 francs from sources that included dues, gifts, subscriptions, and lottery returns. The revenue was spent, typically, on visits to 1,391 poor families, religious instruction, and works of patronage, as well as on the distribution of bread, meat, clothing, firewood, and money.[12] In the Tarn—at Albi, Cordes, and Castres—conferences were created between 1847 and 1865, and in Castres the budget of receipts grew from 2,454 francs in 1852 to 35,654 francs in 1865.[13] At Marseille, the number of families visited grew from 577 in 1848 to 1,000 in 1862, and expenditures rose in the same period from 19,997 francs to 68,874 francs.[14]

Even the smallest communes had conferences. The conference of Rodez, in Aveyron, founded in 1840, grew to 272 active members by 1882, and family visits numbered 204 at their peak in 1856. In the 1850s, *confrères* from Rodez established further conferences in the tiny communes of the region and left small circles of active adherents. In St. Geniez d'Olt, the fifteen-member conference visited 87 families in 1853, apprenticed 3 young workers, and maintained a library of two hundred volumes. In the arrondissement of the Millau, with a total population of just over 15,000 in 1876, the society gave religious instruction to 407 schoolboys out of a male school-age population that could not have exceeded 1,500.[15]

Although the society at times helped care for the orphans and victims of epidemics and civil unrest—usually with the help of the Sisters of Charity—its more customary offerings included elementary religious instruction, common prayer, and especially *visites à domiciles,* in which members went into the homes of the poor, distributed food and other

---

11. Lebrun, *Histoire des catholiques en France,* 344; Société de St. Vincent de Paul, *Documents rélatifs à la Société de St. Vincent de Paul* (Paris, 1862), 33; Duroselle, *Les Débuts du catholicisme social,* 550.

12. Rapport du procureur général de Dijon, October 23, 1854, in BB (30) 410, AN; Tableau Statistique pour 1853, *Société de St. Vincent de Paul: Conseil Central de Dijon.*

13. Faury, *Cléricalisme et Anticléricalisme,* 313.

14. *La Société de St. Vincent de Paul à Marseille,* 54–55.

15. B. Combes de Patris, *La Société de Saint Vincent de Paul en Rouergue* (Rodez, 1960).

necessities like coal and clothing, and tried to gain the goodwill of entire families while evangelizing them. The society occasionally provided the poor with travel money, temporary lodging, and medical assistance, and recommended *assistés* to employers seeking to hire. In 1853, at Dijon, it furnished 5,153 francs in aid to families; that came to only about ten centimes to each one per day for a year.[16] The volume of the provisions distributed was less important to the operations of the conferences, however, than the kind of personal, intimate contact they could offer, exemplifying, members believed, the very essence of charity.

In the society's missionary work, the *confrères* preached a message that blended hope and resignation and was appropriate to an organization more interested in winning converts and exerting moral influence than in finding solutions to social ills. The vice-president of the central council of the Dijon conference, M. Foisoet, outlined the morality-nurturing intent and hoped-for effect of the *visites à domiciles:*

> Instead of tossing into the hand of the begger a sterile alm that blazons the importunity of his suffering, we visit the poor in their cubbyholes, in their naked houses . . . ; we sit by their side, we make ourselves the confidants of their pains, the comforters of their sufferings, the supporters of their frailties and their sadness; we are less benevolent protectors for them than sincere and devoted friends whom providence, in its inexhaustible compassion, has blessed with its loyal care and kind affection. . . . We work without respite, not only to provide the bread that must satisfy their bodily needs but still and above all to cure their souls and their wounds, to lift them from their abasement, to enlighten them about their immortal destiny, to assure them of the bliss of heaven in exchange, and as recompense, for their destitution on earth.

Foisoet proudly noted in his annual report that the "affection" inspired by the *confrères* had probably succeeded in "introducing some good sentiments into . . . hearts" and had encouraged a "good number of conversions." The local clergy had attested a "notable number of returns to Easter communion on the part of persons who had stayed away for many years."[17]

16. Rapport du procureur général de Dijon, October 23, 1854, in BB (30) 410, AN.
17. *Société de St. Vincent de Paul: Conseil Central de Dijon,* 6–7, 19; Rapport du procureur général de Dijon, October 23, 1854, in BB (30) 410, AN. See also Pierre Pierrand, *La Vie ouvrière à Lille sous le Second Empire* (Paris, 1865), 395.

Although the Saint Vincent de Paul Society endured beyond the difficult years of the Second Empire, it represented a rather limited and traditional response to the social question, despite its innovations and its formidable organization. Depending for the most part on private initiative and focusing on the problem of indigence in general rather than specifically on that of the industrial working class, it tended to flourish only in areas where Catholicism was deeply rooted, where local officials were benevolent, and where recruitment was easy. The society's efforts were clearly inadequate in regions like St. Etienne, Paris, and the Nord, where industrialization and a rural exodus had spawned the growth of suburbs and where the lack of a traditional social infrastructure had contributed to the rise of a social democratic labor movement. The society had the same problems as the church in providing a parochial organization adequate to the swelling urban population. The conferences of Paris and Marseille, as widespread as they were, failed to attract large numbers of factory workers and seemed most effective in the old quarters of towns like Toulouse and Lille, where the organization's numerous activities served a relatively well settled artisan population and provided aid to the truly destitute at whom its activities were primarily aimed. Moreover, the society seemed to have won the most categorical praise among Legitimists who, like Ferdinand Béchard and Claude Marie Raudot, abhorred any type of state intervention and saw in the group's private, personal, and localized methods the best means to address the social question in the context of the priorities of administrative decentralization.

Béchard viewed private charitable associations run by notables as a replacement for "aristocratic mores and wealth."[18] His assessment indicates that many Legitimists were convinced that the Revolution had damaged the social order by destroying the ability of intermediary bodies to ameliorate social conditions. Echoing this conviction, Armand de Melun declared that French society had entered an era in which stabilizing institutions no longer existed. "Before the Revolution," he told an international meeting of charitable associations, "powerful institutions still stood, with great wealth and great privileges that brought them important duties: the aristocracy, the clergy, the religious orders enriched by

18. Béchard, De l'administration, II, 197. Béchard preferred that local institutions make up for the insufficiency of private resources, and he denounced those who had an "affection only for public revenues, with an enormous budget." He added, "Two things are necessary for public charity: local liberties and religious liberty" (p. 198).

centuries of piety were wealthy enough, powerful enough to create
schools and hospitals and to ensure their perpetuity. . . . The French
Revolution by striking at the aristocracy, the clergy, and the corporations
all at once . . . destroyed the forces capable of creating and maintaining
well-founded institutions."[19] In other words, capitalism, urbanization,
and institutional reform had permitted many workers and peasants to
live outside the orbit of traditional family and ecclesiastical supervision.

It was on the basis of that line of thought about the social question
that the Saint Vincent de Paul Society and other Legitimist bodies elaborated their strategy of social *encadrement*. Duroselle argued in his important study of the beginnings of social Catholicism in France that although
an important organization, the Saint Vincent de Paul Society "was not,
properly speaking, a manifestation of social Catholicism" because it did
not aim "to reform a defective social structure in order to improve the
lot of the poor."[20] Yet, if Duroselle's definition of social reform as the
reordering of a defective society were accepted, it would become impossible to label any early social Catholic association as reformist. The definition of social reform as a gradual modification of social and economic
relationships through legislative intervention aimed at preventing a complete transformation of existing social structures is a relatively recent
idea. In the nineteenth century, French notables typically defined *réforme*
as either moral regeneration or a simple modification of institutions in
the interest of making them function more effectively.[21] Catholics in particular were apt to see the notion of *réforme* in the same spirit in which
the church approached the Catholic Reformation of the sixteenth century, and thus they intended either an inner renewal of the individual
Christian or a correction of certain institutional abuses that were imped-
ing the clergy's apostolic efficacy.[22] The idea that society could itself be
reformed was altogether foreign to them, since they viewed the social
order as, to quote the abbé Jacques Paul Migne, the "work of time,
events, beliefs, and mores—a historical creation constituted by generations in their respect for traditions, laws, and rights that are founded on

19. Armand de Melun, "La Charité en France," *Revue d'économie charitable*, I (1862),
412.
20. Duroselle, *Les Débuts du catholicisme social*, 173.
21. See Emile Littré, *Dictionnaire de la langue française* (Paris, 1883), 1546.
22. *Encyclopédie théologique; ou, Série de dictionnaire sur toutes les parties de la science religieuse* (7 vols.; Paris, 1846), VII, 745.

preexisting facts independent of the will of its present members."[23] To believe that such a historical creation could be the subject of theoretical examination and conscious reform was precisely the error the Legitimists ascribed to the revolutionaries of 1789. They therefore preferred to speak of regeneration or reparation, to stress the spiritual intent of their actions and their desire to reconstruct the bonds of association and deference they believed the Revolution had destroyed. By adopting a hierarchical pattern and accepting the structure of the French Catholic church, the Saint Vincent de Paul Society signified its identification with the established order.[24] That tendency was already clear in 1844 to one Christian socialist writer who pointed out in the pages of L'Atelier that the aim of the Saint Vincent de Paul Society was "to make the workers accept, for the longest time possible, their inferior social condition."[25]

It was not social reform that Legitimists envisioned but the creation of a network of institutions and associations that would envelop the poor in a web of morally salubrious social influences, teach them the values of forbearance and hard work, and bring them back to the church. What struck them most about modern society was not the growing inequality to be encountered there but the diminishing power of traditional social authorities to influence the lives of the popular classes, and the replacement of the older hierarchical lines of authority with horizontal bonds of solidarity that induced the lower classes to act autonomously to raise their own condition. Cut loose from the forces of family, religion, traditional production, and social obedience, the poor were in their daily social encounters separated from the social agents—the *curés, bons maîtres,* charitable elites, and conscientious landowners—who seriously undertook the lessening of class tensions and who by personal example pointed the way to desirable conduct and prepared the poor to accept the transmission of traditional values. Legitimist social action was accordingly intended to re-create the ligatures of social influence that could orient workers and the indigent away from the dangerous moral influence of café owners and socialists. That required the establishment of social institutions to serve as surrogates for the "powerful institutions" destroyed by the French Revolution.

The Saint Vincent de Paul Society occupied a special place in the his-

23. *Nouvelle Encyclopédie théologique* (47 vols.; Paris, 1852), XIX, 810.
24. Duroselle, *Les Débuts du catholicisme social,* 21.
25. *L'Atelier,* January, 1844, in Pierrand's *L'Eglise et les Ouvriers,* 136.

tory of French social Catholicism because it was the first organization to define solutions to social ills through the *encadrement* of the lower classes within an ever-widening circle of clubs, organizations of patronage, and other private and public social services.[26] That intention required a definition of charity enlarged to accommodate the inexhaustible variety of social encounters that workers and the poor might experience in their passage from birth to death. As Armand de Melun told a friend in 1840, charity was to "replace all the powers and hierarchies abolished by the Revolution; it will reestablish . . . those bonds, those relations of clientage, that in the past were the prerogative of birth and fortune. Charity alone can revive all these fallen powers and can take the place of faltering authority and abolished deference."[27]

In this light, it is easy to see why the Saint Vincent de Paul Society quickly began to diversify its activities by creating ancillary groups. The Saint François Régis Society, founded before the Saint Vincent de Paul Society but later annexed or associated with its conferences, acted to facilitate religious marriages for the lower classes and to legitimize their natural children. Many conferences set up *patronages d'apprentis* to provide working-class youth with religious instruction, access to the principles of wise economy, and edifying ways to occupy their leisure time, all in the interest of seeing that they preserved their faith and "religious habits" and became good workers and Christians. The society also promoted the Oeuvre des Militaires, offering elementary instruction and alms to draftees. The Saint Francis Xavier Society existed primarily to evangelize and instruct adult workers in Lille and elsewhere, and the Oeuvre de Sainte-Famille, founded by the senator Charles Kolb-Bernard, attempted to enroll whole families "under the banner of Saint Vincent de Paul" and form "associations . . . between working-class families, with the objective of allowing them to leave their isolation by establishing between them a union of prayer, bonds of affection, and reciprocal assistance."[28] When, in the 1860s, Amédée de Gouvello sought

26. Pierrand, "Un Grand Bourgeois de Lille," 385. Pierrand writes, "What the worker required was 'permanent education,' that of school, patronage, and *cercle*. . . . The worker is a *patronné*: for the Catholics of Lille the social question came down to that" (*La Vie ouvrière*, 416).

27. Armand de Melun to Anne Sophie Swetchine, July 12, 1840, in Andigné's *Un Apôtre de la charité*, 392.

28. Pierrand, *La Vie ouvrière*, 398–99; Pierrand, "Un Grand Bourgeois de Lille," 387–89.

to build agricultural colonies for rural orphans, he appealed to the general council of the society to help provide political support and funds and to grant him permission to recruit nuns from nearby convent schools.[29]

In Rennes, under the leaderhip of Paul Vert, son of a silk merchant from Lyon and himself director of a *usine à gaz* and president of the local Saint Francis Xavier Society, a similar network of associations to surround, supervise, and instruct poor and working-class youths, adults, and retirees was established. In an attempt to ensure that "even when apprenticeship is finished," young workers would "not be abandoned," the Association de la Providence organized diverse feminine orders and lay Catholic patronesses affiliated with the Saint Vincent de Paul Society to distribute necessities, feed orphans, care for the sick in hospices, hospitals, and asylums, run crèches, and give "free religious instruction" to adult workers.[30]

Patronage d'apprentis for working-class youth of ages eleven to sixteen best exemplified the strategy of *encadrement*. Patronage was meant to guard working-class children from the bad influence of the city, where parents worked long hours seven days a week, where schooling ended at an early age, and where church attendance was low. Although hardly original in its intent, the *patronage d'apprentis* did address typically urban conditions. The first of such undertakings began slowly in Paris in the early 1840s through the initiative of Melun and the general council of the Saint Vincent de Paul Society. By 1848, they had spread to Lille, Lyon, Marseille, Limoges, Nancy, Bordeaux, and other provincial centers of industry. In 1847, the society's *patronage d'apprentis* and Melun's Oeuvre des Apprentis recruited as many as two thousand youths in Paris alone.[31]

According to Melun, efforts of patronage were designed to "overcome some gaps" in public and organized charity, by becoming an "entire system of supervisory action over society," concentrating the objectives of the "upper classes" above all on fashioning a new generation of Christian workers.[32] In 1872, R. P. Vincent de Paul de Bailly de Surcy stated that the essential role of youth patronage was to provide working-class youth with what the family and the corporation had once supplied.

29. See Amédée de Gouvello, *Le Dépopulation des campagnes: Les Asiles ruraux et les Orphelinats agricoles* (Paris, 1869).

30. Paul Sebastien Vert, *Des mesures charitables organisées dans la ville de Rennes contre la mendicité* (Paris, 1856), 3–5.

31. Duroselle, *Les Débuts du catholicisme social,* 186–93.

32. *Ibid.,* 186.

In a "*monde-ouvrier,* separated from the church," he explained, "no great social institution watches over the youth of the workshops." By focusing on the morality and religion as well as the work life of the young labor force, *patronage d'apprentis* promised to prevent the laboring poor from "rising up against society like a devastating wave." Bailly de Surcy told his audience, "Patronage constitutes a little society in the image of the church, designed to re-create the reign of God in the souls of its *patroné.*"[33]

Typically, young workers or working-class *écoliers* were enrolled in an association, given religious and moral instruction by priests or by the brothers of Saint Vincent de Paul, and taught about saving wages and the proper conduct in the workshop. Sometimes they were placed with a *bon maître* whose *atelier* was regularly visited to check on the progress of the *patroné.* The association tried to ensure that bosses were holding up their end of the bargain by running Christian establishments where the Sabbath was observed as a day of rest.[34] On Sundays, the associations provided a day of prayer, meals, and recreation for the young apprentices. According to Maurice Maignen, a typical Sunday at the Patronage de la Rue de Regard followed a structured schedule:

9:00–10:00 A.M.	Recreation and reception of *livrets*
10:00–11:00 A.M.	Drawing class
11:00 A.M.	Dinner of soup, bread, and dessert
11:30 A.M. to 12:00 M.	Recreation
12:00 M.–1:45 P.M.	Religious instruction and mass at Saint Suplice
1:45 P.M.	Reading, appeals for the savings fund, and lottery
2:30 P.M.	Recreation and class in computation
4:30 P.M.	Salutations at Saint Nicolas chapel
4:45 P.M.	Second meal: bread, wine, meat, and fruit

33. Bailly de Surcy, "Rapport sur les patronage d'apprentis," April 4–6, 1872, in *Comité catholique de Paris,* 301–303.

34. Often the Frères de Saint Vincent de Paul ran a *comité de placement* that chose *maîtres* for young men. Contracts were signed between the *maître* and the society to ensure the "moral and material interests of the apprentice." A *comité de patronage* visited the *patronnés* at work and school, "encouraging zeal, reprimanding laziness, rewarding their efforts, backing up or replacing the vigilance of parents, preventing or relieving conflicts that arise from the application of contracts, and fulfilling at once the mission of a *conseil de famille* and that of a *tribunal de conciliation*" (Rapport de Melun à l'assemblée générale de Oeuvre des Apprentis et des Jeunes Ouvriers, 1875, in Andigné's *Un Apôtre de la charité,* 173).

5:15 P.M.	Recreation and singing class
6:00 P.M.	Promenade (in springtime)
8:00 P.M.	Departure

Night courses were offered for those who worked during the hours of regular activities, and libraries were stocked with *bons livres* by such authors as Joseph de Maistre, Louis Veuillot, François de Fénelon, and Jacques Bénigne Bossuet.[35]

The elaborate methods of youth patronage were the first steps beyond pure charity toward a concept of neighborhood rehabilitation that addressed the proletariat directly and sought to restructure the pattern of working-class life. By focusing on the workplace as well as on home and leisure, youth patronage prefigured the Christian workshop that became the heart of Legitimist attempts to update the Old Regime *corps de métiers,* which envisioned making the workplace part of the overall *encadrement* of the working class (see Chapter VII). Before 1871, many social Catholics saw youth patronage as completing the effort that the existing charitable groups made toward surrounding the workers with morally amending influences from childhood to old age. By the establishment of the Oeuvre de Grand Patronage beside the Saint Francis Xavier Society and the Saint Vincent de Paul Society in Lille in 1849, Kolb-Bernard intended to construct a "trilogy that the workers could not evade."[36] Melun, when his own Oeuvre des Apprentis was getting off the ground in 1842, wrote to Madame Swetchine expressing the hope that the new organization would close the "entire circle of a worker's life; after having given him protection and guidance in his infancy and prepared for him a moral and Christian apprenticeship in his youth, we can cultivate the seeds sown in these early years during the age of liberty and family life. Finally, that joy which until now did not come from the schools, and which stopped at the thresholds, can be made to penetrate into the domestic foyer, into the home, and into the habits of the people."[37]

35. Andigné, *Un Apôtre de la charité,* 71–79; Charles Maignen, *Maurice Maignen,* I, 150–51; Duroselle, *Les Débuts du catholicisme social,* 187–95. This schedule conformed to the rules decreed by the Saint Vincent de Paul Society's council in Paris.

36. Pierrand, *La Vie ouvrière,* 405–406.

37. Armand de Melun to Anne Sophie Swetchine, July 25, 1842, in Andigné's *Un Apôtre de la charité,* 179. See also Discours de Henri Jouin, in *Comité catholique de Paris,* May 19–24, 1873, p. 207.

ARMAND DE MELUN AND THE QUESTION
OF STATE INTERVENTION

The Revolution of 1848 brought the social question to the center of political debate and paved the way for the full return of Legitimists to political life. In an atmosphere increasingly marked by a reactionary and defiant antisocialism among the Party of Order, the Legitimists were forced to reexamine their preconceptions about the role of the state in solving social problems. Prior to the Second Republic, when as many as a hundred Legitimists sat in the Assembly, very few conservatives believed the state to have any business in the relationship between workers and *patrons* besides periodic arbitration or repression. The Legitimists were as wary as the Orleanists when it came to using tax revenue for social programs, but their paternalism and their fascination with institutional structures inclined them to tinker with the underbudgeted, and largely secularized and centralized, system of public assistance inherited from the revolutionary period, rather than to reject it outright. As forces on the Right and the Left joined to pass France's first series of social legislation between 1848 and 1851, a sort of consensus emerged among Legitimists on the legitimacy and utility of limited state social programs. Armand de Melun was, through his writings, legislative influence, and social action, more responsible for this change in attitude than anyone else.

During the 1840s, Melun's own views on the social question evolved beyond an initial emphasis on charity and patronage. Before 1848, the discussions within the Société d'Economie Charitable had focused to a large extent on preparing arguments for the legal reduction of the workday for children and for a ban on employing children under eight years of age. Although a law accomplishing those ends was passed in March, 1841, Melun remained critical of the Chamber's unwillingness to increase its effectiveness and stiffen enforcement. In accepting state intervention in principle, the Société d'Economie Charitable began to elaborate the concept of *prévoyance,* which envisioned the encouragement of joint worker-*patron* associations, to sponsor retirement funds and credit facilities and serve as mutual-aid societies. The objective was to assist the proletariat in dealing with some of the involuntary causes of poverty: sickness, unemployment, and death.

Practical considerations led Melun to an increasingly complex view of the social question and to the conviction that intermittent charitable activity would always be insufficient to solve a problem that appeared to have an infinite number of causes and ramifications. Moreover, if, as he believed, social ills were partly manifestations of the institutional wreckage of the Revolution, the monarchy must have played a role in relieving social misery in the past; and if the Revolution destroyed the "powerful institutions" the Old Regime had supported, what agency other than the modern state was wealthy and powerful enough to respond adequately to the resulting collective suffering? Would a civil society damaged by the Revolution ever be resilient enough to generate autonomous solutions to the social question? If rich and poor were ever to be reconciled, if the working class was to be brought back to the church, religious and political elites had to work together and demonstrate that the system was not exclusively geared to the interests of wealth and property. Melun's statism, and that of other social Catholics, arose from the tension between the logic of his own analysis of the Revolution and the apparent inadequacy of private organized charity.[38]

In a famous article entitled "De l'intervention de la société pour prévenir et soulager la misère," published in the *Annales de la charité* in 1848 and widely distributed in pamphlet form, Melun repeated that charity was insufficient and concluded that the state had certain "duties" to fulfill toward alleviating the kinds of misery addressed in earlier debates on *prévoyance*.[39] Even more controversial, though, was the justification he offered of state intervention on the basis of an abstract and collectivist definition of society that challenged not only liberal individualism but the Legitimists' own concept of an organic union of autonomous, hierarchical communities. Melun asserted instead that society was a "great association of mutual defense, assurance, and protection formed by God himself between men, to which each brings a small part of what he can and what he possesses in order to preserve the entire share of the rest and

38. Armand de Melun wrote that private charity, "in the present conditions, after the abolition of religious properties, a part of which formed the patrimony of the poor, would be completely unable to alleviate misery if it were abandoned to its own forces." He asserted that the charitable individual "was limited to the restrained proportions of individual action," and that "in order to develop his works, [he] does not dispose of the social power that alone can turn a good thought into a general public institution. . . . The state alone can change a demand into a reform, an idea into an institution. . . . Often one simple article of law can do more against pauperism than millions [of francs]" (*De l'intervention de la société pour prévenir et soulager la misère* [Paris, 1848], 17). See also Armand de Melun, Mémoire aux Chambre sur quelques questions de charité publique, 1847, in Andigné's *Un Apôtre de la charité*, 362.

39. Armand de Melun, *De l'intervention,* 4.

to obtain by the best employment of their common resources what each in his isolation could never attain."[40] Although he was quick to distinguish between his definition of society as a "great association" and socialism, which envisioned "putting in common . . . all work and all revenue at the expense of property and the human personality," he was no kinder toward liberals, whom he accused of viewing society as a "mechanism without entrails that leaves people to their own uncertain destinies."[41] Nevertheless, by blurring the distinction between state and society that was dear to the liberals and by placing the collective responsibility for society in the hands of the state, which he called the focus of "social force," and not the church, charitable groups, and local communities that were dear to the Legitimists, he engendered bitter resistance from the Party of Order and opened himself to accusations that he was a socialist.

In 1849, Melun was elected to the Legislative Assembly from Ille-et-Vilaine and quickly called for setting up a commission to study the social question and introduce legislation. Coming on the heels of the June Days and the Party of Order's repudiation of the national workshops, Melun's attempts to promote new social legislation estranged him from many leaders of the majority. Liberals like the Comte de Montalembert and Louis Adolphe Thiers protested that state intervention threatened to deprive the *patronat* of its freedom of action, family heads of their authority, and the working class of its *liberté de travail*. Many Legitimists feared that even timid social programs would extend the power of the central bureaucracy and cause increased taxation. Melun, in a letter to his associate, Comte Edouard Le Camus, complained that Claude Raudot and Ferdinand Béchard, both members of his commission, "could think of nothing but exaggerated decentralization."[42] Indeed, the eventual success of Melun and a handful of like-minded Catholics such as Henri de Raincey and Benoist d'Azy in passing legislation that extended public assistance, combated unhealthful housing, and created institutions of *prévoyance*—retirement funds, public baths, and more mutual-aid societies—came only because allies that were gained on the extreme Left compensated for the lack of support on the Right.[43]

---

40. *Ibid.*, 4.
41. *Ibid.*, 21.
42. Parker T. Moon, *The Labor Problem and the Social Catholic Movement in France: A Study in the History of Social Politics* (New York, 1921), 46.
43. Duroselle, *Le Débuts du catholicisme social*, 452–56, 464–74.

The tensions of the moment and weariness of the implications of Melun's argument did not, however, prevent the Legitimists from eventually embracing the practical, if not the ideological, significance of his appeal. In effect, what Melun preached, and what the Legitimists came to accept, was not state control over social services but a more or less comprehensive system of state-supported social welfare designed to work in conjunction with and to fortify private charity and church-sponsored endeavors. State assistance to the poor was accepted as a legitimate public service as long as it supplemented traditional forms of charity that either reproduced earlier forms of institutional paternalism or were consistent with projects already undertaken by conservative social Catholics. Melun's article drew the quasi-obligatory distinction between poverty that resulted from "vice" and "misery" that stemmed from the unforeseen misfortunes of accident, disability, sickness, or unemployment, against which workers were defenseless in a liberal society. A state-supported *économie charitable* had to arm the poor against such disasters by promoting institutions of *prévoyance* and by helping private charity ensure a minimum livelihood for everyone through public assistance. If "ignorance" and "debauchery" were the cause of destitution, so too were disease and high prices. Society, Melun argued, owed itself and its citizens a minimum of protection since the existence of moral deficiencies was no excuse for a kind of institutionally sanctioned callousness that only served to exacerbate class conflict. Melun's "great association of mutual defense" was intended to provide scope not for solutions to the social question that went to the organization of bourgeois society itself but only for admonitions to political elites to discover the "duty of society vis-à-vis pauperism" and to ask in "what measure and by what means must this duty be performed."[44]

By accepting fundamentally statist solutions to the social question, the Legitimists prepared themselves to join the competition between rival elites over the character and control of existing social services under the administrative authoritarianism of the Second Empire. During the Second Republic, all political factions had come to accept the social and political utility of consumer cooperatives, popular credit institutions, mutual-aid societies, *bureaux de bienfaisance,* and state hospices, hospitals, and asylums. In the narrow space afforded to public discussion under

44. See Armand de Melun, *De l'intervention,* 9, 22–23.

Napoleon III, social debate among the notables, including the republicans, turned less to the forms social agencies should take than to the political and social consequences of their administration. Instead of asking how best to raise the lot of the poor, Legitimists began to wonder about how the state-sponsored agencies involved should be organized and operated, and who should run them. With the advent of universal suffrage and, after 1851, the domination of the administration by the Bonapartists, the problem of staffing relief agencies became more important and the social question more politicized than ever before. If the Legitimists agreed that the state had a role to play, they certainly were not pleased with the kind of state that the responsibilities fell to. If the goal remained the *encadrement* and the moral elevation of the workers and the poor, what good did it do to have assistance disbursed by a religiously neutral system run by men who were selected by the central government and did not necessarily respect the rights and doctrines of the church? The problem became still more pronounced once the "godless republicans" began to take over the administration after 1871. The significance of Melun's statism was not in turning the Legitimists into social collectivists but in placing them willy-nilly within an emerging *dirigiste* consensus that put the institutional laicity of what they called *l'état sans Dieu* at the center of the social question. As the Legitimists' debate on the social question came to revolve less around what the state was suited to doing and more around the need to ensure that the state be Christian, their royalism gained political allies among nondynastic Catholics who increasingly saw the virtue of supporting a pretender who styled himself a Christian prince.

LEGAL CHARITY, 1850–1876

Between 1848 and 1871, the Legitimists interpreted Melun's concept of society as a "great association of mutual defense" in a resolutely conservative way. In the commission presided over by Alfred de Falloux to study the national workshops, several members accused Melun of "restraining the domain of private charity" by "giving the state too great a role in the easing of misery."[45] As a political realist, Melun

45. Armand de Melun, *Mémoires,* II, 24, in Andigné's *Un Apôtre de la charité,* 370. Originally, Melun envisioned a hierarchical national system of public assistance guided by

took note of the apprehension expressed and pulled back from the ideas he had enunciated in his article of 1848. In a report by the Commission of Assistance in 1851, he distinguished between a system of public assistance that was a "vast ensemble of institutions and committees" linked together by an "immense administration" extending from the communes to the central government and embracing "every kind of aid," and a more modest arrangement of "legal charity" designed to deprive the state of a carte blanche and to delineate clearly between the roles of private charity and public assistance. Legal charity, he argued, would require only the backing of particular laws drawn up for individual social problems and would work in conjunction with, and not against, the efforts of lay Catholics and the church. His description accorded well with Legitimist and Catholic fears of big government, as well as with the social and political priorities of the Second Empire.

Bending to most conservative objections, Melun urged in the *Annales de la charité* that public assistance be decentralized to the "communal and departmental" levels by placing it under the direction of municipal and general counselors. He also recommended the return "of religion into public *bienfaisance*" through the repeal of an 1830 law that excluded clergymen from local and national committees controlling public assistance. He encouraged that legislation abolish "every trace, . . . every symptom of rivalry between public assistance and private religious charity." He desired private charity to be given clear preference under the law, and its practices to be injected into public assistance as integrally as possible.[46]

Confidence in the "incontestable superiority" of private charity and the acknowledgment that it was insufficient to the magnitude of pauperism and indigence were the Legitimists' two basic justifications for legal charity and for efforts to extend the system into a greater number of communes.[47] If private charity was insufficient and subject to limited

---

a *conseil supérieur* that the National Assembly was to name and extending into each locality through departmental, cantonal, and communal committees appointed by local elected officials. A kind of Falloux Law for public assistance, the system was to keep private and public charity separate but give the bishops a voice on the *conseil supérieur*. See Melun, *De l'intervention*, 60–64.

46. Duroselle, *Le Débuts du catholicisme social*, 462–63.

47. See Anatole de Melun, "Application de la mutualité à l'assistance dans les campagnes," *Revue d'économie charitable*, VI (October, 1873), 8–9. Benoist d'Azy told the National Assembly, "We live in the countryside; we see around us poor people who have neither medical assistance nor the care they need when they are sick. Christian charity, in

growth, the public system would have to shoulder a greater portion of responsibility. That made a reform of its procedures all the more important. The inadequacy of the entrenched practices of public assistance was manifest. In 1848 there were approximately eight thousand *bureaux de bienfaisance* and 1,338 hospitals and hospices serving roughly 37,000 communes. Béchard estimated in 1850 that, out of a population of 36 million, where in times of need as many as one-sixth were indigent or "medicant," the bureaus assisted only 800,000 people, the hospitals and hospices only 700,000 and private charity no more than 1.5 million.[48] In Nantes, during the economic crisis of 1846–1847, as many as 20,000, or 21.3 percent of a population of 94,000, had to rely on public or private charity. In 1848, Paris had twelve bureaus, fifteen hospitals, thirteen hospices, twenty-five asylums, and 11,450 beds serving 600,000 people—and the capital had the most extensive facilities.[49] Things had not improved much by 1875, when the number of bureaus had risen to 13,287 and the number of people aided reached 1,247,722, because despite the expansion, public assistance was very unevenly distributed between cities and rural areas and between rich and poor departments.[50] Of the 13,545 bureaus in existence in July, 1874, 644 were dormant for lack of resources and as many as 1,062 had less than fifty francs in ordinary yearly receipts. Moreover, 22,643 communes lacked a bureau altogether. The total number of indigents assisted in the difficult year of 1871 was 1,608,129, representing 528,242 households.[51] Since the most active and well-endowed provincial bureaus—Lille, Reims, and Rennes—drew an important proportion of their revenue from gifts, legacies, donations, and charitable contributions, the Legitimists could argue that the expansion of the system would be impossible unless generous Catholics received assurances that it would be essentially religious in nature.

Largely excluded from the official discussions on public assistance un-

---

all cases, gives a commendable example; everywhere it is beneficent, but it is not sufficient" (*Annales*, 1872, VII, 3).

48. Béchard, *De l'état du paupérisme*, 13; Armand de Melun, *De l'intervention*, 59.

49. M. de Vatteville, *Statistique des établissements de bienfaisances* (Paris, n.d.), 93.

50. *Annuaire statistique de la France de 1878* (2 vols.; Paris, 1878), I, 146–49. North of the St. Malo–Lake Geneva line, 32 departments had 6,632 bureaus; south of the line, 57 departments had 6,655. Finistère had 29 bureaus; Pas-de-Calais, 592; Landes, 93; and Eure, 175.

51. *Annuaire statistique de la France de 1878*, I, 146–48; Pocquet, *Essai sur l'assistance publique*, 344–45, 358.

der the Second Empire, the Legitimists had to wait until the elections of February 8, 1871, before they could again pursue their goal of Christianizing public assistance. The debates on public assistance in the monarchist-dominated National Assembly, in which Melun's twin brother, Anatole, played a prominent role, had an obvious continuity with the outline of conservative priorities by Melun more than twenty years earlier. By 1871, it had become apparent that the Legitimists' limited and uneven national influence made it impossible for them and their clerical allies to dominate throughout the land a system of public assistance that conservatives had left in the hands of local and departmental officials specifically because they wanted to keep it out of the hands of the central power. The de facto decentralization of public giving meant that local conditions often determined its character and personnel. In regions where the Legitimists were predominant, the administration had been unable in many cases to eliminate their control over local institutions. Thus, in Brittany, Anjou, Lower Languedoc, Marseille, and the Nord, the institutions of public assistance developed into communitarian and religious organs dominated by local Catholic notables and annexed to the preexisting structure of organized private charity.

Indeed, in those areas where the Legitimist presence was paramount and where well-organized charitable associations existed, private charity and public assistance did not share responsibilities, as Melun had envisioned, but underwent a complete merger. Michel Denis has shown that in the Mayenne, for example, the organization of the *bureaux de bienfaisance* remained far inferior to that of local charitable efforts and was intentionally kept in its subordination by "charitable people" who "felt repugnance at putting their funds in the hands of an accountant who received a proportional charitable remission." During the Second Empire, under a system devised by the abbé Jean Baptiste Heslot, curé of Andouille, the funds of each of the bureaus in the department were distributed among rich inhabitants of the communes to be given directly to whomever of the poor and in whatever proportion the benefactor wished. "In these conditions," writes Denis, "it was charity that became in some way institutionalized."[52] In Lille, after 1855, the provisions and

---

52. Denis, *Les Royalistes de la Mayenne,* 349. Abbé Heslot wrote, "The benefactor becomes the natural supervisor, monitor, and tutor of the poor person he assists by choice in his neighborhood. He is not afraid to admonish him and to reprimand him if he strays, to reproach him if he gives in to his negligence, his laziness, or his vices, or to encourage him when he does better. In a word, the benefactor naturally adds patronage to alms."

revenues provided to the bureau, which consisted partly of treasury funds and interests on state bonds, were doled out to *dispensaires,* often members of feminine charitable orders, who served as intermediaries between the state and the poor, for whom they were the only humanitarian contact.[53] On the other hand, in regions where Legitimist and clerical forces were in a minority or were politically ineffective, the bureaus, if they existed, were run by either state appointees or local notables outside the Catholic charitable network who often secularized the system by segregating their work from that of the clergy and the local Catholic *patrons.* Thus, while the number of public *assistés* was relatively small, it was not negligible. In an atmosphere where charity, patronage, and ideology were inseparable—and perhaps decisive in the bitter electoral struggles of the 1870s—Legitimists were aware that their strategy of *encadrement* depended on the ascendancy of the proper social authorities and the Christianization of state institutions. To enable that was the intent of the legislative activity of Anatole de Melun and others in the National Assembly of 1871.

Anatole de Melun's goal was to legislate guarantees that public assistance would not contradict or undermine the principles of private charity elaborated earlier in the century. In his first committee report, he referred to public assistance as "state charity," because its very conception depended on the "divine precept imposed on all men . . . to come to the aid of those less favored." Therefore, he concluded, "the more it approaches private charity in its principles and applications, the better it accomplishes its mission."[54] He and others believed that all state-sponsored social measures should "fortify" and complement private charity and should function as a last resort, after the resources of the family and private generosity were exhausted. In addition, he held that public charity ought never to be allocated by an impersonal bureaucracy but should be an act of direct giving since, in order to "unite two souls before God," those who received had to know those who gave.[55]

In effect, the Legitimists wanted to create a system of public assistance in the image of the Saint Vincent de Paul Society. As Anatole de Melun

53. Pierrand, *La Vie ouvrière,* 236–37.
54. Rapport de la commission chargée d'examiner l'organisation d'une commission administrative de l'assistance publique, par Anatole de Melun, in *Annales,* 1872, VII, 185.
55. *Annales,* June 17, 1873, XXXIII, annexe 1815, pp. 408–409; France, Assemblée Nationale, *Enquête parlementaire sur l'organisation de l'assistance publique dans les campagnes* (3 vols.; Versailles, 1873), I, 4–5, hereinafter cited as *Enquête parlementaire.*

explained, the greatest threat to the institutions of charity, besides its insufficiency, was the "threat of having alms carried to the indigent by a salaried official."[56] The French system had to retain its distinctly Catholic nature and avoid the "Protestant" errors of poor relief, in which the Legitimists saw the antithesis of the religious aspect of charity.[57] Béchard was typical in condemning the English poor tax and the workhouses: they led, he thought, to "crushing taxes" that did less to alleviate poverty than to increase "laziness and vice." The English worker, he asserted, divided "his life between the hovel and the workhouse," where he gained a keener sense of his own "brutalization, misery, and oppression." The liberty of the benefactor alone created the "sublime character of *beinfaisance*," since charity has to be a free gift and not a tax the proceeds of which the poor receive anonymously, demanding them as a right that does not depend on "either prayer or recognition." Society would only suffer, Béchard argued, if the state transformed what had to be a spontaneous and free act of conscience "consecrated by divine law" into a civic obligation.[58] But whereas the poor tax, according to Barthélemy Pocquet, eviscerated charity, "legal charity . . . completes the work of private charity" by giving it "the cohesion and coherence, the stability and durability, it can sometimes lack."[59]

If legal charity was to be personal and direct, it had to be decentralized and community-based, the Legitimist thinking ran. Just as *secours à domicile* helped to preserve the family, decentralization was essential to protect the integrity of the charitable community, since it left the distribution of public funds at the discretion of local authorities.[60] In order to avoid the kind of local variation that developed during the Second Empire, however, the central government had to impose unified administrative regulations concerning financial solvency as well as proper techniques and personnel standards. As Pocquet wrote, the "government has the duty

---

56. *Enquête parlementaire,* I, 12.

57. These views reflected the position of the church. See Catta, *La Doctrine politique et sociale du Cardinal Pie,* 218.

58. Béchard, *De l'état du paupérisme,* 467–70.

59. Pocquet, *Essai sur l'assistance publique,* 212–21. Pocquet, whose study was based in large part on Melun's official reports, felt that the state should "take charge . . . of the incurably ill who need permanent aid. It will equalize the resources among provinces that differ in their wealth. Finally, it can better than anyone else use preventive means and offer to the indigent the alms of work, which are perhaps the best of all. Such is the true and only mission of the state" (p. 219).

60. Rapport de la commission des institutions charitables, par Comte de Melun, in *Annales,* February 19, 1872, VII, annexe 906, pp. 185–88; *Annales,* 1871, III, 158.

to maintain the hierarchical bond" while making sure "that the most unfortunate receive the greatest sum of aid possible."[61]

Anatole de Melun held that the needed regulations should come not from the ministry of the interior but from a high council of public assistance linked to a system of communal and departmental affiliates made up of local notables and clergymen.[62] As the republicans gained control of an increasing number of local councils during the 1870s, the legislative enactment of such central supervision became the only means the conservatives had of counteracting the decline of their predominance at the local level. The turn in the conservatives' fortune meant that even if public assistance remained decentralized, it could not avoid laicization under the control of republican municipalities and general councils. Therefore, Anatole de Melun grew more and more reluctant to allow the municipal councils to elect the administrative commission of the *bureaux de bienfaisance:* "Would it not be dangerous," he wondered, "to abandon completely the management of charitable interests into the hands of the commune, especially in a town where political questions play a large role in municipal elections" and "new elements" ignore the strictures imposed by charity?[63] Ideally, he would have wished that "the task of charity and its destiny . . . be put back in the hands of those who directed it before the Revolution," when, by a decree of Louis XIV in 1698, each *bureau de charité* was placed under an administrative commission composed of agents of the king, local oligarchs, clergymen, a judicial officer, and a proxy of the seigneur. Since public assistance had became "prey to politics," he complained, holders of "dangerous opinions" had begun to use the social agencies to enlarge their influence by distributing favors, while "devoted men" who "had sacrificed their lives to the profit of the poor" were replaced with "new men" whose only qualification was "to have the most advanced opinions."[64] To avoid the republican onslaught, Anatole de Melun proposed that the local regulating commissions always include a bishop alongside other local officials and that a curé be given a permanent place in the bureaus.[65] The presence of a priest, he argued,

61. Pocquet, *Essai sur l'assistance publique,* 229; *Annales,* May 17, 1871, III, annexe 239, p. 60.

62. *Annales,* 1871, III, 158; Anatole de Melun, "Application de la mutualité," 8–9.

63. *Annales,* May 27, 1871, III, 158.

64. *Annales,* March 20, 1873, XVI, 590–91.

65. *Annales,* 1872, VII, annexe 906, pp. 185–88. Of course these maneuvers would become academic after 1879, when the republicans reversed most of these policies, secularizing the system and purging conservatives from local agencies.

would "serve as a link" between public and private charity and would
symbolize that "religious impulse" without which "natural generosity"
could not be sustained or developed.[66]

Thus, by the 1870s, the statist approach recommended by Armand de
Melun and the prevailing competition between Catholics and secularists
had transformed the social question into a question of political power.
With no one left to question the legitimacy of at least some measures of
state intervention, conservative social Catholics began to wonder how
far the state could go not only in providing institutions of *prévoyance* but
in regulating the economy itself. If the *encadrement* of the masses offered
the Legitimists an acceptable response to the social consequences of industrial capitalism, it did nothing to stop industrialization from repro-
ducing the conditions they sought to combat. Many younger social
Catholics tried to address this problem by giving substance to the famil-
iar theme of reviving certain aspects of Old Regime corporatism.

66. *Annales,* May 24, 1872, XI, 533; *Annales,* 1871, III, 60.

CHAPTER VII

 Toward a Christian
Social Order

BY THE 1890s, René de La Tour Du Pin was proudly calling
himself a counterrevolutionary and asserting that Christianity had found
its institutional "recapitulation" in the feudal and corporatist regime of
the Middle Ages.[1] Although his was a relatively extreme position, social
Catholics had come by the time of the centenary of the French Revolution to reject liberalism and embrace a variety of corporatist solutions to
the social question. These reached well beyond organized charity and
Melun's welfare state and rejected the parliamentary and administrative
institutions France had inherited from its revolutionary past. How had
corporatism become the centerpiece of Legitimist social Catholicism in
the 1870s, and how far was the Catholic *patronat* willing to go toward
embracing a social reconstruction that repudiated laissez-faire? What pos-
ture did corporatists take toward the institutions of monarchy as they
attempted to insinuate their social priorities into the royalist struggle to
find a viable alternative to the secular and democratic Third Republic?

CORPORATISM AND LIBERALISM,
1830—1870

Although La Tour Du Pin believed that corporatism and
monarchism were the two pillars of a Christian social order, formula-

1. René de La Tour Du Pin-Chambly, *Vers un ordre social chrétien: Jalon de route,
1882—1907* (Paris, 1921), 16—21, 194, 268.

179

tions like his were highly controversial within the Legitimist movement. Legitimists had always said that the revolutionary abolition of the old *corporations* had left the workers defenseless in the face of liberal capitalism by severing the working class from a monarchy that had worked to protect all social interests. Royal regulations concerning the craft guilds, they argued, had guaranteed the workers' right of association and had given them a kind of political representation they lacked in the era of parliamentary government. But the Legitimist rhetoric raised the specter of a return to the Old Regime, against which liberal Legitimists from Antoine Berryer to Alfred de Falloux had fought in the interest of reconciling the Orleanists to a Bourbon restoration. For that reason, corporatism, whose intellectual roots reached back to the Restoration, remained the ideological black sheep of the Legitimist movement until social Catholics retrieved it from oblivion for its potential toward providing institutional surrogates that might help rechristianize the working class.[2] Nonetheless, the corporatist debate was never free of controversy, and its periodic reappearance sent liberal Legitimists like Melun scrambling to couch it in terms acceptable to public opinion. Melun predicted in 1843, "It will be necessary sooner or later to return to these old corporate entities," but he added, "The important thing is to find in these resurrections a form that, accommodated to our times and our ideas, can overcome its essential antiquity with something new."[3]

It was the rise of an independent labor movement in the 1860s and the revolutionary disaffection revealed by the Paris Commune that made Legitimists acutely aware of how alienated the working class had become from the church and its allies. Reflecting on the causes of the Commune in 1872, Armand Fresneau, a deputy from Morbihan, was struck by the workers' rejection of every legacy of the past and warned that unless workers came to enjoy traditions and institutions of their own, society would be "condemned to enact laws of penal repression."[4] Three months later, in a speech before the newly formed Cercle Catholique des Ouvriers in Montmartre-Clignancourt, Albert de Mun sounded the same theme, accusing the socialists of having invented the word *proletarian* to

2. See Comte de Chambord to M. Léon Harmel, September 6, 1877, in Dubosc de Pesquidoux' *Le Comte de Chambord*, 200–201.
3. Armand de Melun to Edouard Le Camus, August 4, 1843, in Andigné's *Un Apôtre de la charité*, 376.
4. *Annales*, March 12, 1872, VIII, 296.

hide from French workers the reality of their "glorious, . . . ancient, and noble" Christian and corporate past. The real workers' tradition, he explained, resided in "those *corps de métiers* under the protection of the church and the empire of Christian thought."[5]

In the 1870s, the Legitimists became virtually obsessed by the mystique of the *corporation*. They drew up plans for the corporate organization of the electorate, talked of *prévots* and *echevins,* recalled the ordinances of Saint Louis enfranchising the craft guilds, and publicized the idea of mixed associations of *patrons* and workers. Their actuating recollection was not merely nostalgic; the growing hostility of a younger generation of Catholics and Legitimists toward the consequences of 1789 compelled them to search for a serious and distinctly Christian alternative to bourgeois society. Yet, like the monarchy, the *corporation* could not be restored without modification. It had to be made responsive to changed economic circumstances, and it had to be made compatible with the conviction, so prevalent among conservative industrialists, that the Revolution of 1789 had released the productive forces that made the progress of the nineteenth century possible.

When the Legitimists proposed corporatist solutions to the social question in the 1840s, the tone of their writings was frankly anticapitalist and paralleled the mentality of distressed artisans threatened by the spread of factory production. Under the July Monarchy, the Legitimists openly denounced "unlimited competition," the "monopoly" of power that industrialists had over the state and the economy, and the restrictions France's bourgeois masters had placed on the right of association. As an alternative to economic civil war, corporatists recommended the formation of mixed syndicates of workers and *maîtres* based on professional affiliation. These were to operate like "large families" to regulate conditions of labor, modes of access to employment, and wage rates for each craft or industry. Joseph Morand, Amédée de Hennequin, and Henri de Raincey, all writing before 1848, proposed that mixed syndicates or representative industrial councils should govern each sector of production: their roles would include drawing up salary scales, creating common funds for pensions, insurance, and education, acting as arbitration boards, and enacting regulations for hiring, apprenticeship, and religious obligations which would form both a body of rules for each industry and a

5. Mun, *Discours à l'inauguration du Cercle de Montmartre-Clignancourt,* 6–7.

basis for general legislation regulating the economy. The state was legally to recognize the authority of the *corporations* to determine practices and protective measures for each sector and was thereby to afford workers a form of representation based on the community of interests with which they were associated. "In our system," wrote Morand, "the syndics would exercise a veritable magistrature having election as its origin and the sanction of the government for its official character."[6]

With little support among the political class, this early corporatism had small success. After 1852, the Legitimists increasingly turned away from their alliance with lower-class populist elements, while many artisans who had been partisans of Legitimism before 1848 abandoned royalism for other political options. In the climate of reaction and prosperity during the 1850s, the social question lost the prominent place it had had on the agenda of the notables. Under the Second Empire, moreover, economic liberalism enjoyed widespread support among the elite, and the Legitimists, who were not immune to trends, rejected the statist implications of Morand's corporatism in favor of corporatist formulas divested of the baggage of economic restrictions and government intervention. Thus, in the 1860s the idea of mixed associations was inserted into the general debate on the organization of labor and slipped easily into the Legitimists' concern with lifting the moral consciousness of the working class and supervising it.

The renewed interest in corporatist schemes was sparked by the growth of trade unions and especially by the law of 1864 on coalitions. Fearing that trade unions gave workers too much autonomy and sanctioned the disharmony of class interests, the Legitimists proposed labor organizations that placed workers under the guidance of conservative forces. One approach resurrected the *corporation* as a kind of social club in which only the supposed moral function of the *corps des métiers* would be left intact. In 1866, Henri de La Broise advocated a series of independent labor associations of workers and *patrons* to advance mutual assistance and solidarity under the auspices of the church. Directed "by the

6. Duroselle, *Les Débuts du catholicisme social,* 204–207. Joseph Morand, a writer for the *Gazette de France,* published a five-part series in 1843 entitled "Des sociétés humaines et de l'organisation du travail," in which he outlined his ideas. See the *Gazette de France,* April 7, 16, 26, June 12, September 9, 1843. For Henri de Raincey, see *L'Union monarchique,* April 17, 1847. Amédée de Hennequin, born in 1812, was the son of a lawyer and the younger brother of Victor Hennequin, a Fourierist. For Amédée de Hennequin's corporatism, see *La Quotidienne, Le Correspondant,* and the *Annales de la charité.*

spirit of faith," these mixed Christian professional associations were to
have no authority to regulate working conditions but were merely to
afford workers a framework for a new Christian sociability. Workers,
La Broise intoned, could participate collectively in "religious ceremonies . . . under the banner of their *patrons,* surrounded by the prestige of
[their] memories, which cement the association and give it the union that
can only result from moral bonds."[7] In the same period, Emile Keller
rejected the "closed and fiscal *corporations* of the Old Regime" in favor of
mixed associations in the form of large mutual-aid societies designed to
increase the effectiveness of *prévoyance* by creating a "collective and inalienable reserve providing for the needs of their members." For Keller, a
revival of the *corps de métiers* had less to do with economics than with the
reconstruction of the Christian community. Mixed associations "without
any danger of revolutionary affiliations," he argued, should have their
own schools, churches, hospitals, and fetes; their agencies would be
staffed by religious orders "created especially to serve the workers."
These *religieux* would not only "resolve the problems of industry and
labor" but care for children, indigents, widows, and unwed mothers.[8]

The Comte de Chambord got into the act in 1865 with the publication
of his "Letter on the Workers." Speaking as king in absentia, Chambord
claimed that the monarchy would enfranchise the working class, as it had
enfranchised the communes in the past, by granting them "voluntary and
free associations . . . for the common defense of their interests." Going
farther than liberals and Bonapartists, who, though recognizing the right
of association, shrank from granting unions the full right to fight in behalf of their labor demands, Chambord encouraged workers to form
mixed syndicates capable of entering into arbitration with employers

7. La Broise, *Le Vrai et le Faux Libéralisme,* 174–76.
8. Keller, *L'Encyclique du 8 décembre,* 279. Emile Keller, born in 1828 at Belfort, sat in
the legislature from 1857 to 1865, from 1869 to 1881, and from 1885 to 1889. Elected at
first as an official candidate, Keller distanced himself from imperial policy over the Italian
question. Considering himself "Catholic first," he vigorously defended the temporal power
of the pope and became one of the leaders of the clerical party. In *L'Encyclique du 8 décembre,*
published in 1866, Keller passionately defended the Syllabus and, most notably, stressed
that action in favor of social peace and justice was at the heart of faith. He also emphasized
that Catholicism, as outlined in the Syllabus, was irreconcilable with the principles of 1789.
The book had a pronounced impact on Mun and La Tour Du Pin, who were given a copy
by a priest while in the hands of the Germans in 1871. Joining the extreme Right in the
Chamber after 1876, Keller remained active as a member of the Oeuvre des Cercles and
one of its principal liaisons with the Vatican, where he was well connected.

over economic issues. He cautioned, however, that such associations not be used for purposes inimical to public order. Arguing that only the "most capable and conciliatory representatives of both parties" should participate in the envisaged deliberations, he hoped to reassure employers that "peace and order" would prevail. But he was also adamant that employers owed their employees the prospect of "equitable satisfaction," thereby signaling the Legitimist party's public commitment to a kind of economic freedom that was not entirely tilted in favor of those with power and property. He endorsed the idea of making *corporations* the basis for political representation in a corporate national assembly. In the final analysis, however, Chambord left the decision about establishing such associations to the discretion of employers, because in calling for "free and voluntary *corporations*," he envisioned no legal enjoining of the *patronat* to "protect" the working class.[9]

Although it appeared that Legitimists had chosen to put corporatism on the agenda, their proposals did not yet challenge liberal sensibilities by letting the freedom of association restrain economic freedom. According to Hilaire de Lacombe, Legitimists had to understand that the decrepit institutions of the Old Regime could be reformed to provide protection for workers but had to be accommodated to a society in which privileges had been abolished. He supported the corporatist idea of free association and industrial arbitration, but he rejected any suggestion that trade monopolies, price fixing, labor regulations, and trade barriers, all abolished by the Chapellier Law of 1791, could be legally reinstated.[10] J. Bourgeois defended his party against the "economists" who at every mention of the *corporations* "recall the abuses that had led to the fall of *maîtrises* and *jurandes*." "[T]hese abuses," he objected, "were peculiar to their time and are not inherent in all industrial organization. We are not

9. Chambord, Lettre sur les ouvriers, April 20, 1865, in *La Monarchie française*, 87–89.
10. Lacombe, "Le Suffrage universel," 620–21. Lacombe argued that the "menacing multitudes" were demanding merely the kind of associations to protect professional interests which conservatives could support: "If the freedom of commerce and industry is whole and complete, if the *chambres syndicales* are not invested with any exceptional prerogative, if they can hinder neither other *chambres* of the same profession which form against them nor the workers who wish not to belong to any, to be independent of all, if they conduct themselves always according to the rigorous observance of civil and penal laws that would prevent or punish their infractions, what reason would there be to refuse to a part of our fellow citizens the exercise of a right that, not unsuitably, is possessed by all others, usually in the interest of their greater good?"

talking about an archaeological restoration, and it goes without saying that we cannot again proclaim that work is a royal right to be bought with cash. The existence of *corporations* is perfectly compatible with the freedom of labor; it would at once be a guarantee of public order, of security for the worker, and of pacific solutions to questions of wages and of all the differences that can arise between workers and employers." [11]

In the minds of Legitimist moderates in the 1860s, the *corporation* was on its way to becoming a new kind of *conseil de prud'homme* that would protect traditional forms of skilled labor rather than become the basis for the organization of labor in general. But Legitimist corporatism had for a long time been conceived, even in its more statist and antiliberal form, by reference to relatively small, stable, and traditional productive communities that were apt to be defensive about access to the trades, labor mobility, and apprenticeship. In that respect, the corporatist advocacy by the Legitimists mirrored their static view of the economy and its roles. As the Marquis de Franclieu explained, "There must be citizens who are exclusively cultivators, industrialists, merchants, savants, and so on. . . . To pretend the contrary . . . would be to deny all the progress achieved in a thousand years and to affirm that, instead of being essentially specialized, man can become universal and transform his aptitudes at will." [12] Given the protraction of French industrial development, the persistence of traditional forms of production, and the inclinations of the Legitimists' potential constituencies, it is hardly surprising that they should have favored forms of labor organization more appropriate to small-scale production. What made the broad return to corporatist themes in the 1870s and 1880s different was precisely the Legitimists' conscious accommodation of the problems of large-scale factory production. The corporatist model conceived in the 1840s, and even in the 1860s, would have had the effect of excluding unskilled, and often female, labor from traditional sectors; a viable industrial corporatism for the 1870s and 1880s would have to concern itself not only with the changing labor force and an altered work experience but also with technological innovation, worker housing, and community services. It only made sense for the corporatist debate to focus on limiting the relative freedom of the entrepreneur if industrialists were unwilling to take such responsibilities upon

11. Bourgeois, *Le Catholicisme et les Questions sociales*, 191–92.
12. *Annales*, May 9, 1871, II, 877. See also M. C. A. Gimpl, *The "Correspondant" and the Founding of the French Third Republic* (Westport, Conn., 1959), 120.

themselves. Certain wealthy *patrons sociaux* tried to develop factory-based services in order to demonstrate to social Catholics that they could address the questions of labor organization and protection without the passage of industrial legislation. In the process, however, they created a practical model for applying corporate principles to the industrial enterprise.

SOCIAL PATRONS

Catholic *patrons sociaux,* most of whom were rich Legitimist industrialists—like Benoist d'Azy—who had participated in mounting private and public charitable initiatives, gained visibility by integrating measures of *prévoyance* into the factory system.[13] By creating housing facilities, retirement funds, savings banks, life insurance reserves, infirmaries, religious institutions, and schools for their employees, they managed to transform industry into a social entity and make the factory the center of community action and support. Entirely paternalist and not wholly original (the Protestant *patrons* of Mulhouse and the Vosges had been the first to employ the techniques), their accomplishments relied on the support of the clergy and the services of charitable congregations to provide the factory community with a distinctly religious inspiration and purpose.[14]

At the same time that the *patrons sociaux* declared that their factory-based instruments of patronage exhibited that the *patron* was less an absolute master than the "first member of a great family of workers," they discouraged workers from administering the associations established by their companies. Assuming that the workers were incapable of helping themselves except under benevolent guidance, they anticipated that effective factory patronage would be a welcome alternative to inadequately funded cooperatives run by workers suffering the handicap of ignorance and incompetence. Anatole de Melun believed that laborers, besides being inclined to "social heresies," were "too little educated to possess the necessary aptitude" to make cooperatives successful and were "almost always forced to accept a director unacquainted with their

13. Duroselle, *Les Débuts du catholicisme social,* 646–56. The most notable *patrons sociaux* included Augustin Cochin, who sat on the board of the Compagnie du Chemin de Fer d'Orléans (1852) and the Compagnie de Saint-Gobain (1864); Denis Benoist d'Azy and Paul Benoist d'Azy, who owned and directed the forges and foundries at Alais, Azin, and Fouchambault; and Léon Harmel and Jacques Joseph Harmel, who ran a textile factory near Rheims, at Val-des-Bois.
14. *Ibid.,* 654–55.

trades." [15] Benoist d'Azy suggested that workers should learn to profit from the superior knowledge of the upper classes. He recommended that *patrons* could use their position to teach useful lessons, by withholding part of an employee's wages each year, equal to the cost of tobacco or weekly drinks at the cabaret, and placing it in a retirement fund. Factory patronage, he explained, would inevitably spread without legal compulsion if Christian *patrons* voluntarily took initiatives that accorded with their religious obligations. Moreover, workers would abandon their desire for autonomy upon "hearing talk of great dividends" and seeing industry managed by "rich and powerful administrators" whom they could thank for a "clean comfortable house, well-reared children, someone who cares for [their] maladies, and someone who assures [them] an honorable retirement in old age." [16] Benoist d'Azy boasted that the workers at his own foundries at Alais were "attached to their master," never complained about low wages, and rarely quit to find alternative employment. [17]

Robert Locke has referred to the actions of the *patrons sociaux* as a neo-feudal attempt to restrict a "free and uninhibited labor supply" whose "constant turnover . . . seriously impaired efficiency." He argues, "Workers, especially those who had been employed for a long time, were reluctant to leave since they often had to forfeit any money that they had paid into a mutual-aid or pension fund when quitting the company." [18] But factory patronage had other "feudal" aspects that were far more important to social Catholics and that contributed decisively to the elaboration of the industrial *corporation*. The large-scale nature of the enterprises in which the efforts of patronage seemed most effective presented opportunities for the extension of *encadrement* into industry itself and created a new means for Catholics to influence the direction of the economy. Most of the firms practicing patronage were *sociétés anonymes* made possible by reforms instigated under the Second Empire. They not only possessed the resources to support extensive social projects, they were also subject to the pressure of numerous stockholders upon whom Catholics could exert an influence for a wide range of reforms. [19] By making workers

15. *Annales,* July 27, 1875, XLIV, annexe 3283, pp. 103–104, 106.
16. *Annales,* July 27, 1875, XLIV, 103.
17. *Annales,* March 7, 1872, VIII, 227–28.
18. Locke, *French Legitimists,* 133–34.
19. See Anatole de Melun's comments in *Annales,* July 27, 1875, XLIV, annexe 3283, p. 103.

depend on a constellation of social services subject to the discretion of employers, managers, and stockholders, social Catholics saw the possibility of moving beyond private or state-sponsored programs toward forms of intervention that would allow Catholics greater freedom to shape morality and social relations in the work environment, where the classes confronted one another most directly.[20] After reading about the social projects undertaken in Léon Harmel's textile factory at Val-des-Bois, Maurice Maignen declared that factory patronage could turn the "principal cause of the moral and material abjection [of the workers into] the means of moral and material rehabilitation"; "La manufacture, l'enfer, devient une Jerusalem."[21]

The Christian factory promised to forge a new alliance between industry and the church, between labor relations and social Catholicism; it seemed to respond to the social question without coaxing state intervention or challenging the economic efficiency of industrial capitalism. By combining social Catholic methods with laissez-faire and the conditions of factory production, factory patronage appealed, especially in the Nord, to a large number of Catholic manufacturers and industrialists who were reluctant to sacrifice their economic initiative to help their employees. It also represented an entrenching of the will to supervise, which was implicit in conservative social Catholicism from the beginning.

In a report written by Anatole de Melun on behalf of the National Assembly's Legitimist-dominated commission on the condition of the working classes in 1875, the *patrons sociaux* showed a growing desire to reshape the urban and industrial environment by focusing on the workers' habitat.[22] The report not only considered questions of charity and

20. Bourgeois, *Le Catholicisme et les Questions sociales,* 23.
21. Notes on Maurice Maignen to René de La Tour Du Pin, November, 1875, in Charles Maignen's *Maurice Maignen,* I, 487.
22. See *Annales,* July 27, 1875, XLIV, annexe 3283. This report was viewed by Locke and Pierrard as an exercise in self-justification since it concentrated on those aspects of working-class life that conformed to the preconceptions and priorities of the *patrons.* It is true that, as an episode in the history of social legislation, the work of the commission was, at best, without effect. Indeed, its effect may have been negative since it served to reinforce elite prejudices against the dangers of working-class autonomy and elite opposition to any statist reforms that could limit the freedom of the *patronat.* But as a historical document the report reveals the complex attitude of the Catholic *patrons* toward the "workers' question," the extent to which the *patrons* had come to accept the legislative work of previous decades, and the confidence they had in the type of self-reliant solutions proposed by men like Benoist d'Azy and Augustin Cochin. That is why they made no real legislative recommen-

patronage but emphasized that proper housing, small gardens, ventilation, and factory sanitation were essential for improving labor relations, altering the "moral situation" of employees, and defusing working-class radicalism in the wake of the Commune. Echoing a growing ecclesiastical preoccupation with how the proletarian milieu was inhospitable to the process of rechristianization, the Catholic industrialists on the commission came out for legislation supporting the creation of "salubrious housing," industrial ruralization, the regulation of cafés, and restrictions on the freedom of the press. What good would it do to encourage traditional family life or church attendance, they wondered, if the urban environment itself rendered ineffective all efforts regarding the moral level of workers? Their concern led to the contemplation of a kind of social Catholic city planning. Much of the report focused on how the Haussmannization of Paris had bred a disregard for property rights by reducing working-class property ownership and suggested that credit arrangements to help workers purchase company-supplied houses would renew respect for the property of others. The commission also feared that the separation of rich and poor into different districts and the *agglomération* of workers into crowded quarters accentuated social tensions by highlighting class differences, besides preventing workers from encountering the "more civilized mores" of a "more favored society." Greater social contact, they argued, would prove to the lazy and insolent that "joy and contentment" attended honesty and hard work.[23]

Nevertheless, the empire of supervision contemplated by the *patrons sociaux* presented social Catholics with as many problems as opportunities. Factory-based patronage effectively placed all social Catholic initiative in the hands of industrialists who jealously guarded their own autonomy and were under no necessity to follow the dictates of faith or serve the concerns of social Catholic activists. As a solution to the wider social problems attending industrialization, moreover, the paternalism of a small number of conscientious businessmen would be no more adequate than the charity of the Saint Vincent de Paul Society had been in eliminating indigence. If, as many Legitimists acknowledged, the majority of the bourgeoisie were immune to the influence of the church,

---

dations: the state services they accepted were already enacted by other legislation, and the type of paternalist reforms they envisioned required no legislative action. See also Locke, *French Legitimists*, 185–87; and Pierrand, *L'Eglise et les Ouvriers*, Chapter V.

23. *Annales*, July, 27, 1875, XLIV, AP, annexe 3283, pp. 102–104.

how could a Christian response to the social question dependent on their willing compliance ever succeed? These questions were only more troubling in light of the enormous power that had accrued to the industrialists in control of the sort of large-scale enterprises in which patronage might be most useful. There was also the question of how many workers would benefit from actions that produced results only in heavy industry. With a work force made up as late as 1906 primarily of those in establishments employing five or fewer wage earners, social projects that required a volume of capital unavailable to small manufacturers would affect very few French workers.[24] Those were the practical matters that informed the corporatist debate after 1871, when it moved to the center of the attempt by Mun's Oeuvre des Cercles Catholiques des Ouvriers to define the foundations of a Christian social order.

THE CORPORATIST PREDICAMENT

The beginnings of the Oeuvre des Cercles between 1871 and 1875 have been recounted too often to require repetition.[25] What must be noted, though, is the continuity between Mun's organization and earlier-established Catholic groups with a social purpose. The Oeuvre des Cercles did not supplant organizations like the Saint Vincent de Paul Society or Melun's Société d'Economie Charitable, nor was it meant to, but it did draw ideological inspiration, methods, and personnel from them.[26] Although Mun and the directors of the Oeuvre were always careful to maintain their independence from other charitable groups and from direct French ecclesiastical tutelage, their organization initially lacked its own infrastructure and was obliged to graft itself onto operations outside

24. Georges Dupeux, *La société française, 1789–1960* (Paris, 1964), 204.
25. See especially Levillain, *Albert de Mun;* Henri Rollet, *L'Action sociale des catholiques en France, 1871–1901* (Paris, 1946); Charles Maignen, *Maurice Maignen;* Robert Talmy, *Aux sources du catholicisme social: L'Ecole de La Tour Du Pin* (Paris, 1963); Georges Hoog, *Histoire du catholicisme social en France, 1877–1931* (2 vols.; Paris, 1946); Calippe, *Attitude sociale des catholiques françaises* (3 vols.; Paris, 1911–12); Mun, *Ma vocation sociale;* and Benjamin F. Martin, *Count Albert de Mun.*
26. Levillain, *Albert de Mun,* 175. Though similar to earlier charitable groups, the Oeuvre des Cercles was more hierarchically organized and centrally controlled and consisted of a number of councils devoted to organization, propaganda, and theory. In addition, it held yearly congresses and general assemblies. According to the basic plan, each *cercle* "would stimulate a conference of Saint Vincent de Paul to practice charitable action" (Levillain, *Albert de Mun,* 313).

those it had built. Since there were not an infinite number of social Catholic activists, supportive royalists, and socially conscious businessmen, the phenomenal growth of the Oeuvre in the early 1870s was dependent upon the "rapid absorption of the clients" of agencies in place, either through formal alliances or by outright mergers.[27] That is not to say that the new organization brought no new energy to the social Catholic movement. Since Mun wanted to overcome the sporadic nature of earlier social undertakings by making the *cercles* more militant, better organized, and more narrowly directed at the proletariat, he managed to create a level of organizational coherence and enthusiasm that earlier groups lacked. Moreover, the Legitimist party, then engaged in an effort to restore the monarchy through parliamentary action, saw the Oeuvre as possibly providing Legitimism with a new urban base. In addition, Mun's counterrevolutionary rhetoric and ultramontane Catholicism engaged many young Catholics in the monarchical campaign who might otherwise have remained uninspired by the tired intrigue of royalist politics. Still, the Oeuvre was never insulated from the bickering that had hampered Catholics in the past, and the conflicts only grew sharper as the movement struck out in new directions.

Continuity with what had come before was inevitable since, outside Paris—where the newly founded *cercles* organized quickly and maintained their autonomy—the Oeuvre was virtually dependent upon the support of the recently established Comités Catholiques between 1871 and 1873. The Comités were set up by Catholic notables and Legitimist deputies in order to coordinate and support the diverse Catholic organizations that had emerged across the country. On May 25, 1872, the Comités Catholiques de Paris published a circular praising the Oeuvre and saying that the "*cercles* must be taken up as a cause and invigorated by the Catholic participants that our committees can naturally furnish."[28] In many instances, the *cercles* came under the protection of the conferences of the Saint Vincent de Paul Society, connected groups, or the parish clergy. In Josselin, the *cercles* "were an emanation of the Comités Catholiques and had been founded by the bishop of Vannes." At Luçon, the conference of Saint Vincent de Paul founded a *comité des directeurs* of the Oeuvre des Cercles which was presided over by the abbé de Tressay

27. Rollet, *L'Action sociale,* 53.
28. Discours de M. de La Bergassière, May 19–23, 1873, in *Comité catholique de Paris,* 164.

and the bishop. At Grenoble, the chaplain of one parish, with the support of the bishop, created a *cercle* alongside the prayer group that had previously been established by the curé. At Roubaix, the Legitimist-owned *Journal de Roubaix* called on the local Comité Catholique to create a *cercle*.[29] The same ad hoc process was duplicated at Loir-et-Cher and in the industrial districts of the Northeast.[30] In 1872, four Legitimist notables founded five *cercles* in Lille that attracted members mainly among the *patronés* of the Saint Joseph Society. By 1878, the *cercles* counted only 814 members out of a working-class population of more than twenty-five thousand. As in other cases, the *cercles* in Lille borrowed their members from the chronically unemployed and the *patronés* of older charitable societies, many of which had been in decline from the 1860s.[31]

The most important link with the past grew out of Mun's encounter with Maignen in 1871. Maignen, the son of Désiré Adelaïde Charles Maignen, the painter, became a priest in 1839 and, under the pseudonym Le Prévost, founded the Oeuvre de la Sainte Famille in Paris. A member of the Order of Saint Vincent de Paul, Maignen ran a number of successful conferences in Paris before becoming the director of the Cercle de la Jeunesse Ouvriers on the Boulevard Montparnasse. There he created an agency of patronage that was a model of its kind, and he became a favorite of philanthropic Legitimist aristocrats, who provided substantial funding and organizational support for his work. Maignen's association with Mun was a marriage of convenience. Mun, shocked by the French collapse of 1870 and the Commune of 1871, set out to create an organization of social reconciliation but had little idea of how to go about that. Maignen, who was seeking funds to revitalize his faltering Cercle Montparnasse, visited the young, well-connected aristocratic officer at his command post at the Louvre and impressed him with his faith and his conviction that the upper classes could resolve the social question if they were only willing to collaborate directly with the workers. After inspecting the Cercle Montparnasse early in 1872, Mun and a small group of friends launched an "appeal to men of goodwill" to raise funds for Maignen and set up similar *cercles* throughout the ruined neighborhoods of Paris.[32]

29. Levillain, *Albert de Mun*, 402–404.

30. Olivier Martin, *Les Catholiques sociaux dans le Loir-et-Cher: De l'Oeuvre des Cercles Ouvriers au parti Démocratique, 1875–1926*, 32–35; Pierrand, *La Vie ouvrière*, 414–15.

31. Pierrand, *La Vie ouvrière*, 414–15.

32. Mun, *Ma vocation sociale*, 54–74; Benjamin F. Martin, *Count Albert de Mun*, 13–14.

The Cercle Montparnasse, founded in 1865, was a fairly typical agency of patronage for working-class youth. Imitating the *club anglais,* which was the rage at the time, Maignen's group was called a *cercle,* and not an association, to deflect official suspicion like that which beset the Saint Vincent de Paul Society in 1861.[33] For funds, Maignen, with the help of Augustin Cochin, placed the Cercle Montparnasse under the patronage of wealthy Legitimists like Armand de Melun, Alexandre de Lambel, Benoist d'Azy, and Joseph de La Bouillerie and accepted an initial loan of 220,000 francs from the Jockey Club and other *cercles mondains,* which he used to purchase the building on Boulevard Montparnasse as well as a meeting hall and a chapel. In 1869, a subscription supported by nearly six hundred Legitimists and Catholic notables, including Emile Keller and two future Legitimist deputies from Loire-Inférieure, netted another 200,000 francs to cover the cost of needed construction.[34] Thus, when Maignen joined forces with Mun, both were already well integrated into an organizational, financial, and familial network of Legitimist politicians, influential social Catholics, wealthy patrons, and powerful elements within the church.

As a scavenger organization, the Oeuvre des Cercles absorbed not only the people and the mentality but the conflicts, hesitations, and limitations that had shaped the destinies of antecedent groups. From the outset, Mun's operation was dominated by aristocrats, Catholic bourgeois, and Legitimist army officers associated with him and with La Tour Du Pin. Although the group grew to nearly fifty-one thousand members by 1880, it attracted very few industrial workers outside the orbit of the charitable bodies and the factories of the *patrons sociaux.* It came to include groups with different agendas which either insisted on a measure of independence or were committed to forms of social action that conflicted with the goals of the Oeuvre's authoritarian leadership. Too, Mun's close association with royalist politics after he entered the Chamber of Deputies in 1876, and especially his politicization of the *cercles* during the election of 1877, chained the Oeuvre to a brand of militant Catholic royalism that alienated liberal Catholics and Legitimist moderates and diminished the Oeuvre's freedom of action after the republicans took control of the government in 1879.

Mun's inexperience and the importance of his connection with Mai-

---

33. Charles Maignen, *Maurice Maignen,* I, 290.
34. *Ibid.,* 290–91; Levillain, *Albert de Mun,* 236–37.

gnen made the first *cercles* very much like the old youth patronage groups even though they were directed at mature workers. In many respects, the early *cercles* were working-class versions of bourgeois social clubs, where members gathered to pray, read approved books, get a hot meal, smoke, and play cards. According to the basic plan of the Oeuvre, each *cercle* was to embody the "devotion of the directing classes to the working class." A federation of *cercles* in each diocese was to be attached to a *comité des directeurs* constituted by notables and clergymen who were to provide facilities and direct activities through supervisors and a Jesuit chaplain. Upper-class directors were to come to each *cercle* regularly to hold discussions, and all members were to participate in common prayer, attend a special mass for the working class twice a year, and wear a medal proclaiming the immaculate conception of the Virgin.[35] At first, it seems, the leaders hoped simply to nurture a Catholic sociability to reduce the cultural and social barriers between rich and poor. In 1872, Mun described the *cercles* in much the way Armand de Melun had characterized his Oeuvre des Apprentis in the 1840s. There a worker could find a "Christian family" and a "place of reunion where there are all the honest distractions and where he can refresh himself from work through recreation, instead of growing weary from pleasure."[36]

But Mun, Maignen, and La Tour Du Pin had larger ambitions for the Oeuvre. La Tour Du Pin was becoming increasingly preoccupied with corporatist theory, while Mun saw the *cercles* as a way to reconstruct an institutional and moral tradition for the working class. By the early 1870s, Maignen had come to see youth patronage as a "herald, a necessary precursor of a wider organization embracing the entire working class and all the leaders of industry, with the mission of fortifying the moral values of everyone in the workshop and the factory."[37] In this connection, Mun's encounter with Léon Harmel during the pilgrimage at Liesse in 1873 seemed like a revelation.[38] Harmel was the son of Jacques

35. Martin, *Count Albert de Mun,* 34.

36. Mun, *Discours à l'inauguration du Cercle de Montmartre-Clignancourt,* 5. Mun seems to have viewed the *cercles* at first, as "temporary hostels" and as an "information bureau" for migrant workers needing a guide in the large city. At the same time, he fully adopted the model of the Cercle Montparnasse, which he called the "best and first of all" *cercles* (p. 5). See also Albert de Mun, Ouverture du cercle ouvrier de Belleville-Menilmontant, April 4–6, 1872, in *Comité catholique de Paris,* 269.

37. Charles Maignen, *Maurice Maignen,* I, 240.

38. Mun, *Ma vocation sociale,* 216–17.

Joseph Harmel, an early *patron social* who had introduced instruments of *prévoyance* into his textile factory at Val-des-Bois under the joint management of the proprietor and the workers. As heir, Léon Harmel had continued the work of his father by attempting to turn the family business into a true "Christian factory." At Val-des-Bois, Mun and others saw in the synthesis of the divers techniques of patronage a practical model for the reconstruction of the *corporation* in an industrial setting. Convinced that Harmel's factory held the key to reviving the spirit of "Christian association in the world of work," the leaders of the Oeuvre decided to use the *cercles* as building blocks for fashioning mixed associations in as many areas of manufacturing as possible.[39] Their decision unleashed a debate that finally dragged social Catholicism into a serious confrontation with French economic, social, and political realities and revealed many of the contradictions inherent in the Legitimists' project of social reconstruction.

The starting point of the debate was the organization of the factory at Val-des-Bois. Harmel had encouraged his employees to create associations—a men's club, a women's association, a girls' society, a mutual-aid society—that they controlled democratically. The associations elected shop committees and members of a corporate board to consult with Harmel and his foremen on questions of floor management and wage schedules. Although agreeing not to strike and possessing no independent authority, the workers were subject to the policies of the employer only upon their advice and consent. Much of the corporate board's most important activity, however, did not concern conditions in the factory. Various corporate committees were empowered to set up religious facilities, schools, life insurance programs, sickness and accident funds, vocational training, and a savings bank. Others purchased coal and potatoes for the community at wholesale prices, contracted with local merchants to supply workers with food, collectively paid off bad accounts, and secured a 5- to 20- percent discount on bulk orders. In addition, they made medical and pharmaceutical services available and paid for them out of a common fund. Sick and pregnant women were relieved of housework by girls released from work for that purpose. Permanently disabled workers received a lifelong annuity and were allowed to remain on the premises and enjoy all the services there as long as they wished.

39. Charles Maignen, *Maurice Maignen*, I, 393.

Family life was protected by the construction of separate cottages with small gardens, rented for 140 francs per year. Each girl received a dowry of 100 francs at the time of marriage, and wedding festivals were attended by the entire community. Wherever possible, morality and religion were preached to discourage vice and laziness. Company schools were run by chaplains and friars, and workers were strongly encouraged to join only Catholic associations.[40]

When Harmel presented this system of shop-floor cooperation and community organization to the Oeuvre's congress in Lyon in 1874, his speech "was greeted . . . with true enthusiasm." At the same meeting, La Tour Du Pin declared that the Oeuvre "recognized its spirit and its principles in M. Harmel's presentation."[41] The industrial heir met with a cooler reception, however, when he proposed his ideas to the Catholic manufacturers who dominated the Comités Catholiques of the Nord and Pas-de-Calais.[42] In November, 1875, Père Eugène Marquigny, a Jesuit, a former editor of the *Etudes,* and one of the ecclesiastical counselors of the Association Catholique des Patrons du Nord, presented a report to the Congrès Catholique de Lille endorsing Harmel's scheme but stipulating that the introduction of the corporate model had to remain entirely at the discretion of the individual proprietor. Laws regulating work in France, he stated, "need no modification," and any effort "to reduce or suppress the individual freedom of labor and replace it with collectivities, associations, or syndicates charged to watch over the interests of each profession" should be rejected by Catholic employers. He conceded that the "free *corporation*" was consistent with Catholic teachings but warned that a "return to the regime of *corporations, corps de métiers, maîtrises,* or *jurandes*" threatened personal freedom.[43] Marquigny's report soon became the basis for a series of resolutions adopted by the Congrès de Lille and recommended to the Patrons Chrétiens, who had begun to collabo-

40. Moon, *The Labor Problem,* 114–17. See also Georges Guitton, *Léon Harmel, 1829–1915* (2 vols.; Paris, 1927), and Léon Harmel, *Manuel d'une corporation chrétienne* (Tours, 1877).

41. Charles Maignen, *Maurice Maignen,* I, 142, 472–73. At the Assemblée Générale des Comités Catholiques du Nord et du Pas-du-Calais, Harmel stressed the importance that wages be paid on a weekday, that they be handed by the *patron* himself to the head of the worker's family, and that they never be distributed to a worker by another worker. He also recommended that all members of a worker's family belong to the factory associations.

42. Levillain, *Albert de Mun,* 425–26n; Rollet, *L'Action sociale,* 74–77.

43. Charles Maignen, *Maurice Maignen,* I, 536–37.

rate with the Oeuvre des Cercles. Northern manufacturers from then on consistently adopted the views that any revived *corporations* had to be based on the principle of "free Christian association" and that patronage had to be "voluntary, . . . freely accorded, and freely accepted."[44]

Their preemptive strike was made with the knowledge that the Oeuvre had not yet announced a clear position on the *corporation* and that certain elements within the organization were not constrained by the material concerns of the Patrons Chrétiens. In November, 1875, the Oeuvre adopted a report drawn up by La Tour Du Pin endorsing Harmel's system and committing the organization to work toward the practical transformation of the *cercles* into corporate bodies "wherever there is a mass of workers."[45]

Inside the Oeuvre, Maignen was highly critical of turning matters of practice and principle over to bourgeois elements who were blindly attached to economic liberalism and the "false dogma" of 1789.[46] Rejecting liberalism in any form as inconsistent with Christian principles, he based his objections to the position taken by the Patrons Chrétiens on practical as well as ideological grounds. In a letter written to La Tour Du Pin in November, he praised the Harmel factory but questioned whether a system designed for a large operation could incorporate the "population of our *cercles*," which were made up chiefly of artisans and of workers employed in small workshops. The success of the Oeuvre, he argued, depended on its adaptation to the "diversity of social conditions," because the future of the Christian social order lay not only in factory patronage but in the ability of the church to carry its apostolic mission into all sectors of production through the *cercles*.[47] If the Oeuvre's ultimate purpose was to Christianize society, it was an apostolic organization. To adopt Harmel's system on the basis of the principles enunciated by Père Marquigny would be to make the sacred mission of the *corporations* depend exclusively on the initiative of large industrial enterprises and would give the "liberal" bourgeoisie control over the application and extension of the corporatist order. Had not the declarations of the Patrons Chrétiens asked that the "heads of the factories or large workshops, who have all the constitutive elements of the *corporations* in their hands,

44. Levillain, *Albert de Mun*, 596; Charles Maignen, *Maurice Maignen*, I, 538.
45. Rollet, *L'Action sociale*, 58–59.
46. Charles Maignen, *Maurice Maignen*, I, 537.
47. *Ibid.*, 487.

exercise their social paternity in such a manner as to coordinate these elements under their direction"?[48]

Maignen was speaking from experience as well as from principle. His own Cercle Montparnasse had attracted a heterogeneous group of crafts-men, artisans, and shopkeepers; in its composition it represented the makeup of the Parisian working classes. In 1878, when Maignen began to organize the members of the Cercle into distinct professional *corpora-tions,* he sought to reproduce the structure of the old *corps de métiers* by grouping the artisans and masters into sections distinguished by the na-tures of their trades. Tailors, shoemakers, saddlers, and dry cleaners were grouped in Section I (*Vêtements*); carpenters, locksmiths, roofers, plumb-ers, and chimney sweeps were grouped in Section II (*Bâtiments*), and so forth.[49] In his letter to La Tour Du Pin, he observed that the workers at Val-des-Bois, employees of a factory located in the countryside outside Rheims, were "fixed, dependent, grouped by the work of the entire family, and *subservient,*" whereas the workers of the large cities were "in-dependent, nomadic, scattered, separated."[50] In practice, if Harmel and the Patrons Chrétiens insisted on the application of corporatism only in factories, Maignen argued, they were in effect legitimating the social pre-ponderance of a new industrial aristocracy over the social destiny of the nation: "[If] the Marquis de Mun [Albert de Mun's father], a *seigneur châtelain* without feudal rights but a seigneur anyway, holds the popula-tion in his hands, it is M. Harmel who has inherited the feudal rights of the marquis; he is the marquis of the nineteenth century; he holds the populations in his hands, liable at his mercy to the corvée."[51] If corporat-ism was to lead to a qualitatively different social order, Maignen con-tended, the control of the *corporations* had to be the prerogative of all, and if the *corporation* was to accommodate a diverse and mobile popula-tion, there would have to be *corporations* for towns, for villages, for ag-riculture, for artisans, and for the migrant worker as well.[52]

Maignen also pointed out that the management of the *corporations* ex-clusively by Catholic businessmen would prescribe the manner in which ordained ministers of the faith carried the Christian message to the work-

48. *Ibid.,* 539.
49. *Ibid.,* 636–37.
50. *Ibid.,* 487–88. Emphasis in the original.
51. *Ibid.,* 488.
52. *Ibid.*

ers. Only the clergy, he declared, could ensure a *formation chrétienne* to the members of the *cercles* who were to participate in the corporate institutions. This principle he held true for its directors as well as its working-class associates. Why, he wondered, should a *patronat* imbued with the false principles of liberalism be free to exempt itself from the direct spiritual guidance of the chaplains associated with the Oeuvre? If "the church has the secret to all social solutions," the clergy must be free to play an independent role in all undertakings of social regeneration.[53] Many of the services provided by Harmel's corporate board engaged the Sisters of Charity, the Brothers of Saint Vincent de Paul, and other charitable orders; only the church, Maignen maintained, had the right to determine the nature of their participation and the extent of their access to members of the *cercles*. He warned Mun that it would be contrary to orthodoxy to have members of religious congregations attached to the *cercles* under the direction of "committees of men of the world, of laics." The superintendence of the feminine orders, he asserted, "belongs to the bishop and the *curé supérieur* of the congregation." The rule of ecclesiastical jurisdiction was by itself enough to challenge the Patrons Chrétiens and threaten the Oeuvre with censure should it adopt their principles as its own.

Mun was not one to work at cross-purposes with the church, nor was he willing to hand control of his organization over to a group of industrialists who were weary of his royalist politics. At the same time, he understood that Maignen's objections threatened to shatter the Oeuvre's "solid organization." At a meeting of the general secretariat in December, 1875, Mun supported a resolution incorporating Maignen's views on the necessary independence of the clergy.[54] On extending *corporations* into the arts and trades, however, Maignen gained only partial satisfaction. The reason was largely political. Maignen's protests had led to the creation of advisory commissions for industry, arts and trades, and agriculture designed to work out the practical means of transforming the *cercles* into *corporations* in the several sectors of production. For Maignen that was a step in the right direction, but it did not end his ideological battle with the Patrons Chrétiens, because their advisory commission was powerful enough to override the resolutions of any other faction. Under the leadership of Hippolyte André, an ironmaster from Couzances and a

53. *Ibid.*, 489.
54. *Ibid.*, 489–97.

friend of Harmel's, the Commission Consultive d'Industriels had enlisted five thousand business owners by 1879 and had gained the numerical predominance to force the Oeuvre to take their views into account in every major decision.[55]

The conflict, therefore, reached a new pitch as the industrialists pressed their case for "free *corporations*" under the regime of the *liberté du travail,* remained hostile to workers' associations outside the orbit of the *corporations,* and absolutely rejected the idea of national social legislation recognizing mixed syndicates and giving professional associations power to arbitrate industrial disputes. To Maignen and many *chefs d'atelier* it seemed absurd to suppose that professional associations could flourish on a national scale as long as small enterprises lacked the capital to support patronage and laicized businessmen were immune from the influence of the church. Only the state, they claimed, could grant workers the legal right to organize and oblige *patrons* to participate in mixed syndicates, and only social legislation could create minimum standards of social justice and the practical means by which workers in small workshops could benefit from them. By late 1875, the corporatist debate had presented the Oeuvre with a choice: whether social Catholics should be liberals or socialists.[56]

For Maignen, corporatism was synonymous with counterrevolution, that is, with the wholesale rejection of the liberal order. What he required from the bourgeoisie was not so much that they step aside but that they repudiate the "false dogma of 1789" in an act of collective conversion or, rather, in an act of collective contrition for the "crime of the eighteenth century."[57] Before the Revolution, he explained, the working classes were Christian, and their faith was externalized in the way they organized their labor, their leisure, and their relations to other social groups. Workers had not fomented the Revolution; rather, it was the error of heretical and selfish elites who expropriated the Christian *corporation* from the working class to fulfill a preverted vision of an individualistic society or to force the workers to submit to their will. Blinded by pride and their own narrow interests, the bourgeoisie had destroyed the institutions that had ensured the moral development of the working classes and then had

55. Rollet, *L'Action sociale,* 66.
56. *Ibid.*
57. Charles Maignen, *Maurice Maignen,* I, 448–79.

employed force to suppress those who suffered from bourgeois greed. The rebirth of the *corporation,* he therefore believed, would signify the end of the Revolution and the redemption of those responsible for it.[58]

For Maignen and La Tour Du Pin, the juridically obligatory *corporation* was justified because neither workers nor *patrons* had an absolute liberty to violate collective interests. Freedom of labor and entrepreneurial freedom were liberal fictions contrary to the divinely imposed obligation to organize society for the moral and material preservation of its members. Since the *corporation* constituted the joint property of all its members, it could confer equal rights and impose equal duties on all parties. Maignen argued that craftsmen should have the right to protect their professional know-how by regulating the "number of apprentices and masters (and consequently of workers) in each *corps de métiers* in proportion to consumer demand," and that mixed syndicates would be obliged to determine prices, fix wages, and discuss all abuses so that "no serious trouble arises . . . between workers and master." Social peace, he concluded, must be won for one class not at the expense of another but through an institutionalized representation of all social interests. That would engender behavior that conformed to reciprocal rights and duties.[59]

As for the Patrons Chrétiens' objection that compulsory *corporations* would hinder productivity and efficiency, Maignen responded that an "emulation toward progress" would supersede unlimited competition and would be favorable to a "perfection of fabrication" without any harmful social consequences. Mixed syndicates, he held, were in "no way contrary to the wise development of industry," because they could meet frequently to adapt their statutes to industrial innovation while prudently regulating the introduction of mechanization so as to create a wise and humane rhythm of economic progress. "A little less cotton and a bit more unity between classes," he suggested, "would be preferable for the well-being of humanity."[60] Like the *corporations* of the past, Maignen's

58. Maignen concluded in his sketch of the ancient *corporations* that their principal goal had been "to guard the faith in order to save [the worker's] soul from the slavery of sin, to assure work in order to save his body from the servitudes of indigence." That was all the workers demanded from the monarchy in the past, and "it would be the same for the true people of today, if they had not been blinded by the Revolution" (*Ibid.,* 511).

59. *Ibid.,* 512–13.

60. *Ibid.,* 513–17.

updated version was to be more concerned with product quality and labor stability than with profit, efficiency, and volume.

Maignen and other counterrevolutionaries were persuaded, however,
that the institutional arrangements they advocated would be in constant
jeopardy unless they were guaranteed by a paternal Christian monarchy
that had a historic obligation to sanction legislation and authorize regulations consistent with the Christian reconstruction of society. Only a
king working in concert with an *assemblée des métiers* under the spiritual
guidance of the church could justly impose collective restraints, because
in his capacity he would embody the legitimate right of the state to arbitrate in the name of all the various bodies constituting civil society. The
restoration envisioned by Maignen was not only to restore political legitimacy but also to reconsecrate the legacy of Saint Louis and reunite
the French monarchy with the people by enacting the Christian social
order into law.[61]

In November, 1877, Maignen traveled to the stronghold of the Patrons Chrétiens to present to the congress at Lille of the general directors
of the Oeuvre a declaration—drawn up by the *patrons d'atelier* associated
with the Cercles Montparnasse—that called for the reestablishment of
the corporatist regime. After denouncing the Chapellier Law, of 1791,
which in the view of counterrevolutionaries embodied the Revolution's
perversion of social relations, the declaration demanded the authorization
of professional *corporations* in industry, the trades, and agriculture as public utilities, subject to administrative regulations. In that way, all the protection accorded to workers by the *corporations* would be recognized by
law as "public property." In addition, the *patrons* of Montparnasse called
for a ministry of labor "assisted by superior councils composed of the
most notable syndics of the *corporations* and charged with regulating
questions that concern work and workers," as well as "new legislation
restoring to the members of the *corporations* the municipal magistrature
that they had exercised over the centuries under the titles of *echevins* and
prévots de marchands."[62]

As Maignen had foreseen, the declaration was rejected by a heavy
majority, but he succeeded in forcing the leadership of the Oeuvre into a

61. *Ibid.,* 513, 529.
62. See the Déclaration rélative au rétablissement des corporations, *ibid.,* 548–61.

crisis of identity by raising the questions of whether a Christian society could remain capitalist and whether a Christian could continue to support what the French Revolution had wrought. Unable to resolve the questions, or to stem the decline of the *cercles* in the wake of the Legitimists' failure to restore the monarchy, the Oeuvre committed itself to a compromise on the nature of the *corporation* in November, 1878. Rejecting the position of the Patrons Chrétiens, the directors condemned "freedom of labor" and "unlimited competition," but they resisted the conclusion that workers and *patrons* should be obliged to enter into *corporations* and that the state should recognize the regulations adopted by professional associations. Rather, the Oeuvre adopted an opinion prepared by the organization's Conseil des Etudes, headed by the La Tour Du Pin, that recommended the building of *corporations* where possible in the context of a free economy.[63] The conflict therefore continued. In September, 1878, at the congress at Chartres, Mun spoke in favor of the counterrevolutionary position, while Charles Périn, a professor of political economy at the University of Louvain and the spokesman for the Patrons Chrétiens, rejected state intervention and the reestablishment of the *corps de métiers* as a threat to property rights and a reactionary obstacle to economic development. A liberal Catholic, Périn cleverly assured the Congress that Pius IX had opposed the "principle of a return to the old system of privileges favoring a particular class of merchants or industrialists," and he suggested that faith and charity were enough to "surmount obstacles created by human disorder."[64] Liberty and civil equality, Périn said, were not revolutionary accomplishments but the conditions that permitted Catholics to exercise moral influence over society. The counterrevolutionaries would achieve nothing by "repudiating the conditions of liberty," he argued, as long as men were immune to the inspiration of the church.[65]

Mun, who after 1875 was preoccupied with national politics, tried not to provoke either side, by remaining conciliatory in public. At the congress at Chartres, for example, he distanced himself from the liberals by announcing that "we are the irreconcilable counterrevolution," but he

63. Rollet, *L'Action sociale*, 65.
64. Levillain, *Albert de Mun*, 651.
65. Charles Périn, in Levillain's *Albert de Mun*, 618–19. See also Charles Périn to Léon Harmel, April 28, 1877, in Mollet's *Albert de Mun*, Documents, 169.

avoided giving a full endorsement of Maignen's corporatist regime.[66] In private he was painfully aware that the dispute between Maignen and Harmel was not simply one of "application" but was a "fundamental struggle." Mun wanted the Oeuvre to offer an alternative to liberalism based on "clear, firm, and precise principles" rather than to preach an "ill-defined counterrevolution." He leaned in the direction of Maignen; all the same, he feared that the paralysis caused by internal divisions in the Conseil des Etudes had let the leadership avoid decisive questions. That, he felt, served the advantage of industrialists like Harmel and liberal "economists" like Périn, who had produced "admirable results" and controlled the powerful *commission des industriels.* "So as not to be a school," he wrote to Félix de Roquefeuil, "we are more and more becoming the Harmel school"; the Conseil des Etudes remained, he thought, a "machine for compromises between Maignen and Harmel [*sic*]." For a time, he contemplated stacking the Conseil des Etudes with "resolute enemies of the Revolution in all its forms, and of liberalism in all its guises," but that seemed to him less urgent as it became apparent that Christian social reconstruction faced its biggest obstacles outside the Oeuvre.[67] After 1879, republican hostility toward clerical power demonstrated to him that no amount of programmatic coherence could remedy that "we can neither incite the laws to conform to our desires nor control the government in this sense." Instead of arguing about the form of the *corporation,* Mun turned his energies toward persuading the "industrialists to undertake certain reforms, to abolish certain abuses, and to establish certain institutions." He admitted, "That is what is practical; we have to limit our declarations to that. As for the arts and trades, I won't say too much: form professional associations, and don't argue too much about the *corporations.*"[68]

---

66. Discours de Chartres, in Charles Maignen's *Maurice Maignen,* I, 604–609. In this speech, perhaps one of the most important of a long career, Mun was deliberately ambiguous, speaking of the *corporation* as both a "professional association" and a "foyer of Christian activity" rather than merely an "arbitration board." The ambiguity lay in the fact that the Conseil des Etudes had defined a professional association as an informal and voluntary union of workers and *patrons* whereas the notion of the *corporation* implied a system that, whether free or obligatory, went well beyond the idea of an association.

67. Albert de Mun to Félix de Roquefeuil, June 20, 1878, in Mollet's *Albert de Mun, Documents,* 176–77.

68. Albert de Mun to Milcent, September 6, 1879, *ibid.,* 191.

At the time of his letters to Roquefeuil, Mun was being warned by Keller—Mun's mentor and a confidant to the pope—to avoid pronouncements in favor of counterrevolution, which only served to antagonize liberal Catholics by making Mun's program seem a specter of the Old Regime that could supply the enemies of the monarchy and the church with ammunition.[69] "Neither the Old Regime nor the Revolution but the Christian society," enjoined Keller, "that is the true motto." He pointed out that limiting freedom of labor was a "delicate point" on which the church itself hesitated, since no clear doctrine on such matters had yet been established. Keller interpreted the idea of corporate property as a "collective patrimony," that is, as including only the funds and services of *prévoyance* that employers and employees had jointly established. Mun, he suggested, should concentrate on "laying out duties for the state" by pursuing social legislation "to check gross crimes and abuses" such as Sunday work, child labor, long working hours for women, the lack of tariff protection, and the absence of a minimum wage. If such an effort failed to create a new order, at least it would diminish the popularity of socialism.[70]

Weakened by internal conflict and by a sharp decrease in recruitment results, the Oeuvre began to decline after 1883, the year of Chambord's death. As the contours of republican policy began to emerge after 1879, Mun shifted his attention to the Chamber of Deputies. He regained his seat in 1881 and turned to fighting for the kind of legislation suggested by Keller.[71] Like Armand de Melun some thirty years earlier, Mun had concluded that private efforts would never suffice to solve the social question and that it was not enough to profess Christian principles but

69. See Comte Alfred de Falloux, "De la Contre-Révolution," *Le Correspondant,* CXIII (1878), 362–76.

70. Emile Keller to Albert de Mun, September 11, 1878, in Mollet's *Albert de Mun, Documents,* 182–83.

71. On the decline of the Oeuvre, see Charles Maignen, *Maurice Maignen,* I, 677, 738–40; Rollet, *L'Action sociale,* 52–53; and Olivier Martin, *Les Catholiques sociaux dans le Loir-et-Cher,* 32. The Oeuvre supported Mun's efforts in the Chamber despite the opposition of the *patrons* of the Nord. Although the *patrons* accepted the idea of limited social legislation, they wanted any such laws to be accompanied by similar arrangements in other countries. In the Chamber, Mun sponsored a law on accident insurance in 1886. In 1888, he pushed for mandatory retirement funds, and in 1890 he supported a law prohibiting children under thirteen from working and raised the perennial question of Sunday rest. See Mollet, *Albert de Mun,* 80–85.

was necessary to enact them into law so that they might animate the "life of society" and "penetrate the mores" of the people.[72]

THE CHRISTIAN SOCIAL ORDER:
STATE OF LAW OR STATE OF GRACE?

The debates within the Oeuvre between advocates of the free *corporation* and the obligatory *corporation* could have been sustained by social divisions and differences over technical matters alone. Maignen, a member of the regular clergy, was fighting a two-front battle. On the one hand, he spoke for the shopkeepers and craftsmen of the *cercles* against the hegemony of a bourgeoisie that wanted to run the *corporations* as private fiefs; on the other hand, he stood for the clerical element that sought to ground the Oeuvre in pure orthodoxy against the economists who would have turned the organization into a dogmatic school of Christian political economy in defense of liberalism. But the conflict pointed to an even more profound disagreement social Catholics and Legitimists engaged in over the kind of durable Christian transformation of France they ought to pursue. Both sides agreed that the new order should be corporatist, but neither wanted to admit the risks involved in changing society; both sides understood their endeavor as applying faith to society, but neither could gain a consensus on precisely what that meant.

As a counterrevolutionary, Maignen opposed economic liberty and championed the ideal of compulsory corporative organization, because he believed that the old *corps de métiers* had made workers Christian. Since the Republic was both the institutional and the philosophic expression of the Revolution, a corporate monarchy—by definition contrary to the principles of 1789—would have to include a concrete institutional component patterned on the organization of labor during the Christian Middle Ages. Harmel's factory was laudable despite its deficiencies, but neither did it save the working class as a whole nor was it consistent with a Christian political economy, which did not recognize the right of industrialists to flood the market with cheap goods, exploit the workers, and leave most in a state of misery. Inasmuch as only legally sanctioned institutions could force the bourgeoisie to fulfill its social obligations,

72. Discours du comte Albert de Mun: Questions sociales, in Mollet's *Albert de Mun,* 48.

Maignen argued, it was necessary for the Oeuvre to devise a sort of "dictatorship of duty," which would end only when "the religious cadres of a Christian society have reformed their ranks."[73]

To the Patrons Chrétiens, Maignen's position appeared both dangerous and incomprehensible. Harmel and Maignen both believed that the *corporation* had a religious as well as an economic function, but Harmel saw no "religious base" in Maignen's system but only the outline of an oppressive economic and political straitjacket. He understood that Maignen wanted the church to play a special and independent role in the Christian factory community; nevertheless, he feared that Maignen had mistaken the organization of the *corporation* for its essence. For the Patrons Chrétiens, the "religious base" of the Christian social order had to reside in the human conscience; in order for the conscience to be free to embrace the doctrines of the church, the state had to work to remove everything that could obstruct the transmission of Christian values. Christian association and the organization of a more just society would emerge, the Patrons Chrétiens argued, through conversion and not coercion. Thus liberty as constituted in modern society was the prerequisite for effective evangelization and the voluntary establishment of free *corporations*. "The old Catholic spirit," explained Périn, "is not in the return to outmoded forms of labor organization but in the reawakening of charity. . . . The combined action of the church, which inspires and sustains charity, and the state, which lends it the support of the laws, is an overriding necessity for [Catholic] programs."[74]

For Maignen, the *corporation,* which united "Catholic principles . . . to all forms of private and public life" through the dual magistrature of church and state, was the essence of the Christian social order; therefore, an autonomous industrial sector had no place in it.[75] For Harmel, "the *corporations* would return of themselves," once the "Christian spirit" freely animated the social order.[76] That is why, while Maignen drew up blueprints for the reestablishment of a corporatist regime, Harmel

73. Rapport sur l'accord à établir entre les oeurves ouvriers, cercles et patronage (Note manuscrit, 1888, Archives Maurice Maignen, in Levillain's *Albert de Mun,* 594–96).

74. Discours de Charles Périn, in *Union des Associations Ouvrières Catholiques, congrès de Chartes: Compte rendu du onzième assemblée générale des directeurs d'oeuvres, 9–13 séptembre 1878* (Paris, 1879), 52–66.

75. Charles Maignen, *Maurice Maignen,* I, 614.

76. Commission de l'enquête économique: Procès-verbal de la séance de 6 mars 1878, in Charles Maignen's *Maurice Maignen,* I, 580.

stressed Christian education, individual initiative, the paternal character of the *bon maître,* and the evangelization of all classes.[77] As liberals, Harmel and Périn embraced a concept of charity that went in tandem with their demand that civil society retain a complete autonomy from a state whose function they wished to define in negative terms. Liberal corporatism amounted to no more than the completion of the *encadrement* of the working class. The free *corporation* was to allow factory owners to supervise the workers within the framework of their own social power while leaving the clergy free to associate itself with the *patrons'* activities. In 1879, Harmel told the directors of the Oeuvre, "The Christian workshop . . . reestablishes the reign of Jesus Christ in the soul through Christian discipline, the practice of patronage, and the permanent influence of Catholic associations; at the same time, it nourishes and soothes the body by moderate work and through economic and charitable institutions of all kinds. Patronage [and] isolated [acts of charity] do much good, but their influence always remains restrained and intermittent, whereas the Christian workshop completely realizes the hopes to which the union of all charitable works gives rise, because it affects one's life in a continuous fashion from all directions."[78] Maignen, who linked the transformation of civil society to the restoration of a monarchical government committed to the creation of a Christian social order, argued that the prescriptive actions of a Christian prince would in no way be inimical to the interests of society as a whole. The bourgeoisie required no less supervision than the working class.

Thus, a fundamental difference of approach engulfed the Legitimist movement as it set about to define the modalities of a restoration. The Legitimists, like the corporatists among whom they ranked, could never agree on whether the institution of monarchy was necessary for the transformation of society or whether it would be the consequence of that transformation. Unlike the republicans, the Legitimists could not decide whether or not to practice the sort of opportunism that led Léon Gambetta to pursue the republican form of government in a way that carried the risk of violating republican principles, confident that "la forme emporterait le fond." Maignen would have agreed with that dictum and

77. See Discours de Léon Harmel, in *Union des Associations Ouvrières Catholiques, congrès d'Angers: Compte rendu de la douzième assemblée générale des directeurs d'oeuvres, 1–5 séptembre 1879* (Angers, 1879), 94–99.
78. *Ibid.,* 94.

therefore had no second thoughts about the wisdom of fighting for the monarchist cause. Harmel, on the contrary, believed that le fond emporterait la forme and could thus separate his social activity from the immediate political priorities of the Legitimist party. Thousands of Catholics faced the same predicament.[79]

Maignen, who died in 1890, and La Tour Du Pin, who rejected the papal instruction to rally to the Republic in 1891, remained unshakable in their adherence to the monarchy, whereas Harmel became one of the early founders of Christian democracy. Indeed, Harmel's career pointed to some such defection from the royalist movement after the death of Chambord in 1883, since he and other social Catholics had developed a method of social action whose link to dynastic politics was tenuous at best, especially after papal support for a monarchy in France waned under Leo XIII. As for Mun, his effort to institutionalize the Christian social order through legislation, although difficult and incomplete, bore some fruit—as well as some strange political alliances—and demonstrated what could be achieved without the monarchy. The more dynasticism stood in the way of social reform, the closer Mun moved toward a *ralliement* that would allow him to pursue his social priorities and renovate French society from within the boundaries of the established Republic.

The Oeuvre had a commission on agriculture but it was rendered invisible by the movement's preoccupation with industry. That was indicative, perhaps, of the growing relative importance of the industrial sector and the shift in society's attention toward the great nineteenth-century drama of the revolt of the urban masses. Compared with the city, the countryside seemed an oasis of stability and traditionalism needing little reconstructive surgery. Yet there too the Legitimists encountered disturbing problems. Although they might have preferred the tranquillity of their estates, they were not mere spectators at the drama that was unfolding in rural France.

79. See Levillain, *Albert de Mun*, 589–601. Levillain writes, "As in the debate about the egg and the chicken, Maignen considered that the corporation would produce the Christian society [but] Harmel [believed] that Christian affirmation would produce the corporation" (p. 601).

CHAPTER VIII

 The Accomplishments and
Risks of Progressive
Agriculture

ONE WOULD expect the Legitimists, a majority of whom
were *grands propriétaires,* to have looked back on the events of the Revolution of 1789 in rural France with an abiding horror and resentment.
Certainly, they did not forget the burning of châteaux and the expropria-
tion of land that many of their families had experienced. Nonetheless,
the events of the summer of 1789 hardly entered into the debates on the
improvement of French agriculture, and the Legitimists never mentioned
the Great Fear or the Night of August 4 in the context of their hopes and
designs for the regeneration of rural France.

Their apparently clement attitude is understandable when one re-
members that the peasants of the late eighteenth century had revolted
against a seigneurial system that many rural elites had criticized and that
the Legitimists had no intention of reestablishing. At least until the
1860s, moreover, the Legitimists were largely satisfied with the social
and economic structure that had emerged in the French countryside after
the Revolution. It was only when traditional society began to break
down that they started to consider ways to check the deterioration of the
old social order. By then the issues and conflicts that had given rise to
the rural Revolution of 1789 had become a distant memory.

Why should the Legitimists have been relatively content with the results of the Revolution in the countryside when in so many other respects
they considered it to have been a disaster? Why, as the nineteenth century
progressed, were they at once so quick to see in the rural social environ-

210

ment both an antidote to democratization and a barrier to the prosperity its continuance required? As Georges Lefebvre has demonstrated, the Revolution continued rather than broke with the transformations undertaken before 1789 in rural France toward the removal of legal obstacles to commercialization and toward the accumulation of land by rich peasants and the bourgeoisie. The result of the Revolution was not a radically new social order but a rural society capable of only slow economic progress, yet one in which the potential for catastrophic social conflict had been largely defused.[1] In addition, the self-sufficient and localized nature of the rural economy in the early nineteenth century provided an imperfect basis for either rapid industrialization or the structural changes that the growth of industry could impose on the countryside.[2]

On the whole, the Legitimist *grand propriétaires* benefited from the prevailing social and economic equilibrium. In the first place, the aristocracy had managed to keep most of its land, and although roughly 10 percent of arable land changed hands during the Revolution, the size, structure, and composition of the landed elite and the overall hierarchical structure of rural society remained relatively unchanged. France was not a country of great landowners, in comparison with other European societies like England or Prussia; neither did it become a republic of small, independent peasants. In 1826, 6 percent of all landowners still owned 20.8 percent of the cultivated land surface, with estates for them averaging 273 hectares, while 89.3 percent possessed 32.5 percent of the land, with average holdings of less than 2.5 hectares.[3] Small- and medium-size farms were frequently rented from large landowners or held in *métayage* so that roughly 25 percent of the peasantry were directly tied to rural elites and in many cases subject to their social and political influence. What is more, despite the unequal distribution of land, the Revolution had created a diverse group of landowners who shared a common attachment to the rights of property and who constituted a formidable barrier to social revolution. Whatever the Legitimists' feelings about Léon Gam-

1. Georges Lefebvre, "The Place of the Revolution in the Agrarian History of France," in *Rural Society in France*, ed. Forster and Ranum, 41.
2. See Theda Skocpol, *States and Social Revolutions: A Comparative Analysis of France, Russia, and China* (Cambridge, Mass., 1979), 176–77; Trebilcock, *The Industrialization of the Continental Powers*, 134–35.
3. P. Houée, *Une Longue Evolution, 1815–1950* (Paris, 1972), 23, Vol. I of Houée, *Les Etapes du développement rural*, 2 vols. See also Chapter I of the present study.

betta's politics, they would have agreed with him that the Revolution "had created not only *propriétaires* but property itself."[4] In addition, the Revolution had left in place an enormous labor supply comprising *parcelaires,* landless day laborers, and domestics. As late as 1882, *journaliers* and *domestiques* constituted 35 percent of the total active rural population, and although the large number of landless peasants offered the potential for revolution, they were too impoverished, too ill informed, too unorganized, and too well integrated into traditional rural society to pose a real threat to propertied interests prior to the 1880s.

Rural individualism, the defense of property, and the helplessness of the landless poor tended to make the countryside politically safe. The Legitimists knew that the larger part of their popular support came from rural districts and that, despite notable exceptions, the countryside tended to resist anticlericalism and dechristianization better than the cities. But not all trends were encouraging. At midcentury, peasants and landlords still fought over the use of forests and commons, and in 1851 rural areas of the Midi had joined the towns in defending the Republic. Still, in 1849 a majority of the peasants had voted for the Party of Order, thus helping to undermine democracy, and in 1851 they "saved" France from the Reds. Although the peasants helped put Louis Napoleon in power, the Legitimists generally considered the rise of Bonapartism a victory for order.

By the 1850s, the situation in rural France had become more disturbing, in large part owing to changes the Legitimists had encouraged. Although the Legitimists benefited politically from the way the rural social structure impeded rapid industrialization, they were among the most avid promoters of agricultural modernization in the nineteenth century. The duality of their interests presented Legitimist *propriétaires* with a number of difficulties. By expanding the acreage under cultivation and increasing productivity, agricultural modernization made greater demands on the rural labor supply at the same time that commercialization, market integration, and better transportation helped quicken the pace of an industrialization that was attracting laborers to the cities. Even though the Legitimists unequivocally deplored the "depopulation" of the countryside, they clearly profited under the Second Empire, in part because

4. Discours de La Ferté-sous-Jouaire, July 14, 1872, in Pierre Barral's *Les Agrariens français de Méline à Pisani* (Paris, 1968), 38.

the growing urban demand for food created new opportunities for farmers. Thus, while conscientious large landowners saw their incomes rise, the social changes brought about by agricultural improvement and industrialization stimulated what François Crouzet called the "disintegration . . . of traditional society" and the concurrent emancipation of the peasantry from its dependence on traditional authorities.[5] As Claude Nicolet has written, the "Republic in the village" was an "absolute necessity" in the founding of the Third Republic.[6]

The Legitimists were faced with an opposition between their material interests and their desire to safeguard the conservatism of traditional rural society. It was both their acute awareness of this problem and their desire to overcome it that molded their views on the reconstruction of rural France between the 1850s and the 1880s. Rather than accepting the full consequences of industrialization or rejecting all compromises with the modern world, however, they concluded that it was possible to enjoy the benefits of economic progress without harming the social, cultural, and demographic basis upon which their influence rested. This explains why they could at the same moment praise the peasantry for preserving "all the conservative instincts," recommend work in the fields as morally strengthening, and condemn the rural masses for their economic illiteracy and their attachment to outmoded routine.[7] Having embraced the "agricultural revolution," the Legitimists nevertheless tried to alter its social and political consequences. This chapter will concern the Legiti-

5. See Ronald Hubscher, *L'Agriculture et la Société rurale dans le Pas-de-Calais au milieu du XIXe siècle à 1914* (2 vols.; Arras, 1980), I, 9; and Jean Pitié, *L'Exode rural et Migrations intérieurs en France* (Poitiers, 1971), 672; Gabriel Désert, *Une Société rurale au XIXe siècle: Les Paysans du Calvados, 1815–1895* (Lille, 1975), 744.

6. Nicolet, *L'Idée républicaine,* 144.

7. *Annales,* September 14, 1871, V, annexe 659, p. 283. Louis de Ventavon told his colleagues in the National Assembly that agriculture "does not limit itself to enriching man; it builds his character. Work in the fields develops love of family and all the conservative instincts in him. The continuous influence of providence is visible to the eyes of the cultivator, and he maintains better than the inhabitants of the cities the religious sentiments that God has placed in all human consciences." By contrast, Louis de Monjaret de Kerjégu, who shared Ventavon's sentiments, wrote, "Among the twenty-five million men who, it is said, make up France's agricultural work force, twenty million or more are ignorant of the most elementary notions they need in order to study, regulate, and carry out their activities, to the extent that this immobilizes agriculture in a vicious circle, where the low yields produced by an unvarying routine, not by the weather, will continue indefinitely" (*Les Souffrances de l'agriculture: 2e partie, Propriété oblige* [Brest, 1866], 3).

mists' innovative role in the rural economy, and the next chapter will focus on their attempt to compensate for the results to which their economic success contributed.

THE LEGITIMIST *AGRONOMES*

After the political disaster of the July Revolution, a large number of well-educated and prominent Legitimists returned to the provinces to dedicate their energy and newfound leisure to the improvement of their estates. Not all internal royalist exiles became conscientious and diligent farmers, but quite a few did, and they constituted an important segment of that minority of *grands propriétaires* whom Ronald Hubscher has called the "captains of agriculture." Like the English gentleman farmer they so admired, these agriculturists rejected earlier prejudices against farming as a profession and took over the direct management of their estates. Motivated initially by the desire to increase their revenue during a period of falling prices and to extend their influence over the peasantry, many Legitimist *propriétaires* were eager to apply available technical knowledge to their properties and thus in the 1830s helped create a new "agronomic movement."[8] Common social and economic interests became the basis for a fruitful collaboration between Legitimists and other rural notables who sought to extend the agricultural revolution throughout France.[9]

As a group, innovative Legitimist landowners were more liberal, aristocratic, and probusiness than those royalists engaged in projects concerning the urban working classes. A majority (52 percent) of the Legitimists I have looked into were *propriétaires*. Nearly 65 percent of the forty-two Legitimists belonging to an agricultural society or a committee of a *comice*

8. The expression is taken from Denis' *Les Royalistes de la Mayenne*, 245.

9. Legitimists and other notables were able to collaborate in the area of agricultural development with less rancor than in other fields because ideological and political divisions were often submerged in the face of common economic and social objectives. This is important to note, since I do not mean to suggest that the Legitimists were alone in encouraging rural modernization. As Désert explains, "This work of agricultural regeneration was not undertaken exclusively by the nobility. Their reduced numerical strength made a collaboration with the bourgeoisie necessary, and they knew how to set aside political divisions and work hand in hand with those who, like them, believed in agricultural progress, when the economic question was at stake" (*Une Société rurale*, 205).

agricole had agriculture as their exclusive profession. Among this group all but one held an elected political office, and the largest number (seventeen out of forty-two) owned estates in the northwest of France. A significant number of progressive Legitimist farmers—Charles de Bouillé, Louis de Monjaret de Kerjégu, Alfred de Falloux, Arthur de La Borderie, Henri de Puiberneau, Armand Fresneau—were members of the Breton nobility. Nobles made up less than half of my total sample, but they made up nearly 70 percent of the Legitimist *agronomes*. Although rural incomes were generally below those in industry, a majority of the most active progressive farmers—the Vicomte de Vögué, Roger de Dampierre, Eugène de Diesbach, Bouillé—enjoyed yearly incomes of over 200,000 francs, which rivaled those of wealthy industrialists. Fresneau and Monjaret de Kerjégu were both distinguished by their long political careers and their activities in the Chamber in behalf of agricultural improvement. Proprietor of a number of farms in Brittany, Fresneau was the son of the prefect of Corsica under Louis Philippe and became the personal secretary of the minister of the interior in 1847. As a Legitimist deputy in 1848 and again in 1871, Fresneau consistently supported tariff protection for agriculture and the establishment of popular farm credit. Kerjégu, whose father was a cloth merchant and a deputy from 1824 to 1830, had extensive business interests in Brest and owned a number of model farms in the canton of Scaer, Finistère. Along with his brother, Kerjégu directed a *ferme-école* at Kerwozech de Saint-Goazec, presided over the *comice agricole* of Finistère, and was a member of the local agricultural society. As activists within the society of notables, these Legitimists often pioneered in the adoption of modern agricultural practices and set an example for many of their peers.

The great wealth of such landowners was important in ensuring the success of agricultural innovation. Not only did key improvements, like land drainage, irrigation, and the construction of farm buildings, require a substantial capital investment but the great size of an estate and the number of peasants attached to it made it possible for the example and encouragement of a progressive landowner to have a lasting effect. Legitimist nobles were often in an excellent position to facilitate major reorientations in patterns of soil use. Georges Dupeux has calculated that 172 nobles of Loir-et-Cher owned over 22 percent of the department's cultivated land in 1848, often possessing estates of between a thousand

and two thousand hectares.[10] Michel Denis has asserted that in much of the Mayenne, "the large landed properties always retained their expanse, and in some instances they even grew when separately acquired parcels were added to them."[11] In the Pas-de-Calais, a small group of nobles, including the families of Montmorency (1472 hectares) and Havrincourt (1140 hectares), owned 16 percent of the land possessed by individuals; Laurence Wylie has shown that in Chanzeaux in 1841 two Legitimist families, the Quatrebarbes and the Kersabiecs, owned about one-fifth of the commune.[12] Such examples are numerous: the Comte d'Ussel (Corrèze), the Vicomte de Saintenac (Ariège), the Vicomte de Meaux (Loire), Théodore Charles de Longueval (Sarthe), the Comte de Buat (Gers and Landes), the Vicomte Ernest Alexis (Aisne), the Comte de Vassenhac (Aisne), Hélion de Barième (Bouches-du-Rhône), and the Comte de Brettes-Thurin (Haute-Garonne) were all the richest or among the richest *propriétaires* in their departments.[13]

PROGRESSIVE FARMING

The Legitimists' efforts at agricultural improvement fall into two periods. During the first phase, from about 1830 until the economic and political crisis of 1846–1851, large landowners, both individually and through the expanding network of agricultural associations, sought to increase their and their tenants' yields by promoting field clearance, drainage, irrigation, and especially crop rotation and the raising of fodder and root crops that would let them enlarge the number of livestock and the availability of natural fertilizer. At the same time, they used their influence on local councils and in business to encourage the government to improve rural access roads and extend highway and rail networks. These years coincided with the first railroad boom and the availability of a cheap

10. Dupeux, *Aspects,* 102–103. Much of the land owned by nobles consisted of forests and woodlands.

11. Denis, *Les Royalistes de la Mayenne,* 340. In Loir-et-Cher, 1,053 *côtes fonciers* of a hundred hectares or more covered 47.9 percent of the land surface, while those of less than nine hectares, numbering 87,711, covered only 19.3 percent of the land surface. See Dupeux, *Aspects,* 99.

12. Hubscher, *L'Agriculture et la Société rurale,* II, 103–104; Laurence Wylie, ed., *Chanzeaux: A Village in Anjou* (Cambridge, Mass., 1966), 40–43.

13. G. Cougny and A. Robert, *Dictionnaire des parlementaires français* (5 vols.; Paris, 1889); Conseillers généraux de 1870, in F (1) b 230, 1–20, AN.

and plentiful supply of labor in a largely overpopulated countryside. Even though many of the innovations were labor-intensive, they made economic sense. They also tended to strengthen the landowner's hold over the peasantry. The trend toward forage crops and the efficient management of the estates often brought sharecroppers and small farmers more completely into the orbit of large landowners, who were enabled to "fortify the agricultural revolution on the technical level without altering the nature of social relations."[14] In the Gard, where Legitimist landowners were "torn between rationalizing their farmlands to maintain their incomes and maintaining the loyalty of the peasantry . . . by permitting inefficient and unprofitable farming to continue," they often found their way around the problem by helping their tenants to farm more productively or by buying land that was already worked effectively.[15]

The growing of rutabagas, turnips, or potatoes on once-fallow land was a relatively simple affair for those who had a little money to invest. On occasion, however, Legitimist landowners went to great expense to transform their estates. In Finistère, during the 1840s the Comte de Kerouallan, proprietor at Arzano, cleared two hundred hectares of marshland and created twenty new farms. At St. Vougay, M. de Cöatgourden spent ten thousand francs turning 18.5 hectares of waste, a part of which was high forest, into a wheat farm by terracing the land. He then used the lime sand from the diggings to fertilize his crops; the value of the land rose from sixteen to fifty francs per hectare in a few years.[16]

In the 1840s and 1850s, crop rotation, drainage, irrigation, and the use of fertilizer were the foundations of further improvements. Spurred on by financial aid from the government after 1865, rural France experienced an impressive acceleration in land drainage. Between 1854 and 1863, at least five thousand hectares were drained in Calvados alone.[17] Gaston Du Plessis de Grénédan, who as a papal zouave was to be killed at Castelfi-

14. Denis, *Les Royalistes de la Mayenne*, 267. Denis stresses that in the Mayenne, industrial enterprises became less profitable in the mid–nineteenth century as the focus of manufacturing shifted to the northeast. In the Mayenne, "it was the *propriétaires* who drew the best profits from this situation," because "it was agriculture that had become the principal 'industry' of this region." This "new orientation," he continues, was "also the best way to safeguard social structures."

15. Fitzpatrick, *Catholic Royalism*, 124.

16. Louis Ogès, *L'Agriculture dans le Finistère au milieu du XIXe siècle* (Quimper, 1949), 58.

17. Désert, *Une Société rural*, 284.

dardo in 1860, put enormous effort into reclaiming the family's land at
Combrit from the sea.[18] In the Legitimist *Union de l'Ouest,* farmers were
advised to use ashes as fertilizer, and Ernest Le Lasseux, reminding the
notables that "time is money" in the "agricultural industry," encouraged
those who directed the *comice agricole* of Laval to increase the number of
lime furnaces so that farmers would not have to travel long distances to
find a furnace whose supply had not been exhausted.[19] In 1847, Louis de
Kerjégu received a gold medal from the Royal Agricultural Society of
Finistère for his innovative views on irrigation in the plateaus of Upper
Brittany and won praise from his friends for demonstrating the merits of
preserving dung water and keeping dunghills dry. According to Louis
Ogès, Kerjégu was found preaching to two cultivators at the market fair
in Carhaix on the wisdom of keeping rainfall off dung heaps. One man
was instantly converted, but the other remained skeptical:

> Wanting the last word, de Kerjégu led his two interlocutors to a
> tavern, where he prepared some coffee. (Note that at Carhaix, cof-
> fee is prepared by pouring boiling water over grounds placed in the
> bottom of the pot). . . . When all was ready, de Kerjégu did the
> serving. He first offered a cup of the excellent beverage to the con-
> vert, who found it to be perfect, then he served himself. The in-
> credulous one was served last. Only the remaining dregs were
> poured into his cup. He protested vigorously, but before the
> amused smile of Kerjégu, he realized that his land was no better
> apportioned than he when he brought it manure washed by rain.[20]

The improvement of French agriculture depended not only on the
work of a few progressive farmers but also on the adoption by the peasantry of some basic innovations. The Legitimists saw men such as themselves as the most effective catalysts of change. La Boulie considered the
suppression of "blind routine, and the destruction of prejudice," to be
the key to agricultural regeneration, and Claude Marie Raudot vented his
frustration over peasant "conservatism" when, after seeing the reception
the peasants accorded his suggestion that they supplement their poor diet

---

18. Jonathas de Lescöet, *Le Cte Gaston Du Plessis de Grénédan, volontaire de l'armée pontificale: Note biographique* (Rennes, 1861), 72–73.

19. *L'Union de l'Ouest,* October 12, 1858; Ernest Le Lasseux, *Comice agricole de Laval:
Rapport de 1853* (Laval, 1853), 11.

20. Ogès, *L'Agriculture dans le Finistère,* 68–71, 46–47.

with horsemeat, he lamented that "it is easier in France to make two or three political revolutions than so radical a culinary revolution."[21] Falloux, who felt that a cultivator did not need a "course in science" to recognize the benefits of fodder, livestock, and fertilizer, suggested that the example of a wise *propriétaire* was the best teacher.[22] He saw his achievements on his property at Bourg d'Iré, in Maine-et-Loire, as the decisive factor in improving the economy of the area: "The farmers of the area quickly got into the habit of coming to see what was happening on the estate, of noting the results, first with simple curiosity or suspicion, soon with a serious interest and the intention of appropriating for themselves what they judged useful. These visits I greatly appreciated, and far from being considered annoying or a waste of time, they constituted my best reward by proving to me that the entire country would not lag in following the same path."[23] Convinced that with sufficient means, most peasants could profit by improvements "made in small bursts, over ten years," Calemard de Lafayette, in a book entitled *L'Agriculture progressive à la portée de tout le monde*—which was authorized by the ministry of public instruction for use in *fermes-écoles*—wrote that an ounce of wisdom and the will to experiment would yield a "relatively cautious and inexpensive plan of improvement . . . acceptable even to small cultivators." His own "Ten Agricultural Commandments" offered a simple, comprehensible, and practical series of steps, including everything from the removal of rocks from fields and effective crop rotation to hard work and the learning of basic arithmetic.[24]

In the years after the July Revolution, the Legitimists worked to extend elementary techniques of the agricultural revolution that had begun in the eighteenth century. France, Raudot declared in 1858, should be "cultivated everywhere as certain parts of the north are cultivated"—where many basic improvements had occurred before 1789. A few simple advancements, he believed, would double French production in a half-century and create "sixty million better-fed, more robust, and happier people than the thirty-six million [France] possesses today."[25]

21. Camille de La Boulie, *La Régénération de l'agriculture et la Compagnie foncière* (Paris, 1863), 3; Claude Marie Raudot, *De l'agriculture en France* (Auxerre, 1858), 6–7.
22. Falloux, "Dix ans d'agriculture," *Le Correspondant*, LVII (1862), 644.
23. *Ibid.*, 640.
24. Calemard de Lafayette, *L'Agriculture progressive à la portée de tout le monde* (Paris, 1867), 18–23.
25. Raudot, *De l'agriculture*, 7.

After the mid-1850s, and especially after the agricultural slump of the early 1860s, the Legitimists' initiatives were increasingly sensitive to their apprehension over the gathering "rural exodus" and the attendant rise in labor costs (see Chapter IX). Growing increasingly petulant about the social and moral transformation of the French countryside, they nevertheless tried to adapt. Continuing earlier reforms, they turned more and more to the extending of pastureland, to livestock production, and to the marketing of fruits and vegetables or rural industrial commodities like milk, sugar beets, and chemical fertilizers, all of which required less labor and more substantial capital investment. In 1858, the general council of Lot-et-Garonne requested the establishment of a departmental nursery and an *école d'arboriculture* to help large landowners make better use of the vast woodlands they owned, since the small wood-burning foundries had all but disappeared. By the 1880s, the Vicomte de Logeril was urging large landowners to use unproductive land abandoned by migrating peasants for silviculture since raising lumber for construction was relatively inexpensive and required little manpower. "In the present state of our suffering agriculture," he wrote, "afforestation speaks for itself as the most natural prescription against the imminent ruin of landed property."[26]

With the extension of roads, along with the growing urban demand for beef and dairy products, new breeding techniques, and the introduction of larger species of cattle from Great Britain and Scandinavia, many aristocratic landowners in the west turned to the rearing of livestock during the Second Empire. After expanding the size of one of his farms at Menez-Ruland in Finistère and creating pasturage out of the moors, Louis de Kerjégu introduced two cows from Scotland that he had purchased at the Universal Exposition of 1855 to crossbreed with the *race d'Ayr* native to Brittany. By 1858, the farm, which in 1844 was almost two-thirds wasteland, yielded an additional 440 francs in yearly revenue and contained an inventory of tools, equipment, and animals worth 10,222 francs.[27] A more famous shift to livestock occurred in Maine-et-Loire on the property of the Comte de Falloux. After retiring from poli-

26. Déliberations du conseil général, Lot-et-Garonne, 1858, in F (10) 1580, AN; Charles de Lorgeril, *La propriété foncière en face de l'abandon de la culture par les populations rurales* (Saint-Brieuc, 1886), 14.

27. Louis de Monjaret de Kerjégu to bureau de l'Association Bretonne, October 5, 1858, in Ogès' *L'Agriculture dans le Finistère,* 60–65.

tics in 1851, Falloux returned to his sizable estate at Bourg d'Iré only to find a poorly managed operation in ill repair, a farm crisscrossed by dirt paths, and divided into 206 parcels under the care of *métaires.* At considerable expense, he consolidated the estate, evicting tenants—many of whom remained as day laborers—and turned sixty hectares to pasture, using the felled trees to help refurbish the château and selling the wood as heating fuel to finance further improvements. After draining and properly irrigating the land and building a granary, a barn, stables, hogpens, mills, and a shed to house his newly acquired farm machinery, he stocked the pasture with Durham cattle brought from England, a breed that was found to be healthier, larger, faster to mature, more prolific, and better-tasting than local animals. On the adjoining arable land, Falloux turned from local polyculture to wheat cultivation to provide feed and straw for his herd and for commercial sale. By his own account, his work, which earned him a prize at the local *concours,* stimulated the entire economy of Segré by bringing in laborers and increasing the business of local butchers, bakers, and artisans. Convinced that he had found a solution to the idleness of the landed aristocracy and a cure for the troubles afflicting rural France, he published an account of his achievement in the widely read *Le Correspondant.* According to Michel Denis, Falloux had a number of imitators in the Mayenne.[28]

As Falloux' example indicates, the Legitimists were not opposed to becoming rural capitalists. Under the Second Empire, many took advantage of the expanding national market by turning to the commercial production of agricultural products. From 1854 to 1861, Bouillé transformed his 125-hectare "terre de Villars" at St. Parize-le-Chatel, Nièvre—part of 521 hectares owned by the family since 1651—into a model of capitalist agriculture by enclosing much of it, constructing 1,879 meters of access roads, and investing 131,914.97 francs in 1867 to purchase a new Dombasle plow and other costly equipment, as well as 207 bulls, 281 cows of the local variety (which he boasted had been sold not only in Nièvre but in distant departments and even abroad), and 464 head of sheep. As a by-product of breeding livestock, Bouillé produced a considerable volume of quality fertilizer that he sold at the market fairs

28. Falloux, "Dix ans d'agriculture," *Le Correspondant,* LVII (1862), 633–40; Denis, *Les Royalistes de la Mayenne,* 340. According to Denis, Falloux was not the first to introduce Durham cattle to France; he notes that the former émigré to England, the Marquis de Quatrebarbes, brought Durham cattle into Sionnière before 1837.

in Nevers, St. Pierre-le-Moutien, St. Parize, and Magny, all within eighteen kilometers of the estate. Between 1854 and 1861, the net profit from the farm grew from 7,898.33 to 28,841.63 francs.[29]

Bouillé's story was typical of the new spirit of enterprise among some large landowners. Stressing hard work, diligence, and an eye for a good investment, Bouillé recounted how, after finishing his legal studies in 1837, he returned to his family estate to dedicate himself "to a manner of living that seemed to promise me, by its attractions and its character of independence, an existence according to my tastes." Pushing aside all prejudices of the time against agriculture as merely a "matter of caprice or distraction," Bouillé studied agronomy "with the desire to acquire a science for which I ought to find an application in my daily work." Later, he traveled around France and to England "to gather precious information on the best farming procedures and on the management of livestock," and although suffering many setbacks after his return, because of a lack of capital and experience, he persevered, never forgetting the "lessons of English agriculture." He wrote, "Persuaded that there is no possible success without a continuing personal presence, and that it is absenteeism and the lack of perseverance to which one must in large part attribute the misfortunes of most of those owners who have not wanted to work in agriculture, I affixed myself to the countryside and I have since lived there constantly."[30]

The Legitimist *grands propriétaires,* like the urban bourgeoisie they criticized as greedy and materialistic, promoted the commercialization of the French economy. Their repeated calls for higher tariffs, which the manufacturers of the north echoed, indicated not that they opposed commercial expansion but, rather, that they desired to capture the national market, and a greater share of foreign trade, for French agricultural goods at a time of growing competition from abroad. Léopold de Gaillard wanted the wine producers of the Midi to petition the government for the reduction of the *octrois,* since their interests lay in accustoming Parisians and Picards to drink southern wine and Bretons to give up their taste for cider.[31] Fresneau believed that, thanks to new means of trans-

29. Charles de Bouillé, *Mémoire sur l'exploitation agricole de Villers, 25 février 1862* (Nevers, 1862), 1–45.

30. *Ibid.,* 45–48. Locke has cited many other examples of Legitimist agricultural entrepreneurship. See his *French Legitimists,* 124–26.

31. Léopold de Gaillard, *La Crise agricole et la démocratie: Discours prononcé le 20 décembre 1866* (Marseille, 1867), 16.

portation and communication, Brittany was destined to become a
"supply market" for Paris and, especially, for England with its attractive
urban markets. Coastal regions of the northwest had profited from foreign trade, and Fresneau thought that new roads and more efficient farming techniques could do the same for the Breton interior. At Kermadio,
in Morbihan, on a poor seventy-eight-hectare farm, Fresneau turned to
producing peas, green beans, and other market crops in 1859 and by 1868
had realized a net income of 12,738 francs. He also urged Breton landowners to set up joint-stock farming companies that could negotiate
cheaper rates with railroad and shipping lines in order to reduce transportation costs.[32] In the Pas-de-Calais, Diesbach, the son of an émigré,
ran one of the largest commercial milk- and butter-producing enterprises
in the region, using the latest manufacturing equipment.[33]

Having embraced commerce and the hope of regional agricultural development, the Legitimists were not about to restrain the transportation
and communication revolutions. Often speaking for local interests, they
sought advantageous transport links to foster commerce in their regions,
and many engaged in battles with the central government, from which
they appeared to emerge as the protectors of the agricultural community.
In 1866, Falloux and the Duc de Fritz-James told the commission con-
ducting the *enquête agricole* that France had a comparatively inadequate
rail system and argued that, in particular, the *arrondissement* of Segré
needed the proposed *grand traversal,* linking the west to Paris and the east,
to run through the area because the quarry slate, wheat, livestock, lime,
and granite blocks of the region would give rise to a lively commercial
exchange. In a rather stormy hearing, both men demanded the completion of a canal on the Oudan River to help raise market prices for cereals
grown around Segré.[34] In 1868, Edgard de Champvallier told the general
council of the Charente that, though the rail system gave adequate commercial access to Paris, the west could not easily trade directly with the
east and the center. A "more equitable distribution of . . . products"
would occur, he argued, if the new transversal line ran from Niort north
to the Vendée and Deux-Sèvres and then off to the east. "With this cre-

32. Armand Fresneau, *Kermadio, du 1er avril au 15 août 1868: Rapport adressé à M. le Cte
de Ségur d'Aguesseau—comment on peut quintupler le revenu d'une ferme bretonne* (Versailles,
1868), 17–23.

33. Hubscher, *L'Agriculture et la Société rurale,* I, 256–61.

34. Déposition orale de M. de Falloux, in *Enquête agricole,* Série 2, Part 2 (Maine-et-
Loire), 627.

ation," he asserted, "each crossing point becomes an active center that permits communication at the same fixed costs, at whatever distance, with all the provinces and that satisfies all the conditions of demand, be it from Paris, or the east, or the Mediterranean ports, or the regions of the west."[35] Another Charentois, Ramboud-Delaroque, promised in his *profession de foi* to voters in the 1852 local election that he would devote his attention to "protecting agriculture . . . by the creation of new means of communication in the rural communes."[36] In the Variante region of the Garonne Valley, Gabriel de Belcastel organized a group of landowners in support of the construction of the Canal de St. Martory to facilitate transport and help irrigate the "meager plateaus."[37] The Comte de La Rochethulon called rural roads the "arteries of agriculture, which cannot prosper without them," and Edouard de La Bassétière affirmed that French farming could meet the threat of foreign competition only by constructing easier means of transport and lowering the cost of railroad delivery. He believed that with a well-integrated system of roads, rails, and canals it would "be possible to make cereals from the center, from the west, and from the north of France arrive on the markets of the Midi, their natural outlet."[38]

The growing interest in marketing and technological progress convinced many Legitimists of the need to look to the world of science and industry for help in developing chemical fertilizers, farm machinery, and other devices capable of increasing productivity without raising labor costs. Often it was the agricultural societies and the committees of the *comices agricoles* that arranged the marriage between agriculture and technology and disseminated an awareness of new methods and equipment—usually to the already-prosperous farmers. Reviving the initiatives taken under the Old Regime, the agricultural societies began to proliferate under the reign of Louis Philippe. Unlike their eighteenth-century predecessors, which were essentially physiocratic "study groups," the new organizations were constituted as state-sponsored trade associations operating as advisory bodies, pressure groups, and "organs for the

35. Edgard de Champvallier, *Rapport de la commission d'enquête d'utilité publique du chemin de fer de Niort à Ruffec* (Niort, 1868), 1.

36. Belanger, *Les Conseillers généraux de Charente*, 149.

37. Gabriel de Belcastel, *Lettres aux propriétaires riverains de la Variante* (Toulouse, 1861).

38. Déposition orale de M. le comte de La Rochethulon, in *Enquête agricole*, Série 2, Part 10 (Vienne), 55; Documents annexes au déposition de M. de La Bassétière, in *Enquête agricole*, Série 2, Part 3, pp. 156–57.

representation of professional agricultural interests."[39] In 1867, a number of wealthy Legitimists including Vögué, Dampierre, Bouillé, and Gabriel de Saint-Victor, all of whom had a stake in industry as well as agriculture, organized the Société des Agriculteurs de France as one of France's first private lobbying organizations. The SAF effectively represented the interests of large landowners by promoting state subsidies for rural investment and provincial public works; it also fought the free-trade policies of the Second Empire and helped create the protectionist alliance between growers and manufacturers that triumphed under the Third Republic. Vögué, Dampierre, Bouillé, and Saint-Victor were all deputies in the National Assembly of 1871, and while in government they sponsored legislation to revive the Institute Agronomique, create more *fermes-écoles,* fight phylloxera, and encourage scientific research to develop rural industrial commodities. Known as the "rue d'Athens," because of the location of its headquarters, the SAF played a key role in organizing a conservative Catholic peasant syndicalist movement after the passage of the law on associations in 1884.[40]

The committees that conducted the *comices agricoles* were more modest organizations. Under the Second Empire, they came to form the first link in a chain of state-authorized agricultural associations—made up of the local committees, departmental *chambres d'agriculture,* and a national Conseil Général d'Agriculture—that advised the government on rural affairs and, through the *comices,* tried to encourage practical innovations with competitions and the distribution of cash prizes for distinction in the area of cultivation. Between 1840 and 1873, the number of *comices* grew slowly from 566 to 600; by 1870 there were only 353 agricultural societies, which frequently united the same personnel. The *comices* were often dominated by a small group of Bonapartist notables—with the prefects or subprefects sometimes presiding over them as honorary presidents—who were counted on to help the administration to influence local affairs. Some Legitimists sought to avoid complicity in what they saw as a political enterprise. Many others, however, felt that the *comices* served a beneficial practical function and sought election to their organiz-

39. Marc-Henry Soulet, "Les Organisations professionelles de représentation de l'agriculture et l'enseignement agricole, 1830–1940," in *The Making of Frenchmen: Current Directions in the History of Education in France, 1679–1979,* ed. Donald N. Baker and Patrick J. Harrigan (Waterloo, Ont., 1980), 578.
40. See Barral, *Les Agrariens français.*

ing committees. Saint-Victor, who was president of the *comice agricole* of Tarace, Rhône, believed that the *comices* could become the "most legitimate and most natural representation of national agriculture" and convinced himself that a "partisan spirit" had no place when agricultural interests were at stake.[41] Besides, the *comices* were by no means radical institutions and were often effective in promoting the message of progressive agriculture. The *concours* they conducted fitted with the Legitimists' belief in the power of healthy competition and emulation to spread new techniques, and since the event was often accompanied by a *fête agricole*—a kind of small-scale exposition of local agricultural products, combined with religious ceremonies extolling the saintliness of those who worked the soil and the bounties of God's good earth—the *comices* seemed to help keep alive a sense of pride within the rural community by yoking serious pedagogy and the atmosphere of a county fair.[42]

At the departmental or regional level, the Legitimists were often the driving force behind the agricultural societies. Under the Second Empire, Legitimists appreciated the societies not only because they exerted a positive economic influence but because they gave the Legitimists a measure of political and organizational strength, as well as influence over agricultural policy, in circumstances that prevented them from playing a dominant role in the administration. The two most important agricultural societies of the northwest, the Association Normande and the Association Bretonne, were founded in the 1830s by Legitimist aristocrats—including Louis de Kergolay, Arthur de La Borderie, and Vincent d'Audren de Kerdrel, all of whom were influential members of the liberal wing of the Legitimist party. Of the twenty-two inspectors of the Association Normande, in Calvados, ten were nobles, and one-fourth of the entire membership were of the nobility. In the Camargue, Charles de Bouillé, the Vicomte d'Adémar, the Duc d'Escars, and Louis de Saint-Pierre founded the Société Agricole de Desséchement et de Colonisation,

41. Gabriel de Saint-Victor, *De l'enquête agricole: Discours* (Lyon, 1866), 5–6. See also Tudesq, *Les Grands Notables en France*, I, 187.
42. Houée, *Les Etapes du développement rurale*, I, 64–69. Despite links to the central government, the *comices* had freedom to concentrate on the particular problems of local agriculture. In Sarthe and the Mayenne, the *comices* focused on the raising of cattle, horses, and pigs; in Finistère, on drainage; in the dry plains of Bouches-du-Rhône, on irrigation; and in the Var, on the cultivation of fruit trees. See F (10) 1580, AN. Yet, as Désert points out, because only a small minority of farmers were active in the *comices*, the influence of such groups extended only to the most pioneering. See his *Une Société rurale*, 209.

and in the Limousin, aristocratic *propriétaires* and local bankers dominated the Agricultural Society of Haute-Vienne.[43]

In 1858, a subprefect in Haute-Vienne assured the government that
the agricultural associations of the department were "composed of intelligent, devoted, and essentially practical *propriétaires*" who "continue to
support and favor progress by their advice and their pecuniary subsidies."[44] Yet many of the activities of the agricultural societies were practical for only a handful of farmers, since the advanced and sophisticated
projects they promoted contrasted sharply with the underdevelopment
of much of French agriculture. While in certain areas peasants still cultivated the land with archaic equipment, the bulletins of the societies and
trade journals such as the *Journal de l'agriculture practique* were filled with
drawings of the latest farm machinery, complex meteorological tables,
and intricate discussions of animal reproduction. As Hubscher points
out, the societies embraced a "mystique of progress in an era amply
bathed in scientism" and such values were frequently evident in the hu-
bris of the Legitimist *agronomes*.[45] In 1867, Calemard de Lafayette declared that "the art of cultivating the land must today be elevated to the
heights of a science," for "those who exercise this art need to know many
things that science alone can teach." He added, "If primitive agriculture,
backward, marked by routine, has for a long time been content with its
way of furnishing the indispensable products of consumption, agronomy
and agricultural progress henceforth have a more difficult and more rigorous task for which routine and simple craft can no longer suffice."[46] In a
report to the National Assembly on agricultural instruction in higher education, Bouillé and Dampierre explained that it had not been civil equality and the suppression of seigneurialism that had led to improvements
in the material well-being of the rural masses but rather the "transformation, contemporary with the Revolution, of agricultural methods . . .
due to the discoveries of science and the application of these discoveries
to the cultivation of the land." After exhorting their colleagues to "raise,
raise again, and always raise the level of science that can be applied to the

43. Désert, *Une Société rurale*, 204–207; Tudesq, *Les Grands Notables en France*, I, 427;
Corbin, *Archaisme et Modernité*, I, 438–39.
44. Extrait du procès-verbal des séances du conseil général du département de la Haute
Vienne, 1858, in F (10) 1580, AN.
45. Hubscher, *L'Agriculture et la Société rurale*, I, 191.
46. Calemard de Lafayette, *L'Agriculture progressive*, 12.

expansion of production," they called for funds to build model and experimental farms, an agronomic institute, and agronomic stations capable of undertaking botanical, meteorological, chemical, and geological
research in the service of agriculture.[47] In 1874, the Agricultural Society
of Indre opened a facility of the sort they had in mind at Châteauroux,
mostly with private funds, and brought in scientists to do soil testing and
to manufacture chemical fertilizer. By 1877, the station was producing
7,650 tons of phosphoric and nitrite manures each year as well as new
seed hybrids. The society held a yearly "scientific demonstration" to dis-
play the wonders of new mechanical equipment.[48]

On the whole, the societies yielded positive results. In 1858, the general council of the Sarthe reported that despite difficulties, "these institutions have not been without influence on the agriculture of the department."[49] The years 1840 to 1880 were prosperous for French agriculture,
and by the end of the Second Empire even the highlands of the Massif
Central and the Pyrenees had been touched by the introduction of fodder
crops and the rehabilitation of pasture lands. Between 1835 and 1874,
French agricultural production achieved an average annual growth rate
of about 1.2 percent and the absolute value of its products increased from
5.8 million to 9.3 million francs.[50] Although the price of industrial goods
rose under the Second Empire, agricultural prices kept pace, gains oc-
curring in cereals, livestock, and wine. Between 1848–1852 and 1873–
1877, the price of beef rose 81 percent, pork 56 percent, and veal 66 percent.[51] Ground rents rose steadily from 1851 until about 1885, and the
revenue of landowners increased accordingly. In Loir-et-Cher, the in-

47. *Annales,* March 17, 1875, XXXVII, annexe 2959, 141–44.

48. H. Ratouis de Limay, *L'Oeuvre de la Société d'Agriculture de l'Indre pendant la période d'un siècle* (Châteauroux, 1902), 44–52.

49. Extrait du procès-verbal des séances du conseil général du département de la Sarthe, session de 1858, in F (10) 1580, AN. The same report added that the local and national *concours* "interest particularly the highest and richest portions of society," and Désert stresses that "the rural masses remained passive in the face of the theoretical discussions that excited the agricultural societies" (*Une Société rurale,* 210; see also pp. 284–85). Benoist d'Azy noted the intrinsic limits to agricultural modernization when he told the *enquête agricole* of 1866 that it did no good to tell peasants to grow more wheat or raise more livestock, because "in order to put this advice into practice, conditions that [the peasant] does not always have at his disposition are necessary" (*Enquête agricole,* Série 2, Part 9 [Nièvre], 364–65).

50. Jean Claude Toutain, *Le Produit de l'agriculture française de 1700 à 1958* (Paris, 1961), 128, 171, 207.

51. Agulhon, Désert, and Specklin, *Apogée et Crise de la civilisation paysanne,* 230.

come of *propriétaires* increased 105 percent between 1850 and 1885, while that of *fermiers* rose 172 percent.[52] Thus, from an economic point of view the supposedly dormant and declining class of Legitimist squires was doing relatively well and was contributing to agricultural progress that, if not spectacular, helped to end the cycle of famine and disease that had plagued the French countryside as far back as anyone could remember.

Despite the improvements, the Legitimists never ceased to complain about the "suffering of agriculture" under the Second Empire, because the countryside seemed to be losing its status as the repository of France's ageless values and customs. Declining birth rates, foreign competition, the influence of urban ways, and especially the exodus of landless peasants and rural artisans to the cities told the Legitimists that something was amiss in the villages. Falloux attributed the situation in 1866 to "the perpetual rapprochement of the countryside and the city, . . . the development of commercial relations, . . . pleasure, and . . . the continual lure of bad examples available to everyone"; in such an atmosphere, he said, "mores have become more and more difficult to maintain."[53] Yet was it not the Legitimists themselves who, by their sponsorship of progressive farming, contributed to the rural exodus and the cultural transformation of the countryside? In a remark of perspicacity, M. de Chaumontel, the *maire* of Beuville, in Calvados, told the commission of the *enquête agricole*, "Yes, we need more hands in agriculture: this condition is the *sine qua non* of its prosperity. This is so widely recognized that there is a palpable need to moderate the emigration from our countryside by attaching the man of the fields to his village; but, having said as much, we are all guilty of self-contradiction, and all of us, so long as we are, stimulate this emigration."[54]

The Legitimists, conscious of the problem and concerned that too much of a good thing might further jeopardize their social and political predominance in the countryside, held on to certain traditional attitudes and practices that hindered rather than accelerated economic progress. Many landlords kept in their leases restrictive clauses regulating crop rotation and the size of a tenant's herd, thus limiting his initiative. Leases were often short-term (usually for nine years), preventing farmers from

52. Dupeux, *Aspects,* 278, 286–87.
53. Falloux, *L'Agriculture et la Politique,* 22.
54. Déposition orale de M. A. de Chaumontel, in *Enquête agricole,* Série 2, Part 1 (Calvados), 221.

planning for the future, and increasing the leverage of the *propriétaires*.[55]
Landlords discouraged their tenants from borrowing money from anyone other than themselves, so the peasants remained constantly in debt
and little new capital was put into the land. If paternalism could offer
progressive examples, it could also breed dependence and a fear of acting
contrary to "local custom." Moreover, since the Legitimists remained
wedded to the idea that life in the countryside was morally edifying and
that property ownership taught the lessons of probity, hard work, and
frugality, they had little inclination to criticize the peasant who remained
on the land, even if parcellation and individual, scattered holdings undermined economic welfare. Vögué proclaimed that he "preferred the property arrangement that makes a dayworker a sharecropper, later a tenant
farmer, and perhaps one day a *propriétaire*," and Falloux told of how the
small landholding peasant families of Anjou were admirably self-sufficient
and content to "live from one generation to the next in close association"
with their landlord.[56] The Vicomte de Meaux convinced himself that
"small property had enriched the French soil" because the division of
land gave the peasants a love of work unmatched anywhere else in Europe. "Small property," he maintained, was a "source of healthy enjoy-
ment and the occasion of manly virtues, a guarantee of stability for the
entire society, and . . . the most potent instrument of agricultural production and the progress of cultivation."[57]

Retrograde Legitimist attitudes represented social inertia, however,
rather than a concerted effort to subvert progress. Despite the Legitimists' concern for the moral health of rural society, they gave in fully to
their material interests and struggled to find a strategy of modernization
consistent with preserving the traditional rural social structure. To many
it appeared that commercialization and technological innovation could
exist alongside efforts to find practical solutions to the *manque des bras*.
The Legitimists reasoned that if peasants moved to the cities in search of
greater material well-being, an improvement of conditions in the countryside could stem the flow. As Kerjégu explained, scientific agriculture
would stop the rural exodus by helping peasants to a greater prosperity,
which would let them indulge a materialism in the comfort of the village

55. Désert, *Une Société rurale*, 210–11; Ogès, *L'Agriculture dans le Finistère*, 52.
56. Locke, *French Legitimists*, 151–52.
57. Camille de Meaux, "Les Conclusions de l'enquête agricole," *Le Correspondant*,
LXXVII (1869), 103.

foyer.[58] Such illusions readily sprang from the self-inflicted predicament of Legitimists who wanted to become capitalists while remaining traditionalists. The inner tension gave rise to some interesting theories about the cultural impact of progress. The Comte de Villebois argued that a new railway running through La Fleche would have a morally salutary effect since it would allow peasants doing military service to travel home more often, where "relations with relatives preserve among their sons the sentiments and the memories of the family."[59] Falloux, who felt uncomfortable with the "universal locomotion, and the fever of displacement" that the railroads could "bring about in future generations," still believed that "the rails are infinitely more conducive to moral soundness than the old highways," along which travelers stopped frequently to drink at inns and peddlers and vagabonds had an opportunity to harass residents. The railroad, by contrast, "is endowed with a completely opposite temperament" because the traveler "suffers from the shadow of neither excessive food nor drink" and the railroad worker remains near the train and does not venture into town to influence the "habits of the local population."[60]

Technological innovation offered the possibility of solving the problem of rural depopulation by replacing the labor of men with machines. Although there is some debate on the subject, it appears that the introduction of farm machinery did not force emigration to the cities but occurred in response to the shortage of labor and to high wages that developed after the rural exodus was well under way. Where there were enough workers available, landowners often felt that the use of machines was unnecessary, but they sometimes introduced a few to moderate the workers' demands for higher wages. Even though the Association Bretonne assiduously promoted technical progress, its members ignored suggestions made in 1853 by the Agricultural Society of Autun that large landowners replace laborers with machines.[61] As Georges Duby points out, the widespread use of farm machinery did not occur in France until after 1870. Mechanization arrived earliest in the northeast, where there

58. Monjaret de Kerjégu, *Les Souffrances de l'agriculture*, II, 21–22.
59. Comte Felix de Villebois-Mareuil, *Résumé de la discussion sur le double trace du chemin de fer d'Angers au Mans* (Angers, 1857), 1–4.
60. Falloux, *Dix ans d'agriculture*, 37–38.
61. Réponse de la Société Centrale d'Agriculture du Pas-de-Calais, enquête agricole, 1866, in Hubscher's *L'Agriculture et la Société rurale*, II, 660–61; Alain Plessis, *De la fête impériale*, 144.

were large wheat farms and a sparse rural population. It came much later to regions like Brittany and Limousin, "where cereal production was less important and the rural population denser."[62] Because machinery was very expensive, its use before the twentieth century was restricted to the largest estates.[63] In 1855, M. de Crésolles owned one of the only threshers in Combrit, and in Calvados, as late as 1882, there were fewer than five farm machines for every hundred individual plots of land.[64] Although enthusiastic about the ability of machines to save labor costs, Calemard de Lafayette admitted in 1867 that their use was a "question of local experimentation."[65]

Despite the Legitimists' faith in the economic advantages of science and progress, a technological solution to the labor shortage remained elusive. Although they thought economic development essential for maintaining the vitality of French agriculture, they were also convinced that the flight from the countryside gave evidence of a moral crisis calling for solutions that were not purely economic.

62. Agulhon, Désert, and Specklin, *Apogée et Crise de la civilisation paysanne,* 225.
63. See Price, *The Modernization of Rural France,* 362–63; Désert, *Une Société rurale,* 191, 737; and Houée, *Les Etapes du développement rural,* I, 42–43.
64. Ogès, *L'Agriculture dans le Finistère,* 59; Désert, *Une Société rurale,* 194.
65. Calemard de Lafayette, *L'Agriculture progressive,* 204.

CHAPTER IX

Repeopling the Countryside

ECONOMIC HISTORIANS, especially those concerned with the slowness of French industrialization, often stress that the French rural economy was comparatively reluctant to release workers for industrial employment.[1] Undoubtedly, permanent rural emigration in France was less intense and more protracted than in Britain or Germany, yet it was enough to provoke apprehension and a sense of great urgency among Legitimists. Why did they view the yearly outflow of manpower as the greatest threat to French agriculture and to French society in general? What remedies were they willing to entertain in light of their economic interests?

Since the Legitimists and other landowners were responding to French conditions, it would be useless to cite comparative rates of out-migration to show that their fears were exaggerated. In France, where the countryside remained relatively overpopulated until the middle of the nineteenth century, the acceleration of the rural exodus under the Second Empire seemed abrupt and frightening, especially since birthrates were declining in many regions where emigration was pronounced. According to Maurice Lévy-Leboyer, roughly 635,000 peasants had emigrated to the cities between 1801 and 1841; between 1851 and 1871, however, rural France lost 2,123,000 inhabitants. In the next ten years, an additional one million people left the villages.[2] By the 1850s, even Brittany, which had an un-

---

1. See especially Trebilcock, *The Industrialization of the Continental Powers,* 164–65, 191.
2. Statistics cited from François Caron's *An Economic History of Modern France,* trans. Barbara Bray (New York, 1979), 112.

usually high birthrate and a low level of out-migration, began to experience a decline in the rate of demographic expansion. Moreover, while the flight from the countryside was depleting the population of certain regions—the northeastern countryside, the Massif Central, the Alpine region, the Midi-Pyrenees, and parts of Normandy—a handful of departments, like the Bouches-du-Rhône, the Nord, the Gironde, and especially the Seine, were undergoing an unprecedented population growth fueled by immigration as well as natural increases. Although the aggregate statistics represent only a 5-percent shift of the population from rural to urban areas of over two thousand inhabitants, and only a 6.5-percent increase in the population of cities of over five thousand, between 1851 and 1866, the Legitimists clearly anticipated that rural depopulation would be an ever growing trend. Shifts in the nation's demographic—and thus economic—profile, coupled with urbanization, industrialization, and a nascent consumerism, indicated to traditionalists the triumph of the cities over the countryside in determining the economic, political, and cultural destiny of France.

For large landowners and agricultural entrepreneurs the rural exodus was soon translated into an apparent manpower shortage and a rise in the cost of labor, since the development of a market economy and greater demographic mobility occurred while much of French agriculture remained technically backward and labor-intensive.[3] Although varying from region to region, and from one season to another, wages for agricultural day laborers and domestics increased across the country. In Finistère, Aube, Marne, Haute-Garonne, and Aude, salaries for *journaliers* doubled between 1860 and 1876; in Indre-et-Loire, they increased by 300 percent. In Calvados, the average daily wage for a day laborer rose from 1.53 francs in 1852 to 2.60 francs in 1882, and in Loir-et-Cher the increase was roughly the same. Wages for domestics rose as well: 132 percent in Calvados and 120 percent in Finistère for a male worker. Overall, labor represented 40 percent of production costs in 1880, as against about one-third in 1859.[4] Rising wages, the Comte de Perrigny told the *enquête*

3. See Désert, *Une Société rurale*, 186–89; and Price, *The Modernization of Rural France*, 394–95.
4. See Agulhon, Désert, and Specklin, *Apogée et Crise de la civilisation paysanne*, 223–25; Désert, *Une Société rurale*, 546–47; Dupeux, *Aspects*, 260–61; Hubscher, *L'Agriculture et la Société rurale*, II, 571–75.

agricole in 1866, had made "the situation . . . especially difficult for the *propriétaires.*"[5]

To the paternalistic landowner accustomed to the obedience of his workers, the rural exodus signified not only higher labor costs but a breakdown in traditional forms of social deference. Legitimists often complained that the competitive economic advantage gained by laborers, no matter how small, had led to an intolerable supposition of independence among a work force that, besides costing too much, was demanding more freedoms than in the past. The young seemed to the *propriétaires* especially infected by the plague of indiscipline and restlessness. According to the Marquis d'Effiat, a landowner in Chezelles, Indre-et-Loire, "Competition [for jobs] is such that the domestics see themselves as masters and are always ready to demand their account. It is the same with day laborers; everyday they become more demanding, and the young do not replace the old. Work suffers, and I know some landowners who have not been able to dig up their vineyards this year for a shortage of labor."[6] The preference the Legitimists found among *fermiers* and *métayers* for a churchgoing, settled family life was proof enough to them that temporary migrants and emigrants were a threat to their kind of existence. Ferdinand Béchard supposed that "populations attached to traditions and to the soil" loved order and peace and retained "the habit of work, the sentiment of liberty, and of personal dignity," whereas "nomadic populations are the repositories of idleness, corruption, and troubles."[7]

If the apparent breakdown in social discipline impressed the Legitimists as the underlying cause of the rural exodus, they were also aware that the peasant emigration coincided with the growing dependence of French agriculture on national and even international markets. The moral disposition of the masses might be altered in some way, but the consequences of market integration were beyond the Legitimists' control. That signaled to them the loss by *propriétaires* of their monopoly over the rural labor force, as well as the diminishing ability of traditional social cadres

---

5. Déposition orale de le comte de Perrigny, in *Enquête agricole,* Série 2, Vol. VIII (Loir-et-Cher), 285.

6. Déposition orale de M. le marquis d'Effiat, in *Enquête agricole,* Série 2, Vol. VIII (Indre-et-Loire), 271.

7. Béchard, *De l'état du paupérisme,* 68.

to determine the political, moral, and social climate of the nation. What would happen to France, and themselves, they wondered, if the rural environment, which had historically formed the physical setting for the transmission and survival of traditional values, lost its economic and moral sovereignty over a majority of the population? The Legitimists believed that agriculture functioned not only to feed the nation but to preserve the sacred link between the people and the work of creation. Comte Alfred de Falloux, recalling Schiller's *William Tell,* concluded that the Swiss had survived their tumultuous history because they remained an "aggregation of pastoral people, preserving in their mountains their masculine and primitive simplicity."[8] He explained, "Agriculture does not corrupt those who are enriched by it. . . . It is the career in which the creature remains the most constantly in rapport with the Creator. His principal instruments come to him directly from God; the sun and the clouds, the heat and the dew are his primary tools. The gaze of the laborer is, along with that of the astronomer, the one that rises most habitually toward heaven."[9]

Farming, he therefore thought, was the source of a Christian people's physical and spiritual vitality; to abandon it en masse could only mean that a civilization had lost the moral fortitude to preserve what grounded its strength and spirit. If peasants emigrated to the cities, if landowners spent more time in Paris than on the farm, clearly some "moral brake" had been loosened.[10] The Legitimists concluded that the rural exodus reflected not only the rise of insubordination but the collapse of the internalized moral constraints that had prevailed for centuries in the closed society of the rural communes. Emigration and social indiscipline were two sides of a process by which a materialistic culture triumphed over the notions of right and duty inherent in Christian civilization. Was it not

8. Falloux, "Dix ans d'agriculture," *Le Correspondant,* LVII (1862), 659.

9. *Ibid.,* 656.

10. *Ibid.,* 652. Gavardie linked the land to the continuity of values when he wrote, "The land can be acquired and transmitted only through long work and application; mobile wealth rambles about like the desires of man. Landed property was made to steady the heart and the step of a nervous generation in too much of a hurry to enjoy itself. It favors and fortifies the respect for paternal traditions; it calms the passions by daily contact with the majestic serenity of the earth" (*Etudes sur les vraies doctrines sociales,* 182). La Boulie associated the vitality of the rural economy with political conservatism: "The wealth of the countryside is the firmest guarantee of the stability of a government and of the fidelity of a people to conservative principles" (*La Régénération de l'agriculture,* 25). Thus, for the Legitimists the land symbolized the morally salutary trilogy of God, family, and fidelity.

true, they argued, that peasants emigrated to the cities in search of comfort and riches? And did they not thereby demonstrate their preference for temporal pleasure over social and religious obligation? The rural exodus was ultimately the "product of a sensualist and skeptical civilization," a "sign of the times" that many feared was "irresistible."[11]

The nature of agricultural labor convinced the Legitimists of the validity of this argument. As M. de Bee, president of the Chambre Consultative d'Agriculture of Bouches-du-Rhône, pointed out, life in the countryside was inherently difficult and the land gave up riches only to those who most persevered. "Agriculture is modest," he observed. "Its products are obtained with pain and labor; it provides what is necessary, even abundance, but never an exuberance of instantaneous riches. To prosper at it, one must be wise. It demands perseverance of effort, and time for bearing fruit. Abnegation is often necessary for it; privations are common. It repels all illusions, at the bidding of realistic calculation and concrete experience." In a society where the search for pleasure and wealth "had become predominant," how could rural life continue to attract workers, offer an honorable and lucrative career to the sons of landowners, or even retain the people who remained?[12] "To an entire population wanting to be lodged, clothed, and fed like the most well-off, in the wink of an eye," wrote Léopold de Gaillard, "industry alone, and industry aided by powerful machines, can respond. It has responded, . . . but in responding in this manner, it has put into relief, for even the least perceptive, the inferiority of agriculture." He concluded, "Voilà que l'agriculture est restée suspecte d'ancien régime."[13]

But if this "crisis . . . of civilization" was "irresistible," what could be done?[14] Was it necessary to change the "sensualist" mind-set before agriculture could flourish, or could enough vigor be imparted to agricul-

11. Paul Anselme Le Breton, *Département de la Mayenne, congrès agricole de Laval: Compte rendu des séances* (Laval, 1870), 19; Gaillard, *La Crise agricole et la Démocratie,* 8. In 1879, a participant in a session of the Association Normande at Argentan seemed to accuse those assembled of having encouraged a new outlook in the peasant: "You have opened his mind; you have shown him new horizons. Now he finds himself too confined by the circle of his old habits. You have made a new man: he wants new pleasures, new satisfactions" (Désert, *Une Société rurale,* 190).

12. De l'émigration des inhabitants de la campagne dans les grands centres de population, Chambre Consultative d'Agriculture, Bouches-du-Rhône, June 21, 1858, in F (10) 1580, AN.

13. Gaillard, *La Crise agricole et la Démocratie,* 21–27.

14. *Ibid.,* 8.

ture to enable it to satisfy the material desires of the people? If the material improvement of rural life benefited the interests of the rural population, did it not also pander to the sensualism of the rising generation? In fact, the Legitimists sought simultaneously to better the lot of farmers and to promote institutional and educational reforms that could fortify the moral character of the rural masses and convince young rural notables of the economic, social, and moral benefits of an agricultural profession.[15]

THE POLITICS OF RURAL IMPROVEMENT

Gaillard felt that the moral crisis afflicting the countryside could not be remedied by altering government policies. All the same, most Legitimists were quick to lay upon the Bonapartist regime's lack of sympathy for agricultural development much of the blame for the decline of agriculture's relative importance in French life. A change of attitude by policy makers, they were persuaded, would allow the state to manage the economy more wisely, granting to agriculture the place it deserved. According to them, the government of Napoleon III fostered a moral and economic climate that systematically misprized rural life, pampered industry, and exacerbated the flight to the cities.[16] On more than one occasion, Falloux accused the regime of an antirural bias, pointing to its free-trade policies, its conscription policies, its taxation structure, and its public-works programs. In order to be fair to all interests, he argued, a government should do nothing to foment, overexcite, or encourage the "universal tendencies" of the times.[17] The spirit of this criticism can best be seen in the Legitimists' opposition to the Empire's military reforms. Since the new policy expanded the size of the army and lengthened the training period, the Legitimists viewed it as a dangerous drain on rural manpower. The rural notables' "antimilitarism" focused not only upon the maladroit actions in the Italian and Mexican fiascoes but also upon the way that peasant conscripts, once exposed to new ideas and superior

15. Most of the sources for this chapter are inquiries, deliberations, and public commentaries of the 1860s, many of them connected with the *enquête agricole* of 1866, which generated much interest and debate. As Gabriel de Saint-Victor, president of the *comice agricole* of the canton of Tarace in the Rhône, remarked in this period, "Agriculture is à la mode; everybody is talking about it, many are complaining, and everyone seems interested in it" (*De l'enquête agricole*, 6).

16. See Falloux, "Dix ans d'agriculture," *Le Correspondant*, LVII (1862), 653.

17. *Ibid.*, 652; Falloux, "L'Agriculture et la Politique," in *Etudes et Souvenirs*, 263–64.

living conditions in the barracks, lost their taste for rural life.[18] In the
1860s, with the support of national figures like Antoine Berryer and the
Catholic deputies in the Corps Législatif, the Legitimist press launched a
nationwide campaign against the reforms and promoted a series of incen-
tive programs to encourage recruits to return home after their terms of
service. In 1867, for example, the *Journal de Rennes* and *La France centrale*
circulated a petition with the help of the clergy calling the conscription
laws disastrous and explaining that "our farmers need peace to repair
their losses."[19] In Toulon, the committee of the *comice agricole* recommended that peasants be given leave after two years of service on condition that they "deliver themselves to work in the fields" of the areas from
which they came. In Bouches-du-Rhône, the general council suggested
that day laborers and farmers who were still on the land at sixty be given
a "special medallion" indicating "their perseverance in the agricultural
profession," and recommended that the example of the recipients be
broadcast by reading their names at the regional *concours* and posting the
names in each commune.[20]

The Legitimists' interest in offering incentives for remaining on the
land was seated in their conviction that the state could help decrease rural
depopulation by seeking a prosperity in agriculture that would support
the aspirations of people caught up in the moral revolution of modern
times. It made little sense, they reasoned, to oppose economic progress
in the interest of combating the climate of materialism, since the morality
of the peasantry did not depend on the perpetuation of poverty and harsh
living conditions in the countryside.[21] What the Legitimists promoted,
therefore, was a new *politique agricole* that would modify the development
of the French economy through state action meant to let agriculture enjoy some of the economic incentives and fiscal advantages that the industrial sector already benefited from.

18. See Menager, *La Vie politique*, II, 635–36; and Weber, *Peasants into Frenchmen,* 301.
Saint-Victor calculated that French agriculture had lost two million workers between 1851
and 1861, and he believed the "scarcity of labor" to be due in part to the "exaggeration of
the state of arms." The only other cause he cited was the decreasing birthrate. See his *De
l'enquête agricole,* 13–14.
19. Rapport du procureur général de Rennes, March 14, 1867, in BB (18) 1744, AN.
20. Extrait du registre des délibérations du conseil général, Bouches-du-Rhône: De-
mandes en faveur de l'agriculture, August 26, 1858, in F (10) 1580; Chambre consultative
d'Agriculture, Bouches-du-Rhône, June 21, 1858, in F (10) 1580, AN.
21. Falloux, "L'Agriculture et la Politique," in *Etudes et Souvenirs,* 263.

Legitimist objections to the Empire's public-works program were part of a critique of the liberal political economy from a rural perspective. The public-works program, which stressed the redesign of Paris and the construction of public buildings such as the new Opéra, prompted Legitimist accusations that the regime was coaxing workers from the fields and drawing them into the morally destructive environment of the cities, where they became a threat to public order. Typically, the Comte de La Rochethulon, who judged the works to be unnecessary and inexcusably overbudgeted, argued that they caused the "workers of the fields . . . to abandon the plow for the trowel," to leave their families for most of the year, and to "participate . . . in the license of the big cities." [22] What made the public-works policy particularly troubling, however, were not its moral effects—clearly a moral decline had innumerable causes—but the way it demonstrated how the French economy was being deformed in the hands of men with no real ties to the rural economy. To rural capitalists and producers who depended on a favorable investment climate just as much as maufacturers, the grand projects represented an irresponsible use of resources, serving only to redistribute wealth artificially from the provinces to Paris and from agriculture to industry. Not only was the government depriving *propriétaires* of workers, it was draining rural capital as well, by financing ostentatious construction through a taxation policy that hit landed wealth harder than mobile capital. While taxes on securities were mild, land was burdened with inordinate fiscal levies—the inheritance tax, the *impôt foncier, droits de mutation,* the *octrois,* and taxes on beverages—that turned hard-earned francs into public funds to be used at the discretion of blithe administrators. [23] Meanwhile, stockjobbers and securities speculators poured their millions into the Bourse, foreign investment, and the national debt without having to shoulder responsibility for building up the French economy. For Claude Marie Raudot, the support that bankers and financiers received from the central administration seemed to confirm the widespread antirural fiscal bias of the capitalists and bourgeois functionaries who controlled the government. [24] While speculators and functionaries directed capital and manpower to a few privileged departments and made investment capital

22. Déposition orale de M. le comte de La Rochethulon, in *Enquête agricole,* Série 2, Part 10 (Vienne), 52–53.
23. *Ibid.,* 53.
24. Raudot, *De l'agriculture,* 38–40.

available to industry at the expense of agriculture, rural *propriétaires* had no effective means of influencing policy. As M. d'Andigné de Resteau told the *enquête agricole* in Maine-et-Loire, the *chambres de commerce* always got a sympathetic hearing from officials whereas the *chambres d'agriculture* went unheeded and remained underrepresented in the councils of state.[25]

The manifest official preference for industry led a handful of Legitimists to question whether industry and agriculture were compatible. Bourgeois society, liberalism, and industrialism, they argued, posed an unacceptable threat to the traditional rural way of life. For Henri de La Broise, a landowner in the rural department of the Mayenne, centralization and the "exaggerated development of industry" promised to turn a Christian people into egotistic bourgeois or victimized proletarians by "seducing" the population away from the land. For the sake of civilized values, he concluded, industrial growth would have to be moderated.[26] Antoine Blanc de St. Bonnet, an obscure philosopher and committed reactionary of bourgeois origins, argued that landed property was the only true basis of wealth and culture and that the "fictive capital" of industry, with its links to vice and greed, could only destroy the Christian personality of man and society. He therefore recommended a "reasoned but urgent reduction of industrialism" through the strict regulation of the mobility of the work force.[27]

But such proposals were extreme and were ignored by more moderate and influential Legitimists who chose to make a distinction between wealth gained through speculation and invested solely in liquid securities for short-term profit and wealth earned through productive activity and applied to increase the economic health of the nation. For most, unwise financial investment, wasteful speculation, and frivolous government spending that did nothing to enrich the truly productive sectors of the economy were just bad capitalism. Like many other Legitimists, the Vicomte de Meaux regretted that industry offered more gainful employment than agriculture but acknowledged that industrial labor "would continue to increase the national fortune." It was wrong, he wrote, "to attribute the insufficiency of agricultural capital to the increase of industrial and commercial wealth." He continued, "Industry and commerce

25. Déposition orale de M. de Andigné de Resteau, in *Enquête agricole*, Série 2, Vol. II, Part 2 (Sarthe), 570–71.
26. La Broise, *Le Vrai et le Faux Libéralisme*, 168.
27. Blanc de St. Bonnet, *La Légitimité*, 602–609, 329–39.

create wealth, and wealth, once created, always spills over onto the soil. That is why the countries in which industry flourishes most are also those in which land grows in value still more: one clearly sees this in England. How, therefore, can the price of land fall in France by virtue of industrial development? No, what has impoverished the land is not money earned through industry but money consumed by sterile expenditure."[28] It was not industrialization per se that harmed agriculture, he maintained, but rather the abuse of capital by loafers, speculators, and functionaries who artificially disturbed the correct path of capitalist development.

This distinction between development and speculation, between productive investment and "sterile expenditure," was the key to the Legitimists' concept of the relationship between agriculture and industry. What they objected to was not mobile capital, as Locke supposes, but rather economic and bureaucratic practices that effectively reduced the relative availability of capital for investment in agricultural enterprises.[29] The way to unhamper the rural economy, they argued, was not to abandon capi-

28. Meaux, "Les Conclusions de l'enquête agricole," *Le Correspondant,* LXXVII (1869), 108.
29. Locke argues that the Legitimists "generally considered liquid securities to be socially harmful" because, whether they were of the bourgeoisie or the nobility, they tended to identify property with the continuity of their families. He also asserts that they saw stockholders as having no "sense of paternal responsibility toward the workers" and that they considered the joint-stock corporation "to be a threat to the social order." After skillfully documenting the Legitimists' participation in business and their propensity for maintaining a sizable stock portfolio to complement their landed wealth, Locke nevertheless repeats the common view that the Legitimists were hostile to nonagricultural capital. I would suggest that Locke confuses what the Legitimists called speculation, by which they meant the abuse of liquid capital, and liquid capital in general. Although it is undeniable that their attitude reflected the misgivings of modernizing landowners in a period when industrial stocks yielded better returns and when agriculture's relative share of the total amount of national wealth was diminishing, that does not mean that they rejected all forms of capitalist financing. Liquid securities were an important part of the wealth held by *grands propriétaires* as well as by the rich bourgeoisie, and the bourgeoisie often invested part of its industrial profits in land. The consequence was that in the nineteenth century the wealth of the aristocracy and that of the rich bourgeoisie were fairly similar in composition. Moreover, the Legitimists tended to regard stockholding as a legitimate financial device as well as the best way for rich Catholics to influence the social policies of big business. In complaining about liquid securities, they were only pointing out that by discouraging investment in rural enterprises in favor of stocks and bonds that yielded short-term profit, the prevailing financial system led to the undercapitalization of "agricultural industries." Like all capitalists, they understood that capital had to be liquid in order to provide diverse investment opportunities. See Locke, *French Legitimists,* 166.

talism but to pursue policies that ensured a more equitable distribution of capital and human resources and that encouraged rural producers to treat farming like an industry.[30] As Charles de La Monneraye put it, agriculture was an "industry whose basis is in the soil, expressed by landed capital. This capital would remain inert and unproductive without the necessary infusion of mobile capital."[31] A new *politique agricole* built on sound economic principles and administered by leaders who understood the importance of agriculture, the Legitimists believed, would have the double advantage of enriching the land and reinforcing the strength and stability of traditional rural society. It would permit agriculture to meet the challenge of the new materialism. It would also coincide perfectly with the political, social, and material interests of a group that possessed a vast amount of landed wealth along with substantial industrial investments and that sought to replace a ruling class of profiteers and bureaucrats with a coalition of productive and moral leaders—rich landowners and Catholic industrialists—who were naturally best suited to direct the affairs of state. As Gaillard wrote in 1866, what France needed was a "sincere fusion between the progressive elements of agriculture and the conservative elements of industry."[32]

To implant successfully a new political economy implied the power to implement needed reforms, and that required a greater say for rural *propriétaires* in public affairs. Thus, on the political front, the Legitimists sought to remedy the agricultural community's lack of influence by demanding an institutionalized forum in which landowners could make their ideas known on "all the laws and measures concerning the agricultural industry." Not only would an effective representation of rural interests ensure good legislation, it would also increase the voice of conservatives in government. Most Legitimists favored schemes that would grant rural producers the legal right to choose delegates from the committees of the *comices agricoles* and from the departmental *chambres d'agriculture* to sit on a new Conseil Supérieur d'Agriculture with the power to advise the ministries and the Conseil d'Etat on matters such as rural

30. Charles de La Monneraye, *Lettre sur la situation de l'agriculture* (Rennes, 1866).
31. *Ibid.*
32. Gaillard, *La Crise agricole et la Démocratie,* 28. The industrialists and the rural *propriétaires* who elaborated this *politique* saw no real conflict of interest between the primary and secondary sectors. The whole point, in fact, was that if capital—and human—resources were managed equitably, industry and agriculture could enjoy a common prosperity, because the sectors, with their shared interests, could take advantage of similar institutions.

roads, irrigation and hydraulic works, livestock breeding, forest management, and agricultural instruction. In 1871, a number of Legitimist deputies took that idea one step farther by calling for the creation of a "special ministry of agriculture" to regulate "agricultural interests."[33]

Still, there would be extreme limitations on the ability of any such institution significantly to redistribute capital and jobs in a liberal economy. Despite the great power of the administration, the state could do little to alter the existing geography of employment and investment. The flight of labor and capital from the countryside was not due only to moral weakness and government insensitivity; the long-term reduction of employment opportunities in rural areas was at the heart of the problem. Because of the economic constraints produced by French landholding patterns, French agriculture had never been capable of providing full employment, and hence a large number of landless and impoverished peasants were forced to work in nonagricultural trades like weaving and food processing.[34] In the early nineteenth century, rural overpopulation developed in part because of an "interpenetration of agricultural and artisanal sectors" that allowed the poorest inhabitants to survive without emigrating. Cottage production let people stay where they were, and other forms of employment, if they required travel, were often seasonal and produced only temporary migration, enabling a maintenance of ties with the rural economy.[35] After midcentury, however, with the rise of urban factory production and the transportation revolution, dispersed local handicraft and rural industries declined.[36] The result of the rural deindustrialization was a growing instability and irregularity of rural employment, and even widespread unemployment. As temporary migration turned into a rural exodus, the agricultural sector lost large numbers of semiskilled artisans as well as day laborers. Despite substantial rural

33. Déposition écrite de M. de La Bassétière, Documents annexes, in *Enquête agricole,* Série 2, Vol. VII, Part 3 (Vendée), 155; Déposition orale de M. D'Andigné de Resteau, in *Enquête agricole,* Série 2, Vol. II, Part 2 (Sarthe), 570–71; Meaux, "Les Conclusions de l'Enquête agricole," *Le Correspondant,* LXXVII (1869), 122–25; *Annales,* March 7, 1871, I, annexe 41, p. 27.

34. Pitié, *L'Exode rural,* 518.

35. Hubscher, *L'Agriculture et la Société rurale,* II, 139; Weber, *Peasants into Frenchmen,* 213.

36. See Désert, *Une Société rurale,* 420–23, 734–35; Houée, *Les Etapes du développement rural,* I, 36–38; Weber, *Peasants into Frenchmen,* 228–29.

unemployment, landowners complained of a "lack of hands," because it was the youngest, healthiest, and most desirable workers who left.[37]

To arrest this trend, the Legitimists recommended that industry move out of the congested cities and into the countryside. The *chambre d'agriculture* of Bouches-du-Rhône called for an "alliance of agriculture and industry" to persuade wealthy landowners to create "industrial establishments on their properties offering the advantages to the rural population that it looks for in the cities."[38] The large-scale production of commercial goods from raw materials found on the farm was considered a natural agricultural complement to the progressive farming in the age of mobile capital.[39] Camille de La Boulie, the vice-president of the Agricultural Society of Bouches-du-Rhône, pointed to the *compagnie foncière* of M. M. Blanchard and M. Château, which manufactured phosphoric acid and combined it with magnesium salts and manure to make fertilizer, as a perfect example of the union of agriculture and industry. Not only could such chemical factories provide employment by creating rural work colonies, they could also save the French government the cost of importing guano from Peru and provide an opportunity to flush the stench out of Parisian sewers. Moreover, high-grade fertilizers, La Boulie argued, would increase crop yields, slow rural depopulation, and stimulate the birthrate.[40] Anatole de Melun suggested that industrialists follow the example of their colleagues in Lyon and Rouen by dispersing a portion of their manufacturing to neighboring rural villages; Béchard thought that rural public-works projects, distributed "in harmony with the essentially variable needs of the laboring classes," would decrease urban crowding. He even recommended that municipalities limit the number of new industries within their boundaries to conform with a "determined total of the population," by placing "manufacturing sites outside city walls."[41]

37. See Pitié, *L'Exode rural*, 513–15; Wylie, *Chanzeaux*, 52–53.
38. Chambre consultative d'agriculture, Bouches-du-Rhône, Extrait des délibérations, June 21, 1858, in F (10) 1580, AN.
39. See F (10) 1580, AN; and *Annales*, July 27, 1875, XLIV, annexe 3283, p. 103.
40. La Boulie, *La Régénération de l'agriculture*, 10–12.
41. *Annales*, July, 27, 1874, XLIV, annexe 3283, p. 104; Béchard, *De l'état du paupérisme*, 124–27, 340–41. Wylie discusses how in Chanzeaux the Marquis de Quatrebarbes tried to combat the rural exodus with "miniature public-works programs" such as locally funded road maintenence. "It is necessary, vitally necessary," Quatrebarbes argued, "to stop the deplorable uprooting of the rural population. We must attach the people to the soil by

According to the Legitimists, rural reindustrialization would allow industry to prosper in an atmosphere of social peace without draining the
resources of the countryside. By reducing the working population's contacts with the morally deleterious influences of the city and keeping it in
the salutary rural environment, employers would assure themselves a
work force that was more docile, more obedient, and easier to control.
As Melun explained, the social question would be "simplified" if more
large-scale manufacturing took place in the countryside: "There air and
land are not lacking; without too much expense, it is possible to build
detached houses, often surrounded by a little garden, or at least buildings
in which each tenant possesses his own entryway and lives with his
family in complete independence." In the countryside, workers would
become more like good peasants who "love the land and think of the
future in the handling of their savings"; since good habits were "contagious and win over the industrial worker," the level of social discontent
would be considerably reduced.[42] Béchard observed that workers employed outside Rouen earned less than those in the city but "never complained, never revolted," whereas "the others are always the first to join
in disorder and sedition."[43]

Nevertheless, as Melun pointed out, efforts at rural reindustrialization, "despite their success, find few imitators, especially from the cities."[44]
Evidently, if the countryside was to provide more employment and be
more productive, it would have to rely on its own resources. The Legitimists stressed that rural enterprises, like industrial manufacturing, needed

---

giving them the well-being that the cities falsely promised to them, for in the cities they
find too often nothing but disappointment, immorality and ruin" (*Chanzeaux,* 55).

42. *Annales,* July 27, 1874, XLIV, annexe 3283, p. 103.

43. Béchard, *De l'état du paupérisme,* 337. See Locke, *French Legitimists,* 187. Social
considerations also led the Legitimists to prefer cottage industries over factory production
where they were possible, as in sectors of the textile industry. As Anatole de Melun noted,
"Around Lyon, and in the communes neighboring several towns of the Nord, weaving
takes place in the paternal home, where parents and children work together on different
jobs. This system has great advantages from the moral point of view; it tightens the bonds
of the family and preserves it from the dangers of communal life in the workshops. The
paternal eye is always more vigilant than the most active surveillance by strangers. From
the social point of view, the system alleviates the unpleasant incidents of the urban agglom-
erations which easily stir popular emotions. The restructuring of the large manufacturers
that crowd the city of Lyon and their transformation into little workshops scattered
throughout the countryside has produced the happiest results" (*Annales,* July 27, 1874,
XLIV, annexe 3283, p. 104).

44. *Annales,* July 27, 1874, XLIV, annexe 3283, p. 103.

capital in order to flourish. Consequently, they made a steady appeal for more credit institutions to serve rural interests, and they continued seeking new ways to finance agricultural projects. They were dissatisfied with the newly established Crédit Foncier, which they saw as too remote from the ordinary farmer and too closely tied to the Empire's harmful urban construction program. Meaux called for the creation of "free and spontaneous associations" of large landowners and rich cultivators to form vast "financial establishments" to lend money to smaller local farmers.[45] Benoist d'Azy, who felt that agriculture needed credit "because the more it perfects itself, the more it participates in the nature of industry," argued that in addition to the long-term loans offered by Crédit Foncier to large producers for major projects—irrigation and construction—more liquid capital would aid farmers by enabling them to take immediate advantage of price fluctuations in purchasing animals, fertilizers, and tools. He advised landowners, large and small, to lobby for more local farm credit banks capable of making short-term loans; they would allow agriculture to enjoy the same advantages as other forms of commerce.[46] Other Legitimists suggested that producers' cooperatives were the best means of helping small farmers purchase and share expensive machinery, work animals, livestock, and seed.[47]

Rural credit was not the only possible solution, though, to the dearth of capital in the countryside. Armand Fresneau, who reasoned that "landed revenue, once created, becomes a workable and alienable asset like any other," thought that Breton landowners should exploit the Empire's legislation encouraging sociétés anonymes and set up large farming companies run by jointly owned peasant administrative organizations. The new companies could produce vegetables for export. Fresneau wanted landowners to consolidate their estates into joint-production cooperatives organized on the basis of an efficient division of labor. He believed that the agricultural joint-stock companies should be financed through an initial investment of 400,000 francs and the sale of stock annuities at 5-percent interest. The lands of the cooperatives were to be worked by

---

45. Meaux, "Les Conclusions de l'enquête agricole," Le Correspondant, LXXVII (1869), 110.

46. Déposition orale du comte Benoist d'Azy, in Enquête agricole, Série 2, Part 9 (Nièvre), 372–73.

47. Calemard de Lafayette, L'Agriculture progressive, 218–19; Annales, September 14, 1871, V, annexe 659, p. 283.

métayers, and the companies were to try to acquire additional farmland
"suitable for rapid integration into a general system of production." [48]

The major problem with most of these schemes, as Fresneau recognized, was that they were suited only to moderately well-off landowners who already produced for the market and who could shoulder the burden of loans and investments. Accordingly, they did not constitute an effective overall rural social policy. The typical peasant, involved in subsistence farming and often deep in debt from loans contracted in meeting basic expenses, remained on the fringe of the market economy. "Large landowners," wrote Fresneau, "have their own facilities. Only they can sell to industries, cover heavy expenses, and force middlemen to deal with them"; intricate marketing schemes, he asserted, could do "nothing . . . for the small farm." [49] Gaillard believed that large estates were naturally more productive. He could picture the "soil of France . . . shared by seven or eight giant industrial companies having immense capital, an immense battery of equipment, and an immense roster of employees." French agriculture would then, "at the touch of a telegraph machine," be made to function according to grand designs in the "service of an idea." Still, "We are not there yet," he sighed, "and we will never be there if God and the civil code have their way." [50]

His reference to the civil code underlines how it was the desire to bring prosperity to the rural economy, more than anything else, that led the Legitimists to criticize the parcellation of French farms and the effects of the revolutionary inheritance laws. Large landowners, who had learned how to avoid dividing up their properties or at least how to keep their scattered estates in the family, seldom blamed the inheritance laws for ruining the rich, even though the Legitimists liked to repeat maliciously that the revolutionaries had intended to destroy the aristocracy. Many Legitimists argued that equal inheritance had the harmful effect of reducing the authority of the *père de famille* over his heirs, but that did not mean that they wanted to return to the practices of the Old Regime. [51] Raudot felt, instead, that a truly progressive revolution would have more effectively eliminated certain legal practices and attitudes about landownership that were already crippling the landed elite before 1789—including

48. Fresneau, *Kermadio,* 17–23.
49. *Ibid.,* 21.
50. Gaillard, *La Crise agricole et la Démocratie,* 12.
51. See, for example, comments in Dubosc de Pesquidoux' *Le Comte de Chambord,* 244.

the practice of partible inheritance. It was hypocritical, he thought, for the Left to accuse the Legitimists of wanting to restore the *droit d'ainesse,* given that partible inheritance had been even more widely practiced than primogeniture before the Revolution. The revolutionaries, by assuming that they could eradicate the counterrevolutionary nobility and concurrently stimulate commerce and democracy by putting "all properties up for sale, to change hands incessantly," had, according to Raudot, only "adopted and increased . . . what was perhaps worst in the Old Regime." Morevoer, the notion that small holdings would ensure the prosperity of agriculture, the growth of the population, the well-being of the people, and the conferring of human dignity had been proved false; the Revolution, according to its own criteria, was a complete failure, since it had only helped to protect an archaic system of farming whose chief distinctions were not prosperity and dignity but routine, ignorance, and poverty. Rather than safeguarding a truly propitious democracy, the Revolution had made it impossible by stunting the moral and material development of the people. If the French Revolution were to occur in nineteenth-century England, Raudot commented, he was certain that "agriculture would regress."[52]

Inasmuch as the Revolution was a fait accompli, many Legitimists were not optimistic about France's ability to reverse the damage, although they did suggest remedies. Raudot thought that the aim of any reform should be not to "create an impossible aristocracy but to save democracy from the excesses of its triumph." Restoring primogeniture would be beside the point; what France needed was fathers who had the liberty to dispose of their goods freely but who also made economically wise decisions about the future, forestalling the state from stepping in and destroying freedom in the name of some chimerical equality. The state, he believed, should serve good sense by allowing property owners to declare certain properties indivisible, by enlarging the size of the *quotité disponible,* and by encouraging the consolidation of contiguous parcels owned by the same individual or family.

The Legitimists saw little likelihood that such solutions would command wide acceptance in times such as theirs. As Meaux remarked, "Public attitudes, at present, will not lend themselves to this change." On the one hand, peasants would keep dividing their land and avoiding

52. Raudot, *De l'agriculture,* 23.

cooperatives because they would rather have their own piece of earth than entrust it to someone else even if ceding some control could bring higher yields. The peasants, too, would never help in consolidating parcels, because they would quickly exhaust their means if they tried.[53] On the other hand, the rich, on whom the future of French agriculture really depended, were no more inclined to behave wisely and progressively, too many *propriétaires* choosing to become absentee *rentiers du sol,* indifferent to the prosperity of agriculture in general and content to abandon their estates to rent collectors and to the unchanging routine of the past, and preferring the "pleasures of the city" to a simple "sojourn in the country." Worst of all, Raudot complained, many had learned nothing since 1789 and continued to sell off their properties piece by piece to sustain their extravagant life-styles and selfish ambitions. Centralization only encouraged such tendencies, by conferring higher status on nonagricultural professions and by depriving the elite of an effective role in local government. In the final analysis, parcellation was another side of the moral malaise that gave rise to the rural exodus, and absenteeism merely demonstrated that much of the rural elite was no less corrupted than the common people by the lure of easy riches and fame. To Raudot, the reason for the plight of French agriculture was clear and simple: "In France, a landowner must leave his fields and his manor in order to be something: in England, he must stay put. Everything is there. Make the landowners live on their lands, take a liking to rural life, and they will buy instead of sell."[54]

The Legitimists kept encountering frustrations in their attempt to elaborate a successful *politique agricole,* because they embraced contradictory goals. If they acknowledged that the crude chase after riches had led to the undervaluing of nonlucrative agricultural professions and if they chose to address the challenge of the new materialism by stimulating agricultural productivity, they also had somehow to incite a morally debilitated population to act correctly. If it was true that rural prosperity could break the attraction of the cities, it was equally true that economic reforms capable of regenerating agriculture would have to be the result rather than the cause of a profound and general change in attitudes. As Meaux wrote in frustration, the "morality of the countryside" was in

53. *Ibid.,* 13–25; Meaux, "Les Conclusions de l'enquête agricole," *Le Correspondant,* LXXVII (1869), 105.
54. Raudot, *De l'agriculture,* 91; Désert, *Une Société rurale,* 742.

decline despite the increasing use of "agronomic methods" among a handful of conscientious landowners. Every advancement in the economic order, he complained, produced a "direct and visible repercussion . . . in the moral order."[55]

Like the problem of the corporate reconstruction of industry, that of the reconstruction of rural France forced the Legitimists to face questions of freedom and motivation as they related to a largely open society. In effect, most Legitimists accepted the basic liberal assumption that economic choices in civil society were made by free individuals acting in accord with collective standards. With only a few exceptions, the Legitimists would not have suggested that either the state or the landowners had the right to coerce peasants and *propriétaires* to stay on the land. The Legitimist goal was, rather, the creation of social and institutional structures—including the hereditary monarchy—that would engender a collective moral sensibility among free individuals which would impel them to behave correctly. If peasants were free to choose where to live and work, they should not be left free to choose badly. The fact that they were doing so in increasing numbers confirmed for the Legitimists that something had gone wrong since 1789. The Legitimists thus believed that, besides laying the foundations for a renewal of agricultural prosperity, it was necessary to alter rural culture. Béchard put the point explicitly: "It is impossible to forbid the worker from going where a larger salary calls him or to constrain him by direct means from changing his residence to fit the vicissitudes of commerce, but it is possible to contribute indirectly to a satisfactory distribution of the population by working through institutions and mores."[56]

EXODUS OR REDEMPTION

The Legitimists counted on decentralization and improved charitable modalities to play an important role in the regeneration of the countryside. Decentralization was expected to encourage the notables to remain in the provinces once they regained a political purpose there. The Legitimists reasoned, too, that a greater availability of public and private

55. Meaux, "Les Conclusions de l'enquête agricole," *Le Correspondant*, LXXVII (1869), 125.

56. Béchard, *De l'état du paupérisme*, 227–28.

social services would detain the rural poor from seeking better relief facilities in the cities.[57]

With rural assistance, as with legal charity and working-class patronage, the nature of what was to be offered was as important as its availability. One of the Legitimists' favorite rural charitable projects was the
colonie agricole. In 1872, Henri Fournier, a Legitimist deputy from the
Cher, recommended that the state establish colonies or asylums for rural
indigents and orphans on communal properties or uncultivated land in
the countryside, where the poor "could form . . . a permanent reserve
of manpower" that neighboring landowners could look to "in search of
the hands a lack of which often causes them to cancel great projects of
agricultural development."[58] The model of the colonie agricole that the
Legitimists most favored was provided by Amédée de Gouvello, who in
1863 set up an institution for orphans on his own properties at Nourray,
near Vendôme. Rather than being a work camp or a modified rural poorhouse, Gouvello's colony was a complete community under the superintendence of men trained in modern farm management and the patronage of religious orders that ran a hospital, a church, and a school to
provide surrogates for family structures. Gouvello thought that if agricultural colonies were to contribute to the moral and economic development of the nation, they could not be merely "means employed by
bienfaisance to occupy the poor child" but would have to be systems of
encadrement that aimed "to make the most and best of him by enriching
him." For that, costly state orphanages functioned no better than human
warehouses, since children received neither physical nor moral training,
nor did they get the agricultural instruction that might attach them to
the soil. All orphans in state asylums or hospitals, Gouvello argued,
should be either adopted by farmers or sent into private agricultural colonies where they could be trained to make up for the growing "dearth
of men."

The colony at Nourray, which consisted of a hundred hectares of arable land and roughly ten hectares of pasture, was farmed as a métairie by
twenty-five colons brought in from the hospices of Vendôme and Blois.
The orphans, ranging in age from infancy to twenty-five, were taught
farming techniques and given regular religious instruction by three

57. See especially Annales, March 25, 1872, VIII, annexe 1033, p. 262. Gouvello suggested that indigents be transported to the countryside to be cared for by private charitable
organizations. See Gouvello, Le Dépopulation des campagnes, 24–25.

58. Annales, March 25, 1872, V, annexe 1033, p. 264.

brothers of the order of Saint Croix du Mans. The boys were raised from infancy in virtues that would "attach [them] to the soil" and help them to become honest cultivators and good fathers, and the girls, who remained secluded in an area under the care of nuns until the age of seven, worked in the colony until their nineteenth year, when they were placed with *propriétaires* who had need of servants. To instill in the youth the value of work and thrift, the colony awarded them prizes for their performance, the proceeds going into a savings fund or to the local notary to invest. A *colon* who remained until the age of twenty-one received the prize amount with interest.

Gouvello felt that a widespread imitation of his colony would slow down the "vast movement" of the "inhabitants of the countryside into the cities." To promote that end, he founded the Société Générale de Patronage des Orphelinats Agricoles with the assistance of the senator Edmond Drouyn de Lhuys, the Marquis and Marquise de La Rochefoucauld, and the Saint Vincent de Paul Society. The organization sought to gain the support of bishops, general councils, and landowners for the establishment of colonies "on a vast scale." The colony of Nourray was a sort of microcosmic utopia for wealthy landowners who dreamed of being able "to proportion the number of workers to the number of hectares requiring cultivation." As a human nursery designed to train obedient rural workers, docile female domestics, good family farmers, and Christian *contre-maîtres,* the colony was seen as yielding the human material that would allow the countryside to resist the inroads of industrialization and moral decay.[59]

Gouvello's colony also satisfied the Legitimists' preference for the institution of *métayage*. Although detractors saw *métayage* as a form of servitude or as a premodern form of cooperative land tenure that slowed agricultural progress, stunted the personality and moral independence of the *métayer,* and deprived the *propriétaire* of the leisure he required to become a man of the world, the Legitimists viewed it as a "true fraternity of capital and labor" that promoted social harmony and technical innovation better than other systems of land tenure.[60] They argued that land-

59. Gouvello, *Le Dépopulation des campagnes;* Gouvello, *Vues sur la réorganisation de la France;* Déposition orale du marquis de Gouvello, in *Enquête agricole,* Série 2, Part 8, p. 301; *La France centrale,* December 12, 1866. For a further discussion of *colonies agricoles,* see Duroselle, *Les Débuts du catholicisme social,* 602–603.

60. Corbin, *Archaisme et Modernité,* I, 274–75; Belcastel, *Lettres aux propriétaires riverains de la Variante,* 23.

owners who leased their fields on the basis of *fermage* and collected merely a fixed cash rent for a predetermined period were disposed to concern themselves more with lowering expenses than with improving the land.[61] The tenants, on the other hand, who feared that they might do something to increase the value of the owner's land and, consequently, the amount of their rent, were wont to put any extra money in stocks and bonds rather than back into the farm.[62] Inevitably at odds over rents, the landowner and the fixed-rent tenants were "always in a state of antagonism."[63] By contrast, *métayage* was a "voluntary association" in which the *métayer* and the *propriétaire* shared funds and equipment; thus, it assured "reciprocal advantages to the two parties." According to Paul Le Breton, president of the *comice agricole* of Laval, a harmony of interests created a bond of affection and a common desire to improve the productivity of the soil. The *propriétaire,* who usually determined the use to which the land was to be put and collected his rent in kind, had a vested interest in increased yields. In exchange, the *métayer* benefited from the progressive example, the paternal protection, and the wealth of a *maître,* who he could be sure was truly devoted to his interests. A union of capital and labor and an interdependence of interests made "contention extremely rare."[64] Moreover, *métayage* required a "large measure of probity among the population and the continued presence of the *propriétaire* or his representative within reach of the *métayer*." It got landowners to understand "that it is for them a social duty, a patriotic mission, to maintain and develop this healthy association" as a barrier to "socialist utopias."[65]

Although *métayage* offered dubious economic advantages, it accorded well with the Legitimists' confidence in paternalism and reciprocal dependence. Like corporatism in industry, *métayage* promised the possibility of combining economic progress with social precautions against the disruption and class polarization that capitalism seemed to entail. Legitimists knew that *métayers* emigrated less frequently than other peasants

61. Falloux, "Dix ans d'agriculture," *Le Correspondant,* LVII (1862), 645.
62. Paul Anselme Le Breton, *Etude sur le métayage dans la Mayenne* (Paris, 1881), 10.
63. Victor Desvalettes, quoted by Denis in *Les Royalistes de la Mayenne,* 247.
64. Le Breton, *Etude sur le métayage,* 6, 10. General "surveillance" over the conditions of production and the morality of the *métayers* was, for Le Breton, the "very essence of the *métayage* contract" (p. 10).
65. Falloux, "Dix ans d'agriculture," *Le Correspondant,* LVII (1862), 645; Le Breton, *Etude sur le métayage,* 18–19.

because they had few direct contacts with the larger markets.[66] They
were economically dependent on the rich, who operated as their bankers,
creditors, suppliers, and supervisors.[67] Le Breton believed that the vertical solidarity created by *métayage* explained why the number of taxable
arable units increased more slowly in the Mayenne than elsewhere: fewer
landowners sold to intrusive outsiders.[68]

In the long run, neither agricultural colonies nor *métayage* could stop
the rural exodus or check the general tendency toward materialism. Public assistance and rural orphanages affected only a small portion of the
rural population, namely, those who were the least integrated into society and thus the most vulnerable to control. The system of *métayage* was
confined to certain regions of the west and south. Once again, the inadequate reach of private initiatives forced the Legitimists to look to the
state for help. Like the republicans, they eventually turned to education
as affording the best means to affect the mores of the entire population
and instill values in it favorable to agriculture, conservatism, and social
reconstruction.

Far from deeming education unnecessary for the simple peasants, the
Legitimists believed that instruction in agricultural technique would endow the rural masses with *moeurs agricoles* and a real taste for farming.[69]
But if education was necessary, Louis de Kerjégu thought that its content
and form in France only served to destroy in youth a love for the land.
The Legitimists pointed out that the *instituteurs* sent to teach in the rural
communes received only a classical education in urban normal schools
and thus had no training regarding the practical needs of rural life. Moreover, since they probably chose to become educators in order to escape
an ordinary rural existence, they were averse to the numbing routine,
rigidity, and boredom of the countryside and could not help diffusing a

66. See Corbin, *Archaisme et Modernité*, I, 276–77. This defense of *métayage* came at a
time when the system was threatened by emigration, land sales, and the growth of small
property owning. Corbin observed that in the Limousin "small-time notables" preferred
métayage as a way of maintaining their social predominance in the face of a growing number
of small landowners among the peasants.
67. See Le Breton, *Etude sur le métayage*, 10.
68. *Ibid.*, 12. Corbin found that in the Limousin the inhabitants of villages farmed by
métayage did not generally emigrate even though temporary and permanent out-migration
was considerable in the region, especially in communes where fixed-rent tenant farming
predominated. See his *Archisme et Modernité*, I, 182–83, 269.
69. Louis de Monjaret de Kerjégu, *Rapport sur la prime d'honneur de la Mayenne* (Nantes,
1870), 12.

favorable impression of city life, an ambition for social advancement, and a hatred for farming. As Kerjégu noted, peasant families often refused to send their children to schools in the *chef-lieu* of the canton "because, they say, it detaches our children from us" by putting them in "contact with the bourgeois."[70]

Though a system of *fermes-écoles*—most of them established on the land of wealthy landowners—existed to teach elementary agricultural skills, there were too few to meet the need for moral and practical instruction. To incline peasants to follow in their fathers' footsteps, the Legitimists wanted not only an extension of the *ferme-école* program but the placement of a professor of agriculture in each departmental primary normal school. The professor was to train instructors to impart the practical skills and moral advantages of agriculture to peasant children.[71] Gouvello argued that an *instituteur* who was acquainted with the mores and the habits of the countryside could approach the peasants as one who had "also held the reins of the plow." He went on, "No longer [would the *instituteur*] be a danger to agriculture; he would be, on the contrary, a powerful auxiliary to agricultural progress. Then . . . you would see all the inhabitants of the countryside send their children to school. Their parents would go there also to ask for advice, instruction, and counsel from an *instituteur* who had become for them a friend and a treasure."[72] Not only would there be one more agent of moral improvement in the commune, to reinforce the work of the clergy, but a "broader transmission of conservative instruction in religious beliefs" would be assisted by a teacher who could help the peasant to resist "bad advice" and "comprehend the utility and honor of his profession."[73]

70. Louis de Monjaret de Kerjégu, "Quelques Réflections à propos de l'enquête parlementaire agricole, 10 mars 1870" (MS in Bibliothèque Nationale).

71. See Déposition orale de M. le comte de Sesmaisons, in *Enquête agricole,* Série 2, Vol. VII, Part 3 (Loire-Inférieure), 576–77; Marc-Henri Soulet, "Les Organisations professionelles et le Représentation des intérêts de l'agriculture," in *The Making of Frenchmen,* ed. Baker and Harrigan, 578. Comte de Sesmaisons was the vice-president of the *comice agricole* of Loire-Inférieure.

72. Gouvello, *Vues sur la réorganisation de la France,* 53–56. M. A. Chaumontel, *maire* of Beuville, Calvados, thought that it was not indispensable for agricultural laborers "to know how to read and write" though such knowledge was essential for the "well-being of man." But education "could only serve in our fields if, once educated, the children remained in the village" (Déposition orale de M. A. Chaumontel, in *Enquête agricole,* Série 2, Part 1, p. 221).

73. Le Breton, *Département de la Mayenne, congrès agricole de Laval,* 19–20. See also Falloux, "Dix ans d'agriculture," *Le Correspondant,* LVII (1862), 656–58.

The Legitimists applied the same logic to the elites in secondary and higher institutions of learning. Although France had possessed since the Second Republic a system of regional agricultural schools and a National Agronomic Institute for the sons of well-to-do landowners, the system was woefully inadequate and attracted many fewer students than the *lycées* and the *grandes écoles*. To make matters worse, Napoleon III had reduced funding for the regional schools and, in 1852, had abolished the National Agronomic Institute altogether.[74] There remained a number of experimental farms and agronomic stations, but these were not strictly speaking educational facilities. Young aristocrats and bourgeois, meanwhile, went increasingly to the established secondary schools and universities in preparing themselves for professional careers and higher administrative posts. There, neither the classical nor the scientific instruction provided training for a specifically agricultural profession. Kerjégu, who after 1848 had directed an *école d'agriculture* at Trévarez, observed that "the instruction of the colleges produces lawyers, military officers, industrialists, and men of science, but it does not place in the hearts of the sons of cultivators a love for their paternal profession, which, so harsh, so unlucrative, so little honored, so humiliating, thereafter seems to them deadly in comparison with the bourgeois life." What the sons of the elite lacked, he argued, was an "appropriate education that, by revealing to them the grandeur of their profession, by teaching them how it can be for those who are drawn to it a source of respect, material profits, intellectual enjoyments, and moral satisfaction, would make them understand it, practice it with the most active emulation, and love it with passion."[75]

In 1872, as deputies, Charles de Bouillé and Roger de Dampierre sponsored legislation to reopen the National Agronomic Institute and place it at the summit of a system beginning with the elementary *fermes-écoles* and continuing up through the more theoretical regional schools. The institute would crown the arrangement by providing higher education to train true specialists in the science of cultivation. It would also decrease the number who sought careers in the overcrowded liberal and

74. Locke, *French Legitimists,* 168.
75. Monjaret de Kerjégu, *Les Souffrances de l'agriculture,* 11. Patrick J. Harrigan found that in 1864, 29 percent of the fathers who enrolled their sons in secondary schools were landowners or peasants but only 6.6 percent of the students following the classical curriculum and 12.4 percent of those in special education expected to enter agricultural professions. On this, see Robert D. Anderson, "New Light on French Secondary Education in the Nineteenth Century," *Social History,* VII (1982), 154–56.

administrative professions, by offering a truly esteemed and intellectually rewarding career in farming for young men who might otherwise end up consuming more public funds, writing more harmful literature, or worst of all, becoming radicals out of personal frustration.[76]

The Legitimists' objective was to end absenteeism and stop the departure of brains, money, and talent from the countryside. The special role agriculture once played in French society could only be restored, they believed, if the elite of society were "made to appreciate the social utility" and the special mission of farming. Kerjégu reminded the notables that rural property ownership carried with it certain social obligations transcending personal interests.[77] To abandon the fields was "to lack the sense of high patronage" especially required of *grands propriétaires,* whom Falloux placed "at the first rank among the servants, nay the saviors, of a troubled society."[78] The Legitimists hoped that the next generation of bright young notables, by staying in the countryside, or even returning to the land, could reverse the historical process by which one class after another had followed the aristocracy into the "devouring life of the city" and into the arms of the Revolution. The first rural exodus, they believed, had begun in the eighteenth century with the dissolution of "agricultural mores" among the aristocracy, who were smitten by sensualism long before it corrupted the morality of the masses.[79] By joining the trek to the cities, the bourgeoisie and the peasantry were merely following the "grievous example" that came down from the heights of the social order. "Today," wrote Kerjégu, "the sons of the rich or comfortable cultivators imitate the sons of the more powerful *propriétaires,"* and "the

76. *Annales,* August 2, 1872, XIII, annexe 1405, pp. 541–43. In the Ardèche, the general conselors complained that there were too few *écoles régionales* and that those existing were too far from the Midi. Besides demanding their own regional school, the conselors thought that southern schools should specialize in viticulture and the cultivation of mulberry trees. See Département de l'Ardèche, conseil général, August 21–27, 1865, in F (10) 1580, AN.

77. Monjaret de Kerjégu, *Rapport sur la prime d'honneur,* 65; Monjaret de Kerjégu, "Quelques Réflections," 25.

78. Extraits d'une brochure adressée par M. Edouard de La Bassétière à M. le president de la commission, Documents annexes, in *Enquête agricole,* Série 2, Vol. VII, Part 3 (Vendée), 151–52; Falloux, *Dix ans d'agriculture,* 6. Désert has noted that in Calvados absenteeism was widespread, especially among the rural bourgeoisie. See his *Une Société rurale,* 291.

79. La Broise, *Le Vrai et le Faux Libéralisme,* 168; Monjaret de Kerjégu, "Quelques Réflections"; Mailly-Nesle, *La Révolution est-elle finie?* 25.

son of the tenant farmer, he too . . . abandons agriculture." Even "the sons of the day laborer, the laborer himself, often leaving his family in the village, go off to the cities and the factories."[80] Only "the presence and the intelligent and active support" of landowners, ready to act "as wise generals, colonels, and captains" in a war to prevent the "conquest of our territory," might rally an "army of laborers . . . to protect our borders."[81]

Agricultural education, therefore, promised to arm a new generation of progressive and socially conscious *propriétaires* with a knowledge of advanced farming and a sense of Christian duty. Kerjégu believed that the new elite could equal the achievements of Mathieu de Dombasle, Jules Rieffel, and Jean Bodin and change the moral destiny of France: "When this generation of valiant, generous, and educated leaders, who attend to twenty-five million cultivators, who—imbued by religious sentiments—command the respect of the people by the example of a profound respect toward God . . . , come . . . , then, but only then, will the desertion of the countryside end. Agriculture will rise to all the heights of esteem that belong to it and will preserve all its children."[82]

Such prophetic visions bespoke the Legitimists' desire not only to reverse history and halt the rural exodus but also to supply a countermodel of development that reconciled economic modernization with the continuing cultural and political predominance of the countryside. Faced with an erosion of political and social power and with little alternative but to modernize in order to remain prosperous, rural Legitimist notables tried to propagate an ethic of proprietary obligations, along with a myth of the inexhaustible moral and material bounty of the soil.[83] Much more was at stake than profits, cheap labor, and social control: the restoration of the monarchy itself rested on agriculture's providing the con-

---

80. Proposition de loi rélative à la création d'une école supérieure d'agriculture, présentée par MM. le comte de Bouillé, le marquis de Dampierre, in *Annales,* June 24, 1872, XII, annexe 1240, p. 82; Monjaret de Kerjégu, "Quelques Réflections."

81. Monjaret de Kerjégu, "Quelques Réflections."

82. *Ibid.*

83. The Legitimists were not alone in this conviction. In 1905, Méline wrote a book, *Le Retour à la terre et la Surproduction industrielle,* in which he argued that the population would eventually have to return to the "life-giving soil." Industry, he believed, was capable of only limited expansion, because the consumption of manufactured goods tended to fall behind production and thus a decreasing number of people would be able to find employment in the cities. See Barral, *Les Agrariens français,* 33.

stituents of an alternative ruling class as well as a social environment that could sustain ideological support for traditionalism and the church. The Legitimists thought that the more France turned its back on the rural cottage and the village parish, the farther it embarked on an exodus from the promised land and severed itself from its roots in a Christian past. The revitalization of agriculture and a halt to rural depopulation would signify the triumph of morality over materialism and would symbolize, like the restoration of the legitimate monarchy, a France redeemed from the sins of the Revolution.

PART THREE

The Apogee and Decline
of Legitimism

CHAPTER X

 The Monarchy According
to the King

WHEN THE Second Empire fell in 1870 and elections were
called to form a new government in February, 1871, the parties of the
Right, with a striking parliamentary majority of four hundred deputies,
found themselves in control of the affairs of the nation.[1] Arriving in the
provisional capital at Bordeaux during the confusion that followed the
Franco-Prussian War, the delegation of nearly two hundred Legitimists
was no less astonished than the nation at large to see that the French had
turned to the notables of 1815 and 1830 to extract them from the continuing crisis. The apparent resurrection of the old Legitimist party was
undoubtedly the most unexpected result of what had been a highly un-
usual campaign.[2] But as later by-elections revealed, the Legitimists' return to power was to be short-lived, since their election in no way signified the population's desire for a restoration of the Bourbon monarchy.
The Legitimist deputies were swept into the National Assembly as part
of a diverse conservative peace coalition that had won a majority by tap-

1. Jacques Gouault, *Comment la France est devenue républicaine: Les Elections générales et
partielles à l'Assemblée Nationale, 1870–1875* (Paris, 1954), annexe II, pp. 237–38. The number of deputies in each parliamentary group varies slightly from one account to another.
Gouault seems to have made the best estimate. The National Assembly of 1871 included
between 64 and 81 Legitimists of the extreme Right, the *chevaux-légers,* about 130 Legitimists of the moderate Right, 214 Orleanists of the center Right, 78 Thierists of the center
Left, 122 moderate republicans, and 42 members of the social-democratic Left. The by-
elections of July, 1871, added eleven deputies to the center Right, five to the moderate
Right, and three to the extreme Right.
2. See especially Locke, *French Legitimists,* 15–31.

ping the French peasantry's overwhelming support for an end to hostili-
ties. After the election, the monarchist parties, long unable to agree on a
compromise candidate for the throne, split over the nature of any constitutional settlement; the refusal of the Comte de Chambord to sanction
an ideological compromise with the Orleanists that would have produced
what he saw as a detestable hybrid regime dissipated all hope for an immediate monarchical restoration. Meanwhile the republican party built
up enough support in the Assembly and the nation to secure a narrow
victory over the various forces of the Right. In 1880, Emile Zola, relish-
ing the long-awaited triumph of secular democracy, proclaimed that the
once-exuberant royalists belonged to a "lost generation."[3]

The reasons for the Legitimists' failure to restore the monarchy in the
1870s are complex, going well beyond the political shortsightedness of
Chambord. France's prolonged cultural secularization, the confidence of
the liberal bourgeoisie, and the revolutionary tradition had already called
royalist aspirations into question. By the time the Legitimists moved
back onto the political stage, the social and economic transformations of
the nineteenth century had eroded the potential popular base for monarchical traditionalism in both the cities and the countryside. Although the
Legitimists had picked up support among Catholics fearful of marginal-
ization under liberal or republican regimes, the Legitimist appeal to the
range of elements constituting the Right was tenuous and quickly evapo-
rated once Chambord and the extreme right wing of the Legitimist party
frittered away their parliamentary coalition with the other monarchist
groups.

Why did Chambord and his supporters follow the politically disastrous course of insisting on the white flag and what was the relationship
between their insistence on the fleur-de-lis banner and the vision of social
reconstruction that the Legitimists had promoted under the Second Empire and continued to offer during the 1870s? What was it about Chambord's intransigent opposition to the tricolor that led a substantial number of Legitimists, both inside and outside the National Assembly, to
collaborate in his obstinacy and follow him into political oblivion?[4] The

3. Quoted by Gaudin in "Le Royalisme dans les Bouches-du-Rhône," 262.
4. Chambord found his strongest support among the extreme Right within the National Assembly, a group known as the *chevaux-légers* after the location of their *réunion* at
Versailles. Locke estimates that the extreme Right included eighty-one out of a total of two
hundred Legitimist deputies elected between February and July of 1871. See his *French*

monarchical campaign points once again to the centrality of ideological considerations in the politics of nineteenth-century Legitimism. Although devoid of a political rationale, Chambord's rejection of the tricolor possessed a historical resonance and an intellectual coherence that sprang not merely from the desire for a change of regime but from the dream that France might become what it was not: an untroubled and harmonious Christian nation.

THE IDEOLOGICAL CONTENT
OF THE *DRAPEAU BLANC*

Chambord's refusal in 1871–1873 to accept the French throne from a National Assembly that was unwilling to abandon the tricolor was a symbolic act whose motivations remain shrouded in mystery— mystery that Chambord did much to generate by the ambiguity of his language.[5] Even Legitimists like Comte Alfred de Falloux and the Vi-

---

Legitimists, 30–31. Philippe Levillain offers a more cautious estimate by including among the *chevaux-légers* only those sixty-four Legitimists who signed the proposition presented by Charles de La Rochefoucauld-Bissaccia on June 16, 1874, in favor of an immediate restoration. See his "Un Chevau-léger de 1871 à 1875: Joseph de La Bouillerie," *Revue historique,* DXXI (1977), 121–22. There was only a slight difference in social composition between the *chevaux-légers* and the more moderate "liberal Legitimists." Moderates tended to be older, wealthier, and more aristocratic than the intransigent royalists. Both groups included a high percentage of *propriétaires,* but there were a greater number of military officers, lawyers, and journalists among the extreme Right. The moderate Legitimists had a majority among the party's parliamentary delegation in the National Assembly, but many Legitimists, including Chambord, believed that the *chevaux-légers* better represented the views of royalists closely linked to the Catholic masses. Chambord and his entourage generally viewed the moderates as too independent and too closely connected with Orleanism through their links to Berryer and their strong support for monarchical fusion. Chapter XI discusses the issues that divided the moderates from the extreme Right.

5. The available documentation concerning Chambord's views on government and society is limited to scattered archival sources and a small number of manifestos and letters printed in the press or sent as instructions to his supporters in France. The Marquis de Foresta, Chambord's political agent in the Midi, indicated in a letter to Joseph de La Bouillerie that most of the "intimate papers" of "our poor king" were destroyed at Frohsdorf on the orders of the Comtesse de Chambord after the death of her husband in 1883. Documents pertaining to the activities of the *comités royalistes* and the Bureau du Roi were also burned, since, according to Foresta, it would have been "imprudent" to preserve them; nonetheless, certain materials contained in nine trunks sent to Foresta from Frohsdorf were preserved in the Archives du Marquis de Foresta, at the Château des Issarts, in Bouches-du-Rhône. Levillain, in his research on the life of Albert de Mun, has been able to recover a number of letters written by Chambord and conserved in the private papers of other

comte de Meaux, who had been among the most visible supporters of a monarchical restoration in the nineteenth century, were caught off guard by Chambord's obstinacy. In their frustration, they attributed the failure of the Right to the pretender's lack of will. Liberal Legitimists, who made up the moderate wing of the Legitimist party, credited Chambord's clerical education, his long years in exile, and the influence of his wife for his myopia and intransigence, and some even accused him of moral cowardice.[6] It is impossible to deny that the pretender was for most of his life surrounded by sycophants and that they worked in his entourage for decades. In that kind of environment he had no reason to think that liberal dissidents, like Falloux, represented more than a small number of his adherents, and this naturally reinforced his own inclination to eschew compromise. Yet his actions were not simply a reflection of his surroundings or the influence of close advisers. They had a base as well in a mature ideological critique of postrevolutionary France that reached back to the ideas of the Vicomte de Bonald and Joseph de Maistre and that was supplemented by a strident ultramontanism reflecting the "clericalization" of Legitimist thought in the wake of Italian unification and the secularizing impetus of liberalism during the Second Empire.[7] In addition, the critique of industrialization elaborated by the social Catholics strengthened the social component of Chambord's concept of the role of the monarchy. In the crucial years between 1871 and 1873, Chambord presented a careful, albeit questionable and self-serving, reckoning of seven decades of French history. His assessment of events seemed more compelling to many provincial Legitimists than the overwhelming evidence of his unpopularity. Precisely because Chambord articulated, in his own manner, a theory of French politics that implied an explanation of how modern France functioned, Legitimists of the extreme Right were confirmed in their convictions and remained unwilling to relinquish the path they had chosen under the pretender's auspices. The confidence with which they stated their convictions had its effect, since the Legitimists, by virtue of

---

royalist and Catholic leaders. For the present study, I have made a close reading of Chambord's most important published political pronouncements and have used the extensive writings of his closest supporters to explicate his texts more fully. For Foresta's letter, see Levillain, "Un Chevau-léger," 120. The bibliography of Levillain's *Albert de Mun* includes a list of private archival sources containing letters from Chambord.

6. See especially Meaux, *Souvenirs politiques,* 182–83.

7. See Denis, *Les Royalistes de la Mayenne,* and Rials, *Le Légitimisme,* 38–43.

their concrete presence in the National Assembly and the entrenchment of their social influence in the Nord, Brittany, and parts of the Midi, had become part of a national debate on the future constitutional order at a time when the survival of the Republic was in doubt.

According to Chambord, the Revolution had broken the unity between the monarchy and the nation, and had thereby destroyed the foundations of the grandeur and prosperity France had known in earlier centuries. As pretender and heir to legitimate traditions, Chambord considered himself to be the depository of the sacred contract between the king and the nation that Legitimists traced back to the origins of the Capetian state. Since he considered providence to have confided to him the national patrimony of the *droit monarchique,* he believed he had a sacred mission to conserve the hereditary monarchy as a "trust" until the nation, disabused of its revolutionary errors, returned to a full understanding of the necessity of those principles for which he stood. Chambord was also convinced that he was obliged by God and by the law of succession to pass on this patrimony intact to his successor. Since the entire fusionist proposal was predicated on the certainty that Chambord would remain childless and that his heir would be the Orleanist Comte de Paris, he believed it essential that the cadet branch and its supporters renounce the false legitimacy of the "usurpation" of 1830 as well as the traditions of individualism, parliamentary liberalism, and bourgeois skepticism that the Revolution had produced and that the tricolor symbolized.

History therefore had not, in Chambord's view, defined for him an active role in the pursuit of a restoration. As he told Charles Chesnelong, the envoy sent by the monarchists to negotiate the terms of an agreement between king and parliament, "I have never had, nor will I ever have, a vulgar ambition for power for power's sake."[8] For Chambord, the restoration was a matter of making the nation whole again by the reunification of past and present and by the reconciliation of the people, for the sake of their own moral well-being, with a political tradition they ought never have abandoned. His role in this historic reunion was fulfilled, he believed, merely by his preserving the integrity of that part of the nation's sacred inheritance entrusted to him by God. Thus, though Chambord accepted the idea of fusion in principle, his conception of legitimacy as

8. Comte de Chambord, in Charles Chesnelong's *Un Témoignage à l'histoire: La Campagne monarchique d'octobre 1873* (Paris, 1895), 125.

an unshakable religious obligation to respect traditional authority made it impossible for him to sanction a compromise, imposed by transitory political realities, that purported to fuse an immutable and divine principle with the ideological legacy of a revolution that declared itself legitimate by violating the *droit monarchique*.

His prescription for obstinacy and passivity placed the entire burden of initiative on the nation and its legal representatives. According to his reasoning, it was up to France to renounce the errors of the past and proclaim its return to the normal path of historical development by recognizing the right and the social implications inherent in the monarchical principle. Chambord also believed that the restoration could occur only by acclamation, because anything else would be inconsistent with the integrity of monarchical authority and with the obligation of the nation to obey the dictates of history. A restoration imposed by a coup d'etat would be meaningless, in his opinion, since a nation that had to be coerced to recognize its legitimate government would not have moved freely and sincerely to an acceptance of the principle of legitimate authority; a restoration by plebiscite or election would contradict the right of Chambord to rule and would in any case be the most precarious of restorations, since popular sovereignty created a counterlegitimacy and implied that the nation had the right to make and unmake governments at will. For the pretender, only a sincere and voluntary conversion of France to the principle of legitimacy would ensure a long and fruitful reign. Chambord hoped to induce the needful conversion by insisting that the Orleanists and the people accept the fleur-de-lis.[9]

To men reared in the age of science, liberals and republicans who be-

9. The theoretical rejection of a coup d'etat was implicit in the Legitimist critique of postrevolutionary political instability. The restoration was regarded as a voluntary embrace of legitimate authority that would signify a return to social peace and stability. The use of force, whether by an individual or by a revolutionary crowd, was seen as possible or necessary only in a society that had been destabilized by revolutionary doctrines. It appears that Chambord did contemplate in 1879 a proposal that envisioned a seizure of power by General Ducrot in the expectation of "grave events." According to that plan, the general was expected to restore order and reorganize the administration in preparation for the return of Chambord. The scenario, reminiscent of the actions of General Monck at the close of the English Interregnum, had long preserved a measure of respectability in Legitimist circles and was understood, in contrast to the Bonapartist model, as favoring the return to social order rather than the ambitions of one man. See Chesnelong, *Un Temoignage à l'histoire*, 4–5; and Vicomte de Chalvet-Nastrac, *Les Projets de restauration monarchique et le général Ducrot* (Paris, 1909).

lieved in the efficacy of compromise and accommodation between rational and honest citizens, Chambord's obsession with his *principe* and his
characterization of the Revolution as the root of all evil were inexplicable
and merely demonstrated his anachronistic and absolutist conception of
kingship.[10] The Duc de Broglie, who was no radical, once commented
that legitimacy was "only an irrelevant triviality" whose contribution to
political debate was no more useful than the "magic formulas" of a
"charlatan."[11] But for Chambord the stability of power and the cohesion
of the social order were dependent on political institutions that expressed
the collective adherence of a people to immutable principles. He was incapable of understanding how the Orleanists, to say nothing of the republicans, hoped to restore stability by embracing the very principles
that had led to eighty years of ceaseless agitation. Revolutionary doctrines were, in his mind, nothing more than a rationale for the spirit of
insubordination that infected an entire culture avid to separate itself from
the sometimes harsh but eternally necessary values of deference, sacrifice,
and harmony. He believed that the trauma of the postrevolutionary period by itself amply demonstrated the futility of attempting to build a
durable order on the basis of a principle of rebellion that sanctioned all
forms of moral defiance and political revolt. The disintegration of French
society, he argued, was the logical result of a chain reaction of defiance
that arose out of the repudiation of royal authority in 1789. A lasting
restoration built upon principles that had unleashed a permanent rebellion was an impossible illusion.

Chambord believed that France, dispossessed of its traditions and the
values that had protected society from moral and social chaos, had lost
its compass in the turbulent winds of modernity and had descended into
a decadence that resembled the darkest days of pagan barbarism, in contrast to the brilliance and order it had attained under the rule of Christian
kings. Having ceased to conduct its affairs according to the moral laws
of the Catholic church, it had become caught up in an infernal cycle of
riots and coups reminiscent of the late Roman Empire. Violence and the
caprice of unrestrained majorities or self-serving factions reigned with-

10. To the centrist parties, Chambord's attitude betrayed a mentality inimical to parliamentary government. As Emile de Marcère, a deputy from the Nord, wrote, "His integrity
and royal dignity made the path of compromise, which is of the essence for a constitutional
political regime, repugnant to him" (Marcère, *L'Assemblée Nationale,* II, 61).
11. Quoted by Rudelle in *La République absolue,* 31.

out regard for the principles of right and justice. In the absence of a knowledge of divine order and the freedom bestowed by God, charity had vanished, and words like *fraternity* and *liberty* had become excuses for despotism and moral license. Under such conditions, France was destined to alternate between the anarchy provoked by moral disorder and by social dissolution and the servitude that was the inevitable punishment for a nation incapable of restraining its passions. As he told Joseph de Carayon-Latour in 1871,

> We must learn to recognize that the abandonment of principles is the true cause of our disasters. A Christian nation cannot tear out pages from its long history with impunity, break the chain of its traditions, inscribe the negation of the rights of God in the preamble of its constitution, banish all religious ideas from its laws and its public education. . . . Under those conditions, it can never put a halt to disorder; it will oscillate indefinitely between Caesarism and anarchy, the two equally shameful forms of pagan decadence, and it will never escape the lot of peoples unfaithful to their mission.[12]

The contrast between the supposed harmonious development of France under the monarchy and the vicious circle of revolution and reaction which characterized the nineteenth century was the key to Chambord's political obstinacy as well as to that of the extreme Right in the Assembly—a group of some eighty deputies who were referred to as the *chevaux-légers*—whose views he expressed and for whom no lasting coalition of goodwill with the Orleanists was possible. Chambord and the *chevaux-légers* were convinced that bourgeois liberalism had twice, in 1789 and 1830, violated the principle of monarchical authority, legitimated the spirit of rebellion in political and moral conduct, and opened the way to a republican experiment that by its nature undermined conservative safeguards and quickly moved in a progressively more radical direction.[13] The Terror, the June Days, and the Commune had each

12. Comte de Chambord to Joseph de Carayon-Latour, May 8, 1871, in Duc de Castries' *Le Grand Refus du comte de Chambord—la légitimité et les tentatives de restauration de 1830 à 1886* (Paris, 1970), 137–38, Vol. V of Castries, *Le Testament de la monarchie,* 5 vols.
13. For the Legitimists, history had proved the radicalization of the Republic axiomatic. According to La Rochette, the leader of the extreme Right in the National Assembly, this owed to the fact that with France "in revolution, victory always goes to the most violent"

proved that the inevitable result of republicanism in France—call it conservative or radical—was socialism and war against the church.[14] The
Republic was, for them, the ultimate danger, because Jacobin statism
threatened to destroy the autonomy of organic social bodies by absorbing social life completely into the state, while official atheism undermined the ability of the Catholic church to endow civilization, through
its teachings, with the capacity to protect itself from the irretrievable
disaster of permanent revolution.[15] The extreme Right recalled that on
two further occasions bourgeois liberalism had misunderstood the logical
consequences of the revolutionary spirit and had believed it possible to
ward off material threats to property by sacrificing the nation's liberties
to a Bonapartist dictatorship. Pointing out that liberals were wedded to
the Revolution by conviction and blinded by a materialist outlook that
prevented them from seeing the moral causes of perpetual disorder, the
extreme Right accused the Orleanists of preferring to place the crown of
the Revolution on the head of a "Jacobin Caesar" over renouncing their
commitment to the principles of 1789. Recent history, however, had
shown that in order to survive, the Empire needed to perpetuate instability and keep the bourgeoisie in a constant state of fear and obedience. Consequently, although the Empire suppressed the socialist threat,

---

(*Annales,* February 25, 1875, XXXVI, 652). As early as February, 1871, La Broise confidently wrote, "Since no one can foresee what the future holds for us, we are reduced to
conjectures about what the Third Republic will be if it definitely takes root among us. But
since our modern republicans are far from dazzling by their invention and do not go beyond
copying their political ancestors as best they can and are even content to allow imitation to
degenerate into parody, we can expect that the new republic will be a repetition of the
Convention of 1792 or the Republic of 1848" (*République ou Monarchie,* 30–31).

14. Chambord saw no fundamental distinction between the radicals and the moderate
republicans. As he told some visitors in 1872, "Only in vain does one try to establish a
reassuring distinction between this party of violence which promises peace to men by declaring war on God and this more prudent and better disciplined party which arrives at its
goals by indirect means—but the same goals. They differ by their language, but they pursue the same chimera. They do not recruit the same soldiers, but they march under the
same flag: they can only bring upon us the same misfortune" (Quoted by Dubosc de Pesquidoux in *Le Comte de Chambord,* 299).

15. As Charles Dreux-Brézé concluded, "If . . . the Revolution is, in essence, destructive of all constitutive principles of the social order, it must struggle against them wherever
they are found. And, as these principles are encompassed by the Catholic church, it is the
church, their inspiration and guardian, that it must attack first, and the annihilation of the
church will be its final aim" (*La Révolution: L'Unité de son but, sa logique et ses contradictions*
[Paris, 1863], 27).

its reliance on force and state despotism served only to undermine the forces of order and created the conditions for a return to the very sort of republican anarchy that had been responsible for the dictatorship. Chambord once explained to a group visiting him in Venice that Napoleon III based "his rule on fear in order to make himself necessary." Chambord added, "From time to time he stirs up the Red specter, and the bourgeoisie, overcome with trepidation, throws itself into his arms; by the same token, he flatters the people in order better to dominate them. He follows to the letter the Caesarian policy of weakening the people in order to subjugate them—a retrograde and pagan policy that is now augmented with revolutionary maneuvers that in the end must surely corrupt, disunite, and waste the nation."[16] An obscure Legitimist pamphleteer advanced a similar theory when in 1871 he cautioned that "the empire . . . always proceeds from the republic once it declines, because states enslaved by their passions and ready for servitude never lack a despot. . . . If France opposes the empire, it must oppose the republic, because the two, like satellites, follow each other in orbit, and when one vanishes, the other appears."[17]

Despite the antipathy shown toward the Empire and the Republic by this viewpoint, it was the Orleanists whom the extreme Right saw as playing the principal role in perpetuating the revolutionary cycle. Only nominally Catholic and imbued by their prejudices with an illusory fear of a return to the ancien régime, the liberals always opted for the Revolution and repeatedly injected it with new life. To Chambord and the extreme Right, the Orleanists were the "eternal Girondins" who "held the door open to evil" and then absolved themselves of responsibility for what naturally followed.[18] By misreading human nature in considering

16. Quoted by Dubosc de Pesquidoux in *Le Comte de Chambord,* 59. For Véran, the Empire was, in effect, a perpetual reenactment of the coup of 1851. As he explained, "The Empire needs the fear, the passion, and the blindness produced by revolutionary chaos: . . . it imposed itself on the eighteenth of Brumaire and on December 2 under the pretext of repressing it." This, however, he saw as inevitable, since "it comes from the Revolution, but it cannot kill its mother" (*L'Empire plébiscitaire et la Monarchie légitime: Réponse au l'Ordre et au Galois* [Dunkerque, 1874], 23). Writing as early as 1851, without the hindsight Véran possessed, Monsignor Pie expressed a similar theory. The Empire killed the Reds, he said, but it left the "skeptical bourgeoisie," which was the "effective cause of the Reds," in control (Baunard, *Histoire du cardinal Pie,* I, 368). The Legitimists believed that the Empire, because of its very nature, would inevitably give rise to the radical republic.

17. D'Yvon, *Monarchie-République,* 3, 33.

18. Blanc de St. Bonnet, *La Légitimité,* 94. The Legitimist theory of French politics was, in effect, that in every revolutionary situation, the Left would overtake the Center

man's propensity toward good stronger than man's penchant for evil, liberals sought to liberate humanity from the servitude of the past but only emancipated its predominant inclination to disregard the larger duty it had to history and society in favor of immediate gratification. So concerned were the liberals with liberty that they put as much value upon the right to believe in nothing as upon the right of the church to prescribe general rules of social conduct. Thus it seemed to Chambord's followers that liberalism's pretended neutrality turned into a deliberate negation of the liberty of Christians, who were forced in the name of freedom to accept the rights of incredulity and error.[19] By flattering human passions with the exaltation of material progress and by removing the obstacles the church and authority had established to check the evil inherent in man's limitations, liberalism permitted an inextricable confusion between good and evil, from which evil alone profited. The Revolution, the Legitimists argued, inevitably benefited from the permissiveness preached by the revolutionary parties, since it was natural for people to prefer sensation to abnegation. They considered the liberals woefully mistaken in believing that the emancipation they promised would create a world ruled by reason. Blinded by their presuppositions, liberals were, they judged, incapable of understanding that their deceptive doctrines had become, as Gustave de Bernardi explained, "the principal solvent of French society, and the war machine by which the Revolution has produced this predominance of evil among us, by which the people end up, miserably, in an incurable disorder." Elsewhere he wrote, "To believe that the Revolution will stop in the liberal oasis of the parliamentary regime is a childish dream. We soon perceive, in the riots that in each instance trouble the bourgeois regime, that the revolutionary spirit has not spoken its final word. The middle classes, by attaching themselves to anti-Christian skepticism and by decreeing that natural and social laws can depend on unaided reason and the human will, place new and irresistible aspirations in the spirit and the heart of the French."[20]

    Thus, for Chambord and the extreme Right, liberals were at once the

unless the Center sincerely embraced the Right. The Legitimists considered France to have been in a revolutionary situation since 1789, and therefore discounted any possibility of a lasting centrist coalition. What divided the Legitimists was whether the Center's embrace of the Right should be a submission or a transaction.

    19. See La Broise, *Le Vrai et le Faux Libéralisme,* 130–31, 51–52; Bernardi, *La Révolution,* 144.

    20. Bernardi, *La Révolution,* 137–39.

most dangerous and most gullible of revolutionaries: their doctrines represented the revolution in its most moderate form and made evil palatable to otherwise honest men, whose diminished fortitude destroyed the barrier to radicalism and socialism.

Such views did not bode well for the future of fusionist campaign. From the time the idea of monarchical fusion was first broached in 1848, Chambord feared that the Orleanists would force him to commit himself and his party to a compromise of principles that would reinstate a regime like that of 1789 or 1830, which would lead inexorably to a recurrence of the revolutionary cycle. Orleanism, as both a personal affront to the monarch and the pivot of the revolutionary process, had turned France into what one Legitimist called a "new Sisyphus . . . condemned to roll the millstone of despair and shame without reprieve."[21] Between the legitimate monarchy and the revolutionary spirit there was no centrist solution, no neutral ground. The *juste milieu* only created what Joseph de La Bouillerie called a "France halfway between the monarchy and revolutionary principles."[22] The bourgeois regime, dedicated "to serving the ideas of the moderate Revolution, dear to the *classes dirigeantes,*" had only proved that "it is above all to the revolutionary temperament of the active part of the nation that one ought to attribute [the] vicissitudes" in the political order.[23] Bernardi said, "French society will be menaced as long as most of the Frenchmen belonging to the *classes dirigeantes* are not convinced of this truth: that the dangers it faces are due less to radical doctrines than to the attachment of conservatives to ideas and institutions that lead logically to radicalism."[24]

Sharing that view, Chambord welcomed the cooperation of the liberal bourgeoisie, but he would not sanction a fusion of political doctrines and preferred to speak of a "reconciliation" that would create a broad conservative alliance, reunite the French royal family, and end all ideological divisions in favor of the principles of legitimacy. As one publicist wrote, fusion itself was a materialist notion, a "concept from chemistry, signifying mixture; to fuse is to compose one thing of diverse elements."[25] Thus, the term suggested something provisional, or to exploit the meta-

21. Marquis d'Auray de St. Pois, *La Royauté est nécessaire: Etude religieuse, politique et historique* (Nantes, 1880), 45.
22. Quoted by Levillain in "Un Chevau-léger," 118–19.
23. Bernardi, *La Révolution,* 93.
24. *Ibid.,* 76.
25. *Henri V et la Démocratie* (Paris, 1873), 58.

phor, something combustible that lacked the permanence and spiritual sincerity that the ideas of reconciliation and perfect harmony suggested. "To fuse principles as one fuses interests," wrote Antoine Blanc de St. Bonnet, "is an idea put forward by businessmen but not by statesmen."[26] The Legitimist principle could not compromise its purity, since that would pervert its truth, destroy it, and render it no more effective than the other defective formulas by which the ruling classes had hoped to bring order to France.

It was convictions like these that informed Chambord's pronouncements during the monarchical campaign of 1871–1873 and placed the white flag at the center of the fusionist controversy. Although it was long apparent that the question of the flag threatened to destroy monarchical unity and extinguish the chances of a restoration, Chambord made the fleur-de-lis the sine qua non of his return to the throne. For him it was not merely a matter of personal honor or preference but a question of whether his accession could fulfill the promise of a lasting and fruitful reign. The white flag was the symbol of the principle of legitimacy, the sign by which Chambord could know whether his authority and his convictions were truly and voluntarily accepted by the nation's representatives. Moreover, it signified a cluster of ideas that concerned not only the constitutional order but the role of the church in society, the possibility of future progress and prosperity, and the relationship between social comportment, culture, and citizenship necessary for durable social and political harmony. What it did not signify—and this had been lost in the ambiguity of language and the confrontation of preconceived ideas—was a return to the Old Regime.

In the immediate political context of party divisions within the National Assembly, Chambord's insistence on the white flag was intended to ensure that he, and not the Assembly, would determine the nature of the restoration. Since the majority was divided and since the monarchist deputies insisted on the right to collaborate in the work of national regeneration, Chambord, who at this time discounted the possibility of a coup d'etat, knew that he needed a guarantee of the Assembly's recognition of his principles if the restoration was to give institutional expression

26. Blanc de St. Bonnet, *La Légitimité*, 620; Dubosc de Pesquidoux, *Le Comte de Chambord*, 452–53. See also Guillaume Véran, *Les Solutions: Place au droit national de la France* (Toulouse, 1871), 39; and Armailhac, *Le Légitimité et le Progrès*, 96–97. The slogan of many on the extreme Right, made popular by H. de Lourdoueix, of the *Gazette de France*, in 1848 was Fusion, but Not Confusion.

to Legitimist ideas. An Assembly that from the outset demanded the right to impose certain conditions on the king would be constrained nei- ther to organize the new regime according to his views nor to recognize his moral authority to define the spirit by which the executive and the legislature arrived at mutual agreements. Amédée de Margerie realized that, by rejecting the white flag or by insisting that the government could defer its validation until after the restoration, the rightist deputies would "in good conscience render suspect the sincerity of [their] adhesion to principle, and [would] deposit seeds of destruction in an edifice" that presumably was to last for centuries.[27] For the pretender, the issue of the flag did not, as the Orleanists believed, concern the precise extent of the king's executive power or even relate to ministerial responsibility but, rather, signified Chambord's desire to obtain the free and voluntary ad- hesion of the nation's representatives to Legitimist principles. The Or- leanists and the Legitimists had long had Chambord's assurance that he would act as a constitutional monarch willing to conduct the affairs of state in conjunction with an elected assembly and who would respect civil equality and civil liberties. Chambord had given his consent without hesitation to these conditions, which formed the legislative and juridicial inheritance of 1789. But he would not under any condition agree to the retention of the tricolor and thereby condone the spirit of rebellion that had overturned so many regimes. From a purely practical point of view, Chambord, along with the deputies, knew that no solid majority existed in the Assembly for a restoration with the white flag but that there was one for restoring the monarchy with the tricolor, if Chambord were willing to defer the issue until after he took power. But if, as the majority held, the flag could "be modified only by the accord of the king and the national representation," Chambord would have had to expect either re- sistance to the white flag and the principle of legitimacy—which would quickly have undermined his authority—or the retention of the tricolor. Chambord knew that if the tricolor were retained, he would have either to legitimate the Revolution or to abdicate shortly after his accession.[28]

27. Amédée de Margerie, L'Urgence (Paris, 1874), reprinted in Ernest La Roche's Les Nationaux et les Partis: Etude des institutions de la France, de son droit national et de la solution constitutionnelle après la guerre de 1870 (Paris, 1876), 429.

28. Chesnelong's Un Temoignage à l'histoire is the fullest account of the fusionist nego- tiations of 1871–1873. During Chesnelong's "visits" to Frohsdorf in 1873, Chambord sug- gested that he could dissolve the Assembly and appeal to the nation if the deputies did not accept the white flag. Chesnelong responded that such an action would be impossible be-

Besides responding to these contingent questions, Chambord's apparently inexplicable combination of constitutional liberalism and ideological obstinacy flowed from a conception of the monarchy that was completely at odds with the distinction of the time between constitutionalism and absolutism. For Chambord and the Legitimists, representative government was not dangerous per se but threatened the stability of power only when the society it represented "became a crowd, by happenstance composed of individuals foreign to one another, incapable of governing themselves or of choosing guides, and suspectible only to the orders of a master or aroused by a voice from the rostrum."[29] In a normal state cured of the revolutionary diseases of individualism and insubordination, the monarchy would complement the natural ordering of social relations. The true function of the state, the Legitimists assumed, was to express the genuine corporative and hierarchical nature of the social order as it had been constituted by tradition. They considered that a legitimate government had its basis in established networks of authority and thus had a vested interest in respecting the nation's values, its interests, and its history. Albert Du Boys, a leading Legitimist in Dauphiné, theorized that the French monarchy had, in its origins, represented an "association of heads of families and of proprietors who sought to guarantee the security of their wives and their children, and the tranquil possession of their herds, their huts, and the fields they had already cleared." This association elected a king who consolidated the "tutelary authority with which they defended their rights." The Capet dynasty became hereditary, remained legitimate, and imposed its rights on future generations precisely because it acted as a "living and tangible image" of the "tutelary principle in which . . . all rights were accustomed to finding their guarantee and their personification."[30] The Legitimists argued that the new monarchy, like the old, "must come from the very entrails of a people and not from the more or less healthy brain of some politician; it must preserve and develop traditional foundations and not make a blank slate of all previous elements of life." Since the king was supposed to act as the "patron of all

---

cause the Assembly of 1871 was a constituent assembly and the king would not have the prerogative of dissolution until a new constitution was written. As long as Chambord felt forced to compromise with an Assembly that had made clear its preference for the tricolor, he would believe that the deputies were setting a trap. On this, see especially *Un Temoignage à l'histoire*, 184–89.

29. Larcy, "La Décentralisation de 1789 à 1870," *Le Correspondant*, LXXXII (1870), 24.
30. DuBoys, *Des principes de la Révolution française*, 21, 34.

social guarantees," he had to be able to "impose his spiritual power on friend and foe alike." His authority, which derived not from coercion but from the synthesis of the nation's legitimate social interests, was to obtain an "enlightened obedience" by persuasion. Jean Dubosc de Pesquidoux, one of the pretender's earliest biographers, wrote that Chambord was "the synthesis of France, the compression of its history, the conservation of the past, the guide of the present, and the guardian of the future."[31] By that conception the Legitimists attempted to fuse together popular and royal sovereignty.

It was in this regard that a preexisting recognition by the Assembly of the principle of legitimacy would signal, according to Chambord, the moral synthesis of the nation and king and would remove the dangers of intractable conflict and shifting coalitions that had previously undermined constitutional regimes and called into question the authority of the executive. It was not, he believed, the precise mechanism of power that mattered but the spirit that animated those who exercised it. Chambord assumed that the nation's acceptance of the white flag would expunge the divisions of the past and reinstate a spirit of cooperation, reciprocal duty, and harmony between the king and his people. He told Chesnelong, "I would rebuild the moral unity of France by effacing the memory of disorders and by uniting in the service of the country all noble-hearted men whom unfortunate circumstances have often separated."[32] Here Chambord was expressing a conviction of many of his followers: that in a truly harmonious nation political factions were an anomaly, and that the antagonisms factions expressed could arise only in a society disorganized by state despotism, moral confusion, and selfish greed. With the white flag, the king would be assured of standing "at the head of a permanent conservative party, which is not a party" but "France itself."[33] One Legitimist writer compared the prospective resto-

31. Dubosc de Pesquidoux, *Le Comte de Chambord*, 86, 134; Ferdinand Béchard, *La Commune, l'Eglise et l'Etat dans leurs rapports avec les classes laborieuses* (2 vols.; Paris, 1851), I, vii. Blanc de St. Bonnet wrote, "What derive from the depths of nations are neither . . . regulations nor principles of power but the customs that determine their form. What derive from the depths of the nation are the legitimacies the king is going to maintain—interests and acquired rights that represent the degree to which the nation has sheltered justice and truth" (*La Légitimité*, 666–67).

32. Quoted by Arthur Loth, *L'Echec de la restauration monarchique en 1873* (Paris, 1910), 369.

33. Le Serrac de Kervily, *Lettre sur la situation politique* (Paris, 1874), 8.

ration to the reunion of a "regiment . . . dispersed, in disarray," that all
at once "catches a glimpse of the flag" and "rallies to it and masses itself
around [the king] against the enemy." He declared, "A symbol, a visible
symbol, and better yet, in flesh and bone," was the "cement of a permanent cohesion."[34] Chambord's faith in the power of his *principe* thus made
it possible for him to disavow any claim to unrestricted power, to agree
dependably to submit the acts of government to the real control of freely
chosen representatives, and at the same time to reject "these sterile parliamentary struggles whence the sovereign comes out, too often, either
impotent or weakened."[35]

Instead of wanting a parliamentary democracy, a *monarchie censitaire,*
or an absolutist regime, Chambord called for a *monarchie représentative*
grounded in a system of universal suffrage designed to represent society
as a *réunion des corps* and project the "nature of things" prevailing in "organized societies."[36] One man, one vote—and the capricious despotism
of an undifferentiated mass of voters—were, according to his plan, to be
replaced by suffrage based on the corporate representation of decentralized local and professional associations; that arrangement would "cause
each to act within the sphere of his knowledge and his relationships."
The resulting legislature would, Chambord hoped, express the solidarity
of vertically integrated communities. Voting would cease to be an engine
of social revolution and would regain its primordial status as simply a
mode of designating representatives with limited mandates whose acts
were constrained by dedication to the concrete and practical interests of
separate yet interdependent constituencies. In the culturally homogeneous and patronage-based communities that resulted, political representatives would cease to be politicians and would become "visible and
responsible beings" whose election rested on the voters' knowledge of
their strengths and qualities.[37] Having arrived at a strange and incongru-
ous adaptation of Rousseau, Chambord imagined that, with a consensus

34. *Ibid.,* 2.
35. Chambord to Carayon-Latour, May 8, 1871, in Castries' *Le Grand Refus,* 137–38.
36. Béchard, *De l'administration,* I, 88. See also Véran, *La Question du XIXe siècle,*
214–15.
37. Henri de Lourdoueix, quoted by Véran in *La Question du XIXe siècle,* 109–11; La
Broise, *République ou Monarchie,* 111. For a presentation of corporatist suffrage as envisioned by Chambord's closest adviser on this matter, see the speeches and proposals of
the Marquis de Franclieu, in *Annales,* July 7, 1873, XIX, annexe 1863, pp. 59–61, November 8, 1875, XLII, 47–51.

arising out of the natural order of society, politics itself would cease to exist and government would become a purely technical matter in which the king could act as moderator and an arbiter between corporate interests. There would be nothing to distort the process by which the wishes of the people reached the king. As a result of a consensus between the chief of state and the nation's representatives, the separation of powers and the issue of ministerial responsibility would lose their importance, and the danger of a parliamentary monopoly would vanish. As Chambord said, the deputies would examine "questions submitted to their jurisdiction" without encroaching upon essential prerogatives of the executive, since the transparency of language and purpose between the nation and the monarchy would reduce institutional regulations to simple technical formulas by which society governed itself.[38]

AN ANTIPOSITIVIST RESTORATION

Still, to believe in the perfect compatibility between state and society assumed that society would be animated by universally accepted rules of conduct. Indeed, the society to which Chambord addressed himself was assumed to be Christian in the largest sense of the word, and he expected that the imperatives of a sincere and serious faith would enforce a collective interior disposition with respect to what Margerie called "certains engagements pour toute la conduite de la vie."[39] For Chambord, the distinction between Christian and revolutionary France lay precisely in the extent to which state and society recognized the function of the church in disseminating the valid rules of conduct upon which a harmonious order must rest. The Legitimists argued that the Revolution, by its obliviousness to the unity of faith, social action, and political conduct, had destroyed the link binding private and public comportment and had encouraged moral relativism. According to their line of thought, politics was grounded in the "moral order" and the stability of the state ultimately depended on the moral constitution of man and his conformity to divine laws. They hence concluded that society should be governed in a Christian sense and that "false" political systems would never have acquired an institutional reality had secular and acquisitive values

38. Franclieu, in *Annales*, November 8, 1875, XLII, 49.
39. Margerie, *La Restauration*, 188.

not corrupted the people.[40] For the Legitimists, moral order implied a collective affirmation of the power of the church over the moral direction of the nation. Chesnelong's view of the church was that "it is the *grande école* of authority and respect. It places moral order in the soul and in turn endows the material order with the only guarantee that can assure it dignity, efficacy, and durability."[41]

Consequently, the relationship between church and state envisioned by Chambord and the Legitimists went far beyond the idea of simple political complicity inherent in the formula of an alliance between throne and altar, because the distinction between the two was one of function rather than purpose. In the final analysis, the state could fulfill its role only if the church succeeded in its mission: the moral order created by the church was nothing less than the totality of perceptions and actions by which society conducted its affairs. To put it another way, moral order was equivalent to Christian culture; that culture, purveyed by the church through its pedagogical, social, and evangelical functions, formed the foundation of a reconstructed monarchical order.

The connection the Legitimists saw between religion and society—a connection that they believed preceded the formation of the state—was manifest in every dimension of their thought. The entire Legitimist effort can be seen as a comprehensive attempt to preserve or re-create a durable Christian cultural life. That objective lay behind not only the Legitimists' persistent and unanimous demand for the *liberté de l'enseignement* but also their attempt to bring the most intimate aspects of family life and popular culture into conformity with Catholic traditions and practices. The most comprehensive effort in this direction was by the Comités Catholiques de France, which met in Paris at the height of the monarchical campaign. The Assemblée Générale des Comités Catholiques de France, held in 1872 and 1873, brought together the leadership of the principal Catholic associations, including a large number of Legitimist deputies, in order to coordinate the work and strengthen the influence of the numerous independent Catholic social and cultural organizations that had emerged in the previous decades.[42] The Comités Catholiques not only sought to pro-

---

40. See Gavardie, *Etudes sur les vraeis doctrines sociales,* 103; and La Roche, *Les Nationaux et les Partis,* viii, iv.

41. Discours de M. Chesnelong, May 19–24, 1873, in *Comité catholique de Paris,* 41.

42. Chesnelong was the president of the Assemblée Générale des Comités Catholiques de France in 1873; Charles Kolb-Bernard, Charles Combier, and Charles du Bodan, all

mote the work of well-established or newly constituted charitable *oeuvres* and Catholic schools but also encouraged the extension of the Catholic press[43] and the creation of a Catholic telegraph and news-gathering service. In that, they demonstrated a willingness to exploit the new technology of mass printing, photography, and mass communications to promote traditional values. Besides helping to coordinate the large national pilgrimages of Lourdes, Paray-le-Monial, and La Salette, which were viewed as evidence of a new religious revival in defiance of the positivist spirit of the age, the delegates drafted legislative proposals aimed, for example, at restricting state activity on Sundays and introducing chaplains into the army barracks. At the same time, they sought to inject the evangelical message into artistic life by holding *concours* to promote Christian iconography, songs, and drama. Legitimists set up libraries and associations to disseminate *bons livres* and to combat the ravages of colportage and the radical press.[44] Many even wrote pious novels and devotional literature accessible to and affordable by the lower classes— works intended to instruct in the virtues of living according to faith and custom.[45]

While taking positive steps to enhance religious cultural values, the Legitimists worked to suppress blatant expressions of cultural radicalism

---

Legitimists, were vice-presidents. Out of a parliamentary delegation of roughly 180 deputies, 60 Legitimists attended the general assembly and 12 others "adhered" to its program.

43. The principal goal of the Comités Catholiques in this regard was to increase the number of dioceses with their own church-controlled publication, *Semaine religieuse*. The first such publication began in Paris in 1853; there were fifty of them by 1868. According to Lebrun, they were designed to substitute for colportage literature, to disseminate writings of edification, and to support the rebirth of clerical erudition. See his *Histoire des catholiques en France*, 296.

44. Both the Saint Vincent de Paul Society and, later, the Oeuvre des Cercles maintained popular libraries and distributed religious literature to their members. In 1848, Le Beschu de Champsavin, Alexandre de Trédern, Armand de Cintré, Jean Baptiste Lesbaupin and Paul de La Bigne-Villeneuve founded the Société des Bonnes Livres when they discovered that those who fought on the barricades got their ideas from "papers costing one sou." One library catalog for the Oeuvre de Cercles listed works by Bossuet, P. Arsene Cahour, Vicomte Chateaubriand, Corneille, René Descartes, Fénélon, Jean Pierre Claris de Florian, Joseph de Maistre, Blaise Pascal, Racine, Madame de Sévigné, and Louis Veuillot. See Rollet, *L'Action sociale*, 33; Duroselle, *Les Débuts du catholicisme social*, 686–89; *La Société de St. Vincent de Paul à Marseille*, 36–37; Le Beschu de Champsavin, *Lettre à l'évêque de Rennes au sujet de la fondation d'une oeuvre de bons livres* (Rennes, 1849).

45. See Pierre Pierrand, "Le Roman pieux; ou, D'édification en France au temps de l'Ordre Moral, 1850–1880," in *La Religion populaire*, ed. Y. M. Hilaire (Paris, 1981), 229–35.

and anticlericalism. In the National Assembly, they not only led the fight to outlaw the Workers' International, restrict civil burials, and apply censorship to the radical press but also sponsored legislation against divorce and public blasphemy.[46] They called for public prayers petitioning God's forgiveness for the sins of the Commune, demanded that the Assembly itself sponsor the construction of the Basilica of the Sacré-Coeur at Montmartre, and insisted upon the suspension of state operations on Sundays. By such measures the Legitimist deputies hoped to get the government to recognize the moral obligation of public institutions and to get it to take the lead in giving expression to the reality of a Christian France.

The use of the state to promote a new moral order constituted the core of what the Legitimists understood as a Christian monarchy. Although they rejected the separation of church and state, they did not envision what their adversaries called a government of priests. Theocracy, they concluded, was an aberrant form of government, since the church was not, properly speaking, a governing body. But though they saw church and state as distinct in their duties, they held that the establishment of a Christian monarchy required a transformation in the spirit by which the state understood its responsibilities to protect the church. Thus, they thought that it was not enough for the state to permit the church to exercise freely "une action individuelle sur les âmes"; the faith of society as a whole needed to be protected by *pouvoirs* that were themselves Christian. "Catholicism," wrote one Legitimist, "expects the protection of civil government" not only in the spiritual domain but also in the public exercise of power. "It is not enough," he continued, "that it not be treated as an enemy; it must be accepted at all times as a superior power, imposing itself on princes and peoples alike, and as the only ally of which the public power can avail itself in order to justify its mission, demand obedience, and finally, perpetuate the social peace that must be on earth the reflection of all celestial harmonies."[47]

Chambord, who called *l'état sans Dieu* the "most incomprehensible

46. Gabriel de Belcastel summed up the rationale behind the regime of Moral Order when he wrote that "evil has no rights and cannot have any, since it is the pure negation of good, which in essence is the inverse. Evil is therefore by its nature subject to repression, and the right of good to preserve itself by driving back evil is absolutely undeniable" (*La Monarchie chrétienne: Lettres d'un catholique à ses contemporains* [Paris, 1884], 100).

47. Auray de St. Pois, *La Royauté est nécessaire*, 9–11.

aberration that can befall a Christian nation in the name of progress," promised the church not only "full liberty . . . in spiritual matters" but a "perfect accord" between church and state in areas of common concerns as they affected "the good of religion and the well-being of peoples"— an astonishing assertion, given the French monarchy's historical record in religious matters.[48] As long as the state recognized the church as its "director of conscience" and the king acted as the sergeant of God, Chambord was certain that there would be no schism in the social consciousness and the moral order between a culture of faith and one of *incroyance*. The unity of church and state in protecting the Christian basis of the social order was to create a society that by its organization and ritual expression would establish a framework within which the people collectively thought and behaved in a Christian manner. Like the external manifestations of the Catholic religion, which permitted faith to take root in the hearts of the people and sowed the seeds of grace and salvation, the white flag was to act as "the symbol, the external expression of principles . . . before the people, the only one it sees, the only one that would have for it a decisive significance." It was to demonstrate the convictions of a Christian monarch whose recognized authority buttressed the "contagious beauty of his personal example."[49]

In most utopian form, the Christian monarchy, far from being a reproduction of seventh-century absolutism, was understood in the manner in which Hegel had described the Prussian state: as a totalizing force capable of abolishing the contradiction between liberty and authority by creating a social and moral harmony in which coercion and conflict became unnecessary. For many Legitimists, Catholicism promised perfect social freedom and a dissolution of the consciousness of class distinctions, or rather, a society in which class distinctions were irrelevant since abnegation, charity, and a kind of collective autorepression reconciled the function and desire of each individual with the social conditions created by inequality. Christian society was portrayed by many Legitimists as a church full of worshipers or a procession of pilgrims in which everyone freely adhered to a common faith and common goals and joined in a new egalitarianism of the spirit that transcended material class boundaries. A

48. Comte de Chambord to A. M. Nicolas, August 16, 1872, in Auguste Nicolas' *L'Etat sans Dieu: Mal Social de la France* (Paris, 1873), ii; Comte de Chambord to M. Cherrières, March 26, 1859, in Chambord, *La Monarchie française,* 58.

49. Chambord, in Chesnelong's *Un Temoignage à l'histoire,* 143; Margerie, *La Solution,* 51.

Legitimist who chronicled the pilgrimage to Lourdes of October, 1872, asserted that "socialists" who spoke "with a superb horror" of social inequalities did so because "they frequent neither our temples nor our celebrations where, everyday, they would have before their eyes the magnificent spectacle of the most touching equality." To the "holy table, the poorest and the most wealthy come, without distinction of rank, to sit side by side; at the pilgrimage of Lourdes, the delegations were composed of all social classes without exception. Every Christian is a gentleman, and every Christian knows it. The place where man lapses most often and most sadly into inequality is where the Revolution reigns."[50] Describing a teeming religious procession through the streets of Rennes at the inauguration of the Voeu de Notre-Dame de Bonne-Nouvelle in 1861, Paul Vert noted the people "deploying themselves along the magnificent lines of our streets with so much order and majesty." For him, faith was the perfect form of crowd control, and it offered a new image of the masses:

Nobody has ever seen a more respectful, more assorted, more sympathetic, and more charming crowd. . . . Where was the force that restrained and disciplined these masses so in a hurry and so eager to see? Nobody was there either to command or to impose such force—not one official uniform, not one municipal magistrate, not one authority military, civilian, or judicial, not a policeman, not a soldier, not even a single fireman. How to control this crowd, to hinder its movement and its clamor? It was the crowd itself that quite naturally kept itself orderly and decent. An invitation by a priest, a wave of his hand, was sufficient to make the most intrusive groups move or retreat. What secret power brought about these wonders? It was that the hearts of the people who watched the procession pass beat as one.

Significantly, it was the Legitimist notables of Rennes who marched at the head of the procession with their children and who, along with the crowd, formed a "single people" partaking of "the same faith, the same love for the holy and solemn ceremonies of the church."[51] For many Legitimists who imbibed the Catholicism of the Syllabus of Errors, this

50. Paul Alexandre de Geslin de Kersolon [Jean Loyseau], *Lourdes: Pèlerinage et Pèlerins* (Paris, 1872), 71–72.
51. Paul Sebastien Vert, *Rélation de la fête du 8 séptembre 1861 pour l'inauguration du voeu de Notre-Dame-de-Bonne-Nouvelle à Rennes* (Rennes, 1861), 41–43.

was true freedom and equality, the inspiration of moral order; it was with such as this in mind that Louis Veuillot's clerical journal *L'Univers* spoke of the capacity of Catholicism to "remake a Christian France."[52]

The voluntary solidarity of all classes was what Chambord felt the Revolution had destroyed. When he proclaimed that he would never consent "to become the legitimate king of the Revolution," he was referring not to the institutional settlement of 1789, as the Orleanists believed, but to the spirit of skepticism, selfishness, and indiscipline that had undermined the moral order, encouraged social disintegration, and made political stability impossible. Chambord had always drawn a distinction between the legitimate achievements of 1789 and the Revolution as an act of collective insubordination meant to affirm the moral sovereignty of man.[53] As Albert de Mun correctly pointed out, the "noble demand for the white flag" had nothing to do with the "resurrection of the Old Regime" but rather envisioned the "repudiation of the revolutionary spirit."[54] In contrast to a process by which societies developed gradually and naturally without uprooting their basic traditions, the French Revolution was, in the sight of the extreme Right, an unprecedented attempt to create new moral laws to replace Christianity. The *principe révolutionaire* was, in their understanding, neither a simple call to reform nor an isolated act of rebellion; rather, it sought to establish the absolute independence of society from the moral direction of the church. As Monsi-

52. *L'Univers*, 1872, in Thomas Kselman's *Miracles and Prophecies in Nineteenth-Century France* (New Brunswick, N.J., 1983), 120. Catholicism provided Legitimists with a substitute for secular nationalism. It was thus natural for the Legitimists to attach political significance to the mass pilgrimages of 1872–1873. In Amédée de Margerie's description of the grand mass in the amphitheater at Paray-le-Monial, it is difficult to distinguish between the religious and the nationalist aspects of the ceremony. See his *La Fête du Sacré Coeur en 1873 à Paray-le-Moniel: Lettre à M. Vagnen* (Nancy, 1873), 5.

53. "The Revolution," wrote Dreux-Brézé, "is not only the demagogic tendency that on certain days excites and arms peoples against their sovereigns, it is the spirit of insubordination that contests all authority, all right, all principle, . . . the need to modify everything, always to innovate, and the revolt of error in rejection of the most well-founded teachings and the most generally admitted doctrines" (*La Révolution*, 19). But Carayon-Latour told the National Assembly, "The salutary reforms of the end of the last century" were the consequence not of the Revolution but of "Christian civilization": "And the heir of our kings is shocked, like an outraged honest man, when one still speaks to him of abuses and privileges. (Exclamations on the Left.—Applause on diverse benches of the Right.) What he wants, he has said it a hundred times, is equality before the law, freedom of conscience, the free access of all. . . . (Laughter and noise on the Left.)" (*Annales*, January 21, 1875, XXXVI, 228).

54. Mun, *Ma vocation sociale*, 189.

gnor Louis de Ségur put it, the Revolution represented the "will of the
sovereign people substituted for the sovereign will of God."[55] This was
not to say that all defiance and change were illegitimate. According to
Henri de La Broise, there was a "radical difference" between the Revolution and "troubles that have, at certain moments, led divers peoples to
revolt." A *jacquerie,* demands for municipal franchise, or a riot against
corrupt local authorities had just and limited goals and could be halted
by a simple redress of grievances. The French Revolution, by contrast,
aspired to be permanent and universal by challenging the idea of authority itself and sanctioning a continuing revision of the entire social order.[56]
For that reason, the Legitimists likened it to the Protestant Reformation
in its scope and consequences rather than to attempts at the limited and
legitimate modifications and institutional refinements envisioned by the
Estates of Dauphiné in 1788 or the *cahiers* of 1789. For Chambord, recognizing the legitimacy of the Revolution would have been tantamount
to condoning future revolutions and future attempts to negate fundamental social principles. It was the revolution of the spirit which the
Tricolor stood for that Chambord could not countenance—the "colors
that presided over so many crimes, that have always been the signal for
the overthrow of legitimate monarchy."[57] The Marquis de Dreux-Brézé,
an important member of Chambord's entourage, accurately explained
that Chambord demanded a repudiation "not of the revolution that
simply modified certain individual situations and grew out of the reformist movement of the last century, which royalty placed itself at the
head of and which Monsieur le Comte de Chambord has declared himself ready to resume," but of the "revolution representing the ascendancy
of the changing will of the nation over tradition, of the aspirations of the
modern world over the principle of authority, of the interests and rights
of the society of 1789 over time-honored necessities."[58]

Distinguishing the moral consequences of the Revolution from much
of the legislative and juridical work of 1789–1791, Chambord was in-
credulous at those who accused him of wanting to return to the institu-

---

55. Louis Gaston Adrien de Ségur, *La Révolution* (4th ed.; Paris, 1872), 55. See also
Bernardi, *La Révolution,* 140.

56. La Broise, *République ou Monarchie,* 39–40.

57. Comte de Chambord to M. de La Ferté, May 24, 1871, in Hélis de Noailles' *Le
Bureau du Roi* (Paris, 1932), 208–209.

58. Charles de Dreux-Brézé, *Notes et Souvenirs pour servir à l'histoire du parti royaliste,
1872–1883* (Paris, 1895), 142–43.

tions of the past. He found it equally incomprehensible that he was charged with being out of touch with the modern era simply because he insisted on the immutability of *la morale*. For the pretender and his followers, there was no correlation between material or economic progress and cultural change; thus, there was no contradiction between age-old values and what Chambord called the "exigencies of our times."[59] As he told the nation in 1871, "I am and I want to be of my times; I render sincere homage to all its greatness." According to Henri de Pène, Chambord was one of the first stockholders in Vicomte de Lessep's Suez Company. But the pretender also cautioned that material innovation did not allow societies to escape "eternal necessities."[60] Unlike the positivists, who assumed that Catholicism would wane as society reached a more rational and scientific stage of development, Chambord and the Legitimists saw the rechristianization of France as the highest expression of civilization and providential design. The Legitimism Chambord represented was more antipositivist than reactionary, since it condemned not industry, science, and reason but the culture of acquisitiveness and materialism which saw progress only as improved physical well-being. Moral fortitude and social peace, the Legitimists argued, were precisely what allowed society to enjoy the fruits of industry without threatening the material patrimony amassed through the ages. There was, they maintained, nothing inherently revolutionary or subversive about modern science and industry, nor was there anything inherent in the Revolution that caused the development of material progress. Railways, the telegraph, steam power, and modern armies, they implied, owed nothing to Robespierre but merely coincided with the nineteenth century; technological advances could be more fully secured if greed, class antagonism, and individualism vanished.[61] La Broise defended the Legitimist view of progress by denying that royalists intended "to stop the march of society." To wish to return to what was fruitful in the past, he contended, in

59. Chambord to M. de La Ferté, May 24, 1871, in Noailles' *Le Bureau du Roi,* 208.

60. Manifeste du 7 juillet 1871, in Castries' *Le Grand Refus,* 149; Henri de Pène, *Henri de France* (Paris, 1884), 364.

61. If the Revolution was the "occasion" for technological development, wrote Monsignor de Ségur, "it was not the cause of it. The violent disruption that it has imposed on the entire world has without a doubt precipitated a certain development of material civilization; the same violence has caused many others to be aborted. The fact remains that the Revolution, considered alone, has not been, properly speaking, the *principle* of any real progress" (*La Révolution,* 8).

no way meant seeking to "recover a long-lost social organization," because society flourished only by making prudent use of the achievements of earlier generations.[62]

Progress, as the Legitimists conceived it, consisted of material improvement *and* moral continuity. Their conception permitted them to reverse the dialectic of their opponents and assert that the material accomplishments of the nineteenth century coincided with an unprecedented moral decline and that the period was thus retrograde. According to Bernardi, "It is not industrial development, material riches, or even number that constitutes the value of a people but rather its moral and intellectual strength."[63] La Broise argued, "True civilization is the perfect equilibrium between our moral nature and our physical nature: if we let the latter encroach, we soon sacrifice everything to it, we destroy the equilibrium and move toward barbarism. Thus it is possible to be persuaded that material progress, when not accompanied by moral progress, soon leads to decadence; we should reject the insane and prideful belief that man can become a god."[64] By flattering human vanity, by questioning religion, by choosing high stock prices and order in the streets over moral order, liberals and republicans had become *les retardataires* while Legitimists, who appreciated the civilizing role the church played throughout human history, had earned the title of "promoters of progress."[65]

It was confidence about being able to reconcile economic modernity and traditional values that permitted the Legitimists to think they had cast off the stigma of the ancien régime. As Legitimism had become more militantly integralist and more conscious of the need to refute the criticism launched against it by the Left, it had developed into a kind of counterpositivism that equated secular materialism with paganism and

---

62. La Broise, *Le Vrai et le Faux Libéralisme*, 294–95.

63. Bernardi, *La Révolution*, 122–23.

64. La Broise, *Le Vrai et le Faux Libéralisme*, 296. See also La Roche, *Les Nationaux et les Partis*, 398.

65. *Henri V, l'Eglise et la Révolution* (Paris, 1872), 179; La Broise, *Le Vrai et le Faux Libéralisme*, 38–50. Monsignor de Ségur drew a distinction between "reactionaries," who were "afflicted spirits, always occupied by a regret for the past, the Old Regime, the Middle Ages," and those who were "men of faith and heart, Catholics above all, who amid blasphemies and revolutionary ruins do not compromise one principle of the social order established by God, do not recoil one step before the demands of a perverted world, but regard the *antirevolutionary reaction* as a duty of conscience" (*La Révolution*, 118).

endowed Catholicism with the same function in history that reason has in the philosophy of Hegel. Reassured by a new intellectual confidence, many Legitimists proclaimed that the principles of 1789 codified a regression of society toward pre-Christian values whereas Legitimism and the Catholicism of the Syllabus held the possibility of emancipating humanity from the surviving fetters of barbarian degradation. As the church came to terms with modern innovations and society returned to faith, they affirmed, an equilibrium between moral and material development would be established, and France would be able to institute a new higher order that abolished the contradiction between the individual and the needs of the community without reverting to the Christian Middle Ages. There would be social peace and material prosperity, because the new Christian society would be able to enjoy the fruits of its ingenuity without tearing itself apart. As one writer put it, the principle of legitimacy solved the problem of reconciling the "immutable laws of order and authority" and the "temperament of modern societies." He rhapsodized, "The past cannot be revived, and the Revolution must die."[66]

In sum, the white flag was not merely a trivial formality for Chambord, nor did it express his rejection of eighty years of national development: it represented an opportunity for the nation to repudiate the entire cultural, political, and social legacy of the Revolution and to obtain the absolution that alone could end the fatal revolutionary cycle. Chambord told La Bouillerie,

> I am not a candidate for the throne, I am a principle of government. If France wants the government that I represent and that is the only one I can offer, I am at its disposal and would very much like to deal with the Assembly of Versailles, which is the legal organ of the nation. But if, on the other hand, they want only a *monarchie de circonstance* to legalize the revolutionary currents and provide them with a temporary dike—which the next generation will breach—it is useless to call upon me. . . . I cannot in sincerity make a pact with what I consider error and the cause of France's disarray.[67]

66. *Henri V et la Démocratie,* 59–60.
67. Comte de Chambord to Joseph de La Bouillerie, in Castries' *Le Grand Refus,* 199. Margerie put it more succinctly when he wrote, "Bad princes make revolutionary peoples" (*La Restauration,* 283).

It was Dreux-Brézé, who knew Chambord better than most Legitimists, who fully discerned the reason for the king's *grand refus*. Seeking above all "to escape from an era of political upheavals," Chambord felt that the Assembly's and the nation's misunderstanding of his principle would only disarm him "against the inevitable difficulties of his reign" and would lay the groundwork for the "subsequent victory of a new revolution in which [he] saw the possibility of his remaining even a hope for France disappear." [68] Chambord preferred to continue loyal to the higher obligation of keeping the monarchical principle intact while awaiting a more propitious occasion, when France, through the work of providence, might realize the necessity of restoring the legitimate monarchy *tout entière*. As he frequently warned the monarchist deputies, a "diminished king" would be an "impotent king." He told the nation, "The demands made heretofore allow me to size up the importunities that would lie ahead, and it is impossible that I would be consenting to inaugurate a strong and restorative reign through an act of weakness." [69] Chambord saw himself as the "sacred repository of our national traditions," the "necessary pilot," the "only one capable of steering the ship into port"; in the end, he believed, it was up to France to recognize his role voluntarily. All he could do was create the opportunity, by being true to his sacred mission: "I have preserved intact the sacred trust of our national traditions and our liberties for forty-three years. I therefore have the right to count on an equal confidence and to inspire an equal assurance. . . . My person is nothing; my principle is everything. France will see the end of its trials when it is willing to understand this." [70]

It is useless to speculate on how differently France would have evolved had Chambord been simply a practical politician, but it is useful to clarify his motivation for insisting on the fleur-de-lis, in order to illumine the internal logic of Legitimist ideology, the persistence of intransigent anti-republicanism after the royalist political collapse of the 1870s, and the subsequent splintering of the Legitimist movement. Chambord's refusal to become the "legitimate king of the Revolution" was not only politically disastrous for the Legitimists, it pointed to the fundamental contradiction in their program of social reconstruction. In renouncing ultimate political authority, Chambord was acting in accordance with the Legiti-

68. Dreux-Brézé, *Notes et Souvenirs*, 141.
69. Chesnelong, *Un Témoignage à l'histoire*, 143.
70. Lettre du Salsbourg, October 27, 1873, in Chambord, *La Monarchie française*, 132.

mists' quest for the perfect fit between civil society and the state, which they believed they could ground in a simultaneous moral transformation and institutional reconstruction. Chambord had come to represent a variety of Legitimism in which monarchy as a form of executive power could not be separated from the social relations, institutional arrangements, and values it was supposed to enshrine and guarantee. The principle of legitimacy, that is, of the obligation of state and society to live in conformity with divine law, became an end in itself, and the priority accorded it seems to have convinced Chambord that a restoration was impossible and even undesirable so long as France remained "revolutionary," since so long as it did, the monarchy could not express the mores and social interests of France without losing its essential link to sacred traditions.[71] That the Legitimists hoped that the restoration would preserve the power of traditional notables against the advance of democracy is clear; the Orleanists had the same goal in mind when they considered the monarchist option. But Chambord invested their practical goal with a sense of historic mission in defining the restoration as an opportunity to repair history by effecting the reunification of the monarchy and the nation. Indeed he envisioned the reestablishment of the monarchy as a marriage between himself and what Antoine Blanc de St. Bonnet called a "virgin nation," and his actions were those not of a psychological cripple but rather of an indignant bridegroom left waiting at the altar.[72] Perhaps Charles de Lacombe put it best when, in irritation with the pretender's obstinacy, he described Chambord as a "bishop *in partibus* who would return to his diocese only when all his diocesans did their Easter duties."[73]

Once the unity of the Right in the Assembly was broken and once the French peasantry began openly to support republican candidates in July, 1871, the failure of the monarchy was a foregone conclusion. Chambord's role in the process was to confirm an already skeptical nation's presuppositions about the likely consequences of a Bourbon restoration. Legitimist candidates, after their unexpected victory in the election of February 8, 1871, lost steadily in the by-elections of 1871–1875; in the national elections of 1876 and 1877 their parliamentary delegation

71. See *ibid.*, 134.
72. Blanc de St. Bonnet, *La Légitimité*, 458. For Blanc de St. Bonnet, it was France and not Chambord that had "declared the impossibility of returning to the monarchy" (p. x).
73. Charles de Lacombe, *Journal politique de Charles de Lacombe, député à l'Assemblée Nationale* (2 vols.; Paris, 1908), I, 77.

dropped from 180 to 24 to 18. The overall proportion of votes for monarchist candidates hovered at about 30 percent for the next ten years.[74] As the republicans consolidated their power, they did not hesitate to use their control over Parliament and the administration to invalidate the election of royalists and purge them from major and minor bureaucratic agencies. Between 1876 and 1877, the republican Chamber invalidated the election of 102 opponents of the regime, 90 of whom were accused of being "official candidates" selected by President MacMahon and the fallen Broglie ministry.[75] At the same time, the number of conservative general counselors fell from 1,532 in 1874 to 1,004 in 1880 and 882 in 1886. Meanwhile, the republicans gained control of roughly 20,000 municipalities, leaving the conservatives in possession of only 9,500 *mairies*.[76] At the national level, the Constitution of 1875 ensured that whoever controlled a majority of the local councils gained the greatest number of seats in the Senate. With the enactment of the laic laws, the affirmation of Jacobin centralization and liberal democracy, the establishment of the supremacy of Parliament, the neglect by republicans of agriculture, and the promotion by them of a policy of official anticlericalism, the Left was on the way to creating a France that contradicted the entire Legitimist project. What was worse, the continued success of the republicans in national elections clearly confirmed that religious beliefs, regional identities, and historical memory did not translate into a majority for the Right and that quite a few Catholics had quietly rallied to the Republic.

The 1880s marked the end of an era. The monarchist notables were replaced in many of their local strongholds by doctors, veterinarians, and notaries. Visible symbols of ultramontane Catholic Legitimism like Veuillot, Monsignor Edouard Pie, and Frédéric Le Play died in 1879, 1881, and 1882 respectively. The Comte de Chambord expired in the summer of 1883, and the mantle of legitimacy passed into the hands of an Orleanist prince. Three years later, a new pope, Leo XIII, issued the encyclical *Immortale Dei* in which he proclaimed that the church had no

74. Rudelle, *La République absolue*, 46.

75. Zeldin, *France, 1848–1945*, 218. Of the twenty-four members of the Legitimist Right elected to the Chamber in 1876, twelve had their election contested or invalidated in Parliament. Nine failed to win reelection in by-elections, and only three were finally reelected, including Albert de Mun. See Levillain, *Albert de Mun*, 476.

76. Rémond, *Les Droites en France*, 145. See also Daniel Halévy, *La République des Ducs* (Paris, 1937), 368–71.

preference for a specific form of government as long as it respected the rights of the church. The 1880s, like the 1830s, witnessed the return of many Legitimists to isolation and abstentionism as the party was decimated by defections from which it would never recover.

Chambord's *grand refus* clearly facilitated the consolidation of the Third Republic and the destruction of Legitimism as an independent and viable force in French politics. Nevertheless, not all Legitimists blindly followed their king to political self-immolation. On the contrary, there was much resistance to his position and, as the dissension became more vocal, different factions of the party sought to define their own ways of achieving the social and political goals of Legitimism. In the movement's death throes, it splintered. The disillusionment of the party's principal leaders not only uncovered latent divisions but gave greater clarity to the range of significance the Legitimists attached to the monarchy. Chambord had provided only one formula for the regeneration of France, a formula that proved inadequate. Many of his supporters were too committed and too disputatious to give him the final word.

CHAPTER XI

 The Fragmentation of the
Royalist Cause

IN THE political essay *La Monarchie chrétienne,* published in
1884, Gabriel de Belcastel took time out from his combative advocacy of
the royalist cause to recall what seemed to him the most significant
achievements of the Legitimist party in the nineteenth century. Omitting
mention of the political struggle, Belcastel pointed with a mixture of
pride and regret to the Legitimists' work as soldiers, judges, priests, and
charitable patrons. He was especially emphatic on the importance of their
contribution in the fields of Catholic education and social activism.[1]

Belcastel's regrets illuminate the extent to which Legitimism had
come to represent a certain vision of French society for which the monarchy was only the guarantor, and Chambord the personification. As a
malleable symbol, the monarchy became an instrument for the construction of various social projects in the hands of Legitimists as diverse in
their temperaments and ideological priorities as Claude Marie Raudot,
Albert de Mun, and the Comte Alfred de Falloux. Since the objectives of
Legitimist social reconstruction reached well beyond the limits of the
constitutional question, the failure to restore the monarchy in the 1870s
did nothing to diminish the attachment of a number of the Legitimist
factions to the social demands they had associated with the restoration of
the monarchy. Without the hope of an immediate political success and,
after 1883, deprived of a unifying symbol, the Legitimist cause fragmented along lines traced by long-standing social and ideological differ-

1. Belcastel, *La Monarchie chrétienne,* 6–7.

295

ences. The separate tendencies eventually merged with the weak and polymorphous conservative movements of the late nineteenth century.

French royalism had always been torn by a certain political schizophrenia. The Legitimists had been able to play a role in determining the political and legal contours of French life only when they worked in a coalition with other conservative forces. Their electoral success in 1849 and 1871, as well as their ability to pass conservative legislation such as the Falloux Law, was possible only because they had been willing to subordinate their dynastic convictions to form a broad conservative union against secularization and democratization. Nonetheless, the inclination of more moderate elements in the party to collaborate with centrists always evoked shouts of betrayal from intransigents who saw any transaction that shook the integrity of Legitimist principles as a capitulation to the forces of the Revolution. The division between "liberals" and "ultras" had plagued French royalism from the time of the emigration and had persisted throughout the nineteenth century.[2] After 1830, rival models of political comportment and ideological expression repeatedly divided the Legitimists between those willing to accommodate the political realities they faced and those preferring the crisis politics of insurrection, internal exile, or abstentionism. The integration of conservative social Catholic and clerical tendencies into Legitimism during the 1860s served only to multiply the possible options for political action, since the Catholics presented the older cadres of the party with allies some of whom preferred social action to electoral politics and others of whom were willing to compromise with any regime that promised to protect the interests of the church. The persistence of Legitimism proved that the party remained a political force and that it retained a loyal following in its regional strongholds, but its tactical failures and outright unpopularity drove home that it would never have sufficient strength to rule alone. The need to forge coalitions resulted in a perpetual reenactment of the cycle of fusions, *ralliements,* abstentions, and schisms as moderates made deals and extremists fled from the prospect of revolutionary contamination. In the process, three distinct Legitimisms were articulated to justify divergent political strategies, and each was invested with an ideological significance that turned discordance within the party into the im-

---

2. See especially Locke, *French Legitimists,* 10–53; and Rémond, *Les Droites en France,* 73–82.

possibility of dialogue, with each faction of Legitimists questioning the legitimacy of alternative restorations.

Chambord's *grand refus* merely intensified the dialectic between unity and division and facilitated the fragmentation of his own movement. By highlighting the incompatibility between Legitimism and liberalism, he encouraged the intransigents and created a storm of bitter recrimination among moderates, who insisted that fusion was the only path to political success. At the same time, Catholic leaders who saw Chambord as the protector of the church or who regarded royalty as a natural adjunct to the Christian social order took note of the hazards of dynastic politics and questioned the wisdom of supporting a political option that had failed so completely in halting the onslaught of anticlerical republicanism. Into what three components did Legitimism split, and how does the fragmentation of the royalist project illuminate the historical evolution of Legitimism and the weakness of French conservatism in the late nineteenth century?

LIBERAL LEGITIMISM AND THE MONARCHY OF THE NOTABLES

On September 5, 1875, in response to the inauguration of a statue honoring Chateaubriand erected at Saint Malo, a number of journals of the extreme Right paid homage to the memory of the great writer and statesman. Charles de Lacombe, a "conservative" who supported the restoration of Chambord, saw only irony in the celebration of a man whose ideas the right wing of the Legitimist party had repudiated. As they "rendered the greatest homage" to Chateaubriand, wrote Lacombe, the monarchical campaign was foundering because Chambord and "those who follow his orders . . . have moved farther and farther from the politics recommended and practiced by Chateaubriand."[3]

For moderate Legitimists like Lacombe, many of whom were the party's most visible spokesmen in France, the spectacle of the crisis of the white flag was an unmitigated disaster. Devoted to Chambord but unable to induce him to follow a more pragmatic line, the moderate Right found itself in the impossible position of advocating a monarchy for which it had no king. Frustrated by the fanaticism and intractability of the ex-

---

3. Charles de Lacombe, *Journal politique,* II, 228.

treme Right and more inclined by temperament and by social back-
ground toward the liberal aristocrats of the Orleanist center Right than
toward the likes of Louis Veuillot, who had become one of Chambord's
most enthusiastic supporters, the moderates were caught between their
animus against the *cheveaux-légers,* whom they blamed for destroying
conservative unity, and their hatred for Louis Adolphe Thiers, who had
opened the way for the consolidation of the Republic.

The moderates reserved their most violent invective for Chambord
himself. It was the pretender, they argued, who had validated the Left's
fears of a reactionary restoration, who had turned public opinion against
the Right, and who had destroyed the dream of a liberal constitutional
monarchy by embracing the ultras and rendering the monarchical option
unpalatable to honest conservatives who might otherwise have welcomed a return to legitimacy without second thought.[4] By undermining
the sort of conservative unity that had provided a measure of stability
under Louis XVIII, Chambord had, they believed, dislodged the basic
elements of a united conservative program and cleared the way for a
repetition of the revolutionary cycle. For the moderates, his blunder was
not only tactical but historic; as Léopold de Gaillard observed, it had
been the disunion of conservative forces under the Restoration that
"produced the movement and the government of 1830; under the July
Regime, it produced the Revolution of 1848." Since then, he argued,

4. See Michel Denis, "Un Aspect du conservatisme en Bretagne au début de la IIIe
République: Le Monarchisme libéral," *Annales de Bretagne,* LXXVII (1970), 395. Although
the moderates made up the majority of the Legitimist delegation in the National Assembly,
it is far from clear that they represented the views of the majority of the party. Having
opposed abstentionism under the Second Empire and having worked actively at the local
and national level to create a viable opposition in the 1860s, moderates like Meaux, Benoist
d'Azy, Larcy, and Audren de Kerdrel were better placed to be included on the conservative
electoral lists drawn up in anticipation of the elections of February 8, 1871. The numerical
weight of the abstentionists is difficult to calculate, but judging by the level of opposition
to the moderates' political activity in the west, it must have been formidable. Although
Legitimists were no longer constrained from voting or running for office after the fall of
the Second Empire, elections subsequent to February, 1871, offer no better indications,
since all varieties of Legitimism were defeated at the polls. Nor is the composition of the
departmental *comités royalistes* illuminating in this regard, since their personnel were appointed by Chambord's entourage and were almost exclusively *grands seigneurs* of the extreme Right. See Denis, "Un Aspect du conservatisme," 391–415; Henri Goallou, "Le
Plébiscite du 8 mai 1870 en Ille-et-Vilaine," *Annales de Bretagne,* LXXVII (1970), 374–77;
Gouault, *Comment la France est devenue républicaine;* Robert R. Locke, "A New Look at
Conservative Preparations for the French Elections of 1871," *French Historical Studies,* III
(1968), 351–58; and Pocquet du Haut-Jussé, ed., *Légitimistes parlementaires,* 181–84.

universal suffrage had twice responded to the "most extreme social peril" by putting its faith in "men of order"; both times, conservative bickering rendered them impotent.[5] According to Falloux, only a "peace treaty between the vanquished of July 28, 1830, and the vanquished of February 24, 1848," could secure a durable monarchical restoration, because throughout the history of the Legitimist party compromise was a political fact of life that no degree of ideological integrity could escape.[6]

By making monarchical fusion and the preservation of a conservative majority the central preoccupation, the moderate Right concentrated on conciliating the Orleanists and persuading the *chevaux-légers* and Chambord to work to preserve the peace coalition that had brought the Right to power in 1871.[7] Consequently, they took a purely pragmatic stance toward the question of the white flag, thereby merely alienating their more ideological allies. Arthur de Cumont, a deputy from Maine-et-Loire and a close associate of Falloux, acknowledged, "The white flag is a noble flag," but he added that "it would decidedly bring defeat" and that, though "Long live the king" might make royalists feel a sense of "honor and glory," it was useless as a "rallying cry of universal suffrage."[8] If garnering public opinion and the support of the center Right required that Chambord accept the tricolor, the moderates were ready to call on him to do so.

The moderate Right's preoccupation with the possible was not entirely new. For a long time liberals in the party had embraced a conception of politics and the monarchy that Chambord was not prepared to brook. The moderate Legitimists of the 1870s saw themselves as the heirs to the eighteenth-century tradition of constitutional royalism that sought to create a monarchy in which the king governed in conjunction with the elite of the nation under the rule of laws collaboratively and rationally

5. Gaillard, *Les Etapes,* ii–iii.

6. See Charles Mazade, *L'Opposition royaliste: Berryer, de Villèle, de Falloux* (Paris, 1894), 287. Falloux returned to this theme in "De la Contre-Révolution," *Le Correspondant,* CXIII (1878), 376. See also Falloux, *Discours de M. de Falloux à l'Assemblée Nationale.* 13.

7. Chesnelong characterized the moderate Right: "United to the extreme Right by its sentiments for Monsieur le Comte de Chambord and by its absolute attachment to the principle of the traditional monarchy, reconciled to the center Right by several of its ideas, it strove to bring about a bond between one and the other and to offer to both an acceptable terrain of conciliation and loyal accord" (*Un Témoignage à l'histoire,* 7–8).

8. Arthur de Cumont, in Guillaume Véran's *Les Habiles: Appel à la raison publique—réplique à l'auteur des "Incurables"* (Angers, 1883), 61.

arrived at through deliberation and compromise. Liberty, national unity, and the preservation of conservative social values were seen as the principal goals of the state, and these were believed achievable only when the monarch sought to preserve civic calm and took the lead in reconciling differences among his most important citizens. Lacombe traced the lineage of this tradition back to the sixteenth-century statesmen who had brought about an end to the Wars of Religion, and he counted Henri IV as the "first among them." He wrote, "The *politiques* were men of compromise. Coming from diverse backgrounds, they felt that France could perish in terrible conflict and that the accord necessary to save it was to be obtained only at the price of mutual concessions. . . . Henri IV made himself their leader. This inspiration brought him to the throne; it also constituted the essence of his reign."[9] If the moderates' reading of history was correct, succumbing to prejudice was the greatest disservice they believed they could do the monarchist cause. Falloux even speculated that if Louis XVI had followed Jacques Turgot's advice and had made an alliance with those who wanted to take sensible steps in 1789 against the "resistance of superannuated traditions," the Revolution might have been avoided.[10]

The moderates therefore hoped to press Chambord into the mold of Henri IV; their wish was for the pretender to follow the example of his royal ancestor. Versailles, after all, was worth a flag. Chambord himself had invited the comparison with Henri IV by stating that Henri V could not abandon the flag of Henri IV. Falloux testified to the "profound chagrin" felt by liberal Legitimists who viewed themselves as loyal supporters and who believed that the "immense power" they were willing to confer on Chambord obliged him to "keep faith with his friends" by yielding "to his subjects in the most solemn matter of all," as Henri de Navarre had done.[11] The moderates also pointed to a more recent instance of royal pragmatism when they noted that Louis XVIII, whom Lacombe called a "true model of constitutional kings," had abandoned the Manifesto of Verône of 1795, which opposed any compromise with the Revolution, had issued the Declaration of Saint Ouen, which called for the reconciliation of the old and new France, and had promulgated

9. Charles de Lacombe, *Journal politique,* II, 336.
10. Falloux, *L'Agriculture et la Politique,* 3–4. See also Pitman, trans. and ed., *Memoirs of the Count de Falloux,* I, 167.
11. Pitman, trans. and ed., *Memoirs of the Count de Falloux,* II, 462–63.

the Charter, which made concessions to parliamentary rule.[12] If the Bourbon Restoration had failed, Falloux argued, it was not a liberal ministry that had brought on the Revolution of 1830: "If the royalists who disapproved of the Ordinances had been successful in dissuading Charles X, they would have saved the monarchy."[13]

Practical considerations made it possible for the moderate Right to assert that Chambord's *principe* was distinct from the white flag and that Chambord did not have the right to jeopardize the future of the monarchy, a "domain that does not belong to him alone," for a personal matter of pride and honor. Chambord had perhaps been correct to fight against a threat to his "necessary prerogatives," but the tricolor did not represent a substantive affront. The fleur-de-lis was merely a personal "consolation" for which the moderates believed he should have traded the far greater reward of "public gratitude."[14] Far from weakening him, a spirit of abnegation and compromise would have gained him respect and increased his political authority, the moderates held.[15]

Why did liberal Legitimists so willfully misread Chambord's motives? In part, by offering themselves simplistic psychological explanations, they made it unnecessary to look deeply into his premises. Unlike the pretender they supported, the moderates could not conceptually detach the social utility of a restoration from the parliamentary means to accomplish it. Chambord's indifference to public opinion and his inflexibility about what seemed to the moderates archaic symbolism indicated to them not an ideological division in their party but personal deficiencies in Chambord that validated their long-held suspicions that he had lost touch with reality. The moderates argued that Chambord, who had been reared in the melancholy atmosphere of Charles X's court in exile and educated by clerics who despised the modern world, was most comfortable with the rigid formalities of the semifeudal court at Frohsdorf and had become a prisoner of his youthful prejudices. His long-standing policy of electoral abstentionism, which the moderates neither accepted nor practiced, revealed his indifference to public service and the practical

12. Charles de Lacombe, *Journal politique,* II, 377, 338–39.
13. Comte Alfred de Falloux, *Du scepticisme politique* (Paris, 1872), 9.
14. Comte Alfred de Falloux, "Du Drapeau," in *Discours et Mélanges politiques,* II, 325–26.
15. Charles Chesnelong to Joseph de Carayon Latour, in Chesnelong's *Un Témoignage à l'histoire,* 34. Chesnelong suggested representing monarchical fusion by a new flag that combined the fleur-de-lis and the tricolor.

needs of the Legitimist movement. "Instead of a monarch," Arthur de La Borderie complained, "we have only . . . an infant who persists in demanding the moon."[16] The Vicomte de Meaux spoke more boldly when he suggested that Chambord feared political responsibility; he concluded, "Deep inside, he does not aspire to reign." He enlarged on that idea: "Like a fish out of water, without direct descendants, and having more than enough reason to be uninterested in his heirs, so that he is disengaged from the dynastic sentiment that among the old kings merged with paternal feeling, he prefers to continue in his way a king *in partibus,* impotent and respected."[17]

As for the extreme Right, to whom the moderates invariably referred as ultras or *pointus,* they were cast as the natural heirs of the émigrés who chose to await the decision of providence rather than remain in France to fight against the Revolution. Guided by "illusions," the ultras, according to Cumont, naïvely demanded a restoration but rejected the practical means to achieve it.[18] Their blind servility, he said, revealed that they were "basically men of the Old Regime" who had forgotten nothing and learned nothing. In any case, the moderates questioned whether the ultras were truly conservative, since their antifusionist tactics only contributed to the success of the Left and their "sentimental foolishness" hampered attempts to hold the tenuous conservative majority together.[19] Moderate doubts were strengthened after the crisis over the white flag in 1873, when the *chevaux-légers* tried systematically to obstruct any attempt by the moderate Right to create conservative safeguards such as a more restrictive electoral law and a Senate dominated by traditional elites. While the extreme Right believed they were prolonging the provisional life of the Republic in order to gain time, the moderates saw their tactics as an obstacle to the establishment of conservative institutions. The longer the extreme Right was willing to wait for a "savior" to fall from

16. Arthur de La Borderie to B. Pocquet, in *Légitimistes parlementaires,* ed. Pocquet du Haut-Jussé, 170.
17. Meaux, *Souvenirs politiques,* 182–83. My point here is not to deny the moderates' assessment of Chambord's personal shortcomings but to suggest that recourse to a psychological interpretation of the pretender's political position allowed the moderates to ignore that they had committed their support to a man who had rejected their strategy and their program.
18. Arthur de Cumont, *Les Incurables: A propos d'un brocheur* (2nd ed.; Angers, 1883), 30–31.
19. *Ibid.,* 27, 7.

the sky and "do their work," the more the moderates feared that the Assembly would "fall into the arms of [Léon] Gambetta."[20]

Such assessments by the moderates ran contrary to Chambord's assumptions about the popular basis of a restoration and the historic role of monarchical institutions, and to his obsession with national redemption. Chambord and the extreme Right assumed that the people would support the restoration because France was Catholic and monarchist by nature, but the moderates perceived that the monarchy was unpopular. Cumont affirmed, "French opinion is halfway between the extremes of Right and Left, both of which it opposes and detests equally."[21] Even in the west, liberal Legitimists observed disturbing signs of antiroyalism and general support for moderation. Vincent d'Audren de Kerdrel explained to the editor of the *Journal de Rennes* that protestations of fidelity to Chambord, though popular in Ille-et-Vilaine, would be disastrous "in many departments [where the people] regard us with horror"; in Coanbre, Hippolyte de La Grimaudière found that the "immense majority" were "neither monarchist nor republican" but were "full of prejudices against the Legitimists," whom they regarded as "housebreakers to be feared as much as the radicals" for opposing the established Republic.[22] Impelled by practical considerations and the drift of public opinion, the moderates argued that concessions to the "foolish demands of the

20. Meaux, *Souvenirs politiques,* 409–10; Arthur de La Borderie to Barthélemy Pocquet, in *Légitimistes parlementaires,* ed. Pocquet du Haut-Jussé, 149.

21. Cumont, *Les Incurables,* 9. See also Falloux, "De la Contre-Révolution," *Le Correspondant,* CXIII (1878), 374. Meaux drew the pessimistic conclusion, "We were monarchists, and the country was not" (*Souvenirs politiques,* 21).

22. Hippolyte de La Grimaudière to Barthélemy Pocquet, in *Légitimistes parlementaires,* ed. Pocquet du Haut-Jussé, 146. From Paris, Audren de Kerdrel wrote to Barthélemy Pocquet concerning the attitude to the extreme Right in Ille-et-Vilaine: "[They] say, 'The king speaks and we submit.' There is no reasoning with such people [*des gens soumis*]. The Comte de Chambord could ask us to support the reestablishment of the aristocracy with its privileges. What would you say: We will reestablish the aristocracy, because your submission does not admit any distinctions? . . . We are a long way from Berryer saying to his friends: Make people like you and they will like your ideas" (pp. 181–82). In 1875, La Grimaudière wrote, "What good have we done with our popularity of February 8? Our conduct during the war was admirable. To what do we attribute our unpopularity today? The reason is this idea, false as it is, . . . that we put the interests of our party before those of France and that we want to lead our country into the abyss rather than let it establish the monarchy or not" (pp. 183–84). Louis-Numa Baragnon, of Nîmes, however, had the different problem of being a moderate in a department where disagreeing with *L'Union,* Chambord's official mouthpiece, opened one to the accusation of being an Orleanist. See Père de Alzon, "Lettres inédites de M. Baragon," *Le Correspondant,* CCV (1901), 125.

extreme Right" would squander whatever popularity the Legitimists had gained during the Franco-Prussian War and the electoral campaign of 1871.[23]

Yet, in the final analysis the moderates were less concerned with mass opinion than with the political sensibilities of the liberal bourgeoisie. If it was clear that France wanted moderation, it was even more certain that the "intelligent and enlightened classes" would never "consider passing under the yoke . . . of intransigents and fanatics." It was therefore not enough, they argued, that the monarchy be restored; it also had to be "in perfect union with modern France."[24] Whereas Chambord seemed to want to punish the bourgeoisie for its ideological sins, the moderates wanted a politics that could cement an alliance between all conservative factions and consolidate a conservative majority behind a monarchy that could reassure the liberal bourgeoisie that the gains of the Revolution were secure. The moderate strategy of working for a parliamentary and elitist monarchy supported by a coalition of *grands notables* was a reincarnation of the constitutional royalism of Antoine Berryer, who before his death in 1868 had been hoping to make the Legitimist party a rallying point for what Lacombe called the "conscientious parties."[25] During the 1840s, Berryer, appalled by the Legitimists' opportunistic and obstructionist electoral alliances with the Left, tried to pull the party in a more moderate direction by fashioning a program designed to regain the confidence of the middle classes. Since Berryer believed that the bourgeoisie was the most vital, most numerous, and most powerful segment of French society, he concluded that the Legitimist party should try to gain a "position of leadership within it" by recognizing the "march of time" and embracing "current attitudes." He knew that a large portion of the bourgeoisie could not be retrieved from republicanism, but he believed that most bourgeois were "attached above all to the ideas of order and to the fear of revolutions"; it was among that contingent that he thought the Legitimists should seek their "true allies."[26]

Parliamentary fusion, however, implied that Legitimism had to divest itself of its alignment with the Old Regime in the eyes of those who

---

23. Cumont, *Les Incurables*, 7–8; Pocquet du Haute-Jussé, ed., *Légitimistes parlementaires*, 183–84.
24. Cumont, *Les Incurables*, 8–11.
25. Charles de Lacombe, *Vie de Berryer*, II, 355–56.
26. Charles de Lacombe, *Journal politique*, II, 338.

cherished the gains of 1789.[27] So long as the house of Bourbon remained a symbol of counterrevolution, it could never enjoy the "benefit of liberal opinions" and would be in competition with the house of Orleans.[28] Berryer observed that although the bourgeoisie feared revolution, it had a "lively revulsion against whatever could revive an inequality between the classes and lead back to the ascendancy of the old nobility and the old royalist party." If the Legitimists could offer the bourgeoisie the "double security" of a "strong and stable government" and of the preservation of the personal and material advances made since 1789, the fusion of the upper classes might, he was persuaded, be achieved under the auspices of the legitimate monarchy.[29]

The fusionist strategy also accorded well with the moderates' conviction that the areas of agreement among conservatives were more numerous and important than the areas of difference. All true conservatives, after all, shared an allegiance to civil liberties, to the freedom of conscience, to the separation of civil and religious jurisdictions, and to the open opportunity for appointment to state employment. Liberal Legitimists saw no reason that the monarchy should be made unpalatable to anyone who wanted to avert further democratic and social change. As Roger de Larcy explained, the Legitimists and the Orleanists were "too weak separately to resist the repeated shocks of revolutionary passions and unrestrained factionalism"; working together, however, they could provide a "point of equilibrium" for a monarchist regime capable of preventing violent political oscillations.[30] Indeed, the Vicomte de Meaux theorized that the Legitimists and the Orleanists constituted two complementary and essential elements of a single ruling class, because the former could make a traditional claim to legitimacy and had the "support of the most conservative class of the nation" and the latter had wide experience in parliamentary government and firm ties to the world of finance and industry.[31] Had not the Legitimists worked successfully with Orleanists in the Party of Order and with liberals and moderate republicans in the Liberal Union of 1863? Was not Thiers's coalition ministry of

---

27. Charles de Lacombe, *Vie de Berryer*, II, 373.
28. *Ibid.*, II, 270–71, III, 249.
29. *Ibid.*, III, 249–50.
30. See especially Larcy, *Des vicissitudes*, 495.
31. Meaux, *Souvenirs politiques*, 151–52. See also Vicomte Marie Camille Alfred de Meaux, "La Chambre Introuvable," *Le Correspondant*, LX (1863), 759.

1871 one of fruitful cooperation between the Right and the center Right? Chambord had himself encouraged optimism about cooperation by repeatedly paying homage to liberal principles in his numerous public pronouncements. When Chambord told Berryer in 1851 that he intended to respect "public liberties" and constitutional practices, most moderates were already convinced that the pretender had embraced the "liberal doctrines in the hearts and minds of the most intelligent and devoted defenders of the royalist cause." [32]

Nor did the moderates see recent French history as obstructing the social and political fusion of elites. Unlike the extreme Right, which viewed the French Revolution as the root of all evil, the moderates conceded that, despite its harmful effects, the French Revolution was a fait accompli that had wrought certain "inalienable and imperishable" changes. [33] Although punctuated by great crimes, the Revolution was in many repects a great success, they argued. A number of its most enduring legacies were neither anti-Christian nor antimonarchical. [34] By hindsight, it was easy for Falloux to see that the consequences of the Terror were transitory and that the "three or four principles" that had "become the basis of modern society" were "born more out of the efforts, thoughts, and reforms of the monarchy than out of the errors it made over two centuries." [35] Since the "conquests of 1789" had become the basis for a "new unanimity" among the elite, it was easy for them to view the Revolution of 1830 as the result of false personal impressions rather than great ideological conflicts. [36] Falloux recounted in his memoirs an informal visit he made with the Comte de Montalembert, Bishop Félix Dupanloup, and Thiers to Berryer's home at Augerville in 1852. As the conversation turned to the events of 1830, the partisans of the two defunct monarchies were astonished to learn that neither side had intended what the other presumed and that the collapse was the result of nothing more than impatience and a lack of communication. The real villians of 1830, they concluded, had been those on the Left who were

32. See Chambord, *La Monarchie française*, 42–43; and Charles de Lacombe, *Vie de Berryer*, I, ix.

33. Falloux, *Discours de M. de Falloux à l'Assemblée Nationale*, 19.

34. See Falloux, "De la Contre-Révolution," *Le Correspondant*, CXII (1878), 372.

35. Falloux, "Le Parti catholique," in *Discours et Mélanges politiques*, II, 113–14.

36. Falloux, *Discours de M. de Falloux à l'Assemblée Nationale*, 19; Gaillard, "L'Obstacle," *Le Correspondant*, LXXVI (1868), 7; Falloux, "Le Parti catholique," in *Discours et Mélanges politiques*, 117; Falloux, "Les Républicains et les Monarchistes," 395–96.

too persistent in their demands for reform and those on the extreme Right who, like Jules de Polignac, "believed [themselves] in supernatural communication with heaven." Afterward, Falloux told Thiers that "the July Revolution was due to a terrible misunderstanding" and concluded that France had to cease to be the "victim of such mistakes."[37]

The loyalty with which the moderates supported the restoration of the monarchy stemmed not from any appeal Chambord held for them but rather from their false impression that his endorsement of constitutionalism implied an attachment to parliamentary institutions and the liberal heritage of 1789. As the descendants of monarchists who had reacted against the absolutism of the Old Regime, the autocracy of Napoleon, and the political and religious intolerance of ultraroyalism, the moderates naturally equated representative government with political liberty and the enduring hegemony of the *grands notables*. Since the Republic had historically been the vehicle for the dangerous social experiments of bourgeois radicals and popular elements, the moderates were convinced that only a strong monarchist government, resting on an enduring conservative majority, could protect the social order and bring about the integration of the aristocracy and the conservative bourgeoisie. What they expected from Chambord was not the moral redemption of the nation but a guaranteed institutional framework through which the traditional elite might continue to enjoy its legitimate political and social predominance.[38] The result of the monarchical campaign, they hoped, would be a solid roadblock to the further democratization of French politics and society; the campaign's failure, they feared, would leave no choice but another Bonapartist dictatorship or a democratic and anticlerical Republic that would destroy "what remains of the influence of the upper classes."[39]

The priority placed on institutional frameworks was confirmed by the reaction of liberal Legitimists to the collapse of the monarchical campaign in 1873. Members of the moderate Right who remained loyal to the monarchy because of long-standing family traditions liked to think of their political choice as springing from reason and experience. Some

37. Pitman, trans. and ed., *Memoirs of the Count de Falloux,* II, 200–205, 350; Mazade, *L'Opposition royaliste,* 200.

38. See Noailles, *Le Bureau du Roi,* 268–69.

39. Comte Alfred de Falloux to Charles de Lacombe, November 6, 1873, in Charles de Lacombe's *Journal politique,* I, 228.

saw the institution of monarchy as a synthesis of order and liberty; others argued that a king provided "a fixed point and an element of perpetuity" to government in times of flux and uncertainty. Audren de Kerdrel, obviously no sentimentalist, told the Assembly that he was a Legitimist because hereditary monarchy assured a "wise preponderance of power and the stability of authority" in a parliamentary regime based on ministerial responsibility.[40] But if institutional safeguards were more important than abolishing the contradictions of modernity, it did not take a great leap of imagination for some moderates to conclude that the form executive power took was not the deciding condition for preserving the social hierarchy. The experience of the Second Republic and the liberal Empire, when a broad union of conservatives and liberals was able to moderate the regime and temporarily defend liberties from the autocratic aspirations of an executive who rejected legislative control, demonstrated that it was at least possible to achieve the ascendancy of liberal institutions without a monarchical restoration. Indeed, in 1851, Raudot thought that the Republic gave the Right a golden opportunity to "prepare the ground for a durable edifice."[41]

After the failure of the restoration and the installation of the ministry of the Duc de Broglie in 1873, the moderate Right joined the cabinet and worked to prolong the Republic while equipping it with conservative safeguards. The republic of the dukes may not have been the ideal of the liberal Legitimists, but they voted in favor of the Septennant, supported the presidency of Marshal Marie de MacMahon, and underwrote Broglie's attempt to create a conservative Senate dominated by wealthy notables. They also sponsored numerous modifications in the electoral laws with a view toward ensuring the preponderance of "intellect, wealth, and quality" in the Chamber at the expense of radical and socialist constituencies.[42] With such measures, the moderates hoped to secure

40. *Annales*, XI, 152.
41. Raudot, *De la grandeur possible de la France*, 14.
42. Meaux, *Souvenirs politiques*, 214–17. According to Meaux, Broglie's Grand Council was to provide a "counterweight to the omnipotence of numbers" and more "maturity in deliberations, more order and method in legislative work," by "disengaging from French society the elements of strength and stability it contains, in order to extract from it a truly conservative senate." In fact, the second chamber was designed to institutionalize the power of the old *pays légal* by assuring representation to former deputies and to general counselors, magistrates, the high clergy, presidents of the *chambres de notaires*, deans and professors of departmental faculties, military officers, high functionaries, recipients of the Legion

an aristocratic republic and forestall the political advent of Gambetta's *nouvelles couches*. Lacombe said, "The monarchy is absent, . . . but society remains." It was, according to Roger de Dampierre, "necessary to seek the means and the opportunity to save France . . . without [the] legitimate monarchy."[43]

Failing to check the drift of opinion toward the republicans, the Right lost control of the Chamber of Deputies in 1876. After the Seize Mai crisis of 1877, when conservatives unsuccessfully tried to engineer a comeback by bringing the full weight of the administration to bear on the electorate, many Legitimists lost hope and returned to internal exile.[44] Numerous leaders of the moderate Right, including Falloux, died in the early 1880s, about the same time as Chambord, only to be replaced by a new generation of liberal monarchists like Baron Armand de Mackau and Henri de Breteuil, who, although committed to the restoration of the Comte de Paris, used plebiscitarian tactics against the liberal, parliamentary Republic. Finally achieving fusion, many Legitimists joined with the Orleanists and other rightists in the Conservative Union of 1885, which benefited from general dissatisfaction with the policies of the Opportunists. Unable to bring down the Republic, the conservative coalition had to be satisfied with a minimal program designed to roll back republican reforms.

By the end of the Boulanger Affair in 1889, the Right had come under the increasing control of younger men whose growing antipathy toward parliamentarianism and an open society would have disturbed men like

---

d'honneur, and the highest taxpayers in agriculture and business. As for the Chamber of Deputies, most moderates suddenly discovered the benefits of corporate representation, and even Falloux, who disagreed with the corporatists on so many matters, concluded that an electoral law based on the representation of interests would be preferable and that, although the former corps of the Old Regime were gone, "modern counterparts" could be found. Along these lines, Dampierre and a number of *propriétaires* from the Gironde suggested dividing citizens into four categories (large landowners and industrialists; proprietors, merchants, and *rentiers;* professionals; and the proletariat), each with an equal number of representatives in the Chamber. See also Falloux to Lacombe, July, 1875, in Charles de Lacombe's *Journal politique*, I, 124; and Pétition à l'Assemblée Nationale déposé par M. de Dampierre, December 18, 1873, in C4260, AN.

43. Charles de Lacombe, *Journal politique*, II, 375; Roger de Dampierre to Comte de Chambord, in Meaux's *Souvenirs politiques*, 132. See also Meaux, *Souvenirs politiques*, 334; Rémond, *Les Droites en France*, 137; Gaillard, *Les Etapes*, ii–xvi; and Denis, "Un Aspect du conservatisme," 394.

44. On the role of the Legitimists in the government's preparations for the elections of 1877, see Levillain, *Albert de Mun*, 551–54.

Falloux and Berryer. Ironically, the liberal Legitimists, who preened themselves on being conversant with modern times, were men of the early nineteenth century in their attitudes, more comfortable with salon politics and parliamentary reports than with *ligues* and mass electioneering. They would have been content to play the role of English Tories within the framework of a constitutional monarchy in which a peaceful *alternance* between rational and civilized elite parties was the basis for stability and gradual reform. In 1873, Audren de Kerdrel had already announced the demise of the Legitimist party and told his friends, "We now become *Tories* devoted as before to the ideas of order and liberty, to decentralization, to the family, to religion, to society; in a word, we should guard and defend the ideas and principles whose vehicle the monarchy once was."[45]

But France was not England. French republicans were far more radical than the party of Gladstone, and the animosity of the Right toward secularization and democracy created a politics too inflexible to allow peaceful shifts from Right to Left. If Falloux and Berryer had lived, they might have decided to join the Ralliés or they might have founded some kind of republican conservative movement to the right of the Opportunists. Indeed, many royalists moved silently toward the center in the twenty years before the First World War in an effort to escape political isolation by accepting a prudent antisocialist Republic.[46] This "discreet *ralliement*" was no doubt belated and painful, but it was perhaps inevitable for those who cherished the exercise of power as much as they respected France's monarchical tradition.

SOCIAL CATHOLIC LEGITIMISM: FROM COUNTERREVOLUTION TO *RALLIEMENT*

By placing their hopes for the stabilization of French society in the assured hegemony of the *grands notables,* the liberal Legitimists had sought a political solution to the menace of secular democracy. Agrarian, aristocratic, and more concerned with decentralization than with the morality of the capitalist system, the liberals offered little that chimed with the preoccupations of other Legitimists who believed that the threat to the traditional social order lay in the problems associated with urbaniza-

45. V. de Kerdrel to Barthélemy Pocquet, in *Légitimistes parlementaries,* ed. Pocquet du Haut-Jussé, 167.
46. See Denis, *Les Royalistes de la Mayenne,* 529–30.

tion and industrial expansion. As early as 1849, Armand de Melun had only been irritated by the clamor for decentralization and budgetary restraints, since it worked against proposals to extend public assistance. Mun, who never got on well with the older royalist cadres, had accorded the Legitimist obsession with decentralization and administrative reform an entirely secondary importance. Intent above all upon questions related to the industrial era, Mun was a spokesman for a brand of royalism that had little resonance for rural oligarchs who wanted the freedom to rule their social subordinates in peace. For many younger Legitimists, largely sympathetic to the extreme Right in political matters, the social question and the philosophic combat against the Revolution appeared infinitely more exciting and relevant than the prosaic constitutional and administrative details that absorbed Raudot's life. For them, the monarchy of the notables did not sufficiently address modern social and moral issues, nor did it satisfy their desire to confront what they saw as the disintegration of civil society.

Although the moderates were apt to remember the Chambord of 1849–1851, who declared his allegiance to liberal principles and sided with Berryer in the struggle between parliamentarians and intransigents for control of the party, many royalists of Mun's generation recalled the "Letter on the Workers" of 1864 and embraced the pretender's growing antipathy toward liberalism and bourgeois society. Chambord had throughout his political career, tried to strike a balance between the different factions in the party, but by the 1870s he had clearly come to sympathize with the extreme Right. His shift in sentiment was reinforced by the crisis of the white flag, and in 1878 Chambord explicitly adopted the term *counterrevolution*. He became increasingly reliant on the political advice of Mun and Joseph de La Bouillerie, and he concluded that "for France to be saved, God must reign there as a master before I can reign there as a king."[47] Mun, confident of the pretender's blessing and increasingly hostile toward the Legitimist parliamentary leadership—whom he judged "almost entirely liberal" and prone to "political and social conceptions" that "came close to openly Orleanist tendencies"—awaited a restoration which would inaugurate the Christian regeneration of society.[48] Like the moderates, Mun endorsed a monarchy that complemented his priorities, and he saw in Chambord exactly what he wanted to see.

47. Mun, *Ma vocation sociale*, 181–82.
48. *Ibid*.

Yet the marriage between counterrevolutionary social Catholicism and the monarchy proved precarious. Mun, like many of his colleagues, was too young to remember the debates of the Restoration, or even the conservative rapprochement of the 1840s. Indeed, his encounter with royalist politics began in 1870 through the medium of the social Catholic and clerical movements—both of which had maintained only a fraternal relationship with the Legitimist party—and his intellectual inspiration derived not from the Vicomte de Chateaubriand, Pierre Paul Royer-Collard, and Alexis de Tocqueville, but from the Syllabus of Errors and the works of Emile Keller. Keller, who considered himself "Catholic first," equated faith with the search for social justice and saw the "principles of 1789" as the greatest obstacle to the construction of a Christian social order. During the Second Empire, clerical leaders had tried to distance themselves from dynastic politics and had sought to create unanimity among conservatives in favor of legislative and policy reforms that would protect religious interests.[49] At a time when overt opposition to the regime of Napoleon III was risky, many Legitimists got used to speaking about the need to preserve "eternal" social and religious values that existed "above political forms and . . . inseparable from any form of government whatsoever."[50] Monsignor Edouard Pie wrote in a pastoral letter in 1870, "Jesus Christ did not dictate to Christian nations the form of their political constitutions," because politics was contingent and Catholics recognized the "relative equal value of all constitutional systems." If Pie and many in the French episcopate preferred Chambord after Sedan, they did so for practical religious reasons, having determined that the Republic would be a threat to the church and that legitimacy could help bring the "social reign of Jesus Christ."[51]

In October, 1879, the papal nuncio, Archbishop Czacky, tried to modify Legitimist strategy when he told the Comte de Balcas and the Marquis de Dreux-Brézé, two of the pretender's political officers, that the monarchists were "definitively defeated" and that "religious interests" could best be served if the royalists united around a program de-

49. See Discours de Dr. Frédault, April 4–6, 1872, in *Comité catholique de Paris*, 44–45.

50. See Gavardie, *Etudes sur les vraies doctrines sociales*, 11, 104.

51. Lettre pastorale et Mandement portent publication de la bulle apostolique annoncer la suspension du concile oecumenique, October 13, 1870, in Catta's *La Doctrine politique et sociale du Cardinal Pie*, 321; Baunard, *Histoire du cardinal Pie*, II, 478–79; Gadille, *La Pensée et l'Action politiques des évêques françaises*, I, 57.

signed to defend the church. Since France had chosen the Republic, he argued, the Legitimists were likely to lose what was left of their influence if they continued to work for a restoration. Dreux-Brézé, who claimed that Legitimist candidates had obligations to constituents who despised the Republic, rejected Czacky's proposition. But the suggestion that a monarchical restoration was neither the only nor the wisest means of attaining Catholic social and religious goals had been sanctioned by the authority of the Holy See.[52]

Deferential toward Rome and predisposed to view conditions in France from the perspective of religious and social issues, the leaders of the Oeuvre de Cercles also questioned the value of conventional Legitimist electoral politics. Mun and other socially oriented Legitimists believed that the political solution the liberals sought for France's social crisis was bound to fail because the monarchy could not be restored until society had been regenerated. Catholics, they felt, should turn their attention away from the senseless attempt to change the government and concentrate on propaganda and social action. After 1877, Mun sought to disassociate the Oeuvre from the royalist political committees that were controlled chiefly by conservative landowners beholden to the traditionalists in Chambord's entourage. Those men did not share Mun's social radicalism. Although some social Catholics, like René de La Tour Du Pin, wanted to remain active in the royalist struggle, others argued that the "Oeuvre should not become a political party, nor the organ or the instrument of a political party." They feared that too great an association with the monarchist cause would impede them in the task of Catholic social reform, tarnish reputations, and divide and weaken the organization.[53]

Mun recommended that, instead of trying to court the liberal bourgeoisie without converting it, the royalists embrace the interests of the masses through the "Christian reform of society," which would create "the basis and the condition of the reestablishment of the monarchy."[54] As Léon Harmel told La Tour Du Pin in 1880, "If all Catholics worked to raise the morality of those around them and to Christianize them, if

52. Dreux-Brézé, *Notes et Souvenirs*, 178–81. Chambord responded to the news of this proposal by commenting, "I thought the church forbade suicide" (Brown, *The Comte de Chambord*, 169). Maurras made the same reply when the Vatican condemned Action Française in 1926.

53. Levillain, *Albert de Mun*, 575; P. Hubin to Louis de Villermont, January 5, 1878, in Mollet's *Albert de Mun*, Documents, 172.

54. Mun, *Ma vocation sociale*, 185. See also Rollet, *L'Action sociale*, 152.

they sought to attach the people to themselves through creative [social] institutions, they would form a Christian people and the king would return without needing the support of newspapers or of illusionists who render his governance impossible."[55]

Since Mun looked toward finding support for the restoration of the monarchy in an alliance between the Catholic elite and the masses rather than in a coalition of notables, he used the term *counterrevolution* freely and discounted liberal fears that such rhetoric would scare the Orleanists. Naturally, the moderate Right saw an emphasis on counterrevolution as the surest way to scuttle the fusionist campaign; in an open letter in *L'Union de l'Ouest,* which circulated in Mun's electoral district in Morbihan, Falloux denounced the "supreme blindness" of using "this symbol" and argued that the counterrevolutionaries were abandoning Legitimist principles and helping the adversaries of the monarchy.[56]

By the late 1870s, the two factions of the Legitimist party had ceased to speak the same language. Unlike Falloux, who saw the principal reforms of 1789 as the basis for a conservative consensus, Mun and other "clericals" viewed the Declaration of the Rights of Man and Citizens as unholy writ for the establishment of a society founded on merely human volition. In place of the society created by the Revolution, Mun wanted a society reconstructed according to the "will of God." Counterrevolution did not imply a return to the Old Regime but a "social transformation that will be contrary to the Revolution, because it will be supported upon clearly opposed principles."[57] By his own account, Mun needed a slogan that would "designate clearly and in a gripping and immediate way the work of social and political reform that we pursued, which had as its object the founding of institutions inspired by a spirit diametrically opposed to that of the Revolution."[58] He argued, "The Revolution already existed in the Old Regime . . . in the form of rationalist philosophy, social egotism, class antagonism, . . . and state persecution of the church." The Republicans had become the "executors" and "natural heirs" of an abusive and corrosive social and political order that Catholics had always opposed. In 1789, he claimed, the nation had wanted to re-

---

55. Léon Harmel to René La Tour Du Pin-Chambly, July 26, 1880, in Xavier Vallet's *La Croix, les Lys et la Peine des hommes* (Paris, 1960), 24.

56. Falloux, "De la Contre-Révolution," *Le Correspondant,* CXIII (1878), 363–77.

57. Quoted by Charles Maignen in *Maurice Maignen,* II, 966.

58. Albert de Mun to Paul du Lac, 1884, in Levillain's *Albert de Mun,* 623–24.

turn "frankly to its Christian vocation" but was thwarted by the Revolution; thus, the true revolution, the counterrevolution, had yet to occur. The Republic, having perfected the regime of economic privilege, class conflict, and the philosophical intolerance born of the Enlightenment, needed to be replaced, like the corrupt Old Regime, with a new order that broke definitively with the errors of the past.[59] As a counteroffensive against the application of revolutionary principles to society, the new Christian society, based on "the principles of the Catholic church and the infallible teachings of the sovereign pontiff" would be antiparliamentarian, anti-individualistic, and antimaterialistic; it would be "guaranteed by the devotion of the strong to the weak" and thus would be able to do without the support of the liberal capitalist bourgeoisie.[60]

It was far from clear, however, whether a counterrevolutionary struggle could be mounted in conjunction with a faltering monarchical campaign dominated by liberal monarchists who cared little about social and economic reform. Aware of the difficulties, Mun supported leaders of the Oeuvre who wanted to separate their activities from Legitimist politics, and he remained suspicious of the social conservatives who sat on the Right in Parliament.[61] He was truly devoted to Chambord, but his devotion was premised on his belief that the pretender had embraced his counterrevolutionary program. Although a Legitimist "by habit" rather than "by reflection," Mun reasoned in the early 1870s that Chambord represented his best personal choice because "at the time the monarchy, such as the Comte de Chambord presented it, seemed to me to be the political expression of the ideas germinating in my mind." He added, "I understood it as the antithesis of the Revolution, and . . . I wanted to see it triumph with this program."[62]

59. *Annales de la Chambre des Députés,* November 16, 1878, IX, 294–95.
60. Texte de l'Extractum Liebig, in Mollet's *Albert de Mun,* Documents, 169; Albert de Mun to Félix de Roquefeuil, July 27, 1878," *ibid.,* Documents, 178–79.
61. See Albert de Mun to Félix de Roquefeuil, June 20, 1878, in Mollet's *Albert de Mun,* 174; Discours d'Albert de Mun, June 2, 1877; *ibid.,* 48, L'Extractum Leibig, *ibid.,* 169. In 1881, at the beginning of the Republic's first anticlerical campaign, Mun, then a deputy from Morbihan, delivered a speech at Vannes, at the request of Chambord, in which he attacked the Republic as the enemy of the church and the workers, and called for a monarchy that would "strive to solve . . . the social question." At the same time, he notified the leaders of the Oeuvre that this "political speech" was only an expression of his personal opinions and "not a headline for our common work." See Mun, *Ma vocation social,* 242. The text of the speech can be found in Moon, *The Labor Problem,* 90–91.
62. Mun, *Ma vocation sociale,* 55–57.

Although the new Christian social order might have had natural links
to the Legitimist tradition, it was impossible for Mun to reconcile Chambord's political inaction with the social mobilization needed to forge a
base for a counterrevolutionary restoration. According to Mun, the
monarchy would not be restored through principled obstinacy or party
transactions; it would require a "long struggle" to build a vast popular
movement working to regenerate the social order and willing to call
upon a Christian prince to act as the guarantor and "social expression"
of a nation in the process of redemption.[63] In order to remain a monarchist and actively work for the restoration of the monarchy, Mun had to
try to transform the royalist movement into the organized vanguard of
the coming Christian social revival. That task was greatly complicated
by Chambord's death in 1883, because in the absence of a sympathetic
pretender Mun had grave doubts about whether the monarchy he was
working to restore would be truly Christian.[64] Though he pledged to
support the Comte de Paris, he had no great enthusiasm for the new
pretender's liberal proclivities and even less for the group of Orleanists
and Legitimist moderates who controlled the political direction of the
movement and whom he characterized as an "elite of academicians, literary hacks, and cabinet politicians whose influence does not extend beyond the salons of Paris and the corridors of assemblies."[65] He joined the
Conservative Union in the early 1880s and participated in the Boulanger
fiasco, but he was aware that the leaders of the Right, clinging to their
conservative social views, stubbornly opposed the social legislation he
introduced in the Chamber.

Before deciding to follow an independent course, however, Mun tried
to bring the monarchist leadership to his program by outflanking it politically. Certain in 1885 that the Conservative Union's parliamentary tactics and its indifference to social issues had exhausted its electoral appeal,
Mun decided to launch a nondynastic Catholic party capable of rallying
a new majority behind a program of religious defense and social reform.
In its attempt to get the Comte de Paris to see the light and in its aim of
demonstrating to the monarchists that social royalism could win on the
electoral terrain, the Catholic party was a complete failure.[66] The project

63. Discours d'Albert de Mun, June 2, 1877, in Mollet's *Albert de Mun,* 49; Albert de
Mun to Félix de Roquefuil, July 26, 1877, *ibid.,* 170.
64. See Albert de Mun to Hyroix, July, 1883, in Levillain's *Albert de Mun,* 745.
65. Levillain, *Albert de Mun,* 758.
66. *Ibid.,* 866, 1020.

immediately provoked opposition from conservative leaders like Keller, Mackau, Charles Chesnelong, and the Comte d'Haussonville, who were either jealous of their political positions, concerned about maintaining unity on the Right, or weary of the threat Mun's ideas posed to their material interests. Meanwhile, the Vatican, hoping to protect the French church from further anticlerical legislation, thought that a confessional party that challenged the hegemony of the republicans would only invite more persecution. The pope consequently let it be known that he viewed Mun's plans as inopportune. Defeated and more isolated than ever, Mun quickly tried to patch up relations with the leaders of the Right and turned his attention once again toward the Oeuvre.

As politically unsuccessful as the attempt to create a Catholic party was, it represented a real threat to the royalist establishment, because it deemphasized constitutional issues and gave concrete form to Mun's thesis that the monarchical form of government could be reinstated only as the result of a social transformation requiring the support of a Catholic mass movement. Mun's actions underlined the proposition that the Conservative Union could never be the vehicle for accomplishing the counterrevolution and that the majority of the people, tired of the bourgeois Republic, would never rally to a bourgeois monarchy dominated by notables who merely desired an "Orleanist-style restoration." The social order, he argued, could be saved only if the impetus for change came not from "discredited . . . political milieus" but from "centers of intellectual and social activity among men of work, study, and action, and [from] the popular milieu more sensitive to [the people's] interests and . . . needs than to parliamentary preoccupations."[67] Benjamin F. Martin has suggested that Mun "saw himself as a French Ludwig Winsthorst, leading a nation-wide, society-wide Catholic movement, a Catholic party in which he could move the focus of conservative politics [away] from the restoration of the throne."[68] This allusion to the German Zentrum is a tenuous analogy at best, since Mun envisioned a more radical movement that would draw its principal support from urban sectors of the population and that in France would likely tend toward the Right and embrace some sort of constitutional revision. Moreover, his conception of the role of the Oeuvre was more similar to that of Lenin's vanguard than to that of a parliamentary leadership in parties accepting the rules of a bourgeois

67. *Ibid.*, 343. See also Albert de Mun to Gicquel de Touches, in Alexander Sedgwick's *The Ralliement in French Politics, 1880–1898* (Cambridge, Mass., 1965), 16.
68. Benjamin F. Martin, *Count Albert de Mun*, 58–59.

democracy. But Mun's experiment was bound to fail quite apart from the attitude of the papacy or the jealousy of the Right because, though it involved political independence from established conservatives, it required a mass following that had to include traditionally conservative constituencies. In France, any Catholic party that tried to unite aristocrats, Catholics, clerical elements, and workers while refusing to commit itself to loyalty to the Republic would inevitably appear suspect to the Left and would thus have to seek allies among the royalist notables who Mun believed were incapable of attracting real popular support. Mun encountered the same predicament during the Boulanger Affair, when he found himself working to tap the "popular reaction against the omnipotence of financiers [and] the power of Mammon" while cooperating with conservative aristocrats whom he viewed as "too imbued with their bourgeois spirit [and] too involved with high finance . . . to espouse resolutely the cause of the masses."[69] Even after he joined the *ralliement* in 1892 and tried to relaunch the Catholic party, he remained cut off from monarchists who did not adhere to the papal encyclical, from republicans who detested his opposition to the principles of 1789, and from conservative Ralliés like Etienne Lamy and Jacques Piou, who thought that the best way to help the church and secure an alliance with the Opportunists was to renounce demands for social reform. As Mun admitted in 1908, the second attempt at a Catholic party failed because of the "difficulty of bringing together a sufficient number of adherents."[70]

Ultimately he had to circumvent that impediment by working alone to solicit fraternal support for social legislation on the extreme Left. By his own admission, he had lost his "political faith" in the 1880s but remained a social Catholic the rest of his life. After 1885, he became an "opportunist," accepting allies wherever he could find them.[71] On October 10, 1889, he gave an interview to the *Pall Mall Gazette* in which he elaborated a government program stressing religious and social concerns. On October 13, he broke openly with the Comte de Paris, and the next day he told *L'Univers* of his willingness "to offer the example of a pacific

69. *L'Univers*, October 13, 1899, in Mollet's *Albert de Mun*, 104–105n; Levillain, *Albert de Mun*, 961–62.

70. Albert de Mun, *La Conquête du peuple* (2nd ed.; Paris, 1908), 21. See also Benjamin F. Martin, *Count Albert de Mun*, 96–97; Sedgwick, *The Ralliement*, 59; Talmy, *Aux sources du catholicisme social*, 288–89.

71. See Levillain, *Albert de Mun*, 452–53.

acceptance of the de facto government if that government became stable, honest, respectful of religion, and mindful of the true interests of the people."[72] Already inclined to obey papal instructions that French Catholics accept the existing political constitution, Mun rallied to the Republic in May, 1892, vowing to "accept the form" but "change the substance" of the regime.[73]

Alienated from a royalist movement that many liberal Legitimists found congenial after 1883, Mun abandoned the monarchical *forme* to save the *fond* of the Christian social order. Like the liberals who had defected in the 1870s, Mun concluded that the monarchy was an obstacle to the type of social reconstruction he desired.

PROPHECY AND FANTASY:
THE "BLANCS D'ESPAGNE"

One faction of the Legitimist party that experienced no such loss of faith were the Blancs d'Espagne, a handful of Chambord's most ardent supporters who eventually abandoned the French royal family for its Spanish cousins in order to preserve the integrity of Legitimist principles. Led by Guillaume Véran, Joseph Du Bourg, and Maurice d'Andigné, the Blancs adhered to the old principle of *droit national,* inspired by the obscure theories of the Abbé de Genoude and Henri de Lourdoueix, who edited the *Gazette de France* and led the intransigent wing of the Legitimist party in the 1830s and 1840s. These future partisans of the house of Anjou had enthusiastically supported Chambord's *politique des principes* as the only way to forestall the advent of a radical republic. They believed that the Assembly and the nation, which in their opinion had a historical obligation to recognize the legitimacy of the monarchical principle, should simply have proclaimed Chambord king of France without opposing his demand of the fleur-de-lis. Having failed to do so, France was bound, they thought, to suffer the consequences of Orleanist intrigue and republican treachery. As Véran wrote in 1883, "The fall of Marshal MacMahon and the triumph of Jacobin despotism . . . have justified the great policy of the king. . . . The monarchy was not formed:

72. See *ibid.,* 956–57; *L'Univers,* October 14, 1889, in Mollet's *Albert de Mun,* 105n.
73. Speech to the Ligue de Propaganda Catholique et Sociale, May, 1892, in Sedgwick's *The Ralliement,* 59.

the dukes, leaders of the centrist parties, provided the obstacle. The fall toward the leftist Republic had begun."[74]

The Blancs' inflexibility was grounded in convictions the polar opposite of Mun's that social reform had to precede the restoration of the monarchy. Since the legitimate monarchy signified, guaranteed, and consecrated the religious principle of social authority necessary for maintaining order in the family and society, intransigent Legitimists argued, it had been the attack launched against the Bourbon monarchy in 1789 that had destroyed the social order in the first place. If the sovereign exercise of authority by a legitimate and hereditary monarch was inseparable from "all the relationships upon which God had founded society," it was useless to set about the task of social reconstruction until the legitimate monarchy had been restored.[75] As Emmanuel Lucien-Brun, a *chevau-léger* from Ain, asked the social reformers in Frédéric Le Play's *Union de la paix sociale* in 1872,

> How . . . do you hope to reestablish authority and order in the family, the workshop, and the communes as long as order does not reign at the summit of the state—as long as the primary social authority is not reestablished? Nothing is assured for tomorrow, and you wish to undertake the long work of social restoration! Tomorrow, perhaps, the government will be in the hands of the enemies of all order, all honest custom, all rules. Each day, each hour can lead to an upheaval that will leave nothing standing of what still remains. Is it wise to undertake repairs on an edifice assailed by a horde of demolishers and incendiaries? First remove the most pressing peril; at least assure yourselves of some good protection and some security against the invaders for a few days. Extinguish the flames before returning to work on the shaken foundations of your house. The political question precedes all others; it dominates everything. Resolve it first, and the rest will come in time.[76]

Since "the Republic [was] the form of government of the enemies of God and of the Christian social order," it was foolish to think that Catholics

74. Véran, *Les Habiles,* 72.

75. See Gavardie, *Etudes sur les vraies doctrines sociales,* 280; Muller, *La Légitimité,* 284; and Véran, *La Légitimité devant le catholicisme,* 18.

76. Discours de Emmanuel Lucien-Brun, in *L'Union de la paix sociale,* II (Tours, 1872), 6–8.

could ignore the constitutional question; thus, Mun's Catholic party, according to another *chevau-léger,* was an "error twenty times condemned by experience and no less harmful to religion than to the monarchy."[77]

Moreover, Legitimists of the extreme Right wanted an immaculate restoration because, as the political incarnation of universal truth, the monarchy could brook no error without leading people astray.[78] Earlier French monarchies, including the Restoration regime, had ended in disaster because they were inconsistent with national tradition and the ancient origins of the kingdom. Unlike the liberal Legitimists who believed that Chambord had endorsed modern constitutional government, the extreme Right paid homage to a pretender who promised to return the monarchy to its true character by embracing the "national movement of the end of the last century."[79] Ernest La Roche advanced the idea that the Revolution had begun as an effort to recover France's ancient constitution from the wreckage of feudalism and absolutism but had been perverted by a small faction that "introduced the revolutionary spirit into the government of France and . . . brought all the misfortunes . . . from which we have suffered for eighty years."[80] The regime produced by the first National Assembly was, he affirmed, criminal and could never constitute a point of departure for a new restoration.[81] Véran argued, rather, that it was the *Cahiers de Doléances* that recalled the fundamental laws of the kingdom and that the Estates General had been obliged to use as a reformist blueprint. As the last authentic expression of the national will of a free people assembled under its natural institutions, the *Cahiers* affirmed the inviolability of the hereditary monarchy, proved that France's aspirations were perfectly consistent with tradition, and demonstrated that the masses had never abandoned the king. Thus, according to Véran, it was through the *Cahiers* that the ancient constitution might find "its way back to its proper historical state of development, despite the inter-

77. Emmanuel Lucien-Brun, *La Politique des expédients et la Politique des principes* (Paris, 1881), 9; Edouard de Cazenove de Pradine, *L'Espérance du Nantes,* October 4, 1885, in Levillain's *Albert de Mun,* 840.

78. See Véran, *Les Habiles;* Le Serrac de Kervily, *Manifeste d'un légitimiste,* 86–87; La Roche, *Les Nationaux et les Partis,* 492–93; Guillaume Véran, "Lettre fraternelle à M. H. Lassere, directeur du journal contemporain," *Revue Indépendante,* III (October 15, 1864), 193–201.

79. See Chambord's Manifesto of July, 1871, in Castries' *Le Grand Refus,* 151.

80. La Roche, *Les Nationaux et les Partis,* 112–13. See also Armailhac, *La Légitimité et le Progrès,* 96.

81. See also Andre Barbès, *Les Traditions nationales autrefois et aujourd'hui dans la nation française* (Paris, 1873), 292–93.

ruption of feudalism, the civil and religious wars, and the absolutist regime that, after the Estates of 1614, encompassed the reigns of Louis
XIII, Louis XIV, and Louis XV and ended up at the convocation of the
nation by Louis XVI."[82] Since all acts taken by the Third Estate that
exceeded the specific mandate tradition sanctioned were criminal, the extremists maintained, it was a revolutionary minority that had violated
the people's trust and destroyed the "accord between the nation and the
king." When the delegates took the Tennis Court Oath, La Roche explained, they usurped legitimate authority based on divine law and replaced it with a revocable social contract that legitimated all manner of
insubordination and left society exposed to permanent revolution. The
repercussions of that act ranged from the Terror to the advent of socialism and from party divisions to realism in the arts.[83]

The extremists' point, of course, was that the notables should have
learned from their own history that the abandonment of integral principles leads to national and social suicide. The experience of the Revolution, the extremists insisted, was eloquent testimony that it was impossible to find a remedy for revolutionary ideas in the ideas of the
Revolution itself.[84] That is what had brought about the failure of the
Restoration of 1815, since the "fabricated English Charter" broke with
tradition, accepted parliamentary sovereignty, deprived the people of a
role in the framing of the laws, and turned the government over to "men
of the Revolution" who believed in the wisdom of compromises.[85] By
limiting the electorate to a small minority, Louis XVIII gave political
ascendancy to wealthy notables imbued with the "philosophical, skeptical, and antireligious spirit" while depriving the faithful masses of
the political rights they had enjoyed under the ancient constitution.
Thus, the monarchy isolated itself from the people, grew unpopular,
and helped the "Orleanist faction" usurp royal authority with impunity
in 1830.[86]

82. Véran, in *Revue Independante*, III (August 1, 1864), 33; Véran, *La Légitimité devant le
catholicisme*, 28–29; Véran, *Les Solutions*, 64–65.

83. La Roche, *Les Nationaux et les Partis*, 132–35, ix. See also Armailhac, *La Légitimité
et le Progrès*, 60–64; and Véran, in *Revue Independante*, III (August 1, 1864), 34–42.

84. La Roche, *Les Nationaux et les Partis*, 140–41.

85. Henri de Lourdoueix, in Véran's *La Question du XIXe siècle*, 436–39; Muller, *La
Légitimité*, 225–26; Barbès, *Les Traditions nationales*, 311–15; Véran, *Les Solutions*, 13.

86. Véran, *La Question du XIXe siècle*, 439, 249; Henri de Lourdoueix, *La Révolution,
c'est l'Orléanisme* (Paris, 1852), 235–36; Véran, *Les Solutions*, 12–13; Véran, *L'Empire plébiscitaire*, 57–58; Muller, *La Légitimité*, 271–72.

The extreme Right believed that it was therefore a testament to Chambord's great wisdom and historical insight that he intended to avoid a repetition of earlier fatal compromises in 1873, by insisting on the white flag.[87] Véran felt that the moderates should have recognized the virtue of Chambord's position and worked to convoke the "nation in its primary assemblies in order to elect a new National Assembly armed with regular powers and, in accord with royal authority, ready to undertake the work of restoring the political constitution of France."[88] Instead, he observed, the *habiles* tried to fuse legitimacy and the Revolution, thereby placing the future monarchy in the hands of Orleanists who never intended "to save France, but only this Revolution, which ideological passions or calculations of interest would once again identify with the destiny of the country."[89] Fearing Chambord's popularity and his intention to create a truly just and national regime, the Orleanists used the white flag as a pretext to isolate the extreme Right and trap the wavering moderates in a center Right majority that would be positioned to "choose a king who was, above all, a partisan of the principles of eighty-nine and who would recognize their right to overthrow him."[90] Such intrigues, the Extremists explained, resulted in the Septennant, which was meant to give the parliamentary monarchists latitude in the event of Chambord's abdication or death, after which an "Aumalian stadholder" would pave the way for a restoration of the regime of 1830. The revolutionary cycle would have begun all over again, since the Septennant was the "vestibule of the Orleanist monarchy" and the "revolutionary monarchy" was the "quickly traversed antechamber of the socialist republic."[91] Throughout the regrettable farce, Véran maintained, the liberal

87. See Bernardi, *La Révolution*, 67–68.

88. Véran, *L'Empire plébiscitaire*, 10–11.

89. Bernardi, *La Révolution*, 68. See also the speech by the Marquis de La Rochejacquelein, in *Annales*, February 24, XXXVI, 621.

90. Bernardi, *La Révolution*, 76. See also Loth, *L'Echec de la restauration monarchique*, 306–307, 452–54.

91. Robinet de Clery, *Les deux fusions, 1800–1873* (Paris, 1908), 245; Le Serrac de Kervily, *Manifeste d'un légitimiste*, 67. See Loth, *L'Echec de la restauration monarchique*, 105–106, 526–27, 534–35; Véran, *Les Habiles*, 98–99; Discours du G. Véran, in Maurice d'Andigné's *Le Roi légitime* (Paris, 1884), 96–97; and *Les Légitimistes à Ste-Anne-d'Auray, le 29 séptembre 1887* (Paris, 1887), 55. The extreme Right maintained that it was the Orleanists who voted for the Wallon Amendment and made the Republic possible. Rudelle, however, found that the Right's majority had been overturned by defections and by a number of by-elections after February, 1871. Unlike the centrist majority that supported Thiers' Pact of Bordeaux, the majority that voted in favor of the constitutional laws of 1875 sat on the left-hand side

Legitimists, obsessed with *royalisme à la anglaise,* were the "unconscious accomplices" of the Orleanists, who were the dupes of the republicans.[92]

When Chambord died, many on the extreme Right were loath to recognize the Comte de Paris as heir to the throne. During the 1870s, an enormous amount of ill will had built between Legitimist factions, each of which blamed the other for the failure of the restoration. According to Robinet de Clery, certain *chevaux-légers*—most notably Mun and Belcastel—feared that the royalist cause could not survive an extended quarrel over succession at a time of great danger and reluctantly rallied to Philippe VII. Many others, like de Clery himself, concluded "that the true monarchy . . . died with the king" and retired from politics altogether or, bowing to papal encouragement, joined the struggle against the Republic's religious and educational policies.[93] A minority of dissidents, too small to be politically effective, refused either to give up the fight or to accept a place in a royalist movement dominated by liberals and incarnated in a usurper whom they viewed as antipathetic to true Legitimist principles. These last, the Blancs d'Espagne, contested the succession of Philippe VII by citing certain irregularities in the Treaty of Utrecht of 1713—which was supposed to have barred the Spanish Bourbons from claiming rights to the French throne—and swore allegiance to Don Jaime of Spain. Led in the main by Breton aristocrats and Chambord loyalists based in Paris, the Blancs launched the *Journal de Paris* in October, 1883, under the editorship of Henri Marchand, who called it the only true Legitimist paper left in France. With a handful of adherents drawn mainly from the nobility and the Parisian petite bourgeoisie, the Blancs held their first "Legitimist congress" on July 27, 1884. There, Véran and Andigné argued their case concerning the succession question and called for a restoration based on the "principles of Catholicism, monarchy, and representative liberty demanded by the French nation in 1789 as the foundation of its natural constitution."[94]

---

of the National Assembly. There was no *conjunction des centres* in favor of the Third Republic. If some Orleanist were "guilty" of making the constitution of 1875 possible, the democratic and laic Republic was not their creation. See Rudelle, *La République absolue,* 37–39.

92. Véran, *Les Habiles,* 2–3, 6–7, 50–51, 96–97; Loth, *L'Echec de la restauration monarchique,* 525.

93. Robinet de Clery, *Les deux fusions,* 324–29.

94. Discours de M. Véran, in Andigné's *Le Roi légitime,* 92–93. This volume contains the *compte rendu* of the Congrès du Comité Populaire Légitimiste de Paris. For the history

Such talk about forgotten treaties, collateral branches, and natural constitutions masked the Blancs' desire to be liberated from the annoying distortions and subtle compromises imposed by the exigencies of coalition politics. By taking refuge in pure orthodoxy and by severing all ties with bourgeois liberalism, and thus with those who would sully the Legitimist idea, the Blancs hoped to recapture a vision of the monarchy that bypassed the heretical middle class and established a direct link with the people they believed providence had chosen to demolish the Revolution and reverse the misfortunes of history. Like the old *école du droit national*, the Blancs d'Espagne called for an alliance between the monarchy and the people, against the narrow class rule of the Orleanist bourgeoisie. Whereas national traditions and religious principles retained "all their vigor among the popular classes," Lourdoueix argued in 1849, the middle class hated the presbytery and the château and were infected with the spirit of the Revolution.[95] Elitist liberal aristocrats, the Orleanized middle class, and parliamentary monarchists had all favored fusion and rallied to the Comte de Paris, the Blancs held, because they feared that a monarchy built upon a direct association between the "incorruptible virtue of the king" and the people's "integral affirmation of political and religious truth" would jeopardize their stock portfolios and upset the revolutionary system that allowed them to get rich and exploit the masses.[96]

Since the Blancs were sure that the people were with Chambord, they held the moderate Right and the center Right responsible for the failure of the restoration; they denied that the strength of the republicans rested on the popular will. Véran claimed, "Numbers are not an obstacle to a return of royalty," because providence "wants the people to save themselves through the principles they have created and conserved."[97] The task of the true Legitimists was to follow Chambord's example and remain absolutely loyal to integral principles so that the "power that uses

of the Blancs d'Espagne, see Guy Augé, *Succession de France et Règle de nationalité; Le Droit royal historique français contre orléanisme* (Paris, 1979), 81–87; and Guy Augé, *Les "Blancs d'Espagne": Contribution à l'étude d'une composante du royalisme français contemporain, mémoire de science politique* (Paris, 1977).

95. Lourdoueix, *La Révolution, c'est l'Orléanisme* (Paris, 1852), 209–15.

96. See Loth, *L'Echec de la restauration monarchique*, 93; Gabriel de Charnace, in Denis' *Les Royalistes de la Mayenne*, 300; Robinet de Clery, *Les Prétentions dynastiques de la branche d'Orléans* (Paris, 1910), 8–9; and Véran, *Les Habiles*, xix.

97. Véran, *Les Habiles*, 65, 59; La Roche, *Les Nationaux et les Partis*, 320.

them" might possess the "honest example of the most perfect politics" by which to elicit the latent royalism of the masses. According to the theory of *droit national,* the people and the king were jointly under the sovereign obligation not to violate tradition, since both were bound by faith to respect the *droit primitif* by which the people had delegated a portion of its original liberty to the Capetian dynasty. Though the monarchy itself was not a divine creation, they argued, the principle of legitimate authority it embodied was; thus, all peoples had a moral and religious obligation to respect their own *droit national.* As long as the form of government that embodied this authority guarded the historic rights and interests of the nation, the "primitive delegation" of the people's sovereignty remained binding on all subsequent generations and could not be rescinded. God may "respect human liberty," La Roche contended, but God also "inclines hearts toward obedience" and "obliges freedom according to the moral law, which is to say . . . that a people is duty-bound to impose on itself the law it has recognized and applied" in the past.[98] According to Véran, a people recovers its full original sovereignty only when the legitimate power expires or when a dynasty becomes extinct; since the Bourbon dynasty continued and the Revolution was illegitimate for having violated the *droit national,* France had no choice but to recognize freely the divine injunction to restore the legitimate monarchy.[99] "What does it matter," asked La Roche, that true Legitimists "are so few in number?" For Chambord had already "morally restored" the Christian monarchy by preserving his portion of France's *droit national* intact; the rest was up to God working through history and through the people.[100]

The consolidation of the Republic, therefore, was no reason to despair: "providential events," it was thought, would soon present France with an opportunity to undo the evil wrought by the unfaithful.[101] The Blancs were certain that God would not allow France to succumb once again to the ravages of "triumphant Radicalism." He would instead use the "irresistible grandeur of events" to bring about the "quick and ter-

98. La Roche, *Les Nationaux et les Partis,* 165, 259.

99. Véran, *La Question du XIXe siècle,* 41–42, 177; Véran, *L'Empire plébiscitaire,* 3–4; Véran, *Les Solutions,* 86–87.

100. La Roche, *Les Nationaux et les Partis,* 320. See also Discours du Joseph du Bourg, in *Les Légitimistes à Ste-Anne-d'Auray,* 29; Véran, *L'Empire plébiscitaire,* 21; and Véran, *La Question du XIXe siècle,* 644.

101. Véran, *Les Solutions,* 91; Véran, *Les Habiles,* 126, 54.

rible crisis" into which the Republic would plunge in order that the nation might come to "glorify the truth."[102] At a time when the "eschatological mood" created by the Franco-Prussian War, the Commune, and the giant national pilgrimages of the 1870s still bred a "catastrophic optimism" in some Catholic circles, prophecies and apparitions pointing to the imminent redemption of France and Europe through the restoration of the monarchy and the temporal power of the pope were not infrequent.[103] In 1889, Marchand, the editor of the *Journal de Paris,* offered his readers an ominous scenario. After condemning Mun's Catholic party and the Boulangism of the parliamentary monarchists, he prophesied that the Republic would soon sink into the anarchy of a new reign of terror. He predicted, however, that at that moment the Germans and Italians would join in invading France's rotting corpse as it suffered the final bouts of revolutionary turmoil. Just as all seemed lost, the white flag would appear in the blue heavens beyond the flames of pillage and war; a strong and valiant young prince, surrounded by a phalanx of papal zouaves wearing the sacred heart on their chests, would spark a great national uprising and expel the invaders. Upon the prince's return to

102. Véran, *Les Habiles,* 127–30, 73; Véran, *La Question du XIXe siècle,* 13–14; La Roche, *Les Nationaux et les Partis,* xvi–xvii; Charles Marie Tresvaux Du Fraval, *La Comédie du radicalisme* (Laval, 1875), 77. In 1873, Blanc de St. Bonnet affirmed, "This entire order of things risen up against God will perish. The Revolution is the avenging curse. For some time to come, there will be the consecration of envy, the accomplishment of hatred, the extinction of liberty, the apotheosis of atheism, and the practice of death. But God has never permitted so much evil all at once! In witnessing these horrors, men will cease to be blinded. After the cataclysm, they will remain stupefied by their inaction. Then God will take them by the hand and lead them toward the light" (*La Légitimité,* 43).

103. Véran, *Les Habiles,* 126; Blanc de St. Bonnet, *La Légitimité,* 43; Rials, *Le Légitimisme,* 44–45. See also Kselman, *Miracles and Prophesies.* In 1871, the *comité royaliste* of Mayenne told those contributing to the erection of a statue at Notre Dame de Pontmain that the message of the apparition of Pontmain pointed to the imminent return of Chambord to the throne: "No! France will not perish . . . and in order for her not to perish she must have the king chosen by God to be her savior." A more mysterious message was related by Paul de Foresta in 1874 when he reported that a *brave fermière* in the village of Fontêt, Gironde, had had a vision of God and the virgin Mary, in which Mary announced the return of the king by January 1 but only after a very short and very violent crisis. See P. de Foresta to Maxence de Foresta, December 14, 1874, in Gaudin's "Le Royalisme dans les Bouches-du-Rhône," 188. Another of Foresta's letters told of how the prophecy foresaw the restoration coming after the "deliverance of Rome," when the king would return to France to do battle with the Prussians, who were to have invaded and made their way to the gates of Paris. The war was to continue "until their complete expulsion from France." Foresta refused to "contest these revelations" (P. de Foresta to Maxence de Foresta, January 19, 1875, in Gaudin's "Le Royalisme dans les Bouches-du-Rhône," 189–90).

Paris, an immense crowd crying, "Vive le roi Bourbon," "Vive le lis," and "Vive le drapeau blanc," would clamor tearfully and joyously for the restoration of the monarchy. Not one voice would protest, and the ruinous Revolution would be forever expunged from the pages of history.[104]

104. Henri Marchand, "Une Prophétie," in *Les Légitimistes à Ste-Anne-d'Auray,* 60–63.

Conclusion

FRENCH LEGITIMISM entered the *fin de siècle* fragmented and was to leave only vestiges of itself in the twentieth-century political landscape. Memories of the Restoration and the struggle with the Orleanists, as well as Chambord's protracted tenure as the avatar of principled resistance to modernity, made adherence to the monarchy an intensely personal lifelong experience for thousands of Legitimists whose political faith had been profoundly shaken by the failure of the monarchical campaign in the early 1870s and the death of Chambord in 1883. Those who remained convinced of the possibility and the necessity of a restoration in the 1880s saw the fortunes of their cause decline throughout much of the decade. The collapse of the Boulangist campaign in 1889, itself an act of political desperation, the death of the Comte de Paris in 1893, and the advent of a new pretender, the Duc d'Orleans, who was held in low esteem, buried what remained of the old royalist tradition in the personal frustrations of a handful of forgotten aristocrats. Charles Maurras resurrected a form of monarchism during the Dreyfus Affair, but that remained largely a movement of intellectuals and urban youth who had no use for the aristocratic liberalism and rural paternalism at the heart of the Legitimist program. Action Française had clear ideological roots in the Legitimism of the "white Midi," but its political anti-Semitism, integral nationalism, and skeptical empiricism expressed intellectual and political currents foreign to nineteenth-century royalism.[1]

1. See Gérard Gaudin, "Chez les Blancs du Midi: Du légitimisme à l'Action Française," *Etudes Maurrassiennes,* I (1968), 59–70. I have found no occasion of the Legitimists' using

Legitimism left more subtle and long-lasting marks. The territorial reorganization advocated by Claude Marie Raudot and Ferdinand Béchard finds its echo in contemporary regional divisions. Modern Catholic social services and Catholic youth organizations, as well as the church's social teachings and even Christian Democracy, have their roots in nineteenth-century social Catholicism.[2] The Association Catholique de la Jeunesse Française and the Confédération Français des Travailleurs Catholiques grew directly from Albert de Mun's Oeuvre des Cercles, and one of the first major rural syndicalist movements, the Union Central des Syndicates Agricoles, had its origins in efforts by Legitimist landowners to secure protection for agricultural interests. Under Vichy, fascists fought a losing battle with traditionalists over the shape of the National Revolution as the regime made Catholic corporatism and the promotion of time-honored rural values official policy. Neither Charles de Gaulle nor Valéry Giscard d'Estaing would have rejected the Legitimists' critique of socialism or their preference for a government run by a natural elite of wealth, talent, and education. A kind of cultural and religious fundamentalism prevails among Catholics who, like Monsignor Lefebvre, reject Vatican II, and a counterrevolutionary intellectual tradition persists among neoroyalist scholars like Guy Augé, Alfred Néry, and Stéphane Rials, who see the French Revolution as a horrible debacle. On the Boulevard St. Germain, in the Church of Saint Nicolas du Chardonnet, there is a chapel in honor of refractory priests killed during the Reign of Terror; on Sundays, copies of Action Française' *Aspects de la France* are sold on the sidewalk outside.

As a viable electoral force, though, Legitimism died quickly in the age of mass politics that emerged in the 1870s and 1880s. Universal manhood

---

overt anti-Semitism as a political weapon. Although royalist leaders in the late nineteenth century, many of whom began their political careers as Bonapartists, frequently used anti-Semitism as a strategy of mass mobilization, Legitimists prominent in the mid–nineteenth century distrusted democracy and had no use for the political action of urban crowds. Moreover, the conditions for the diffusion and manipulation of popular anti-Semitism did not exist until the 1880s. Despite the racial myths favored by members of the French aristocracy, and despite the suspicions many nineteenth-century Catholics harbored toward Jews, anti-Semitism was all but absent from Legitimist discourse. See William D. Irvine, *The Boulanger Affair Reconsidered: Royalism, Boulangism, and the Origins of the Radical Right in France* (New York, 1989), 157–76.

2. See Jean Marie Mayeur, *Catholicisme social et Démocratie chrétienne: Principes romaines, expériences française* (Paris, 1986), 17–32.

suffrage, urbanization, mass-circulation newspapers, and an integrated national market eroded the political influence of traditional social elites and rendered the Legitimists' reliance on paternalism and on the loyalty of traditional peasant constituencies ineffective. As public opinion replaced hierarchical social deference and outright intimidation, the monarchy suffered from a bad reputation, a fading national memory, and poor public relations.

The Legitimists' tactical failures in the 1870s and 1880s, and their unwillingness to embrace mass politics, were related to their distaste for democracy and their shabby political organization. As William Irvine has recently made clear, royalists were ill equipped to compete with the republicans for votes in the early years of the Third Republic.[3] Yet their practical limitations are in large measure beside the point, since the Legitimists never sought seriously to adjust to the new political realities of a democratic society. Where democracy was concerned, the Legitimists looked backward rather than forward and remained fixated on efforts, begun after February, 1848, to create the conditions for a permanent counterrevolution. Moreover, they belonged to the tradition of utopian idealism that shaped the sensibilities of political romantics on both the Right and the Left in the 1830s and 1840s. Having spent the years of the Second Empire resisting positivism and realpolitik, the Legitimists continued to pursue utopian aims in an era when even the most idealistic learned that political power was not an abstraction. They consequently gained no purchase on the less subtle methods of political coercion with which other parties were able to consolidate their bureaucratic and electoral successes.

UTOPIAN CONSERVATISM IN THE AGE OF UNIVERSAL SUFFRAGE

Democracy for the Legitimists was inalterably associated with the experience of the Second Republic and the Second Empire. The years 1848 and 1851 together represented a series of lessons that shaped their understanding of conservatism in an age of democratization. In contrast to the situation of the 1870s, the Party of Order that emerged in response to the collapse of the *monarchie censitaire* was able to dominate

3. Irvine, *The Boulanger Affair Reconsidered,* 48.

the Republic through the ballot box with relative ease and therefore learned very little about electioneering in the process. In 1848 and 1849, conservative notables maintained a firm grip on most rural communes and won elections simply by organizing electoral committees, monopolizing the nomination process, and using their considerable journalistic resources to badger republican administrators and to denounce republican policies as a threat to the social order.[4] The great challenge of 1848 was not the loss of social power, or even the brief collapse of conservative political control, but the threat socialism and democratic egalitarianism posed to a conservative ideological hegemony. For the moment, peasant constituencies remained loyal to entrenched elites, but the seeds of an alternative social order had been planted; to prevent them from bearing fruit, the Legitimists hoped to contain the agencies of subversion. As for the masses, the Legitimists regarded them as uneducated, apolitical, and passive. Since the people were not expected to express autonomous opinions but to receive direction from above, the Legitimists saw the matter of winning votes as a putting to use of the moral and social pressure that the wealthy, the clergy, and local officials were capable of by virtue of their social position. If that failed, they resorted to repression, even if they insisted that a durable solution to social disorder could not rest on the fear of force.

From a purely practical point of view, the Legitimists viewed universal suffrage as an unfortunate product of the times which they could turn into a malleable tool for the designation of public officials. It was frightening to them only insofar as it opened a window on society that disclosed the extent to which revolutionary subversion had eroded the moral fabric of the nation. The disorder confirmed by the electoral process pointed to the need to strengthen agencies of social conservation and weaken the forces of revolution; thus, religious education, restrictions on press freedom, and the reduction of lower-class access to the ballot box seemed necessary in order to reverse what the Legitimists saw as the steady moral disintegration of the masses. The problem of democracy, they concluded, lay not so much in its participatory nature as in the way it allowed the anarchic social passions of a morally untethered society to be instantly translated into laws and institutions hostile to the preserva-

4. Tudesq, *Les Grands Notables en France,* II, 1028–72.

tion of conservative instincts. If, as Léopold de Gaillard observed, democracy was capable of "changing a political fact into a . . . social fact in so little time," the restoration of order had first to occur in the moral complexion and the habits of the people before it could be given institutional expression.[5] In 1851, Raudot questioned whether monarchical legitimacy had any meaning or held any promise as long as it was not recognized "by the great majority of the nation." He suggested, "If one attacks, denies, and destroys legitimacy in the spirit, it can produce nothing in fact."[6]

It was, practically speaking, therefore almost irrelevant that the Legitimists believed in the preexisting right of the monarchy to claim legitimacy. Doctrinal purity on that point did not absolve them from the task of shaping social values and governing public opinion, precisely because they gave equal credence to the idea that political institutions were a reflection of the moral condition of society. But, they had to ask, could the needed social and moral reconstruction be achieved by campaigning for votes? Selling a conservative program to an electorate that was deemed free to accept or reject "eternal values" would put them in the position of conceding to the people the right to challenge the legitimacy of the entire social order. Legitimist social reconstruction, they decided, had to be authoritarian and pedagogic rather than open and democratic; it would have to seek to reinforce conservative institutions through wise reforms and practices that would gain the consent of the governed not because they were debated in the open political arena but because social and moral attitudes had been changed. The advent of universal suffrage prepared the Legitimists to think in terms of ideological hegemony and social reconstruction rather than mass electioneering. They sought neither approval nor popularity but only the opportunity to transform French social institutions and to secure ideological conformity in preparation for the restoration of the monarchy. "Does social reform," asked Albert DuBoys, "not precede and take precedence over political reform? Is it not necessary to cure a sick people before asking from it deeds that suppose health and strength?"[7]

5. Gaillard, *La Crise agricole et la Démocratie*, 8.
6. Raudot, *De la grandeur possible de la France*, 6.
7. Albert DuBoys, in Stéphane Rials's "Les Royalistes français et le Suffrage universel," *Pouvoirs*, XXVI (1983), 6.

Ironically, the experience of the Second Republic and the Second Empire made Legitimism resemble republicanism more than Bonapartism or Orleanism. Frustrated by a failure to translate the formal practice of democracy into an enduring victory for republican institutions, many on the Left concluded that it would be necessary to reeducate the electorate before universal suffrage could be made to yield what they desired of it. Like the Legitimists, the republicans believed that political institutions gave expression to the moral interior of a people. Consequently, after 1848 they sought to employ an enlightened pedagogy, with the aid of new social and civic associations, to liberate the French conscience from the weight of tradition. Only in that way, they believed, might the masses come to use political freedom effectively. Since the Second Empire offered little opportunity for meaningful electoral competition, royalists and republicans spent the 1850s and 1860s locked in ideological combat over secularization and clericalism while concentrating their organizational efforts on such matters as education, social assistance, and the right of association. By the 1870s, partisans of the Republic and of the monarchy had developed political orientations equally grounded in the conviction that political success must be prefaced by the reshaping of civic values.

Yet the convergent strategic approach brought more restricted practical benefit to the Legitimists than to the republicans. When universal suffrage was revived in 1871, the republicans, less hampered by social prejudice and doctrinally inclined to embrace the free competition of ideas, launched a vigorous and well-organized electoral campaign based on image-conscious slogans, mass meetings, and direct contact with the voters.[8] Though a handful of Legitimists saw a need to copy republican tactics, most denounced the new mass politics as crude demagoguery and counseled conservative notables to return to their estates and rely on their social position and the influence of the clergy to counteract the republican assault on France's rural communes. Amédée de Margerie was convinced that "the patron in his workshop and the proprietor on his properties" would, "like the head of a family," find a "thousand occasions . . . to contribute little by little to the education of citizens."[9] Even after it had become clear that monarchism was immensely unpopular,

8. See Locke, *French Legitimists*, 224–59.
9. Margerie, *La Restauration*, 314–15.

members of Chambord's political bureau refused papal advice to drop the dynastic label, because people who voted for royalist candidates "liv[ing] in their midst" would feel betrayed if the Legitimists did not announce their fidelity to the monarchy.[10]

Continued reliance on the clergy and monarchist prefects proved inadequate as the Moral Order collapsed in the face of repeated republican electoral victories. The electoral activity of the clergy in behalf of Legitimists had always been controversial and was increasingly discouraged by church leaders and Catholic politicians as royalism became a political liability. In regions where clerical influence was a hindrance, royalists rather cynically counted on their control of the administration during the MacMahon presidency to exert pressure on the voters. When that failed to produce results in the elections of 1876 and 1877, the royalists lost control of state patronage through the ministries, the prefectures, and the courts, and came to face a formidable network of republican electoral agents as the victors filled upper- and lower-level administrative positions with politically reliable officials. MacMahon's resignation in 1879 marked the transition to an assertive republican administration that "sharply diminished the ability of conservatives to translate their superior social and economic position into political power." In the 1880s, the royalists were consequently forced to rely on methods and skills that contradicted their contempt for the democratic process and their paternalistic instincts.[11] As William D. Irvine points out, the royalists' involvement in the Boulanger Affair was a symptom of the decay of royalism in the face of mass society and political democracy. The failure of their attempt to make of Boulangism a way to compensate for their inability to win the confidence of the masses was fatal for the old royalist movement and ended the era, begun in 1848, during which the Legitimists attempted to forge a durable rapprochement between French society and the monarchical form of government.[12] Maurras' preference for the coup de force and his willingness to mobilize urban crowds acknowledged the absence of a royalist mass base and testified to the temperamental and ideological distance between nineteenth-century Legitimism and Action Française.

10. Dreux-Brézé, *Notes et Souvenirs,* 53, 71.
11. Irvine, *The Boulanger Affair Reconsidered,* 53, 71.
12. *Ibid.,* 16–17, 162, 180.

UTOPIAN CONSERVATISM
IN THE AGE OF FORCE

The Legitimists not only failed to adopt the democratic practices of the republicans, they also rejected the plebiscitarianism and secular nationalism of the Bonapartists. The Legitimists' unwillingness to adopt Bonapartist tactics and Chambord's reluctance to accept an *appel au peuple* or a coup d'etat exhibited the conviction that sustained centralized administrative coercion and revolution from above were ultimately in contradiction with the reconstruction of society and the pedagogic strategies of permanent counterrevolution.

The refusal to sanction a politics grounded in naked repression was not necessarily symptomatic of a lack of resources. Bonapartism might have been more attractive to a mass electorate, but it never sank the kind of deep roots that Legitimism had in the West, the Midi, or French Flanders. Bonapartists were in no better position to dominate the army or the bureaucracy during the July Monarchy or the early Third Republic than the Legitimists who had come to see participation in the military and local government as an appropriate means to exercise social status and political influence.

The Revolution of 1848 had inspired all conservative notables to mobilize for a counterrevolutionary offensive against socialism and democracy. Although their counterrevolution took many forms, from armed repression to educational reform, the systematic use of the bureaucratic and police powers of the centralized state became the most characteristic feature of the long-term effort by French elites to prevent social and political change. The Legitimists participated in the protracted counterrevolution, but they alone among the parties of the Right consistently questioned the utility of the normative reliance on police power, the central administration, and periodic armed confrontation with the revolutionary masses. As their preoccupation with decentralization, Catholic education, and public assistance attests, they preferred, through a mobilization of the elite, to try to spark the durable moral and social regeneration of the nation. Their choice, their distaste for the politics of overt domination, made Legitimism unpopular in an era when moral order contradicted the egalitarian and democratic sensibilities of the people, and unattractive to many Orleanists and Bonapartists who were more impressed with the results of preemptive and chronic repression than with paternalism and Catholic moral pedagogy.

That is not to say that the Legitimists did not consent to and support the repression of the June Days or the Paris Commune or that they opposed the creation of agencies of surveillance for keeping radicals at bay. But armed force, centralized administrative pressure, and police tactics could not, according to the Legitimists, serve as a permanent preventive against revolutionary upheavals. The kind of coercive methods used by Orleanist and Bonapartist elites to contain revolution permitted the institutionalization of a bureaucratic command structure and the development of confrontational authority patterns that the Legitimists associated with the destruction in 1789 of the harmony and integrity of the social order. Sustained bureaucratic repression was not in their view the antithesis of revolution but a sign of the continuing revolutionary disintegration of society. Moreover, the Legitimists argued, Jacobin and Bonapartist institutions undermined civil society's capacity to generate its own spontaneous mechanisms of control, by disturbing traditional patterns of authority and by interposing the state between the people and its natural protectors. Brute repression only led to perpetual insecurity and to the installation of "ephemeral governments surviving a few years in fear of disorder and eventually succumbing to some violent intervention." [13] Reacting to the violence of the June Days, the Vicomte d'Arlincourt commented that it was not enough to have reestablished "order in the streets" without having "reestablished it in people's minds." [14] Armand de Melun warned that as long as the spirit of order had "not penetrated the hearts" of the workers, "we can write good books, pronounce beautiful speeches, we can even give the worker a veneer of civilization, but on the first occasion he'll grab a rifle and burn down our houses." [15] Armed vigilance could never be better than a necessary evil; once it became a means of governing, it legitimated an endless cycle of violence and counterviolence that undermined all efforts needed to reconstruct the social order.

According to the Legitimists, the Second Empire, which came to power through force and which succumbed to war and revolution, was a

13. Cadoudal, *Esquisses morales, historiques et littéraires,* 214.
14. Vicomte Charles Victor d'Arlincourt, *Dieu le veut* (Paris, 1848), 30.
15. Armand de Melun to Prince de Chalais, in Andigné's *Un Apôtre de la charité,* 380.

case in point. In 1851, many Legitimists supported the coup d'etat, reasoning, along with Henri de La Rochejacquelein, that sometimes "dictatorship is necessary in order to save society." Others, like Ferdinand Béchard, expected that the conditions for decentralized monarchical institutions would return "the more we distance ourselves from the revolutionary crisis."[16] By the late 1860s, though, most Legitimists had concluded that Bonapartism was not an antidote to revolutionary disorder but a manifestation of Jacobinism in another form. The Napoleonic police state did not disappear but found its raison d'être in a policy of systematic social disruption that fomented unrest in order to justify dictatorship in the eyes of the materialist bourgeoisie. For Guillaume Véran, Bonapartism represented one face of the Revolution and its tactics were nothing more than the "hypocrisy of order."[17]

The Legitimist critique of Orleanism and Bonapartism centered less on institutional arrangements and economic development, and more on how neither grasped the need to reshape the moral constitution of the French people in order to achieve a political settlement that expressed France's rejection of the dominant cultural tendencies of the nineteenth century. Decentralized government, Catholic social activity, rechristianization, the revitalization of agriculture, and the restoration of an openly Christian monarchy were intended to promote not just more efficient social control, and certainly not just a depressing catalog of blue laws, but primarily the spontaneous self-effacement of the modern democratic, egalitarian, and material aspirations of the French people. It was felt that monarchical legitimacy had to be internalized before it could offer an abiding response to revolutionary republicanism and the materialism of the industrial era. In a sense, French Legitimism was the mirror image of French republicanism, since the republic embodied the hope of secular democrats that the internal liberation of the individual would ultimately emancipate France from the royalist tendencies and the religious superstitions of the past.

16. Henri de La Rochejacquelein, *La France en 1853* (Paris, 1853), 127–28; Béchard, *De l'administration*, II, 304–305.
17. Véran, *L'Empire plébiscitaire*, 14–15.

Bibliography

GOVERNMENT DOCUMENTS

Annuaire statistique de la France de 1878. 2 vols. Paris, 1878.

Annuaire statistique de la France: Résumé rétrospectif. Paris, 1966.

France. *Annales de la Chambre des Députés.* Vol. IX. Paris, 1878.

France. Assemblée Nationale. *Annales parlementaires: Annales de l'Assemblée Nationale.* 48 vols. Versailles, 1871–76.

France. Assemblée Nationale. *Documents parlementaires: Annexes au procès-verbaux des séances, projets et propositions de loi, exposé de motif et rapports.* Versailles, 1871–76.

France. Assemblée Nationale. *Enquête parlementaire sur l'organisation de l'assistance publique dans les campagnes: Avis des conseils généraux.* Vol. I of 3 vols. Versailles, 1873.

France. Assemblée Nationale. *Enquête sur l'insurrection du 18 mars 1871: Annexes des séances du 26 au 30 mars 1872.* 10 vols. Versailles, 1872.

France. Ministère de l'Agriculture. *Enquête agricole: Enquêtes départementales.* Série 2. 38 vols. Paris, 1867–72.

Archives Nationales, Paris

Archives Privés: Série AP (Fonds privés).

Archives de la famille de Kergolay, AP 97.

Archives des familles de Noailles, de Beaumont et de Grossolles-Flamarens, AP 111.

Archives d'Enterprises: Série AQ.

Papiers Benoist d'Azy, AP 161.

Dossiers des Magistrates: Série BB 6 II 1848–83.

Ministère de la Justice: Série BB 18 (Correspondances générales), Nos. 1214–
       1794.
       Série BB 30 (Rapports des procureurs généraux, 1849–
       1870), Nos. 368–570.

Archives de l'Assemblée Nationale: Série C.
       Pétitions des amis du droit national en 1850, C 2299.
       Procès-verbal de la commission sur l'agriculture, C 2802.
       Procès-verbal de la décentralisation, C2866.
       Le travail des enfants, C 2878.
       Enquête parlementaire sur les élections générales de 14 et 28 octobre 1877,
       C 3225–67.
       Pétitions pour la rétablissement de la monarchie, C 4259, 4260, 4271.

Conseillers Généraux de 1870: Série F (1) b 230, Nos. 1–21.

Série Départementale: Série F (1) b II (Personnel administrative), Nos. 6–11.

Conseils Généraux: Série F (1) c V (Délibérations généraux, voeux et documents
       divers—classement départementale), Nos. 4, 8.

Ministère de l'Intérieur: Série F 7 (Police générale).
       Agissements cléricaux, No. 12477.
       Agissements cléricaux, No. 12478.
       Congrès catholiques: Assemblées régionales, 1872–1873, No. 12479.

Ministère de l'Agriculture: Série F 10.
       Comices et sociétés agricoles, 1850–1880, Nos. 1580–84.
       Voeux des conseils généraux, 1836–1881, Nos. 1577–81.

Assistance Publique: Série F 12.
       Sociétés de secours mutuels: Demandes d'autorisation, status, contentieux,
       1850–1912—dossier départemental, Nos. 5347–5404.

Ministère de l'Instruction Publique: Série F 17.
       Voeux des conseils généraux rélatif à l'instruction, 1850–1871, No. 1395.

Microfilm: Série Mi (Fonds de Larcy).
       Archives du Château de La Tour, 484 Mi, Nos. 1–37.

ATLASES, BIOGRAPHICAL DICTIONARIES, AND OTHER REFERENCE WORKS

Angot. *Dictionnaire historique de la Mayenne, 1900–1914.* 4 vols. Laval, 1975–77.
Biré, Edmond. *Biographies contemporaines, XIX siècle.* Lyon, 1905.

Coston, Henri, ed. *Dictionnaire des dynasties bourgeoises et du monde des affaires.* Paris, 1975.

Cougny, G., and A. Robert. *Dictionnaire des parlementaires français.* 5 vols. Paris, 1889.

Danican-Philidor, Eugène. *Dictionnaire du personnel administratif; ou, Etats de service permanents par ordre alphabéthique des 768 fonctionnaires de l'administration départemental.* Epinal, 1870.

Encyclopédie théologique; ou, Série de dictionnaire sur toutes les parties de la science religieuse. 7 vols. Paris, 1846.

Goguel, François. *Géographie des élections françaises de 1870 à 1951.* Paris, 1951.

Jolly, Jean. *Dictionnaire des parlementaires français.* 8 vols. Paris, 1960.

Littré, Emile. *Dictionnaire de la langue française.* Paris, 1883.

Nouvelle Encyclopédie théologique. 47 vols. Paris, 1852.

Pascal, Jean. *Les Députés bretons de 1789 à 1983.* Paris, 1983.

Rémond, René, and P. M. Boyer, eds. *Atlas historique de la France contemporaine, 1800–1965.* Paris, 1966.

Ribeyre, Felix. *Biographie des représentants à l'Assemblée Nationale.* 2nd ed. Angers, 1872.

Vapereau, Gustave. *Dictionnaire universel des contemporains contenant toutes les personnes notables de la France et des pays étrangers.* 6th ed. Paris, 1893.

PERIODICALS

Annales de la charité, 1848–49.
Bulletin de la Société d'Agriculture et Arts de la Sarthe, 1854–80.
Bulletin de la Société d'Agriculture, Sciences et Arts d'Agen, 1850–60.
Bulletin de la Société d'Agriculture, Science, Arts et Commerce du Puy, 1852–70.
Bulletin de la Société de Saint-Vincent de Paul, 1864–66.
Le Correspondant, 1852–80.
Journal de l'agriculture pratique, 1855–70.
La Réforme sociale: Bulletin de la Société d'Economie Sociale et des Unions de la Paix Sociale, 1872–76.
Revue catholique des institutions et du droit, 1888.
Revue de Berry, 1864–66.
Revue de Bretagne, de Vendée et d'Anjou, 1857–88.
Revue d'économie charitable, 1871–73.
Revue des deux mondes, 1851–80.
Revue indépendante, 1864–65.
Revue provinciale, 1848–49.
La Vérité universelle, 1871.

NEWSPAPERS

Amis de la religion, 1860–62.
La Décentralisation, 1865.
Espérance du peuple, 1853–62.
La France centrale, 1852–64.
Gazette de France, 1843–73.
Journal de Rennes, 1861–75.
La Quotidienne, 1843–47.
Union de l'Ouest, 1871–73.
L'Union monarchique, 1843–47.

WORKS BY LEGITIMISTS:
BOOKS, MEMOIRS, AND PAMPHLETS

Andigné, Maurice d'. *Le Roi légitime*. Paris, 1884.
Arlincourt, Vicomte Charles Victor d'. *Dieu le veut*. Paris, 1848.
Armailhac, Louis d'. *La Légitimité et le Progrès, par un économiste*. Bordeaux, 1871.
———. *L'Ouvrier économiste; ou, Causerie d'économie politique et morale*. Poitiers, 1871.
Aubry, Maurice. *Programme chrétien d'économie politique: Discours prononcé dans l'Assemblée des Catholiques, le 5 avril 1877*. Paris, 1877.
———. *Théorie et Pratique; ou, Union de l'économie politique avec la morale*. Paris, 1851.
Auray de Saint-Pois, Marquis d'. *La Royauté est nécessaire: Etude religieuse, politique et historique*. Nantes, 1880.
Barbès, André. *Les Traditions nationales autrefois et aujourd'hui dans la nation française*. Paris, 1873.
Becdélievre, Lieutenant de. *Souvenirs de l'armée pontificale*. Paris, 1867.
Béchade, A. de. *Le Noeud gordien: Légitimité au radicalisme*. Bordeaux, 1873.
Béchard, Ferdinand. *Autonomie et Césarisme: Introduction au droit municipal moderne*. Paris, 1869.
———. *La Commune, l'Eglise et l'Etat dans leurs rapports avec les classes laborieuses*. 2 vols. Paris, 1851.
———. *De l'administration intérieure de la France*. 2 vols. Paris, 1851.
———. *De l'état du paupérisme en France et des moyens d'y remédier*. Paris, 1852.
———. *Du projet de décentralisation administrative annoncé par l'empereur*. Paris, 1864.
Belcastel, Gabriel de. *A mes électeurs: Cinq ans de vie politique, votes principaux, propositions, lettres et discours*. Toulouse, 1876.
———. *Lettres aux propriétaires riverains de la Variante*. Toulouse, 1861.

————. *La Monarchie chrétienne: Lettres d'un catholique à ses contemporains.* Paris, 1884.

Belcastel, Gabriel de, Charles Chesnelong, and Albert de Mun. *L'Aurore du salut de la France dans les trois oeuvres des Cercles Catholiques d'Ouvriers, des comités catholiques et du Voeu National au Sacré Coeur.* Perpignan, 1878.

Belleval, Louis de. *Souvenirs de ma jeunesse.* Paris, 1895.

Bernardi, Gustave de. *La Révolution.* Paris, 1873.

————. *La Vérité divine et l'Idée humaine; ou, Christianisme et Révolution.* Paris, 1870.

Berryer, Pierre Antoine. *Oeuvres de Berryer: Discours parlementaires.* 6 vols. Paris, 1872–91.

Blanc de St. Bonnet, Antoine. *De la restauration française: Mémoire présenté au clergé et à l'aristocratie.* Paris, 1851.

————. *La Légitimité.* Tournai, 1873.

Bouchage, Auguste. *Sauver la France: De 1789 à 1871, quel a été le meilleur gouvernement?* Toulouse, 1871.

Bouillé, Charles de. *Mémoire sur l'exploitation agricole de Villers, 25 février 1862.* Nevers, 1862.

Bourg, Joseph du. *La Vérité et le Légende: Les Entrevues des princes à Frohsdorf.* Paris, 1910.

Bourgeois, J. *Le Catholicisme et les Questions sociales.* Paris, 1867.

Cadoudal, Georges de. *Faits et Récits contemporains: Nouveau Recueil anecdotique.* Paris, 1860.

————. *Esquisses morales, historiques et littéraires: Souvenirs de quinze années, 1845–1861.* Paris, 1862.

Calemard de Lafayette. *L'Agriculture progressive à la portée de tout le monde.* Paris, 1867.

Carayon-Latour, Joseph de. *Mémoires sur la propriété de Virelade: Concours pour le prime d'honneur à décerner dans le département de Gironde.* Bordeaux, 1867.

Chalvet-Nastrac, Vicomte de. *Les Projets de restauration monarchique et le général Ducrot.* Paris, 1909.

Chambord, Comte de. *Etude politique: Correspondance de 1841 à 1879.* 5th ed. Geneva, 1880.

————. *Lettres de M. le comte de Chambord: Discours de MM. de Falloux et Berryer.* 2nd ed. Bordeaux, 1851.

————. *La Monarchie française: Lettres et Documents politiques, 1844–1907.* Paris, 1907.

Champvallier, Edgard de. *De l'organisation de l'assistance publique dans le département de la Charente.* Angoulême, 1866.

————. *De quelques questions de vicinalité: De l'assimilation des chemins de grande communication de la Charente aux routes départementales.* Niort, 1868.

———. *Rapport de la commission d'enquête d'utilité publique du chemin de fer de Niort à Ruffec.* Niort, 1868.

Chantrel, Joseph. *Histoire contemporaine: Complément de l'histoire de la France et des cours d'histoire universelle.* 3 vols. Paris, 1864.

———. *Le Père Dimanche.* Paris, 1867.

Chaulnes, Alfred de. *Nouveau Projet de réforme électorale pour annihiler l'Intérnationale, par un français.* Le Puy, 1874.

Chaurand, Baron de. *De l'enseignement de l'agriculture.* Paris, 1867.

Chesnelong, Charles. *Les Comités catholiques et la Défense religieuse et sociale.* Paris, 1877.

———. *Les Derniers Jours de l'Empire et le Gouvernement de M. Thiers.* Paris, 1932.

———. *Un Témoignage à l'histoire: La Campagne monarchique d'octobre 1873.* Paris, 1895.

Cintré, Baron Huchet de. *A messieurs les membres du conseil général d'Ille-et-Vilaine: Au sujet des routes départementales et chemins de grande communication.* Rennes, 1880.

Clozel de Boyer, A. *Monarchie ou Anarchie, ni spectre rouge, ni spectre blanc: Par un légitimiste.* Paris, 1851.

Croy-Chanel, Prince Auguste, de. *La Noblesse et les Titres nobiliaires dans les sociétés chrétiennes.* Paris, 1857.

Cumont, Arthur de. *Les Incurables: A propos d'un brocheur.* 2nd ed. Angers, 1883.

Dreux-Brézé, Charles de. *De la liberté d'enseignement en 1850 et en 1864.* Paris, 1865.

———. *Notes et Souvenirs pour servir à l'histoire du parti royaliste, 1872–1883.* Paris, 1895.

———. *Quelques mots sur les tendances du temps présent.* Paris, 1860.

———. *La Révolution: L'Unité de son but, sa logique et ses contradictions.* Paris, 1863.

Dubosc de Pesquidoux, Jean. *Le Comte de Chambord d'après lui-même: Etude politique et historique.* Paris, 1887.

DuBoys, Albert. *Le Centenaire de l'assemblée de Vizille et son véritable esprit.* Lyon, 1888.

———. *De l'influence sociale des conciles.* Paris, 1869.

———. *Des principes de la Révolution française considérés comme principes générateurs du socialisme et du communisme.* Lyon, 1851.

Falloux, Comte Alfred de. *L'Agriculture et la Politique.* Paris, 1866.

———. *De l'unité nationale.* Paris, 1880.

———. *Des élections prochaines.* Paris, 1869.

———. *Discours de M. de Falloux à l'Assemblée Nationale.* Paris, 1851.

———. *Discours et Mélanges politiques.* 2nd ed. 2 vols. Paris, 1882.

———. *Dix ans d'agriculture.* Paris, 1863.

———. *Du scepticisme politique.* Paris, 1872.

————. *L'Enquête agricole.* Paris, 1866.

————. *Etudes et Souvenirs.* 2 vols. Paris, 1885.

————. *Mémoires d'une royaliste.* 2 vols. Paris, 1888.

————. *Le Parti catholique: Ce qu'il a été, ce qu'il est devenu.* Paris, 1856.

————. *Questions monarchiques: Lettre à Laurentie.* Paris, 1873.

————. *Souvenirs de charité.* Tours, 1857.

Fresneau, Armand. *L'Atelier français en 1879.* Paris, 1879.

————. *Kermadio, du 1er avril au 15 août 1868: Rapport adressé à M. le Cte de Ségur d'Aguesseau—comment on peut quintupler le revenu d'une ferme bretonne.* Versailles, 1868.

————. *Une Nation au pillage.* Châteauroux, 1882.

————. *La Planche du salut.* Paris, 1851.

Gaillard, Léopold de. *La Crise agricole et la Démocratie: Discours prononcé le 20 décembre 1866.* Marseille, 1867.

————. *Les Etapes de l'opinion, 1871–1872.* Paris, 1873.

Gautier, Léon. *Histoire des corporations ouvriers.* Paris, 1874.

Gavardie, Henri de. *Etudes sur les vraies doctrines sociales et politiques.* Pau, 1862.

Geslin de Kersolon, Paul Alexandre de [Jean Loyseau]. *Lourdes: Pèlerinage et Pèlerins.* Paris, 1872.

————. *Pouvoir et Liberté.* Paris, 1872.

Gouvello, Amédée de. *Les Colonies agricoles pour les enfants assistés.* Blois, 1862.

————. *Le Dépopulation des campagnes: Les Asiles ruraux et les Orphelinats agricoles.* Paris, 1869.

————. *Société des agriculteurs de France: Rapport de M. le Cte de Gouvello . . . fermes-écoles.* Paris, 1869.

————. *Vues sur la réorganisation de la France.* Vannes, 1871.

Henri V, l'Eglise et la Révolution. Paris, 1872.

Henri V et la Démocratie. Paris, 1873.

Henri V et la Monarchie traditionnelle. Paris, 1870.

Henri V et les Classes sociales. Paris, 1872.

Henri V et la Véritable Monarchie. Paris, 1872.

Henri V peint par ses adversaires républicains, bonapartistes, orléanistes: Témoignages recueillis par un enfant du peuple. Paris, 1872.

Hervé-Bazin, Ferdinand Jacques. *La Monarchie selon le programme du roi.* Paris, 1882.

Keller, Emile. *L'Encyclique du 8 décembre 1864 et les Principes de 1789; ou, L'Eglise, L'Etat et la Liberté.* Paris, 1866.

Kolb-Bernard, Charles. *Dogme et Politique.* Paris, 1881.

————. *Société de Saint Vincent de Paul de Lille: Discours prononcé par Kolb-Bernard.* Lille, 1869.

La Bassétière, Edouard Morisson de. *Réponse à l'enquête agricole.* Nantes, 1867.

La Borderie, Arthur de. *Les Elections départementales en 1867: Lettre à un électeur.* Rennes, 1867.

La Boulaye, Vicomte de. *Les six solutions.* Paris, 1851.

La Boulie, Camille de. *La Régénération de l'agriculture et la Compagnie foncière.* Paris, 1863.

La Broise, Henri de. *République ou Monarchie.* Laval, 1871.

———. *Le Vrai et le Faux Libéralisme.* Paris, 1866.

Lacombe, Charles de. *Journal politique de Charles de Lacombe, député à l'Assemblée Nationale.* 2 vols. Paris, 1908.

Lacombe, Hilaire de. "Le Suffrage universel et la Représentation des intérêts." *Le Correspondant,* CV (1876), 648–61.

La Monneraye, Charles de. *Discours prononcé par M. de La Monneraye, président du congrès de l'Association Bretonne, réunis à Vannes en 1853.* Rennes, 1853.

———. *Lettre sur la situation de l'agriculture.* Rennes, 1866.

La Pervanchère, Baron Richard de. *L'Agriculture en Bretagne.* Nantes, 1867.

———. *Des vicissitudes politiques de la France: Etudes historiques.* Paris, 1860.

———. *Le 18 Brumaire.* Paris, 1876.

———. *Louis XVI et les Etats-Généraux.* Paris, 1868.

———. *La Restauration.* Paris, 1878.

La Roche, Ernest. *Les Nationaux et les Partis: Etude des institutions de la France, de son droit national et de la solution constitutionnelle après la guerre de 1870.* Paris, 1876.

La Rochejacquelein, Henri de. *La France en 1853.* Paris, 1853.

La Tour Du Pin–Chambly, René de. *Le Centenaire de 1788: Le Centenaire de Romans.* Paris, 1889.

———. *Le Centenaire de 1789: Etude d'économie sociale.* Paris, 1888.

———. *Cercles catholiques d'ouvriers: Discours prononcé . . . le 10 séptembre 1871.* Paris, 1871.

———. *Vers un ordre social chrétien: Jalon de route.* Paris, 1921.

Laurentie, Pierre S. *L'Athéisme social et l'Eglise: Schisme du monde nouveau.* Paris, 1869.

———. *Souvenirs inédits, publié par son petit-fils.* Paris, 1892.

Le Beschu de Champsavin. *Examen du communisme, dédié aux cultivateurs et ouvriers.* Rennes, 1850.

———. *Lettre à l'évêque de Rennes au sujet de la fondation d'une oeuvre de bons livres.* Rennes, 1849.

———. *La Peur des revenants: Des privilèges, des droits féodaux et des dîmes.* Rennes, 1851.

Le Breton, Paul Anselme. *Association libre des agriculteurs de la Mayenne: 5e session—compte rendu de la séance du 23 octobre 1875.* Laval, 1875.

———. *Association libre des agriculteurs de la Mayenne: 7e session—compte rendu de la séance du 4 mai 1878.* Laval, 1878.

————. *Département de la Mayenne, congrès agricole de Laval: Compte rendu des séances*. Laval, 1870.

————. *Etude sur le métayage dans la Mayenne*. Paris, 1881.

Le Camus, Comte de, ed. *Correspondance du vicomte Armand de Melun et de Madame Swetchine*. Paris, 1892.

Les Légitimistes à Ste-Anne d'Auray, le 29 séptembre 1887. Paris, 1887.

La Légitimité. N.p., n.d.

Le Lasseux, Ernest. *Comice agricole de Laval: Rapport de 1853*. Laval, 1853.

————. *Comice agricole du canton de Grez-en-Bouée: Enquête parlementaire*. Château-Gontier, 1870.

Le Serrac de Kervily. *L'Hérédité est le salut du peuple*. Paris, 1849.

————. *Lettre sur la situation politique*. Paris, 1874.

————. *Manifeste d'un légitimiste*. Paris, 1851.

Lestourgie, Auguste de. *Conseil général de la Corrèze, séance du 29 août 1872: Rapport sur l'assistance publique dans les campagnes*. Tulle, 1872.

Lorgeril, Charles de. *La Propriété foncière en face de l'abandon de la culture par les populations rurales*. Saint-Brieuc, 1886.

Loth, Arthur. *L'Echec de la restauration monarchique en 1873*. Paris, 1910.

Lourdoueix, Henri de. *Le Droit national*. Paris, 1851.

————. *Fusion mais pas de confusion*. Paris, 1854.

————. *La Révolution, c'est l'Orléanisme*. Paris, 1852.

Lucien-Brun, Emmanuel. *Introduction à l'étude du droit*. Paris, 1879.

————. *La Politique des expédients et la Politique des principes*. Paris, 1881.

————. *L'Union de la paix sociale*. Tours, 1872.

Maignen, Maurice. *Chroniques du patronage*. Paris, 1862.

Mailly, Comte Adrien de, Marquis de Nesle. *La Révolution est-elle finie?* Paris, 1853.

Margerie, Amédée de. *La Fête du Sacré Coeur en 1873 à Paray-le-Moniel: Lettre à M. Vagnen*. Nancy, 1873.

————. *La Restauration de la France*. Paris, 1872.

————. *La Solution*. Paris, 1880.

————. *L'Urgence*. Paris, 1874.

Mayol du Lupé, Comte Henri de. *La Politique des expédients et la Politique des principes: Discours prononcé à Lille, le 20 mars 1881 par Lucien-Brun et le Vte de Lupé*. Paris, 1881.

Mayol du Lupé, Jéhan de. *La Maison de Mayol: Mémoires familiaux*. Rome, 1913.

Meaux, Vicomte Marie Camille Alfred de. *L'Assemblée Nationale de 1872*. Paris, 1872.

————. *Les Conclusions de l'enquête agricole*. Paris, 1869.

————. *Une Déposition à l'enquête agricole*. Paris, 1866.

————. *Eloge de M. de Falloux prononcé au Collège de Juilly, le 11 mars 1888*. Paris, 1888.

──────. *Rapport présenté à la Société d'Agriculture de Montbrison sur le dessèchement des étangs insalubres*. Montbrison, 1853.

──────. *Souvenirs politiques, 1870–1877*. Paris, 1905.

Melun, Armand de. *De l'intervention de la société pour prévenir et soulager la misère*. Paris, 1849.

──────. *Vie de Soeur Rosalie, fille de la charité*. Paris, 1857.

Merveilleux de Vignaux, Charles. *Un Peu d'histoire à propos d'un nom: Ernoul*. La Chapelle, 1900.

Monjaret de Kerjégu, Louis de. "Quelques Réflections à propos de l'enquête parlementaire agricole, 10 mars 1870." MS in Bibliothèque Nationale.

──────. *Rapport sur la prime d'honneur de la Mayenne*. Nantes, 1870.

──────. *Les Souffrances de l'agriculture: 2e partie, Propriété obligé*. Brest, 1866.

Monnet, Alfred. *Compte rendu de la fête agricole de Bressuire, 10 séptembre 1854*. Niort, 1854.

Muller, Charles. *L'Empire et les Légitimistes*. Paris, 1864.

──────. *La Légitimité*. Paris, 1857.

Mun, Comte Albert de. *Le Centenaire de 1788*. Paris, 1889.

──────. *Conference à Bordeaux, 9 juin 1882*. Bordeaux, 1882.

──────. *La Conquête du peuple*. 2nd ed. Paris, 1908.

──────. *La Contre-révolution: Discours prononcé à la séance de clôture de l'assemblée générale des membres de l'Oeuvre, 8 juin 1878*. Paris, 1878.

──────. *Les Derniers Heures du drapeau blanc*. Paris, 1909.

──────. *Dieu et le Roi: Discours prononcé à Vannes, le 8 mars 1881*. Paris, 1881.

──────. *Discours et Ecrits divers*. 7 vols. Paris, 1888–1904.

──────. *Discours prononcé par Albert de Mun à l'inauguration du Cercle des Brotteaux (Lyons), 1 décembre 1872*. Paris, 1873.

──────. *Discours prononcé par le comte Albert de Mun à l'inauguration du Cercle de Montmartre-Clignancourt, le 16 juin 1872*. Paris, 1872.

──────. *Ma vocation sociale: Souvenirs de la fondation de l'Oeuvre des Cercles Catholiques d'Ouvriers, 1871–1875*. Paris, 1908.

──────. *Oeuvre des Cercles Catholiques: Pèlerinage de N. D. de Liesse, le dimanche 27 août 1873*. Paris, 1873.

Nettement, Alfred. *Causeries sur l'histoire de France, suivies d'une causerie sur la Révolution*. 2 vols. Paris, 1879.

──────. *Nouvelle Histoire de la Révolution de 1789*. Paris, 1862.

──────. *Quiberon: Souvenirs du Morbihan*. Paris, 1869.

Nicolas, Auguste. *L'Etat sans Dieu: Mal social de la France*. 3rd ed. Paris, 1872.

──────. *La Révolution et l'Ordre chrétienne*. 2nd ed. Paris, 1874.

Pène, Henri de. *Henri de France*. Paris, 1884.

Pitman, C. B., trans. and ed. *Memoirs of the Count de Falloux, from the French*. 2 vols. London, 1888.

Pocquet, Barthélemy. *Essai sur l'assistance publique, son histoire, ses principes, son organisation actuelle.* Paris, 1877.

Pontèves, Comte de Sabran de. *A travers les champs de la pensée: Simple Esquisses religieuses et philosophiques.* Paris, 1869.

————. *Mon pèlerinage à La Salette.* Marseille, 1874.

————. *Sur le banc de la grotte de Lourdes.* Marseille, 1878.

————. *Venez, ne tardez pas!* Marseille, 1873.

Pontmartin, Armand de. *Les Elections de 1876.* Avignon, 1876.

————. *Nouvelles samedis.* 20 vols. Paris, 1866–1881.

Poujoulat, Jean Joseph François. *Histoire de la Révolution française.* 6th ed. 2 vols. Tours, 1877.

————. *Lettre à M. de Persigny à l'occasion de sa circulaire contre la Société de St. Vincent de Paul.* Paris, 1861.

————. *Le Roi légitime.* Paris, 1872.

Puységur, Auguste de Chastenet de. *La Fusion.* Toulouse, 1851.

Raincey, Henri de. *Les Catholiques sont-ils de leurs temps: Discours prononcé . . . au congrès catholique de Malines, 1864.* Paris, 1864.

————. *Célébrités catholiques contemporaines.* Paris, 1870.

————. *Histoire critique et législative de l'instruction publique et de la liberté de l'enseignement en France.* 2 vols. Paris, 1844.

Raudot, Claude Marie. *La Décentralisation: Seconde Partie.* Paris, 1858.

————. *De la décadence de la France.* 4th ed. Paris, 1851.

————. *De la grandeur possible de la France, faisant suite à la décadence de la France.* Paris, 1851.

————. *De l'agriculture en France.* Auxerre, 1858.

————. *La France avant la Révolution: Son état politique et social en 1787 à l'ouverture de l'assemblée des notables et son histoire depuis cette époque jusqu'aux Etats Généraux.* Paris, n.d.

Robinet de Clery. *Les deux fusions, 1800–1873.* Paris, 1908.

————. *Les Prétentions dynastiques de la branche d'Orléans.* Paris, 1910.

Le Roi légitime: Discours prononcés par M. le Cte Maurice d'Andigné, M. Sebastien Laurantie . . . 27 juillet 1889. Paris, 1889.

Saint-Albin, Alexandre Denis de. *Les Francs-maçons.* Paris, 1862.

————. *Les Libres-penseurs et la Ligue de l'Enseignement.* Paris, 1868.

Saint-Victor, Gabriel de. *De l'enquête agricole: Discours.* Lyon, 1866.

Ségur, Louis Gaston Adrien de. *La Révolution.* 4th ed. Paris, 1872.

Soi'han de Kersabiée, Alain. *Les Soldats du pape: Journal de deux zouaves bretons— allocation du Saint-Père aux soldats pontificaux, rapport du général Kanzler à N. S. P. le pape.* Nantes, 1867.

Le Testament politique d'un ancien légitimiste. Paris, 1889.

Tresvaux Du Fraval, Charles Marie. *La Comedie du radicalisme.* Laval, 1875.

———. *Le Plébiscite; ou, L'Ornière de l'Empire.* Château-Gontier, 1870.

———. *Halte-là; ou, Le Bord de l'abîme: Etude suivre de quelque poèsies politiques sur nos petits grands-hommes.* Laval, 1872.

Trevéneuc, Henri de. *Abolition du serment politique.* Paris, 1844.

Vedrenne, Prosper. *Vive le roi!* Toulouse, 1871.

Véran, Guillaume. *L'Empire plébiscitaire et la Monarchie légitime: Réponse au l'Ordre et au Galois.* Dunkerque, 1874.

———. *Les Habiles: Appel à la raison publique—réplique à l'auteur des "Incurables."* Angers, 1883.

———. *La Légitimité devant le catholicisme.* Angers, 1880.

———. *La Question du XIXe siècle.* Paris, 1866.

———. *Les Solutions: Place au droit national de la France.* Toulouse, 1871.

Vert, Paul Sebastien. *Des mesures charitables organisées dans la ville de Rennes contre la mendicité.* Paris, 1856.

———. *Question des incurables: Réponse au rapport de M. le maire de Rennes.* Rennes, 1859.

———. *Rélation de la fête du 8 séptembre 1861 pour l'inauguration du voeu de Notre-Dame-de-Bonne-Nouvelle à Rennes.* Rennes, 1861.

Villebois-Mareuil, Comte Felix de. *Résumé de la discussion sur le double trace du chemin de fer d'Angers au Mans.* Angers, 1857.

Villeneuve-Bargemont, Alban de. *Economie politique chrétienne; ou, Recherche sur la nature et les causes du paupérisme, en France et en Europe, et sur les moyens de le soulager et de le prévenir.* 3 vols. Paris, 1834.

Vinols de Montfleury, Jules de. *Mémoires politiques d'un membre de l'Assemblée Nationale constituante de 1871.* Le Puy, 1882.

Vögué, Léonce de. *A messieurs les électeurs du canton d'Aubiguy, 23 avril 1870.* Paris, 1870.

———. *Aux électeurs du Cher.* Bourges, 1850.

———. *Lettre à M. le président de la Société d'Agriculture du Cher sur le concours de Chelmsford en 1856.* Bourges, 1856.

Yvon, P. d'. *Monarchie-République: Quelques Vérités sur la situation politique de 1871.* Bordeaux, 1874.

CONTEMPORARY PRINTED SOURCES AND BIOGRAPHIES

Batjin, Nicolas. *Histoire complète de la noblesse de 1789 à 1861.* Paris, 1862.

Baudon, Adolphe. *Lettre aux membres des conférences de St. Vincent de Paul.* Paris, 1862.

———. *Lettres aux présidents des conférences de St. Vincent de Paul.* Paris, 1862–1866.

Baunard, Louis. *Histoire du cardinal Pie, évêque de Poitiers.* 2 vols. Paris, 1901.

Baunard, Monsignor. *Kolb-Bernard: Sénateur du Nord.* Paris, 1899.

Bernard, Ferdinand. *Le Parlementairianisme, la Dictateur et la Monarchie légitime.* Poitiers, 1882.

Bigot, Charles. *Les Classes dirigeantes.* Paris, 1875.

Bittard des Portes, René. *Histoire des zouaves pontificaux.* Paris, 1895.

Bouillet, Adolphe. *L'Armée d'Henri V: Les Bourgeois-gentilshommes de 1871.* Paris, 1872.

Bucquet, Paul. *Enquête sur les bureaux de bienfaisance: Documents recueillis par les inspecteurs généraux des établissements de bienfaisance.* Paris, 1874.

Cahiers de 1889: Assemblée générale des délégués des assemblées provinciales en France. Paris, 1889.

Charles-Brun, Jean. *Le Régionalisme.* Paris, 1911.

Comité catholique de Paris: Assemblée générale des comités catholiques de France, 1872–1873. Paris, 1872–73.

Desjoyeaux, Claude Noel. *La Fusion monarchique, 1848–1873, d'après des sources inédites.* Paris, 1913.

Dupont, Charles. *Les Républicains et les Monarchistes dans la Var en décembre 1851.* Paris, 1883.

Dupont-White, C. B. *La Centralisation.* Paris, 1860.

———. *L'Individu et l'Etat.* Paris, 1863.

Fadeville. *La République, le Comte de Chambord, Louis-Napoléon et un Prince d'Orléans.* Paris, 1851.

Gautherot, Gustave. *Une Demi-Siècle de défense nationale et religieuse: Emile Keller, 1828–1909.* Paris, 1922.

Guitton, Georges. *Léon Harmel, 1829–1915.* 2 vols. Paris, 1927.

Hanotaux, Gabriel. *Histoire de la France contemporaine.* 6 vols. Paris, 1900.

Harmel, Léon. *Manuel d'une corporation chrétienne.* Tours, 1877.

Lacombe, Charles de. *Vie de Berryer, d'après des documents inédits.* 3 vols. Paris, 1895.

La Gueronnière, Arthur de. *Etudes et Portraits politiques contemporains.* Paris, 1856.

Lavergne, Léonce de. *L'Agriculture et la Population.* Paris, 1865.

———. *Economie rurale de la France.* Paris, 1877.

Le Liepvre, E. *Charles Kolb-Bernard.* Lille, 1893.

Le Play, Frédéric. *La Réforme sociale en France.* 2 vols. Paris, 1864.

Lescöet, Jonathas de. *Le Cte Gaston Du Plessis de Grénédan, volontaire de l'armée pontificale: Note biographique.* Rennes, 1861.

Littré, Emile. *Restauration de la légitimité et ses alliés.* Paris, 1873.

Maignen, Charles. *Clement Myionnet, premier membre de la Congrégation des Frères de St. Vincent de Paul d'Angers: Sa vie, ses oeuvres, d'après son autobiographie annotée et complétée.* Paris, 1925.

————. *Maurice Maignen, directeur du Cercle Montparnasse, et les origines du mouvement social catholique en France, 1822–1890.* 2 vols. Luçon, 1927.

Marcère, Emile de. *L'Assemblée Nationale de 1871.* 2 vols. Paris, 1904.

Marcey, M. de. *Charles Chesnelong: Son histoire et celle de son temps.* 3 vols. Paris, 1908.

Maurras, Charles. *L'Enquête sur la monarchie.* Paris, 1900.

————. *L'Idée de la décentralisation.* Paris, 1898.

Mazade, Charles. *L'Opposition royaliste: Berryer, de Villèle, de Falloux.* Paris, 1894.

Monti de Rézé, René de. *Souvenirs sur le comte de Chambord.* Paris, 1930.

Nancy: Un Projet de décentralisation. Nancy, 1865.

Noailles, Hélis de. *Le Bureau du Roi.* Paris, 1932.

Périn, Charles. *De la richesse dans les sociétés chrétiennes.* 2 vols. 1861.

————. *Les Lois de la société chrétienne.* Paris, 1875.

Quatre-Solz de Marolles, Victor de. *Maurice Maignen: Les Oeuvres ouvriers.* Paris, 1895.

Ricard, Antoine. *Les Pèlerinages de la France à Notre-Dame de Lourdes en 1872.* Paris, 1873.

Simon, Jules. *L'Ouvrier.* Paris, 1861.

————. *La Politique radicale.* Paris, 1868.

Société de St. Vincent de Paul. *Documents rélatifs à la Société de St. Vincent de Paul.* Paris, 1862.

Société de St. Vincent de Paul: Conseil central de Dijon. Dijon, 1854.

Society of St. Vincent de Paul. *Manual of the Society of St. Vincent de Paul.* London, 1857.

Thureau-Dangin, Paul. *Royalistes et Républicains: Essai historique sur des questions de politique contemporaine.* Paris, 1874.

Tocqueville, Alexis de. *Correspondances d'Alexis de Tocqueville et de Louis de Kergolay.* Edited by André Jardin. Paris, 1977. Vol. XIII of Tocqueville, *Oeuvres complètes.* 27 vols.

————. *The Old Regime and the French Revolution.* Translated by Stuart Gilbert. Garden City, N.Y., 1955.

Tourtoulon, Charles de. *De la noblesse dans ses rapports avec nos moeurs et nos institutions.* Paris, 1857.

Union des Associations Ouvrières Catholiques, congrès d'Angers: Compte rendu de la douzième assemblée générale des directeurs d'oeuvres, 1–5 séptembre 1879. Angers, 1879.

Union des Associations Ouvrières Catholiques, congrès de Chartres: Compte rendu de la onzième assemblée générale des directeurs d'oeuvres, 9–13 séptembre 1878. Paris, 1879.

Vatteville, M. de. *Statistique des établissements de bienfaisances.* Paris, n.d.

SECONDARY SOURCES

Books

Agulhon, Maurice. *Marianne into Battle: Republican Imagery and Symbolism in France, 1789–1880.* Trans. Janet Lloyd. Cambridge, Mass., 1977.

———. *The Republic in the Village: The People of the Var from the French Revolution to the Second Republic.* Trans. Janet Lloyd. Cambridge, Mass., 1982.

Agulhon, Maurice, Gabriel Désert, and Robert Specklin. *Apogée et Crise de la civilisation paysanne, 1789–1914.* Edited by Etienne Juillard. Paris, 1976. Vol. III of Georges Duby and Armand Wallon, eds., *Histoire de la France rurale.* 4 vols.

Aminzade, Ronald. *Class, Politics, and Early Industrial Capitalism: A Study of Mid-Nineteenth-Century Toulouse, France.* Albany, N.Y., 1981.

Anderson, Robert D. *Education in France, 1848–1870.* Oxford, 1975.

Andigné, A. d'. *Un Apôtre de la charité: Armand de Melun.* Paris, 1962.

Armengaud, André. *Les Populations de l'Est-Aquitaine au début de l'époque contemporaine, 1845–1871.* Paris, 1961.

Augé, Guy. *Les "Blancs d'Espagne": Contribution à l'étude d'une composante du royalisme français contemporain, mémoire de science politique.* Paris, 1977.

———. *La Légitimité monarchique au XIXe siècle: Mémoire d'histoire du droit.* Paris, 1964.

———. *Succession de France et Règle de nationalité: Le Droit royal historique français contre orléanisme.* Paris, 1979.

Auspitz, Katherine. *The Radical Bourgeoisie: The Ligue de l'Enseignement and the Origins of the Third Republic, 1866–1885.* Cambridge, Mass., 1982.

Baker, Donald N., and Patrick J. Harrigan, eds. *The Making of Frenchmen: Current Directions in the History of Education in France, 1679–1979.* Waterloo, Ont. 1980.

Barbant, Herbert F. *The Beginnings of the Third Republic: A History of the National Assembly, February to September, 1871.* New York, 1940.

Barral, Pierre. *Les Agrariens français de Méline à Pisani.* Paris, 1968.

Basdevant-Gaudemet, B. *La Commission de Décentralisation de 1870: Contribution à l'étude de la décentralisation en France au XIXe siècle.* Paris, 1973.

Beck, Thomas. *French Legislators, 1800–1834: A Study in Quantitative History.* Berkeley and Los Angeles, 1974.

Belanger, Michel. *Les Conseillers généraux de Charente sous la IIIe République.* Paris, 1970.

———. *Les Conseillers généraux de Charente sous le Second Empire.* Angoulême, 1969.

Bellanger, Claude, *et al. L'Histoire générale de la presse française.* 5 vols. Paris, 1969–76.

Bergeron, Louis. *France Under Napoleon*. Translated by R. R. Palmer. Princeton, 1981.

──────. *Les Grands Notables du Premier Empire: Notice de biographie sociale*. Paris, 1978.

──────. *La "Masse de Granit": Cent mille notables du Premier Empire*. Paris, 1974.

Boesche, Roger, ed. *Alexis de Tocqueville: Selected Letters on Politics and Society*. Translated by James Toupin and Roger Boesche. Berkeley and Los Angeles, 1985.

Bois, Paul. *Paysans de l'Ouest: Des structures économiques et sociales aux options politiques depuis l'époque révolutionnaire dans la Sarthe*. Paris, 1971.

Boulard, F. *Essor ou Déclin du clergé français*. Paris, 1950.

──────. *An Introduction to Religious Sociology: Pioneer Work in France*. London, 1960.

Boulard, F., and Jacques Gadille. *Matériaux pour l'histoire religieuse du peuple français, XIX–XX siècles*. Paris, 1982.

Boutry, P., and M. Cinquin. *Deux pèlerinages au XIXe siècle: Ars et Paray-le-Monial*. Paris, 1980.

Braudel, Fernand, and Ernest Labrousse, eds. *Histoire économique et sociale de la France*. 4 vols. Paris, 1970–82.

Briollet, Maurice. *Les Zouaves pontificaux du Maine, d'Anjou et de la Touraine* (Paris, 1968–69).

Brown, Marvin L. *The Comte de Chambord: The Third Republic's Uncompromising King*. Durham, N.C., 1967.

──────. *Louis Veuillot: French Ultramontane Catholic Journalist and Layman, 1813–1883*. Durham, N.C., 1977.

Calippe. *Attitude sociale des catholiques françaises*. 3 vols. Paris, 1911–12.

Cameron, R. E., ed. *Essays in French Economic History*. Homewood, Ill., 1970.

──────. *France and Economic Development, 1800–1914*. Princeton, 1961.

Castries, Duc de. *Le Grand Refus de comte de Chambord—la légitimité et les tentatives de restauration de 1830 à 1886*. Paris, 1970. Vol. V of Castries, *Le Testament de la monarchie*. 5 vols.

Catta, E. *La Doctrine politique et sociale du Cardinal Pie, 1815–1880*. Paris, 1959.

Changy, Hugues de. *Le Soulèvement de la duchesse de Berry, 1830–1832: Les Royalistes dans la Tourmente*. Paris, 1986.

Chalmin, Pierre. *L'Officier français de 1815 à 1870*. Paris, 1957.

Chapman, Guy. *The French Third Republic: The First Phase*. London, 1962.

Chaussinand-Nogaret, Guy. *The French Nobility in the Eighteenth Century: From Feudalism to Enlightenment*. Translated by William Doyle. Cambridge, Mass., 1985.

──────, ed. *Une Histoire des élites: Recueil de textes présentés et commentés*. Paris, 1975.

Cholvy, Gérard. *Religion et Société au XIXe siècle: Le Diocèse de Montpellier, 1802–1894.* Paris, 1976.

Cholvy, Gérard, and Y. M. Hilaire, eds. *Histoire religieuse de la France contemporaine.* 3 vols. Paris, 1986.

Collins, Ross W. *Catholicism and the Second French Republic, 1848–1852.* New York, 1923.

Combes de Patris, B. *La Société de Saint Vincent de Paul en Rouergue.* Rodez, 1960.

Corbin, Alain. *Archaisme et Modernité en Limousin au XIXe siècle.* 2 vols. Paris, 1975.

Daumard, Adeline. *Les Fortunes françaises au XIXe siècle: Enquête sur la réparation et la composition des capitaux privés à Paris, Lyon, Lille, Bordeaux et Toulouse, d'après l'enregistrement des déclarations.* Paris, 1973.

Debray, Pierre. *Comment peut-on être royaliste aujourd'hui.* Paris, 1970.

La Décentralisation: 6ème Colloque d'histoire, Aix-en-Provence, 1961. Gap, 1964.

Denis, Michel. *Les Royalistes de la Mayenne et le Monde modern, XIXe–XXe siècles.* Paris, 1977.

Désert, Gabriel. *Une Société rurale au XIXe siècle: Les Paysans du Calvados, 1815–1895.* Lille, 1975.

Droite et Gauche de 1789 à nos jours: Colloque du centre d'histoire contemporaine de l'Université Paul Valéry. Montpellier, 1975.

Dubois, Jean. *Le Vocabulaire politique et social en France de 1869 à 1872.* Paris, 1962.

Dupeux, Georges. *Aspects de l'histoire sociale et politique du Loir-et-Cher, 1848–1914.* Paris, 1962.

———. *La Société française, 1789–1960.* Paris, 1964.

Duroselle, Jean Baptist. *Les Débuts du catholicisme social en France.* Paris, 1951.

Duverger, Maurice. *La Démocratie sans le peuple.* Paris, 1967.

Elwitt, Sanford. *The Making of the Third Republic: Class and Politics in France, 1868–1884.* Baton Rouge, 1974.

Estèbe, Jean. *Les Ministres de la République, 1871–1914.* Paris, 1982.

Faury, Jean. *Cléricalisme et Anticléricalisme dans le Tarn, 1848–1900.* Toulouse, 1980.

Fitzpatrick, Brian. *Catholic Royalism in the Department of the Gard, 1814–1852.* Cambridge, Mass., 1983.

Forster, Robert, and Orest Ranum, eds. *Rural Society in France: Selections from the Annales Economies, Sociétés, Civilisations.* Translated by Elborg Forster and Patricia M. Ranum. Baltimore, 1977.

Foucault, Albert. *La Société de St. Vincent de Paul: Histoire de cent ans.* Paris, 1933.

Furet, François. *Interpreting the French Revolution.* Translated by Elborg Forster. Cambridge, Mass., 1981.

Furet, François, and Mona Ozouf, eds. *A Critical Dictionary of the French Revolution.* Translated by Arthur Goldhammer. Cambridge, Mass., 1989.

Gadille, Jacques. *Albert DuBoys: Ses souvenirs du concile du Vatican, 1869–1870.* 2 vols. Louvain, 1968.

———. *La Pensée et l'Action politique des évêques françaises au début de la IIIe République, 1870–1883.* 2 vols. Paris, 1967.

Ganier, Jean Paul. *Le Drapeau blanc.* Paris, 1971.

Gavignaud, G. *Propriétaires-viticulteurs en Roussillon: Structures, Conjonctures, Société, XVIII–XX siècles.* Paris, 1984.

Gibson, F. J. *Les Notables et l'Eglise dans le diocèse de Perigueux, 1821–1905.* Lille, 1979.

Gildea, Robert. *Education in Provincial France, 1800–1914: A Study of Three Departments.* Oxford, 1983.

Gimpl, M. C. A. *The "Correspondant" and the Founding of the French Third Republic.* Westport, Conn., 1959.

Girard, Louis. *Le Libéralisme en France, 1815–1848.* Paris, 1967.

———. *La Politique des travaux publiques du Second Empire.* Paris, 1952.

Girard, Louis, et al. *Les Conseillers généraux en 1870: Etude statistique d'un personnel politique.* Paris, 1967.

Goguel, François. *Géographie des élections françaises sous la Troisième République.* Paris, 1970.

Gouault, Jacques. *Comment la France est devenue républicaine: Les Élections générales et partielles à l'Assemblée Nationale, 1870–1875.* Paris, 1954.

Greer, Donald. *The Incidence of the Terror During the French Revolution: A Statistical Interpretation.* 1935; rpr. Gloucester, Mass., 1966.

Halévy, Daniel. *The End of the Notables.* Translated by Alain Silvera. Middletown, Conn., 1974.

———. *La République des ducs.* Paris, 1937.

Harrigan, Patrick J. *Mobility, Elites, and Education in French Society of the Second Empire.* Waterloo, Ont. 1980.

Higgs, David. *Nobles in Nineteenth-Century France: The Practice of Inegalitarianism.* Baltimore, 1987.

———. *Ultra-Royalism in Toulouse from Its Origins to the Revolution of 1830.* Baltimore, 1973.

Hilaire, Y. M. *Une Chrétienté au XIXe siècle? La Vie religieuse des populations du diocèse d'Arras, 1840–1914.* 2 vols. Lille, 1977.

Hoog, Georges. *Histoire du catholicisme social en France, 1877–1931.* 2 vols. Paris, 1946.

Houée, P. *Une Longue Evolution, 1815–1950.* Paris, 1972. Vol. I of Houée, *Les Etapes du développement rural.* 2 vols.

Howorth, Jolyen, and Philip Cerney, eds. *Elites in France: Origins, Reproduction, Power.* New York, 1981.

Hubscher, Ronald. *L'Agriculture et la Société rurale dans le Pas-de-Calais au milieu du XIXe siècle à 1914.* 2 vols. Arras, 1980.

Huot-Pleuroux, P. *La Vie chrétienne dans le Doubs et la Haute-Saône de 1860 à 1960*. Besançon, 1966.

Irvine, William D. *The Boulanger Affair Reconsidered: Royalism, Boulangism, and the Origins of the Radical Right in France*. New York, 1989.

Isambert, F. A. *Christianisme et le Monde ouvrier*. Paris, 1975.

Jacquier, Bernard. *Le Légitimisme dauphinois, 1830–1870*. Grenoble, 1976.

Kent, Sherman. *Electoral Procedure Under Louis Philippe*. New Haven, 1937.

Kselman, Thomas. *Miracles and Prophecies in Nineteenth-Century France*. New Brunswick, N. J., 1983.

LaCapra, Dominick, and Steven L. Kaplan, eds. *Modern European Intellectual History: Reappraisals and New Perspectives*. Ithaca, N.Y., 1982.

Lambert-Dansette, J. *Quelques Familles du patronat textiles de Lille-Armentières, 1789–1914*. Lille, 1954.

Le Bras, Gabriel. *Etudes de sociologie religieuse*. 2 vols. Paris, 1956.

Lebrun, François, ed. *Histoire des catholiques en France du XVe siècle à nos jours*. Toulouse, 1980.

Levillain, Philippe. *Albert de Mun: Catholicisme français et Catholicisme romain, du syllabus au ralliement*. Rome, 1983.

Lhomme, Jean. *Le Grande Bourgeoisie au pouvoir, 1830–1880*. Paris, 1960.

Locke, Robert R. *French Legitimists and the Politics of Moral Order in the Early Third Republic*. Princeton, 1974.

Lukacs, John, ed. *The European Revolution and the Correspondence with Gobineau*. Gloucester, Mass., 1968.

Marcilhacy, C. *Le Diocèse d'Orléans au milieu du XIXe siècle: Les Hommes et leurs mentalités*. Paris, 1964.

———. *Le Diocèse d'Orléans sous l'épiscopat de Mgr Dupanloup, 1849–1878: Sociologie religieuse et Mentalités collectives*. Paris, 1962.

Marker, G. A. *Internal Migration and Economic Opportunity in France, 1872–1911*. New York, 1981.

Marlin, Roger. *La Droite à Besançon de 1870 à 1914*. Besançon, 1965.

Martin, Benjamin F. *Count Albert de Mun: Paladin of the Third Republic*. Chapel Hill, N.C., 1978.

Martin, Olivier. *Les Catholiques sociaux dans le Loir-et-Cher: De l'Oeuvre des Cercles Ouvriers au parti Démocratique, 1875–1926*. Blois, 1984.

Marx, Karl, and Friedrich Engels. *The Communist Manifesto*. Translated by Samuel Moore. Middlesex, Eng., 1967.

Maurain, Jean. *La Politique ecclésiastique du Second Empire*. Paris, 1930.

Mayer, Arno. *The Persistence of the Old Regime: Europe to the Great War*. New York, 1981.

Mayeur, Jean Marie. *Catholicisme social et Démocratie chrétienne: Principes romaines, expériences françaises*. Paris, 1986.

———. *Les Débuts de la IIIe République, 1871–1898*. Paris, 1973.

Mehlman, Jeffrey. *Revolution and Repetition*. Berkeley and Los Angeles, 1979.

Menager, Bernard. *La Vie politique dans le département du Nord de 1851 à 1877*. 3 vols. Dunkerque, 1983.

Mollet, Charles. *Albert de Mun, 1872–1890: Exigences doctrinales et Préoccupations sociales chez un laic catholique*. Paris, 1970.

Monti de Rézé, René de. *Souvenirs sur le comte de Chambord*. Paris, 1930.

Moon, Parker T. *The Labor Problem and the Social Catholic Movement in France: A Study in the History of Social Politics*. New York, 1921.

Nicolet, Claude. *L'Idée républicaine en France: Essai d'histoire critique*. Paris, 1982.

Niebuhr, Reinhold, ed. *Marx and Engels on Religion*. New York, 1964.

Ogès, Louis. *L'Agriculture dans le Finistère au milieu du XIXe siècle*. Quimper, 1949.

Osgood, Samuel M. *French Royalism Since 1870*. The Hague, 1970.

Palmade, Guy. *French Capitalism in the Nineteenth Century*. Translated by Graeme M. Holmes. London, 1972.

Parrot, Jean. *La Représentation des intérêts dans le mouvement des idées politiques*. Paris, 1974.

Pelloux, Robert. *Libéralisme, Traditionalisme et Décentralisation*. Paris, 1952.

Pierrand, Pierre. *L'Eglise et les Ouvriers en France, 1840–1940*. Paris, 1984.

———. *Histoire de Lille*. Paris, 1982.

———. *La Vie ouvrière à Lille sous le Second Empire*. Paris, 1965.

Pinchenel, P. *Structures sociales et Dépopulation rurale dans les campagnes picardes de 1836 à 1936*. Paris, 1956.

Pitié, Jean. *L'Exode rural et Migrations intérieures en France*. Poitiers, 1971.

Plessis, Alain. *De la fête impériale au mur des fédérés, 1852–1871*. Paris, 1979.

Pocquet du Haut-Jussé, Barthélemy A., ed. *Légitimistes parlementaires: Correspondance politique de Barthélemy Pocquet, rédacteur du "Journal de Rennes," 1848–1878*. Paris, 1976.

Price, Roger. *The Modernization of Rural France*. London, 1983.

Puy de Clinchamps, Philippe du. *Le Royalisme*. Paris, 1967.

Ratouis de Limay, H. *L'Oeuvre de la Société d'Agriculture de l'Indre pendant la période d'un siècle*. Châteauroux, 1902.

Reece, Jack. *Bretons Against France: Ethnic Minority Nationalism in Twentieth-Century Brittany*. Chapel Hill, N.C., 1977.

Régions et Régionalisme en France du XVIIIe siècle à nos jours: Actes publiés par Christian Gras et Georges Livert. Paris, 1977.

Rémond, René. *Les Droites en France*. 4th ed. Paris, 1982.

Rials, Stéphane. *Le Légitimisme*. Paris, 1983.

———. *Révolution et Contre-révolution au XIXe siècle*. Paris, 1987.

Ringer, Fritz. *Education and Society in Modern Europe*. Bloomington, Ind., 1979.

Rollet, Henri. *L'Action sociale des catholiques en France, 1871–1901*. Paris, 1946.

Roy, Joseph Antoine. *Histoire du Jockey Club de Paris*. Paris, 1958.

Rudelle, Odile. *La République absolue: Aux origines de l'instabilité constitutionelle de la France républicaine, 1870–1889*. Paris, 1982.

Schall, Abbé J. *Un Disciple de Saint Vincent de Paul au XIXe siècle: Adolphe Baudon, 1819–1888*. Paris, 1897.

Sedgwick, Alexander. *The Ralliement in French Politics, 1880–1898*. Cambridge, Mass., 1965.

Sherman, William. *Le Corps des officiers français sous la Seconde République et le Second Empire: Aristocratie et Démocratie dans l'armée au milieu du XIXe siècle*. 2 vols. Lille, 1978.

Siegfried, André. *Tableau politique de la France de l'Ouest sous la Troisième République*. Paris, 1913.

Singer, Barnet. *Village Notables in Nineteenth-Century France: Priests, Mayors, and Schoolmasters*. Albany, N.Y., 1982.

Skocpol, Theda. *States and Social Revolutions: A Comparative Analysis of France, Russia, and China*. Cambridge, Mass., 1979.

Smith, Bonnie. *Ladies of the Leisure Class: The Bourgeoises of Northern France in the Nineteenth Century*. Princeton, 1981.

La Société de St. Vincent de Paul à Marseille: Histoire d'un siècle, 1844–1944. Marseille, 1944.

Talmy, Robert. *Aux sources du catholicisme social: L'Ecole de La Tour Du Pin*. Paris, 1963.

———. *Une Forme hybride du catholicisme social: L'Association catholique des patrons du Nord*. Lille, 1962.

———. *Le Syndicalisme chrétienne en France, 1871–1930: Difficultés et Controverses*. Paris, 1966.

Toutain, Jean Claude. *La Population de la France de 1700 à 1959*. Paris, 1963.

———. *Le Produit de l'agriculture française de 1700 à 1958*. Paris, 1961.

Trebilcock, Clive. *The Industrialization of the Continental Powers, 1780–1914*. London, 1981.

Tudesq, André Jean. *Les Conseillers généraux en France au temps de Guizot*. Paris, 1967.

———. *Les Grands Notables en France, 1840–1849: Etude historique d'une psychologie sociale*. 2 vols. Paris, 1964.

Vachat, Pierre du. *1877: La Crise du seize mai; ou, L'Etrange République*. Paris, 1981.

Vallet, Xavier. *La croix, les Lys et la Peine des hommes*. Paris, 1960.

Vigier, Philippe. *La Seconde République dans la région alpine: Etude politique et sociale*. 2 vols. Paris, 1963.

Weber, Eugen. *Peasants into Frenchmen: The Modernization of Rural France, 1870–1914*. Stanford, Calif., 1977.

Wylie, Laurence, ed. *Chanzeaux: A Village in Anjou.* Cambridge, Mass., 1966.
Zeldin, Theodore. *France, 1848–1945: Politics and Anger.* Oxford, 1979.
————. *The Political System of Napoleon III.* London, 1958.
————, ed. *Conflicts in French Society: Anticlericalism, Education, and Morals in the Nineteenth Century.* London, 1970.

Articles

Anderson, Robert D. "New Light on French Secondary Education in the Nineteenth Century." *Social History,* VII (1982), 147–65.
————. "Secondary Education in Mid Nineteenth-Century France: Some Social Aspects." *Past and Present,* LIII (1971), 121–46.
Bécarud, Jean. "La Noblesse dans les Chambres, 1815–1848." *Revue internationale d'histoire politique et constitutionnel,* XI (1953), 189–205.
————. "Noblesse et Représentation parlementaire: Les Députés nobles de 1871 à 1968." *Revue française de science politique,* XXIII (1973), 972–99.
Beck, Thomas. "Occupation, Taxes, and a Distinct Nobility Under Louis-Philippe." *European Studies Review,* XIII (1983), 403–22.
Bossis, Philippe. "La Propriété nobiliaire en pays vendéen avant et après la Révolution." *97e Congrès de la sociétés savantes de Nantes, 1972: Section d'histoire moderne,* LXXVII (1977), 173–94.
Briollet, Maurice. "Les Zouaves pontificaux du Maine, d'Anjou et de la Touraine: Biographie de zouaves." *La Province du Maine,* 3rd ser., IX (1968), 236–48, LXXXI (1969), 516–32.
Castries, Duc de. "Grand Avocat, légitimiste fervent: Berryer." *Revue de Paris,* LXXVI (1969), 47–60.
Cobban, Alfred. "The Survival of the French Nobility During the French Revolution." *Past and Present,* XXXIX (1968), 169–72.
Cox, Marvin R. "The Liberal Legitimists and the Party of Order Under the Second French Republic." *French Historical Studies,* V (1968), 446–64.
Daumard, Adeline. "Les Elèves de l'Ecole Polytechnique de 1815 à 1848." *Revue d'histoire moderne et contemporaine,* V (1958), 226–34.
————. "L'Evolution des structures sociales en France à l'époque de l'industrialisation." *Revue historique,* DII (1972), 325–46.
————. "Les Fondements de la société bourgeoise en France an XIXe siècle." In *Ordres et Classes: Colloque d'histoire sociale, St.-Cloud, 1967,* edited by D. Roche and C. E. Labrousse. Saint-Cloud, 1974.
————. "La Fortune mobilière en France selon les milieux sociaux XIXe et XXe siècles." *Revue d'histoire économique et sociale,* XLIV, (1966), 365–92.
Démoulins, E. "Les Doctrines sociales de M. le comte de Chambord." *La Réforme sociale,* VI (1883), 289–97.

Denis, Michel. "Un Aspect du conservatisme en Bretagne au début de la IIIe République: Le Monarchisme libéral." *Annales de Bretagne*, LXXVII (1970), 391–415.

Dogan, Mattei. "Les Filières de la carrière politique en France." *Revue française de sociologie*, VIII (1967), 468–93.

Droz, Jacques. "Le Problème de la décentralisation sous le Second Empire." In *Festgabe für Max Braubach* (Münster, 1964), 789–94.

Estèbe, Jean. "Les Gouvernantes de la IIIe République et leur fortune, 1871–1914." *Revue d'histoire économique et sociale*, LIV (1976), 212–37.

Forster, Robert. "The French Revolution and the 'New' Elite, 1800–1850." In *The American and European Revolutions*, edited by J. Pelinski, 182–207. Iowa City, Iowa, 1980.

———. "The Survival of the French Nobility During the French Revolution." *Past and Present*, XXXVII (1967), 71—86.

Gaudin, Gérard. "Chez les Blancs du Midi: Du légitimisme à l'Action Française." *Etudes Maurrassiennes*, I (1968), 59–70.

Gildea, Robert. "Education in Nineteenth-Century Brittany: Ille-et Vilaine, 1800–1914." *Oxford Review of Education*, II (1976), 215–30.

Goallou, Henri. "Les Déboires de la candidature officielle." *Annales de Bretagne*, LXXVII (1970), 297–314.

———. "Le Plébiscite du 8 mai 1870 en Ille-et-Vilaine." *Annales de Bretagne*, LXXVII (1970), 374–77.

Grubb, Alan. "The Dilemma of Liberal Catholics and Conservative Politics in the Early Third Republic." *Proceedings of the Western Society for French History*, IV (1977), 368–77.

Harrigan, Patrick J. "Elites, Education, and Social Mobility in France During the Second Empire." *Proceedings of the Western Society for French History*, IV (1976), 334–41.

———. "The Social and Political Implications of Catholic Secondary Education During the Second Empire." *Societas*, VI (1976), 41–60.

———. "The Social Appeals of Catholic Secondary Education in France of the 1870s." *Journal of Social History*, VIII (1975), 122–41.

———. "The Social Origins, Ambitions, and Occupations of Secondary Students in France During the Second Empire." In *Schooling and Society: Studies in the History of Education*, edited by Lawrence Stone, 206–35. Baltimore, 1976.

Hervieu, Bertrand. "Le Pouvoir au village." *Etudes rurales*, LXII–LXIII (1976), 15–30.

Higgs, David. "Politics and Charity at Toulouse, 1750–1850." In *French Government and Society, 1500–1850*, edited by J. Bosher, 191–207. London, 1975.

————. "Politics and Landownership Among the French Nobility After the Revolution." *European Studies Review,* I (1971), 105–21.

Higonnet, Patrick J., and B. Higonnet. "Class, Corruption, and Politics in the French Chamber of Deputies, 1846–1848." *French Historical Studies,* V (1967), 204–24.

Hohenberg, P. "Changes in Rural France in the Period of Industrialization, 1830–1914." *Journal of Economic History,* XXXII (1972), 219–40.

————. "Migrations et Fluctuations démographiques dans la France rurale, 1836–1901." *Annales ESC,* XXIX (1974), 461–97.

Jones, P. M. "Political commitment and Rural Society in the Southern Massif-Central." *European Studies Review,* X (1980), 337–56.

Levillain, Philippe. "Un Chevau-léger de 1871 à 1875: Joseph de La Bouillerie." *Revue historique,* DXXI (1977), 81–122.

Lévy-Leboyer, Maurice. "La Croissance économique en France au XIXe siècle." *Annales ESC,* XXIII (1968), 788–807.

Locke, Robert R. "A New Look at Conservative Preparations for the French Elections of 1871." *French Historical Studies,* III (1968), 351–58.

Locke, Robert R., and M. Cubberly. "A New *Mémoire* on the French Coup d'Etat of December 2, 1851." *French Historical Studies,* III (1968), 564–88.

Mayeur, Jean Marie. "Catholicisme intransigeant, Catholicisme social, Démocratie chrétienne." *Annales ESC,* XXVII (1972), 483–99.

Morel, Henri. "Charles Maurras et l'Idée de la décentralisation." *Etudes maurrassiennes,* I (1972), 109–33.

Pierrand, Peirre. "Un Grand Bourgeois de Lille: Charles Kolb-Bernard, 1799–1888." *Revue du Nord,* XLVIII (1966), 381–425.

————. "Le Roman pieux; ou, D'édification en France au temps de l'Ordre Moral, 1850–1880." In *La Religion populaire,* edited by Y. M. Hilaire, 229–35. Paris, 1981.

Prial, Frank. "France Loosens Centralized Rule." New York *Times,* July 17, 1981, Sec. I, Part I, p. 1.

Renan, Ernest. "Philosophie de l'histoire contemporaine: La Monarchie constitutionnelle en France." *Revue de deux mondes,* VI (November–December, 1868), 71–104.

Rials, Stéphane. "Les Royalistes et le Suffrage universel." *Pouvoirs,* XXVI (1983), 1–8.

Richard, Guy. "La Noblesse d'affaires en France de 1750 à 1850." *Revue internationale d'histoire de la Banque,* XIII (1976), 1–58.

Silver, Judith. "French Peasant Demands for Popular Leadership in the Vendômois (Loir-et-Cher)." *Journal of Social History,* XIV (1980), 277–304.

Sontade-Rouger, Mme. "Les Notables en France sous la Restauration." *Revue d'histoire économique et sociale,* XXXVIII (1960), 98–110.

Tudesq, André Jean. "Les Survivances de l'ancien régime: La Noblesse dans la société française de la 1er moitié du XIXe siècle." In *Ordres et Classes: Colloque d'histoire sociale, St.-Cloud, 1967,* edited by D. Roche and C. E. Labrousse. Saint-Cloud, 1974.

Theses and Dissertations

Carpentier de Changy, Hugues. "Le Parti légitimiste sous la monarchie de juillet, 1830–1848." Thèse, 3rd cycle, Université de Paris XII, 1980.

Gaudin, Gérard. "Le Royalisme dans les Bouches-du-Rhône, 1876–1927." Thèse, 3rd cycle, Université de Aix-en-Provence, 1978.

Gillen, James F. J. "The Christian Monarchy in France, 1870–1880: A Study of the Nature and Influence of Legitimism." Ph.D. dissertation, Harvard University, 1954.

Gourinard, Pierre. "Trois théoriciens du légitimisme vauclusien de 1836 à 1893: Armand de Pontmartin, Léopold de Gaillard et Gustave de Bernardi." Thèse, 3rd cycle, Université de Aix-Marseille, 1977.

Millon, Charles. "René La Tour Du Pin et la Philosophie sociale du catholicisme au XIXe siècle face au libéralisme et au socialisme." Thèse, 3rd cycle, Université de Paris IV, 1974.

Index

Action Française, xvii, 2, 313n, 329, 330, 335
Agricultural colonies, 252–53
Agricultural education, 255–59, 257n
Agricultural societies, 214, 224–28
Agriculture: production and prices in, 56, 61, 228–29; as occupation of Legitimists, 137n, 214–16; effects of Revolution on, 210–12; progressive, 212–13, 216–32; and *comices agricoles*, 214–15, 225–26, 239; and land drainage, 217–18; and rural exodus, 220, 229, 230–31, 233–38, 244–45, 250–52, 258; and breeds of livestock, 220–21; and commercial production, 221–23; and transportation and communication systems, 222–24; and science, 227–28; and social structure of rural areas, 229–31; and farm machinery, 231–32; and wages for agricultural day laborers and domestics, 234; and moral value of rural life, 236–38, 236n, 250–51, 259–60; and politics of rural improvement, 238–51; and joint-production cooperatives, 247–50; and education, 255–59, 257n
Agulhon, Maurice, 61, 80
Alexis, Vicomte Ernest, 216
Aminzade, Ronald, 81
Andigné de Resteau, Maurice d', 140n, 241, 319, 324
André, Hippolyte, 199–200

Anticlericalism, 82–83
Anti-Semitism, 329–30, 330n
Arlincourt, Vicomte d', 337
Armailhac, Louis d', 36
Association Catholique de la Jeunesse Française, 330
Association Catholique des Patrons du Nord, 196
Association de la Providence, 164
Associations, 80–83, 82n, 156–65, 181–83, 186, 190–95, 204, 204n, 281–82. See *also* names of specific associations
Aubry, Maurice, 23
Audren de Kerdrel, Vincent d', 62n, 76, 226, 298n, 303, 303n, 308, 310
Augé, Guy, 330
Auspitz, Katherine, 80

Babeuf, François, 101n
Bailly de Surcy, Vincent de Paul de, 157, 164–65
Balcas, Comte de, 312
Banking, 100–101, 240–41
Baragnon, Louis-Numa, 23
Barante, Prosper, 141
Barième, Hélion de, 216
Barrot, Odilon, 97n, 113, 133n
Batbie, Anselme, 109
Baudon, Adolphe, 138, 157
Beaulieu, Le Clerc de, 112n
Beauvilliers, Duc de, 35

reason4